CONTEMPORARY GEORGIA

Lawrence R. Hepburn, Editor

Carl Vinson Institute of Government
The University of Georgia

Contemporary Georgia

Editing: Emily Honigberg
Coordination: Inge Whittle
Design, maps, graphic production: Reid McCallister
Typesetting: Anne Huddleston
Proofreading: Susan McLain, Dorothy Paul

Library of Congress Cataloging in Publication Data

Contemporary Georgia.
    Includes index.
    1. Georgia. I. Hepburn, Lawrence R., II. Carl Vinson
Institute of Government.
F291.2.C66   1987   975.8'04   87-21672
ISBN 09-89854-123-9

Foreword

An annual rite-of-passage at the University of Georgia is the "new faculty tour." Every summer, in August, the University sends 40 to 50 of its new professors on a five-day, 1,200-mile trek through Georgia. The tour is meant more to inform than to entertain. Participants visit farms, factories, research facilities, utilities, museums, campuses, parks, and historic sites. The professors talk with people in politics, business, education, and the arts, as well as with just plain folks. The purpose of the tour is to familiarize the professors, many of whom are new to the South, with the social and cultural life of Georgia and to give them a head start in understanding contemporary Georgia.

Several years ago, S. Eugene Younts, vice-president for services at the University and originator of the faculty tour, suggested preparing a book that would serve all the people who might like to know about contemporary Georgia—not only professors but also business executives, public servants, social workers, journalists, preachers, teachers, students, and others—newcomers and natives alike. The book would be the next best thing to a new faculty tour. From that suggestion, *Contemporary Georgia* was born.

The Carl Vinson Institute of Government, a public service unit of the University of Georgia, is pleased to publish this book. The principal author is Dr. Lawrence R. Hepburn, research associate in the Governmental Research and Services Division of the Vinson Institute.

Melvin B. Hill, Jr.
Director

Acknowledgments

Gratitude is expressed to the following people for reviewing the chapters and for their comments and suggestions in the revision stages. Their help was invaluable in the development of this book. Of course, each chapter reflects the views of the author (or authors), who is responsible for its content.

Lonice C. Barrett (and staff members), deputy commissioner—program, Georgia Department of Natural Resources

Phyllis J. Barrow, assistant professor, Department of Sociology, University of Georgia

Numan V. Bartley, professor, Department of History, University of Georgia

John C. Belcher, professor emeritus, Department of Sociology, University of Georgia

Richard W. Campbell, division head, Governmental Research and Services, Carl Vinson Institute of Government, University of Georgia

John W. English, professor, College of Journalism and Mass Communications, University of Georgia

Paul T. Hardy, legal research associate, Carl Vinson Institute of Government, University of Georgia

Michael W. LaMorte, professor and associate dean for services, College of Education, University of Georgia

H. Max Miller, associate professor, Department of Sociology, University of Georgia

Albert W. Niemi, director of research and dean, College of Business Administration, University of Georgia

T. M. (Jim) Parham, professor, School of Social Work, University of Georgia

Charles E. Tidwell, former executive counsel to the governor, State of Georgia

Joseph W. Whorton, Jr., director, Institute of Community and Area Development, University of Georgia

Jeffrey D. Williams, program analyst, Georgia Legislative Education Research Council

Research Assistants: Lynne M. Cabe, Lisa E. Honigberg

Photo credits: Jerry Burns, 315; Patricia I. Cooper, 278; Georgia Department of Archives and History, 15, 145, 153, 156, 165, 167, 189, 223; Georgia Department of Human Resources, 29; Georgia Ports Authority, 94; Hargrett Rare Book and Manuscript Library, University of Georgia Libraries, 28, 179; Lawrence R. Hepburn, 61, 87, 131, 211, 243, 269, 277, 280, 282, 303, 307, 309, 321, 323; Edwin L. Jackson, 248, 281, 327; Jean Keller, 236; Library of Congress, 25, 30, 33, 185, 194, 226, 230, 232; Reid McCallister, 141, 267, 271; Walker Montgomery, 57, 198; W. Robert Nix, 265; Savannah Landmarks, 329; U.S. Army Corps of Engineers, 45.

Cartoon: Clifford "Baldy" Baldowski, from the Baldowski Cartoons Collection, 151. Courtesy of Georgia Department of Archives and History.

Contents

FIGURES

TABLES

Preface

Ralph McGill, longtime *Atlanta Constitution* editor and publisher, once described a conversation he had with an old north Georgian. As the two admired the beauty of the Georgia mountains, the old man told McGill, ". . . for me, this is Georgia. You can have the rest of it." McGill then recalled that in Italy, during World War II, a man had asked him to describe Georgia and the South. He had responded that there were many Souths, not one, and that Georgia itself was something like Italy with a north and a south of its own. The old man agreed with McGill. "There are two Georgias, and many Souths," he said. "You told him right. . .I didn't know Italy was like that, too." (Ralph McGill, *The South and the Southerner* [Boston: Little, Brown and Company, 1964], p. 14.)

McGill sought to refute a popular notion: that the South, including Georgia, was a monolith—socially and culturally. On the contrary, diversity characterized the southern states. The monolith notion emerged from the mid-nineteenth century schism between North and South, cultivated by generations of writers—including southern apologists as well as northern detractors—and fed by a regional distinctiveness that remained peculiarly sharp despite a near century of momentous changes that had blurred the distinctiveness of other regions of the United States.

Unfortunately, distinctiveness lends itself readily to stereotyping. Media-makers generalized the salient features of much of the South to all of the South. The media-South was characterized by sameness: a rural population, a biracial society, and economic depression everywhere. Overlooked were the cities where two of five southerners lived, the sub-regions that had few or no black people, and the prosperous places. Religion, family, climate, and adherence to tradition were also stereotyped. The South was at once the cotton belt, the bible belt, the black belt, the Coca-Cola belt, and most recently, the sun belt.

A purpose of *Contemporary Georgia* is to dissuade the reader from holding any lingering notion that Georgia shares an overriding sameness with its southern neighbors or that any such sameness characterizes Georgia itself.

American state boundaries were drawn along lines of latitude and longitude and to conform with natural features, such as rivers and seacoasts, with little regard for the location of native populations. Yet, each state has developed its own character. The mix of people who settled within its boundaries determined each state's personality. Democracy, laissez-faire economics, and a federal system of government encouraged people of each state to go their own way and forge their own identity within the context of American society and culture. And they did, depending on the time they arrived, their purpose in coming, the cultural baggage they brought with them, how they chose to use whatever natural resources were at hand, and whether they chose to live close to their neighbors or in splendid isolation.

Georgia's complex personality continues to develop. Georgians have a long tradition of identifying with their state as a whole while holding, like McGill's old mountain man, a strong local loyalty. Georgia is so large a state, with such varied resources, economic activities, and patterns of community life, that no completely integrated state personality was ever possible. And today? Contemporary Georgia is marked by increasing social and cultural diversity born of a population growing by in-migration as much as by natural increase, and nurtured by expanding economic opportunity.

A second purpose of *Contemporary Georgia* is to capture for the reader some sense of the momentous change that is upon Georgia.

Eliot Wigginton, creator of the Foxfire program and Georgia's best known high school teacher, addressed the difficulty of understanding change within one's own culture:

> One of my most vital tasks as students begin to wrestle with their own culture is to lead them toward objectivity; . . . (and) to help them understand that culture is not an artifact but is a living, breathing, changing organism that has no end product per se but constantly evolves over time; to help them understand that they're part of a thrust into the future—not a stopping point, or a beginning, but a continuation; . . . (Eliot Wigginton, *Sometimes a Shining Moment* [Garden City, New York: Anchor Press/Doubleday, 1985], p. 397.)

Capturing a continuation is, of course, impossible. At best, one can capture some sense of change by comparing elements of culture—art, education, social relationships, and so forth—at different points in time. For the most part, the chapters of this book have a "then and now" orientation: Georgia today compared with Georgia yesterday. Knowing where contemporary Georgia came from is crucial to interpreting why things are as they are today and to assessing the prospects for change tomorrow.

The chapter authors are all members of the University of Georgia faculty. Lawrence R. Hepburn is a research associate at the Carl Vinson

Institute of Government and author of two textbooks, *The Georgia History Book* and *State Government in Georgia*. James E. Kundell is senior associate at the Institute, science advisor to the Georgia General Assembly, and author of more than 50 articles, book contributions, and policy reports on environmental and natural resource policy. Charles F. Floyd is professor of real estate in the College of Business Administration, author of *Real Estate Principles* and *The Georgia Regional Economies*, and has assisted the Georgia Department of Transportation in planning highways designed to promote economic development. K. Imogene Dean is associate professor emerita in the Department of Sociology and coeditor of *Georgia Today*, a forerunner of this book. Sam Mitchell is head of the Human Services Division, Carl Vinson Institute of Government, and consultant to human service agencies in research and management development. John D. Burke, associate vice-president for services, served as arts consultant for nine years with the Institute of Community and Area Development. Allen B. Moore is associate professor in the College of Education and joint appointed with the Institute of Community and Area Development.

Any collective bias evident in this book emanates from the authors' experience in public service at the University of Georgia. In addition to their teaching and research activities on campus, the authors have worked with private businesses, farm groups, trade associations, labor organizations, cities, counties, state government agencies, public and private schools, churches, charities, and social clubs—to seek ways to make life better for all Georgians. We all share two assumptions: things could be better, and improvement can come from informed decision making and wise planning.

We have left much of the interpretation of Georgia today and almost all the assessment of Georgia tomorrow to the reader. From the outset of our writing project, the authors intended this book to be a tool useful to decision makers and planners in business, education, government, and community service, as well as a source of information to serious and casual students of Georgia society and culture. Not since the days of James Edward Oglethorpe has the notion of planning for an improved way of life had such wide acceptance in Georgia as it does today. Oglethorpe's plans were based on ideology and failed. Planning today is based on knowledge. Whether the plans made for improving life in Georgia tomorrow succeed or fail will depend in large part on having the best knowledge available. We trust this book makes a useful contribution to that knowledge.

Lawrence R. Hepburn

CHAPTER ONE

Historical Setting

By Lawrence R. Hepburn

> You'd expect a lot of diversity in the largest state east of the
> Mississippi River. Georgia has it.
>
> From misty Appalachian peaks to unspoiled coastal island beaches,
> Georgia offers a spectacular variety of attractions and resources.
> It is a land of toe tapping and sorghum syrup, of wildflowers and
> wild rivers, of computers and jet aircraft. (*Georgia, No Place Quite
> Like It*, Georgia Department of Industry and Trade, 1984.)

Hyperbole has been a standard feature in the promotion of Georgia for
a very long time. In 1717, before Georgia had even been named, an
Englishman, Sir Robert Montgomery, proposed to the Proprietors of
Carolina that he build a buffer colony between them and the hostile
Spanish in Florida. To attract investors and potential immigrants, he
rhapsodized thusly about the land:

> It lies in the same Latitude with Palestine Herself, that promised
> Canaan, which was pointed out by God's own Choice, to bless
> the Labours of a favourite people. . . .
>
> The Air is healthy, and the Soil in general fruitful, and of
> infinite Variety; Vines, naturally flourishing upon the Hills, bear
> Grapes in most luxuriant Plenty. They have every Growth, which
> we possess in England, and almost every Thing that England wants
> besides. . . .The Air is found so temperate, and the Seasons of the
> Year so very regular, that there is no Excess of Heat, or Cold, nor
> any sudden Alteration in the Weather.

Despite his talent as a poet, Montgomery was unable to realize his
colony.

A few years later, however, other Englishmen, who called themselves
the "Trustees for Establishing the Colony of Georgia in America," ob-

tained a charter from the Crown to do just that. Although they, too, intended to thwart the perfidious Spaniards down in St. Augustine, the Trustees were more concerned with creating a model society to which they would send the "worthy poor" of London to start a new life. The Trustees named their colony after the king and described its location much as Montgomery had: "The Air is healthy, being always serene, pleasant and temperate, never subject to excessive Heat or Cold, nor to sudden Changes. . . ."

Its promoters claimed Georgia would neatly fit the mercantilist economic theories then in vogue and produce "almost everything that England wants" (but at that time had to buy), such as olives, oranges, grapes, rice, and silk. Parliament, the Church of England, and entities such as the Society for the Promotion of Christian Knowledge chipped in and on February 12, 1733, the first boatload of English immigrants to be sent "on charity" were led ashore by Trustee James Edward Oglethorpe, the "Father of Georgia." He negotiated land deals with the natives, laid out the town of Savannah according to the ideal community he had in mind (see Figure 1), and set his colonists to growing the produce England wanted.

The realities of life in coastal Georgia quickly gave lie to the promoters' claims. The year after the colony's start, John Martin Boltzius, pastor of the Salzburger community of Ebenezer some 20 miles upriver from Savannah, complained that "the cold is so severe that we can hardly find protection either by day or night. This is the case because we were not prepared for a rough winter. Nothing was said about it, quite the contrary." Neither had the Austrian immigrants been told about the heat; by the middle of June 1735, Boltzius wrote in his diary, "last year was hot, to be sure, but not as burning and stinging as it is now." The pastor duly noted the quick shifts of hot and cold weather and that "rain and wind appear at times so unexpectedly and are so violent that we cannot be careful enough." Finally, Boltzius reported, there were the insects, which came out with the warm weather "to give the people of this colony much discomfort."

In sum, life in the Georgia Colony proved to be no promised land to most of the early settlers. As the settlers were plagued by "fever and ague" and "hemorrhoidal and habitual fluxes" (most likely malaria and dysentery) and driven off to other colonies by the Trustees' utopian strictures against liquor, large landholdings, and slavery, the population stagnated. No Georgia olives or oranges were shipped, no Georgia vintages were cellared, and only a scanty silk output was ever realized. Rice culture did flourish, but that was after the Trustees gave their charter back to the Crown and plantation agriculture and slavery were instituted.

Oglethorpe and the other Trustees were not fools, but their limited

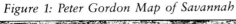

Figure 1: Peter Gordon Map of Savannah

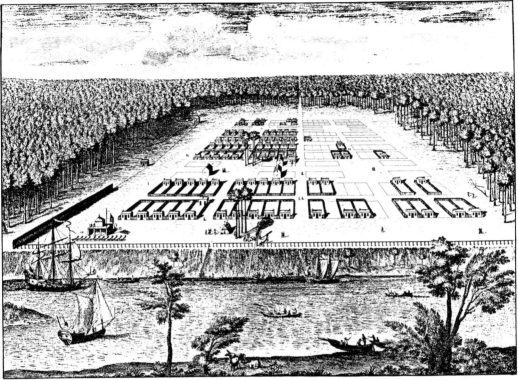

knowledge of Georgia's geography (and probably their own enthusiasm) fooled them into making the plans they did. In fact, Georgia does lie at the same latitude as the promised land. Oglethorpe sited Savannah at nearly the same latitude as Jerusalem (and Shanghai, so why shouldn't Georgia produce silk?). Despite being at the same latitude, Savannah doesn't have the dry Mediterranean climate of Jerusalem. And, while Georgia's environment could support growing mulberry trees, and thus silk production, the environment held out better prospects for other pursuits.

Georgia's founders naturally focused their attention on developing the coastal region where waterborne shipping was at hand and where the authorities could keep an eye on the colonists. But, it was not the coastline of the 1700s but the coastline of prehistoric times, the so-called fall line bisecting middle Georgia, that attracted the newcomers and would define the future of Georgia. At the fall line, where rapids and shoals first impeded navigation upstream on Georgia's south-flowing rivers, were the natural jumping-off spots for overland transportation, trading centers, and in due time water-powered manufacturing sites. Above the fall line was an immense territory whose upper reaches, and riches, were little known to the Trustees, though their grant from the king gave them rights all the way to the Pacific Ocean! In those upper reaches, the Creeks and Cherokees held sway, and as long as the Indian trade in furs and deerskins was profitable, these forested lands were reserved to the native population.

Many who came to Georgia saw that the Indians occupied lands far better than the swampy lowlands and pine barrens out from Savannah, and they pressured the colonial authorities to open the better lands to them. The pioneers who came to Georgia saw where the future of Georgia lay: it was destined to become an inland empire, not a coastal empire. That empire would be based on upland agriculture dominated by a crop of only minor importance in colonial days.

Georgia today, of course, evolved from Georgia yesterday. The events of yesterday and today have been and continue to be conditioned by Georgia's location. The next few pages of this chapter present an overview of where Georgia exists in space: the physical setting. The rest of the chapter provides the historical setting. The economic and social life of the people and the 100 years following the Civil War receive the greatest attention, for in those subjects and in that period lie the clues to understanding contemporary Georgia.

Location and Climate

As the 1984 promotion says, "you'd expect a lot of diversity in the largest state east of the Mississippi River." Massive and compact in form, Georgia encompasses somewhat over 58,000 square miles of land. Its greatest length north and south is about 320 miles; greatest width east and west is about 260 miles. The geographical center of the state is about 20 miles southeast of Macon, near Jeffersonville. Georgia takes in parts of five major physiographic divisions of the eastern United States (see Figure 2). The southern part of the state (below the fall line) lies in the Atlantic Coastal Plain, a region of gently rolling to low flat relief. Above the fall line, Georgia takes in four divisions of the Appalachian Mountain System: the Piedmont, the Blue Ridge, the Ridge and Valley, and the Plateau. The Piedmont, or foothills of the mountains, drew the bulk of newcomers between the Revolution and the Civil War. Today, this broad band across middle Georgia is the magnet for the "Sunbelt immigrants" and holds over one-half of the state's population. It also has most of Georgia's financial, commercial, manufacturing, and higher education resources.

Figure 2: Physiographic Divisions of Southeastern United States

But, as important as the Piedmont was in attracting pioneers to Georgia, another aspect of the state's location drew migrants, commodities, money, and armies *through* Georgia and influenced its destiny. Located just at the southern end of the Appalachians, which impeded westward migration in the late eighteenth and early nineteenth centuries, Georgia stood directly in the path of a stream of migrants who came down the valleys of the eastern slope of the mountains. And, near present-day Dalton, Georgia boasted the first easy gap in the Appalachians for hundreds of miles. Through that gap the state would build a railroad, Grant would send Sherman, and I-75 would whisk snowbirds to Florida.

As much as location itself, climate has helped to steer the course of Georgia history. Georgia lies between 30°21′20″ and 35°00′00″ north latitude and thus corresponds with Algeria, Iran, Afghanistan, and much of China. More importantly, the 4½ degrees of latitude that

Georgia embraces, plus an elevation that ranges down from those "misty Appalachian peaks to unspoiled coastal island beaches," ensure a diversity of climate (and, of course, climate-related human activity). Moreover, Georgia lies between 80°50′24″ and 85°36′00″ west longitude in the southeastern corner of the southeastern section of the United States, a geographic section which features a relatively warm and moist climate.

Georgia's proximity to the Atlantic Ocean and Gulf of Mexico and the frequent movement of air masses across the state ensure that changeability in weather that Pastor Boltzius noted some 250 years ago. Air masses originating over the ocean and gulf dominate the summers, and continental air masses flowing down from Canada heavily influence the winters. Of all the seasons, Georgia's winters are exceptionally changeable as warm moist air masses drift in from the south in place of rapidly moving cold masses from midcontinent. One result is winters almost as rainy and humid as summers, notable for their rain and humidity. Another result is the regular occurrence of unseasonable weather.

It is easy to overstate the influence of climate on social and cultural developments. True, Oglethorpe's "worthy poor" came to Georgia in part because of its climate (or at least the Trustees' inadequate understanding of it), and Georgia's heat and humidity influenced the development of plantation agriculture and slavery. But historical causes and effects are not so simply drawn. The cotton kingdom of nineteenth century Georgia was made possible by climate, but as much so by the invention of the cotton gin. The proliferation of U.S. military facilities in Georgia in the early twentieth century was influenced by climate, but as much so by the influence of politicians in Washington. The relocation of New England manufacturing to Georgia was influenced by climate, but as much so by the South's cheaper labor costs. And, the exodus of Americans from the Snowbelt to the Sunbelt in the last two decades is certainly attributable in part to climate, but also to the ready availability of air conditioning.

In sum, the physical environment provides a setting, a context, in which people make choices. To some extent it circumscribes those choices, but it does not determine them. For over 250 years, the people living on this land have made choices, made decisions, which influenced not only their own lives but also the lives and the choices open to future Georgians.

From Colony to State

In 1752, the Trustees turned their colony over to the Crown. Henceforth, it would be maintained for economic reasons, not philanthropy. Under the Crown, lumber, rice, and meat, plus the hides and furs from the Indian trade were exported. Whites from Virginia, the Carolinas, and New England moved into Georgia. Some brought black slaves with them. By 1766, there were 10,000 whites and 8,000 blacks in the colony. Ten years later, there were 50,000 people, about half of them black slaves.

With population growth and removal of restrictions on private enterprise, some small farms became great plantations. As agriculture expanded, Savannah became a bustling port.

Because Georgia was the weakest of the colonies and still open to Indian attack, Parliament spent more money on it than any other colony. In 1763, the colonial authorities secured for white Georgians a vast tract of Indian land that more than doubled the area of settlement. Ten years later, more Indian land was opened to whites (see Figure 3). Not surprisingly, when her sister colonies to the north gradually moved toward revolution, Georgia lagged behind. Then, as Parliament imposed new taxes on the colonies, Georgians split into pro- and antigovernment factions. After the Lexington and Concord battles in 1775, Georgia patriots began taking over the colony and in 1776 set up a state government. The revolutionary war in Georgia was a civil war; communities were split down the middle and some were all but destroyed.

Georgia as a Frontier State

In the decades immediately following the revolutionary war, Georgia was frontier country. Most of the territory claimed by the state (including what is now Alabama and Mississippi) was sparsely inhabited by Indians. To encourage white settlement, the new state government granted 200 acres of land to heads of families plus 50 acres for each family member. War veterans were given "bounties," additional land ranging from 200 acres for privates to 2,000 acres for generals. From the Carolinas, Virginia, and states farther north, settlers poured into Georgia. Augusta, not Savannah, was their main gateway and in 1786 became the capital. Letters sent back home, such as the one written in 1798 by Pennsylvanian Abner Davis, probably spurred immigration.

> The quality of the Soil in Georgia is Various, in different parts of the state. In the upper part, and adjacent to large Water Courses, in all parts, the soil is generally black and very fertile. Will produce from 40 to 50 bushels of corn to the Acre. This quality, may, be had now at from one to four Dollars an Acre.
>
> About the middle, and from that to the lower part of the State, the Soil is not so rich, being for the most part, what is called Pine Barren, very sandy, and of a yellowish Colour. Will produce from

Figure 3: Georgia 1733, 1763, 1773

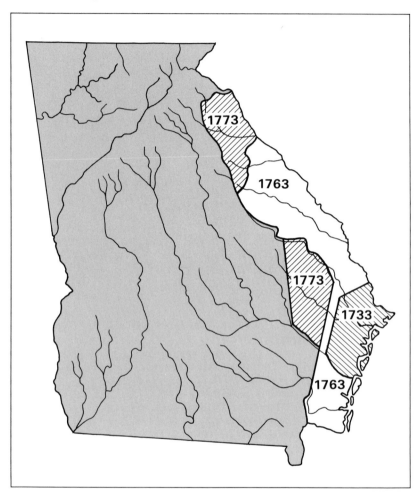

10 to 15 bushels of corn to the Acre. This quality may be had at
12½ and from that to 50 cents per Acre....

The ease with which the soil is cultivated and the Mildness
of the Winters are very considerable advantages. The Farmers in
this Country, Seldom think of putting more than one Horse in the
plough, and that frequently is a small *Tacky* (as they call them)
that may be had here for about 20 Dollars...I am fully of the
opinion that it don't cost the Georgians more than half, or perhaps,
one third, of the labour, or expense, that it does the Pennsylvanians
to raise the same quantity of grain....

In 1790, the first U.S. Census showed there were 82,548 white and black Georgians. (Indians were not counted.) In 1795, the tiny state was rocked by scandal—the Yazoo Land Fraud. The legislature had connived with land speculators to practically give away 35 million acres of the state's western lands for less than two cents an acre. Fearing for their lives, some of the scheming legislators fled the state. The next year, a newly elected legislature, meeting at the new state capital, Louisville on the Ogeechee River, repealed the Yazoo law. However, the claims of the speculators took many years and the intervention of the United States government to settle.

In the wake of the Yazoo scandal, the legislature devised a lottery system for distributing public lands. From 1804 to 1832, the state held six lotteries and gave away about 22 million acres to more than 100,000 settlers (see Figure 4). The state's population rapidly increased to 691,392 by 1840. As the frontier was pushed westward, the state capital was once again moved, this time in 1807 to Milledgeville, newly laid out at the fall line on the Oconee River.

Georgia's population growth was accompanied by an equally startling economic growth. The basis for much of that growth was cotton. In 1793, on a plantation outside Savannah, a Connecticut Yankee named Eli Whitney invented a machine to separate cotton seeds from cotton fibre. The cotton gin [gin from engine] brought a revolution in agriculture. Previously, the costly and slow hand labor required to pick seed from fibres had prevented cotton from being more than a minor crop in the South. Whitney's invention made cotton cheap to process, and the demand for it soared. For growing cotton, Georgia's Piedmont had the right climate and the right soil. The great forests which had supported the Indians for thousands of years were put to the axe to be replaced by cotton fields from horizon to horizon.

Most white Georgians thought that the Indians themselves were the biggest obstacle to economic development. From 1783 on, they increasingly demanded that the Cherokees, Creeks, and smaller tribes be removed from their protected lands to the West, where the national government had relocated the Indians of other eastern states. Removal, which involved three-way negotiations among the governments of Georgia, the United States, and the Creek and Cherokee nations, was marked by broken treaties, bribery, and bloodshed.

After the Yazoo Land Fraud, the state of Georgia had given up its claims to lands west of the Chattahoochee River. In return, the state got $1,250,000 and the federal government's promise to remove all Indians from within its new boundaries. However, the United States government had, in its treaties with the Creek and Cherokees, more or less agreed to protect their lands from white takeover.

Figure 4: Land Lotteries

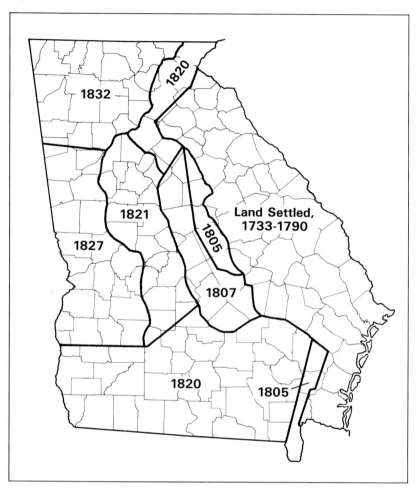

In the 1820s, the pressure of westward migration increased and the Creeks were in the way. Georgians didn't let the government in Washington forget its promise to remove all Indians. Gov. George Troup even threatened war with the United States if the Creeks were not removed. War was avoided, some Indian leaders were bought off, treaties were signed, and by 1827 the Creeks were gone. A lottery was held and whites moved onto the land.

The Cherokees held out for another decade in the north Georgia mountains, out of the main path of white migration to the west. More than the Creeks, the Cherokees were considered by many eastern whites to be "civilized" Indians. Independently of whites, the Cherokees had developed their own system of writing, had written a constitution for their nation (patterned after the U.S. Constitution), and had published a bilingual newspaper, *The Cherokee Phoenix.*

Although the federal government approved the established government of the Cherokees, the state of Georgia refused to recognize it and events of 1829 doomed it. First, Andrew Jackson, no friend to the Indian, was inaugurated as president of the United States. Second, gold was discovered at Dahlonega in the Cherokee country and the nation's first gold rush began. Pressure to remove the Cherokees increased. The Indians took their case to the U. S. Supreme Court and won in 1832, but Jackson refused to enforce the court's ruling.

Jackson's decision sealed the Cherokees' fate. The state of Georgia surveyed the Cherokee land and distributed it by lot to white Georgians. Some Cherokees gave up and moved west, but others held out in remote parts of the mountains. Finally, in 1838, the U.S. Army rounded up the last 15,000 Cherokees in Georgia and forced many to march on foot to the west in the dead of winter. Thousands of men, women, and children died. In the same year, the federal government opened a mint at Dahlonega to coin the Georgia gold.

Another obstacle to Georgia's growth was poor transportation. Georgia's rivers were navigable only up to the fall line. From the big trading centers there—Augusta on the Savannah River, Macon on the Ocmulgee, and Columbus on the Chattahoochee—flat-bottomed pole boats and barges carried cotton and other produce downriver to seaports, the most important of which was Savannah. (From there, in 1819, the first steamship, the *Savannah,* crossed the Atlantic to Liverpool.) Later, steamboats operated on the rivers up to the fall line. But, overland transportation was desperately needed to get products to riverside docks and to move east and west across the state. In the early 1800s, most Georgia roads followed old Indian trails, twisting and turning through forests and fields. Even the best road—from Savannah to Augusta—was so bad it took two to four days to make the trip. And for cotton towns of middle Georgia far from navigation, such as Sparta, Greensboro, Forsyth, and Covington, shipping by wagon over rough dirt roads was slow and expensive.

Then, in the early 1830s, the first rails were laid from Augusta and Savannah into the plantation counties, to be followed by the building of the Western & Atlantic—the so-called "state road." In December 1836, the Georgia General Assembly voted to build a railroad from a point on the Chattahoochee River in DeKalb County to the Tennessee line. It was perhaps the General Assembly's most historic decision. The purpose of building the 138-mile state-owned railroad was economic development: to funnel the products of the Midwest through Georgia to the port of Savannah. That "point" on the Chattahoochee located by state surveyors some 95 miles north of the state capital, Milledgeville, marked the hub of the Deep South's rail network by 1860 (see Figure 5), a strategic target of Union forces in the Civil War, and the new state capital by 1870. Ultimately, the effect of the 1836 General Assembly vote was to center the future growth of Georgia in the northern third of the state around the new state capital, Atlanta. Moreover, that decision helped to determine future transportation patterns for the Southeast and an industrial structure for Georgia based on commerce.

Figure 5: Transportation in Georgia, 1830-1860

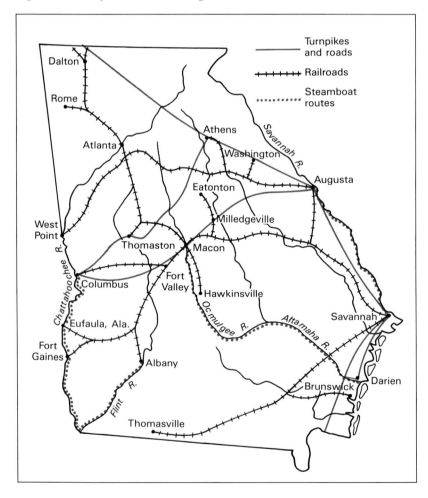

Empire State of the South

By 1830, Georgia was the leading cotton-producing state and well on its way to becoming the "Empire State of the South." Cotton, the basis of the state's prosperity, was so valuable that an acre of it might bring 10 times the price of an acre of wheat. From only 1,000 bales in 1790, cotton production grew to 400,000 bales in 1840, and to over 700,000 bales in 1860. As more land was given over to growing cotton, the number of slaves grew. In 1790, fewer than 30,000 slaves lived in Georgia; by 1860, there were more than 460,000. Across the center of the state were huge plantations worked by gangs of slaves. Here were Georgia's highest land values, highest black population, and highest cotton production (see Figure 6).

However, by the 1840s fertile soils such as Abner Davis had praised back in 1798 had all but disappeared from the older counties of middle Georgia. Worn out from too many cotton crops and too little care, the old lands were deserted by many farmers for land in southwest Georgia and beyond. By 1850, a sometime Georgia poet, Henry Jackson, turned out a bit of doggerel which described the change and became immensely popular in the state.

> The Red Old Hills of Georgia!
>   So bold and bare and bleak—
> Their memory fills my spirit
>   With thoughts I cannot speak.
> They have no robe of verdure,
>   Stript naked to the blast.
> And yet of all the varied earth,
>   I love them best at last.

Agriculture in antebellum Georgia was not composed in the main of huge plantations like those in middle Georgia. Far more common were the small farms of the upland whites, who were often called "crackers."[1] In 1860, over 6,000 farms and plantations had 20 or more slaves, but most white cotton growers depended more on the labor of their own families than of slaves. Yet, by the time Georgia earned the nickname "Empire State of the South," the cotton planter and slave interests increasingly dominated the state's economy and politics. As the abolition movement gained popular support in the North, proslavery sentiments hardened. Apologists for the "peculiar institution" used the Bible, biology, and most of all geography to bolster their arguments. Said Thomas R.R. Cobb of Athens, "So long as climate and disease,

---

1. A term dating from colonial days, used (sometimes derisively) in referring to common white folk. It may have originated with a Scottish term meaning "boaster."

Figure 6: Georgia Black Belt

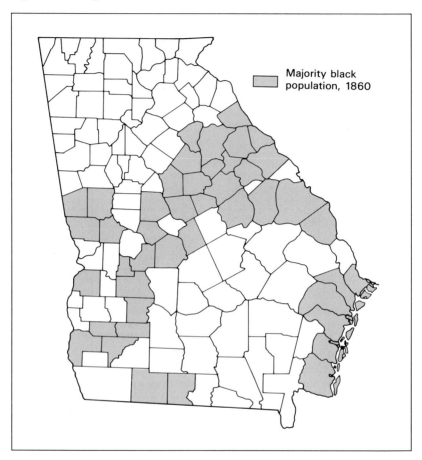

and the profitable planting of cotton, rice, tobacco, and cane, make the negro the only laborer inhabiting our Southern savannahs and prairies, just so long will he remain a slave to the white man." There were anti-slavery sentiments among the people, but by the end of the 1850s—with the emergence of the Republican Party, which appeared to stand only for the abolition of slavery and the dominance of northern industry over southern agriculture—such views were rarely expressed publicly.

Civil War and Reconstruction

The 1860 election of Republican Abraham Lincoln to the presidency of the United States sent shock waves through Georgia. White Georgians

Headquarters 1st Reg't Partizan Rangers,

Blairsville, Union County, Georgia,
May 5th, 1862.

I have been authorized by the Secretary of War to raise a Regiment of

PARTIZAN RANGERS,

For three years or the war. The non-commissioned officers, musicians and privates will receive a bounty of Fifty Dollars each, and are entitled to the same pay and organization as other troops.

Men of the Mountains! The same sanguinary and relentless foe who is visiting the cities and seaports of the Confederate States with fire, sword and devastation, is now approaching with slow but measured tread your own mountain-begirted homes. Can you supinely await longer their approach? Nay: up, up, my Countrymen, and to arms!

Three hundred Spartans, fighting for the sanctity of home and fireside, dared meet, in mortal combat, the armed millions of a Persian despot. Is home, country and liberty less dear to you than to them, and the *men* of 1776? If nay, then let us in this the hour of our country and freedom's peril, rally to their standard, and swear to make each pass in the grand bulwark of mountains which God has upheaved around our homes, a Thermopylæ in which the heroic deeds of the noble Spartans shall be emulated.

We can defend our country, repel the foe, and transmit the priceless heritage of freedom to our children if we *will.* Failing we can but die. Death in such a struggle is glory. Submission to the Federal tyrant is infamy and slavery.

Parties wishing to form a portion of my Regiment, will address me at Blairsville, Union County, Georgia.

S. J. SMITH.

Generally, mountain Georgians were neither slaveholders nor ardent secessionists, which probably explains the peculiar slant of this Confederate recruitment poster.

split over what to do: planters and townspeople were generally for secession, mountain and coastal plain farmers for the Union. At Milledgeville, after three days of hot debate and close procedural votes, an elected convention voted 208 to 89 to adopt an "Ordinance of Secession." It stated, ". . . the Union now subsisting between the State of Georgia and other States, under the name of the 'United States of America' is hereby dissolved. . . ." The next month, Georgia joined with other seceding states to form the Confederate States of America.

For over two years, the major fighting was far from Georgia, but Georgians suffered as the Union blockade of their ports tightened and battles elsewhere claimed the lives of their sons. Meanwhile, because of its location and transportation resources, Georgia became the heart of the Confederacy's war production and supply system.

Early in 1864, the full fury of war came to Georgia. On April 4th, from Washington, D.C., General Ulysses S. Grant wrote to General William T. Sherman, commander of a Union army of 99,000 men camped at Chattanooga, Tennessee:

> . . . get into the interior of the enemy's country as far as you can, inflicting all the damage you can against their war resources.

Through the late spring and early summer, Sherman's army relentlessly pushed south toward Atlanta, the hub of Georgia's rail network and the location of factories, warehouses, and supply depots. After 40 days of pounding the city with artillery, the Federals occupied it on September 1. In mid-November, the "workshop of the Confederacy" was put to the torch. With Atlanta in flames, Sherman's army began its "march to the sea," gathering up grain, vegetables, and meat; appropriating horses, mules, and wagons; destroying cotton gins, houses, mills, railroads, bridges, and depots (see Figure 7).

On December 21, 1864, with his army in Savannah, General Sherman telegraphed President Lincoln, "I beg to present you as a Christmas gift the city of Savannah, with one hundred and fifty heavy guns and plenty of ammunition, also about twenty-five thousand bales of cotton." The general reported that $100,000,000 worth of food and other resources had been destroyed on the march through Georgia. In a few months, the Civil War was over.

In the spring of 1865, the Empire State of the South was no more. Some 40,000 persons were killed or missing and thousands of homeless blacks and whites flocked to the cities seeking food and shelter. Most Georgians faced a bleak future: no mules or horses, no supplies, no equipment, no money.

The war had not only destroyed material resources but also had forced changes in the social and economic structure. In agriculture, various forms of tenancy emerged. Large plantations were divided into tenant farms onto which poor families, black or white, were moved. A family raised the crop and paid a share of it (sharecropping) or paid money (renting) to the owner for use of his land, a "shack," and perhaps for supplies.

Hand-in-hand with sharecropping came the crop lien system. To ensure tenants would pay their debts once the cotton crop was in, the General Assembly passed crop lien laws giving landowners a first claim

Figure 7: March to the Sea

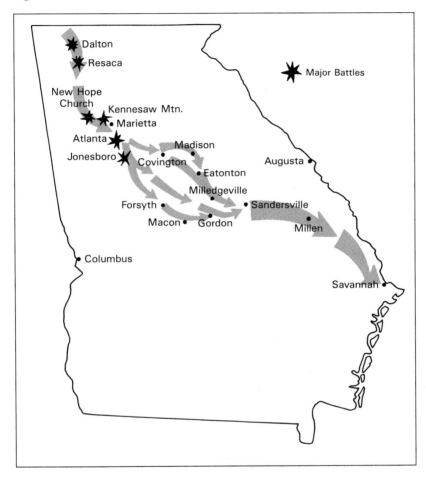

on the crop. Sharecropping and the crop lien system, together with the almost total dependence on cotton, would mean that the Georgia farmer—the bulk of the population—would remain impoverished until the coming of the New Deal and World War II.

The abolition of slavery, which had structured all relationships between Georgia's white and black populations, required that some new social structure emerge from the chaos following the war. The U.S. Constitution and radical Republican strength in Washington guaranteed the former slaves a political status equal to that of whites, the majority of whom only grudgingly tolerated that status. Notions of *social* equality, then touted in the North by preachers and the press, were unequivocally rejected. Although the tenets of white supremacy weren't forged into law for another 30 years, they began hardening into doctrine in the postwar years, undergirding a biracial social structure that would endure for a century.

The transformation of the state prison system—essentially from a penitentiary that was established for the humane treatment of convicts to chain gangs that featured the brutal exploitation of convicts—illustrates one effect of abolition. The state penitentiary at Milledgeville was damaged in the war, and in 1866 the General Assembly authorized local courts to use convicts to build roads, bridges, and other public works or to hire them out to private contractors engaged in such projects. This action set the stage for the beginning in 1868 of the long-term leasing of state convicts. Before the Civil War, the penitentiary's population was virtually all white. (Blacks, being slaves, received corporal punishment, or capital punishment for murder or other heinous offenses, locally.) Fifteen years after the war, the population of convict lease camps was 90 percent black.

Georgia, along with Florida, Louisiana, Mississippi, and Tennessee, used the criminal justice system to make former slaves toe the line or be cast into another form of involuntary servitude. Whether working for private lessors—in brick yards, sawmills, turpentine distilleries, or railroad construction—or for the counties on public roads, convicts were usually shackled to prevent escapes. To be imprisoned meant to be "on the chain gang."

From 1865 to 1871, the years of "reconstruction," government in Georgia saw the intermittent imposition of federal military rule, the election and disqualification of white officials here and black officials there, on-again off-again readmission to the Union, two new state constitutions, the rise of the Ku Klux Klan, and the hurried departure of the state's one and only Republican governor. One political legacy of the period was an almost century-long aversion to the Republican Party among most white Georgians.

The period also saw the removal of the state capital from Milledgeville to Atlanta after Milledgeville innkeepers refused lodging to black delegates to the 1867 constitutional convention. Although the initial move was effected under the federal military authorities, Georgians ultimately ratified it and dedicated a fine new capitol (now gold-domed) in 1889.

Also in 1867 began Atlanta's rise as a center of black culture in the United States. In that year, the American Missionary Association chose the city for a higher education institution for blacks. Over the next two decades, Atlanta University was joined by Clark, Morehouse, Spelman, and Morris Brown colleges and Gammon Theological Seminary to make

Atlanta the nation's largest center of education for black men and women. In time, black-owned newspapers, publishing houses, insurance companies, banks, and other enterprises would also give Atlanta one of the nation's major concentrations of black wealth and influence.

The New South

One conclusion that some Georgians drew from the outcome of the Civil War was that the South had to become more like the North. Maybe not in politics or social relationships or religion, but certainly in commerce and industry; the only way to beat the Yankees, they claimed, was to join them. Continued reliance on agriculture in producing raw materials for northern industry would mean dependence on the North.

On the national scene, the best-known proponent of the "new South" was journalist Henry W. Grady. From his editorial office at the *Atlanta Constitution* and in speeches before audiences of northern businessmen and investors, Grady promoted Georgia and boosted its accomplishments. At a banquet of the New England Club in New York City in 1886, he told his audience:

> . . .we have sowed towns and cities in the place of theories, and put business above politics. We have challenged your spinners in Massachusetts and your iron-makers in Pennsylvania. . . .We have learned that one northern immigrant is worth fifty foreigners; and have smoothed the path southward. . . .We have let economy take root and spread among us as rank as the crabgrass which sprung from Sherman's cavalry camps, until we are ready to lay odds on the Georgia Yankee as he manufactures relics of the battlefield in a one room shanty and squeezes pure olive oil out of his cotton seed, against any down-easter that ever swapped wooden nutmegs for flannel sausage in the valleys of Vermont.

By the time Grady spoke those words, northern money had already poured into the state, especially for railroads and especially in Atlanta. New lines connected it to the Northeast and Southwest by 1875, and its future as a city of commerce and transportation was foretold in the business census for that year. It listed seven banks, 17 cotton brokers, 23 wholesale companies, and 63 insurance agents. Five years later, the population census revealed that Atlanta, with 37,409 residents, had surpassed Savannah, 30,709, to become the largest city in the state. More rail lines, including new roads to the Midwest and to Florida, were built in the last decades of the nineteenth century, and by 1900, 44 railroads had Atlanta branch offices (see Figure 8). Reflecting its transportation status, Atlanta sported the nickname "Gate City of the South," and travelling salesmen joked that "whether you're going to heaven or hell, you'll have to change trains in Atlanta."

Figure 8: Railroads in Georgia, 1902

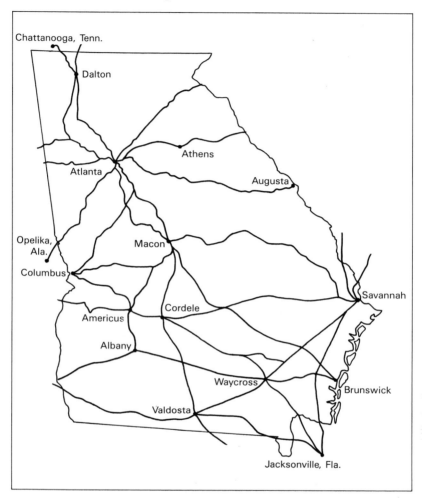

To boost economic development, Atlanta held three great expositions, or world's fairs, in a span of 14 years. In 1881, over a quarter million people visited a three-month long "World's Fair and Great International Cotton Exposition." A highlight was Gov. Alfred Colquitt's touring of the grounds in a suit of cotton—picked, ginned, woven, and tailored in one day. The stunt showed what Georgia could do, and the Exposition Cotton Mill kept on running after the fair closed. The press gave the city good coverage of its second show, "The Piedmont Exposition," in 1887, when President Grover Cleveland attended. But the biggest and most successful show of all was the 1895 "Cotton States and International Exposition." A million and a quarter visitors flocked to see what the southern states had accomplished in the 30 years following the Civil War. Some of them heard Booker T. Washington give a principal address at the fair. The address, which pleased most whites but dismayed many blacks, became known as the "Atlanta Compromise." In it, Washington counseled his fellow blacks to eschew the struggle for social and political equality and put their brains and skill into common labor.

Not all Georgians shared Henry Grady's vision of a new South of railroads and mills or agreed that the agrarian life of the South was inferior to the North's business life being touted in Atlanta. Opposition came early from the reactionaries, led by Georgia's "unreconstructed" Confederate, Robert Toombs. Toombs controlled the 1877 constitutional convention which produced a document that effectively proscribed government involvement in economic development until World War II. From east Georgia, Tom Watson, champion of the small farmer, railed against Wall Street, the railroads, and eastern "plutocrats." Watson knew what most farmers only dimly realized: that with the new industrial order, Georgia's relationship to the North was indeed that of colony to mother country. As Watson and others pointed out, few of the railroads, cotton mills, and other industrial enterprises were owned by Georgians, and most of the profits from them were shipped North. And, through discriminatory freight and credit rates, Georgians were effectively prevented from manufacturing most finished goods, which they paid dearly to obtain from Northern suppliers.

On another plane, Georgia's best-known man of letters, Joel Chandler Harris, also weighed in against the scramble after the "bright dollar." Ironically, this bashful writer, who at night in the privacy of his home penned the "Uncle Remus" stories in which human values and life on the land are celebrated, was by day a friend and colleague of Henry Grady in the editorial office of the *Atlanta Constitution*. After Grady's death, Harris regularly satirized the business culture being imported into Georgia. Shortly before his own death, in 1908, he wrote a satire in which

> . . . the farmer fell to amusing himself with wondering if the great majority of men who are leading or trying to lead a strenuous business life are not actually missing something that is really worth having. Is the game worth the candle that is burning at both ends? And the wonder grew when a casual visitor, who had been in New York during the recent financial excitement, told him of a curious spectacle that fell in his way. He saw prosperous-looking men sitting in automobiles before the closed doors of a bank, crying as though their hearts were broken—and some of them were young men in the very blush and bloom of their prime! To the farmer the tale was more astonishing than any narrative taken out of the Arabian Nights. . . .

However, the modern age was upon Georgia, or at least upon Atlanta. The year after Harris died, and only five minutes from Harris's home in the city's West End neighborhood, Henry Ford opened his southeastern distribution center. Also in 1909, the National Association of Automobile Manufacturers chose Atlanta for its third automobile show (New York and Chicago had hosted the first two), and Asa G. Candler, Coca-Cola magnate and auto enthusiast, bought 300 acres of land on the city's south side for auto racing. The site would later become famous for another mode of transportation.

In 1911, when 2,000 businessmen gathered in Atlanta at the Southern Commercial Congress to hear three men—William H. Taft, Theodore Roosevelt, and Woodrow Wilson—who would compete for the presidency the next year, Atlanta was on its way to becoming the "city of conventions."

The national government provided an economic boost, too, beginning in 1889 when the army made Ft. McPherson a permanent post. A decade later, soldiers were in training in Atlanta, and *entraining* from Atlanta, for the Spanish-American War. In 1900, the government located one of three new federal prisons in Atlanta. The federal presence grew as Atlanta was chosen over New Orleans and Birmingham for a district bank of the Federal Reserve System, established in December 1913.

While Atlanta's growth was based primarily on commerce, manufacturing was also a component. New factories turned out textiles, cottonseed oil, farm machinery, furniture, pianos, and above all, Coca-Cola—first concocted in 1886. Around the state, investment in manufacturing rose from a mere $14 million in 1870 to $202 million in 1910. Nonfarm employment rose from under 20,000 in 1870 to over 120,000 in 1910, and gave rise to Georgia's first labor unions in the 1880s, and, in 1899, the Georgia Federation of Labor. Clay works in Macon and Augusta, iron foundries in Columbus, and innumerable turpentine stills in the Coastal Plain all contributed to the "new South" economy. Savannah boomed as a cotton and naval stores port.

By far, cotton textile manufacturing led the way. Rome, LaGrange, West Point, Dalton, Gainesville, Augusta, Macon, and Columbus had big mills, but more common were the small country mills built along rivers and streams for waterpower. To entice the "crackers" or poor whites to leave their hardscrabble farms to work in the mills (blacks were not allowed in the mills), mill owners provided "free" housing. In the mill village, wherein all the necessities of life came from the mill owner, generations of families owed their lives to the "company store," sometimes never seeing hard cash from year to year.

At the turn of the century, these mill workers were among the most economically depressed of Americans. Whole families, age five and up, worked side by side in the mill, subsisting on diets of corn meal, molasses, and fatback, and plagued by malaria, hookworm, pellagra, and rickets. Their cousins who continued to sharecrop cotton suffered the same afflictions and were far more numerous, for Georgia's industrialization never reached the level that Henry Grady envisioned. Atlanta was one thing, most of Georgia was another.

Practically all of Georgia's farmers, black and white, were the children of those who grew cotton before the Civil War. Unlike the states of the Northeast and Midwest, Georgia received few of the European immigrants who poured into America between 1870 and 1920. But like their counterparts in other parts of the country, Georgia's small farmers rebelled in the 1880s and 1890s. They resented the crop lien laws which favored their creditors, the high interest rates those creditors charged, the high prices merchants charged for fertilizer and supplies, and the high shipping rates the railroads charged. They resented the politicians who favored the bankers, the merchants, and the railroads.

From the farmers' revolts grew a political movement, populism. In Georgia in 1890, so many candidates favoring farm interests were elected to the General Assembly that it was nicknamed the "farmers' legislature." This legislature passed laws to tighten business regulations and fund the farmers' schools. But it also passed the state's first "Jim Crow" laws providing for racial segregation. White supremacy hardened and took precedence over any common interests poor white farmers might have with poor black farmers.

The New Century

After the turn of the century, things improved somewhat for the farmers, who represented over 80 percent of Georgia's population. Between 1900 and 1910, the average value of a Georgia farm doubled, from $816 to $1,657, even though its average size shrank from 118 to 93 acres. In 1911, Georgia farmers planted 5.5 million acres in cotton, up from 2.6 million in 1879. In the latter year, cotton production broke the two-million-bale mark for the first time, reaching a whopping 2,794,295 bales— second only to Texas cotton production.

In those marginally better times, progressive Georgians moved to change their society. In 1908, the state abolished the corrupt convict lease system. Henceforth, it would maintain its own prisoners. The dreadful chain gang, however, was kept. The long campaign against children working in the mills finally resulted in a child labor law in 1914. The law forbade mill employment for boys and girls under 14. The most politically explosive progressive measure was prohibition. The state's biggest denominations, the Baptists and Methodists, led the campaign. Beginning in the 1880s, local and state candidates for office won or lost by virtue of their stance on liquor. In referendum after referendum, localities switched back and forth between wet and dry. In 1907, the

General Assembly finally voted the whole state dry, preceding national prohibition by more than a decade. About the same time, the racist aspect of progressivism resulted in the disfranchisement of black voters.

One month after the Democratic primary of 1906, which featured almost hysterical agitation for disfranchisement, a race riot left 25 blacks and one white dead in Atlanta. Hundreds of others were injured. Across the United States and in Europe, newspaper accounts of the riot added weight to an already bad reputation Georgia had for racial violence.

While disfranchisement, segregation, convict leasing, and the chain gangs defamed Georgia, no aspect of racism brought more shame than lynching. While lynching was not unknown in most states in the 1800s, in the latter part of the century it became an increasingly southern phenomenon directed overwhelmingly against blacks. In 1890, Georgia led all states but Texas with 18 lynchings; and in 1899, 27 black men were recorded lynched in Georgia. (The real numbers are unknown.)

Lynchers continued to act with impunity into the twentieth century, despite the General Assembly's passage of antilynch laws in 1893 and 1895. Few local authorities were willing to stand up to lynch mobs. Despite the fact that the identities of mob members were commonly known in a community, the coroner's jury usually reported that lynch victims died "at the hands of parties unknown." In 1905, a mob took nine prisoners, one white and eight blacks, from the jail in Oconee County, tied them to fence posts and shot them. Ten years later, in the case that brought Georgia the most notoriety and that remains controversial to this day, 25 men took Leo M. Frank from the state penitentiary at Milledgeville, drove 100 miles to Marietta, and hanged him. The lynching of Frank, a white Atlanta factory manager and a Jew, foreshadowed the 1915 rebirth of the Ku Klux Klan at Stone Mountain. (All told, between 1882 and 1968—the years for which records were kept—531 persons were lynched in Georgia; the victims were blacks in 492 cases.)

World War I brought greater demands for Georgia products. Cotton prices shot up and farmers took out loans to buy more land on which to plant more cotton. The 1918 crop reached a record value of $291,831,000. Other farmers planted more acres in corn, wheat, potatoes, and peanuts. Meanwhile, Ft. McPherson was expanded and Camp Gordon opened in Atlanta to train soldiers. At Columbus, Ft. Benning was established as the "home of the infantry."

A sure sign of prosperity were all the Model T's. Henry Ford had opened a full-scale assembly plant in Atlanta in 1915, and shiny black "Tin Lizzies" were everywhere, bumping along Georgia's country roads.

Yet while some Georgians prospered, in the early 1920s, some 75 percent of the Georgia population were still living in the countryside and

At the cotton gin. In the 1920s, Athens, home of the University of Georgia, was more dependent on cotton marketing than college students.

were on the brink of disaster. At the end of the war, cotton prices had plummeted. Then came a worse calamity—the boll weevil. The long-snouted insect that had crossed the Rio Grande into Texas in 1894 entered southwest Georgia by 1913. Within 10 years, the state cotton crop dropped to 588,000 bales. In Greene County alone, the crop dwindled from 20,000 bales in 1919 to just 333 in 1923. Frantically, farmers turned to peanuts, tobacco, and livestock. Never again would cotton account for two-thirds of the value of Georgia agriculture.

Thousands of Georgia's farmers abandoned their fields. Between 1920 and 1925, the farm population dropped by 375,000. In one year, 1923, some 100,000 rural folk packed their meagre belongings and boarded trains to look for work in Atlanta, or in Chicago, Detroit, New York and other northern cities. Others piled into old cars and headed for Florida.

As the farmers lost out, so too did the country merchants who supplied their goods and the bankers who gave them credit. Savannah's port activity dwindled. The severity of Georgia's depression in the 1920s is shown in its median annual per capita income for the years 1920-1930: it was only $244. For the same years, $605 was the median for all states and in New York and Illinois (where so many Georgians flocked) it was $852.

Yet, some positive changes occurred in the 1920s. Yankee tourists heading for Florida helped to stimulate the drive for paved roads in Georgia. Since its earliest days, the state had left road-building to local governments, but the automobile had rendered that arrangement obsolete: good connecting roads between cities became a necessity. After Congress in 1916 established federal aid for highway construction, the Georgia legislature created a State Highway Commission to establish a network of state roads. By 1925, the first urban centers, Atlanta and Macon and Savannah and Brunswick, were linked by paved roads. (As Figure 9 suggests, Florida traffic had first priority.)

In 1925, transportation, which had been at the heart of Atlanta's growth from the beginning, took on a new dimension as the city leased Candler Racetrack for an airfield. The city put up buildings for the Weather Bureau and the Post Office. In 1928, regular air mail service began between Atlanta and New York. The next year, Delta (then based in Louisiana) launched passenger service between Dallas and Atlanta; and in 1930, Eastern added passenger service between Atlanta and New York. Atlanta's initiative in air transportation was perhaps the biggest factor as it outpaced its commercial rivals in the Southeast, Birmingham and Charlotte, after World War I.

A new surge of economic boosterism also helped lift Atlanta above its rival cities. In the wake of the cotton failure and the exodus of Georgians to Florida, a "psychological depression" (according to one report) had infected the Atlanta business community. To turn things around, the Chamber of Commerce organized the "Forward Atlanta Movement," launching a nationwide campaign to advertise the city "just like a commodity." The copy for one ad asked, "Can You Get Along Without An Atlanta Branch?" The growing southern market, the decentralization of American industry, and of course Atlanta's transportation facilities all supported the appeal for "permanent new business houses and branch factories." Forward Atlanta was a smashing success: from 1926 through 1929, 679 new firms—including a Chevrolet plant—located in the city. With them came the new people, many of them from New York where more often than not the home office was located. By 1930, Atlanta counted 270,366 residents.

The New Deal

One prominent New Yorker who came to Georgia was Franklin D. Roosevelt. Searching for a cure, the polio-stricken Roosevelt came at

Figure 9: Paved Roads in Georgia, 1925

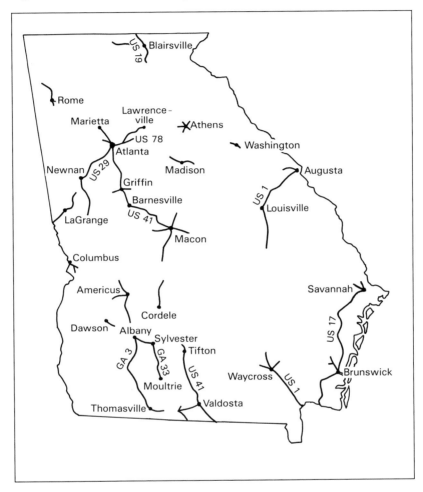

the behest of Georgia friends in October 1924, to a rundown west Georgia spa in whose waters, 88 degrees and laden with mineral salts, the Creek Indians first bathed. He felt some relief there and subsequently put $200,000 of his own fortune into establishing the nonprofit Georgia Warm Springs Foundation in 1927, turning the old spa into the nation's leading research and treatment center for polio. Roosevelt went on to become governor of New York and president of the United States.

FDR's choice of Warm Springs for his therapy had a great impact on Georgians' fortunes during the Great Depression. From his years of close contact with rural Georgia neighbors, Roosevelt could argue from

THIS IMPATIENT AGE!

Cancellations come to him whose goods arrive last!

A FUNDAMENTAL change has taken place in the American people. They will not wait for anything. They have no patience with delay. "They want what they want when they want it" —in the words of the old song.

And that change has created a new situation in merchandising. Merchants are buying hand-to-mouth. Wholesalers warehouse less and order oftener. They both expect the producer to have the goods handy, ready for quick delivery.

Speed, then, is the essence of selling under the new conditions. Availability of the goods. Strategic centers of distribution — preferably branch manu-facturing plants—are essential. For the cancella-tions come to him whose goods arrive last.

In the South—America's fastest growing market— the logical, strategic location is Atlanta. Says the conservative Department of Commerce —"Atlanta is generally recognized as the principal headquar-ters city of this region." More than 900 nationally known concerns have confirmed this judgment by investing millions here in branch equipment.

And why?

Transportation for one thing. 15 main railroad lines radiating from Distribution City to reach seventy million prosperous people within a day's run.

Production economy for another. Economies in labor, power, taxes, raw materials, building costs— and a host more that enable the Atlanta producer to go into market with a better price, *and a better profit.*

Study the facts about Atlanta that apply to your business. They will be gathered especially for you, without charge or obligation, if you will write —

INDUSTRIAL BUREAU, CHAMBER OF COMMERCE
Chamber of Commerce Building

Send for this Booklet! It contains the funda-mental facts about Atlanta as a location for your Southern branch.

ATLANTA

Industrial Headquarters of the South

- 93 -

A typical example of "Forward Atlanta" advertising during 1926-29, this ad was directed at marketing executives.

personal knowledge that the South was "the Nation's No. 1 economic problem." Ideas for federal assistance—including rural electrification, soil conservation, and farm-purchase loans for sharecroppers—emerged from the president's Georgia experiences. (In 1935, of 250,000 farms in Georgia, 164,000 were worked by tenants—102,000 white and 62,000 black.)

Not far from "The Little White House" at Warm Springs, FDR personally oversaw development of Pine Mountain Valley, a model farm complex where grapes, tomatoes, chickens, and cattle were showcased (to show the feasibility of abandoning cotton) and poor rural families were resettled. Up in Atlanta, federal slum clearance was inaugurated and at Thanksgiving, 1935, the president dedicated the New Deal's first housing project, "Techwood."

Across the state, work relief projects paid Georgians the highest wages they'd ever seen and resulted in public facilities—brick schoolhouses and courthouses, concrete roads and bridges, state parks, hospitals and health clinics, even community swimming pools—the likes of which their local politicians could never, or would never, consider. (Gov. Eugene Talmadge called it "wet nursing.")

Farmers might encounter FDR in the big touring car with staff and photographer—or driving his little specially equipped roadster.

Near Macon, 1937, an out-of-work sewing machine repairman and his family are hitchhiking to Alabama.

In sum, the New Deal boosted Georgians (and other Southerners) in the 1930s more than any other regional group of Americans. Compared to others, they got no more help in absolute amounts, but given their meagre economic base and the New Deal policy of closing the income gap among the regions, Georgians gained relatively more than their northern counterparts.

In the 1930s, the rest of the nation learned more about Georgia, not only from the extensive press coverage of FDR's sojourns in the state but also from two books-turned-films: *I Am a Fugitive from a Georgia Chain Gang* by Robert Elliot Burns and *Gone with the Wind* by

Margaret Mitchell. Burns's true-life horror story (Hollywood's first "social conscience" film) outraged the nation and led to the demise of the chain-gang system in the South. But Mitchell's romanticized story of the Civil War thrilled the nation. After the film premiere of GWTW in 1939, Atlanta became a tourist as well as a convention favorite; frustrated northern visitors searched high and low for the fictional Tara and other sites where Scarlett and Rhett cavorted.

In 1939, the city hosted almost 500 conventions. Most conventioneers arrived on one of the 65 daily trains run into Atlanta by the eight rail systems serving it. Many flew in, for in that year Candler Field serviced eight major airlines and ranked third in the United States in air passenger service.

World War II and After

What the New Deal hadn't accomplished for Georgia's economy, the war did. The existing federal establishment in the state, the railroads, the warm climate, the president's own fondness for his adopted home-state, and the political clout and specialization in naval and military affairs of two Georgians in Washington—Rep. Carl Vinson and Sen. Richard B. Russell—helped to create an inordinate amount of war-related activity in the state. Stimulating the Georgia economy were the huge training facilities, including Ft. Benning at Columbus, Ft. Gordon at Augusta, Hunter Field and Ft. Stewart near Savannah; and war production plants, most notably the nation's largest at Marietta where the Bell Aircraft Company turned out B-29 bombers. The state's farms and mills all cranked up to meet wartime demands for foodstuffs and textiles. The income of the average Georgian rose from $424 in 1941 to $882 in 1945.

At the end of the war, much of the wartime infrastructure remained in place to contribute to Georgia's economy in later decades. For example, the B-29 plant was reopened by the Lockheed Company during the Korean War, employed 30,000 workers during the Vietnam War, and produced one of the world's largest planes, the C-5A and B, into the 1980s. Moreover, new postwar technology brought revolutionary changes.

On the farm, the tractor and the mechanical harvester displaced men, women, and mules. With mechanization, sharecropping faded away and displaced tenants headed for the cities to find jobs. By 1970, the number of farms had dropped from 200,000 to 70,000, with those remaining doubled in size from 100 to 200 acres.

In the postwar decades, the development of synthetic fibers and the planting of new cotton lands in the West brought the demise of King

Cotton in Georgia. Farmers found they could make more money raising poultry, peanuts, soybeans, and corn than cotton. Across the Piedmont, other landowners put their old fields into pines: in a few years highways that once ran for hundreds of miles through open cotton vistas were walled in by trees.

Most of the farmers who came to town found jobs for the asking. Into the 1950s and 1960s, diversified manufacturing transplanted from New England located around the state (but mainly near Atlanta). Georgia's mild climate, low taxes and fuel costs, and a largely nonunionized workforce willing to work for lower wages than what prevailed in the North lured companies south. To further enhance the business picture, a state authority took over the decaying docks at Savannah, starting a revitalization that would make it the South's major port.

Along with the companies came people. Moving into Georgia after World War II, they reversed the 75-year-old pattern of south to north migration. Besides the attraction of newly developed jobs, air conditioning made office work and just plain living in summer months bearable to Yankees. Furthermore, DDT and other pesticides that became available after the war practically eliminated the miseries caused by the South's notorious insects, especially the disease-carrying mosquito. Later, the moderation of racial discrimination would bring black as well as more white immigrants to Georgia.

On the negative side was race. Since Reconstruction, the imposition of white supremacy in Georgia political, social, and economic affairs had visited injustice and violence on black people, stigmatized the white people, retarded everyone's progress, and engendered hostility to anyone inside or outside the state who dared criticize the practice. Racial discrimination naturally brought a continuing out-migration of Georgia's black people. But in the postwar years, those who remained began to challenge white supremacy and the Jim Crow laws. In the wake of the 1954 Supreme Court ruling against school segregation *(Brown v. Board of Education),* came the reactionary politics of "massive resistance" and the sometimes violent white backlash that had the potential to cut short Georgia's new-found prosperity.

The campaign against racial discrimination was led nationwide by a Georgian, Martin Luther King, Jr., and his Atlanta-based Southern Christian Leadership Conference. King advocated "non-violence"; in the early 1960s, "sit-ins," "freedom rides," and "demonstrations" became the techniques for ending segregation and discrimination. In 1963, King led 250,000 people in "The March on Washington" —the largest mass protest of the civil rights movement. On the steps of the Lincoln Memorial he told the crowd,

I have a dream that one day on the red hills of Georgia, sons of former slaves and the sons of former slave owners will be able to sit down together at the table of brotherhood. . . .

The next year, Congress passed the Civil Rights Act of 1964 and King received the Nobel Peace Prize.

Meanwhile, in Atlanta, Georgia's business elite took the lead in helping to defuse the potential for violence by seeking accommodation between blacks and whites. Atlanta avoided the kind of racial strife that rocked other southern cities and called itself "the city too busy to hate." Atlanta was all business in the 1960s; as new companies moved in, blacks gained access to jobs, as well as to public facilities and accommodations, formerly closed to them.

Almost inevitably, however, with school desegregation, nondiscrimination in housing, and increased opportunities for blacks came white flight. Through the 1960s and into the 1970s, Atlanta's middle-class white families moved in droves to the surrounding counties of DeKalb, Gwinnett, Cobb, and Clayton, leaving most of the city's residential neighborhoods virtually all-black. And, except for conventioneers, downtown Atlanta became almost deserted at night as the suburbs became the scene for shopping and entertainment.

The train station at Manchester, Georgia. Such segregated facilities were the rule through the 1950s.

Atlanta changed physically, too. The wrecker's ball demolished old landmarks to make room for office buildings, hotels, convention facilities, shopping centers, and expressways. Concerned that the city was becoming "major league" in everyway but sports, politicians and businessmen got together, built a stadium, and in 1966 lured the Braves baseball club from Milwaukee. About the same time, the city dedicated the Memorial Arts Center. On the south side, the Atlanta airport grew close to being the nation's busiest, and air travellers were joking that "whether you're going to heaven or hell, you'll have to change *planes* in Atlanta."

The Changing Countryside

Meanwhile, in the countryside, the red hills of which Martin Luther King spoke in 1963 were undergoing changes as dramatic as those wrought by cotton-growing a hundred years before. Prime movers behind those changes were the automobile and a growing population.

Immediately following World War II, Americans were eager to hit the road. For Georgia in particular, 1947 was an auspicious year in the age of the auto. Correctly gauging the potential market, General Motors opened a new assembly plant on Atlanta's north side, at Doraville, to produce Buick, Oldsmobile, and Pontiac cars. Not to be outdone, Ford dedicated its first new postwar operation at Hapeville on Atlanta's south side.[2] Also in 1947, Atlanta authorities set up a commission to oversee the construction of an expressway system to relieve local traffic congestion. In the same year, federal and state officials agreed to build a 40,000-mile network of highways to link the nation's principal cities.

Because of Atlanta's location and commercial status, federal highway planners chose it as the southeastern hub on which the interstate system would be built. It shared a distinction with only four other American cities: it was a point of convergence of three interstate highways, I-75, I-85, and I-20. The bulldozers levelled the red hills not only for highways, but also for highway-attracted suburban industrial parks, office complexes, shopping centers, and housing developments. In the process, they helped to create a flattened out type of urbanization characteristic of cities that saw their greatest growth *after* the automobile became the dominant form of transportation.

By the 1970s, one out of every five Americans was within an overnight delivery of Atlanta shippers, and about half the nation's population resided within a two-night radius of the city. By the 1980s, more

---

2. By 1982, Georgia would become the third leading auto-producing state.

than 430 of the *Fortune* 500 companies had located offices in the metropolitan Atlanta region. Along with rail and air transportation, the highways made Atlanta more than ever a "city of commerce."

Interstate highways helped metropolitan Atlanta become a magnet for more people and more business (see Figure 10). They also caused headaches for highway planners. Expressways only a decade or so old were quickly overburdened by through and local traffic and required widening and rebuilding. Between 1975 and 1985, almost all interstate highway construction in Georgia occurred on or within the I-285 perimeter around Atlanta.

Figure 10: Georgia Interstates

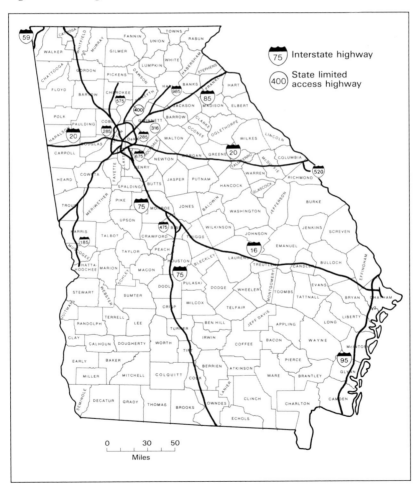

Though not so dramatic in degree, interstate highways also had an important influence on the growth of nonmetropolitan areas of Georgia. The 1980 census showed that of the 62 counties through which interstate highways (or their four-lane limited-access feeders) pass, only three lost population. Exactly half of the 62 exceeded the state's growth rate of 19.1 percent, and in 45 of the 62 counties, growth rates outpaced the national increase of 11.4 percent.

While the interstate highways helped to industrialize and urbanize Georgia, they also helped to maintain much of its traditional rural character. The new highways accommodated those who desired to live in the country while taking job opportunities in town. The 1970s witnessed population movement away from the central cities to rural counties.

The movement of population and industry into Georgia during the 40 years following World War II placed heavier demands on the land's resources, especially water. Although Georgia has no natural lakes, a land with many rivers and valleys lends itself to construction of artificial lakes. Since 1950, almost a half-million acres of land in Georgia (and adjacent lands in bordering states) have been inundated to meet the demand for water resources. Second only to new highways in changing the countryside of Georgia have been the new lakes.

The land is the setting for contemporary Georgia. The prehistoric Indians hardly marked the land, leaving only the huge earthen mounds they heaped up at a few sites. But the Europeans who came to Georgia, and the Africans brought by them, changed the land in ways that continue to influence life. The Indians retreated as the great dark forests which covered nine-tenths of the land were cleared away, opening the land to great bright vistas. The deep topsoil of the Piedmont raised up a cotton kingdom, but its subjects were poor stewards of the soil. They allowed the riches of the Empire State of the South to wash away to the oceans. Impoverished by war, the people struggled on the land for almost a century, working the poor red subsoil for meagre return. But, with new industry and new technology on the land the people broke the shackles of their long depression. The land was changed: the forests returned, and lakes and great cities appeared where before there were only poor farms. New people moved in to inhabit the land.

The geographical setting, altered by both human exploitation and human ingenuity, provides the backdrop against which the story of contemporary Georgia unfolds.

CHAPTER TWO

Environment and Natural Resources

By James E. Kundell

A Land of Five Regions

Georgia is a large state in land area, including some 37.6 million acres
or 58 thousand square miles. It is the largest state in area east of the
Mississippi River, encompassing parts of five major physiographic
regions: the Blue Ridge Mountains, the Ridge and Valley Province, the
Cumberland plateau, and the Piedmont and the Coastal Plain provinces
(see Figure 1). One can begin to understand the land and its uses by
looking at each region separately.

The Blue Ridge Province

The Blue Ridge Mountains are an old mountain range extending from
Pennsylvania to North Georgia. The highest point in elevation in Georgia
is Brasstown Bald at 4,784 feet above sea level. Although their aerial
extent is limited, the mountains in Georgia have considerable impact
on the state. These mountains serve as the first major land obstacle to
warm, moist air masses moving northeastward from the Gulf of Mexico.
The air masses rise to go over the mountains, temperatures cool, and
precipitation results. Part of this region receives about 80 inches of annual
precipitation, making it one of the wettest areas east of the state of Washington. This heavy precipitation falling in a mountainous region could
cause major problems related to erosion and flooding. Fortunately, the
mountains are generally forested, much of the land being in the Chattahoochee National Forest. This forest cover not only reduces erosion but
also modulates the release of water to streams. Thus the flood and
drought cycle that might be found in a region of this nature is avoided.

  The mountains are also important for recreational purposes. Their
proximity to metropolitan regions makes them ideal for weekend excur-
sions. It also makes them desirable for second home development.

Figure 1: Physiographic Regions of Georgia

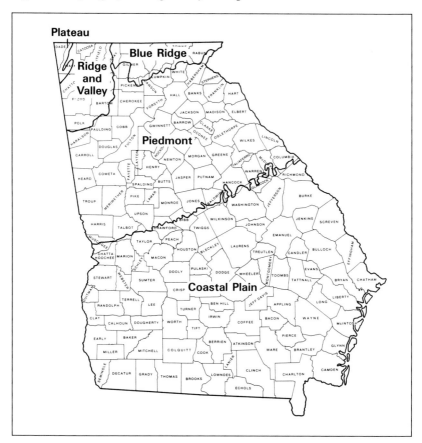

Recreation opportunities in the mountains include camping, canoeing, hiking, hunting, fishing, skiing, and other outdoor activities. As long as they are maintained in a healthy condition, the mountains of Georgia not only protect the water supply of most Georgians but also provide them with a "wild and wonderful" playground at their backdoor.

The Ridge and Valley Province and the Cumberland Plateau

The Ridge and Valley Province in Georgia lies between the Atlanta metropolitan area and Chattanooga, Tennessee. The region is an urban/industrial area with the second highest population density in the state and a concentration of textile industries. The Ridge and Valley Province lies to the west of the Blue Ridge Mountains. Its ridges and valleys are the result of past compression forces from the southeast pushing northwestward and causing the rock layers to fold and buckle as a rug might do if it were pushed from both ends. The result was the formation of parallel southwest-trending ridges and valleys. The compression pressure decreased in a northwesterly direction and resulted in uplifting in the extreme northwestern portion of the state, which is the easternmost extension of the Cumberland plateau. Only a very small portion of this plateau extends into Georgia.

The Piedmont Province

The Piedmont Province is a distinct geological region that lies south of the Blue Ridge Mountains. Like the mountains, it is underlain by hard, crystalline bedrock, but unlike the mountains, it is covered by a rather deep layer of soil, the characteristic "red clay" of Georgia. The Piedmont has generally rolling hills and valleys and increases in altitude toward the mountains.

The Piedmont Province, along with the Ridge and Valley Province, is the major urban/industrial region of the state. More than one-half of the population of Georgia lives in the Piedmont Province. This region, which at one time was the heart of the old "cotton belt," is now important for forest products and animal products (poultry, beef). Textile, pulp, and various other industries are located throughout the province. Major agriculture crops include wheat, corn, and soybeans.

The Coastal Plain Province

The Coastal Plain Province encompasses two rather distinct regions: the upper coastal plain and the lower coastal plain. The upper coastal plain is the major agricultural region of the state. It contains the highest concentration of prime agricultural land and is underlain by plentiful groundwater sources. This region has experienced a major increase in irrigation during the past decade. In the early 1970s, irrigation was a minor user of water in the state, but by the early 1980s over one million acres of land were under irrigation, making irrigation the major consumer of water in Georgia.

The lower coastal plain differs from the upper coastal plain in being flatter and having poorly drained soils. As a result, the area is more forest oriented than agriculturally oriented and is the center of pulp production and naval stores such as pine resin.

The coastal region of Georgia is important for industrial purposes, fishing, and recreation. Deep water ports, generally plentiful water, and proximity to resources such as forest products have supported industrial development along the coast and extending up the Savannah River to Augusta. The coastal marshes serve as nurseries for the commercial fishing industry. The marshes are protected by the chain of barrier islands which extend along the entire coast of Georgia. These coastal resources are discussed in more detail in a later section.

In sum, Georgia is not only a large state, but also a diverse state. From the mountains in the north to the coastal plain in the south, natural resources vary. The igneous and metamorphic rocks of north Georgia are replaced by sedimentary deposits in the Coastal Plain; the red clays of the Piedmont give way to sands and peat below the fall line; whitewater streams of the mountains become meandering rivers toward the coast; hardwood forests merge with pine and cypress stands; wildlife ranges from deer, bear, and quail to alligators, egrets, and red-cockaded woodpeckers.

Natural Resources and Environmental Quality

Because of the diversity of the state, the natural resources of Georgia are varied. This section is a discussion of the natural resources, how they are used, and concerns related to their use.

Land Resources

Since Georgia is a large, geologically diverse state, it has substantial and varied land resources. Sunbelt development and increasing demands for agricultural and forest products will, however, place escalating demands on the land. A rule of thumb is that for each additional person in the state, added either through natural increase or immigration, three-quarters of an acre of land will be needed for roads and houses, schools, and shopping centers. Since the population of the state is increasing by about 80,000 to 100,000 people per year, 60,000 to 75,000 acres per year will be required to meet the additional land needs. Of this, an estimated 25,000 acres per year of prime agricultural land will be diverted to nonagricultural purposes.

At the same time that land is being taken out of biological productivity, indications are that the demand for agricultural and forest products from Georgia will increase. This will place added stress on the land to meet these new demands. If agricultural and forest practices degrade the soil base upon which they are dependent, productivity will decline.

The USDA Soil Conservation Service estimates that some 3.2 million acres of land in Georgia are above the soil loss tolerance level. In other words, soil is eroding from these areas at a rate that will result in a decrease in productivity. This erosion removes soil from where it is beneficial (on land) and deposits it where it is detrimental (in water). Thus it is both a land and water quality problem.

Major points of erosion are commercial and residential development sites and agricultural fields, especially row crops such as corn and cotton. To help combat erosion problems, the Georgia General Assembly passed the Erosion and Sedimentation Control Act, which requires erosion control plans for major developments. The Metropolitan Rivers Protection Act further controls land-disturbing activities within a buffer zone along the Chattahoochee River in order to protect the water supply for the Atlanta metropolitan region. The Soil Conservation Service works with the Soil and Water Conservation districts to decrease erosion from agricultural operations.

Water Resources

Georgia is located in the humid Southeast and receives abundant precipitation. Overall the state receives an average 50 inches of precipitation yearly, ranking fifth among states in annual precipitation. As presented in Figure 2, the northeastern portion of the state (the southern tip of the Blue Ridge Mountains) receives the greatest amount of precipitation; the Augusta area receives the least.

Surface Water

Surface water quality in Georgia is generally good. Of the 20,000 miles of streams in Georgia, 95 percent are rated as being of good to excellent quality. Most of the streams appear reddish-brown in color, however, because of the clays suspended in the water. Although it does color the streams, the transport of very fine clay particles would be difficult to prevent and has minimal impact.

Rivers and Streams. Figure 3 presents the major rivers and reservoirs of the state. These basins generally lie in a north-south direction with whitewater streams in the north enlarging to form meandering rivers in the south. A major watershed divide which follows the eastern edge of the Chattahoochee and Flint basins divides the state into two major drainage regions; rivers receiving precipitation from the north and west of this divide flow to the Gulf of Mexico while rivers to the east and south flow to the Atlantic Ocean. The fact that this divide runs through the Atlanta metropolitan region is a cause for concern regarding the sufficiency of water to meet the area's needs.

Atlanta's location in the Piedmont is an anomaly. Among cities of its size, Atlanta has the second highest elevation in the United States (Denver, Colorado, has the highest). The location of other major cities along the coast or along major rivers was related to water transportation, but Atlanta's location resulted from rail transportation. As a result, lack of water is a concern for Atlanta. Since Georgia is located in the humid Southeast, the prospect of Atlanta facing water shortages may seem unlikely, but four factors in the Piedmont region may indeed contribute to such shortages:

Figure 2: Georgia Mean Annual Precipitation

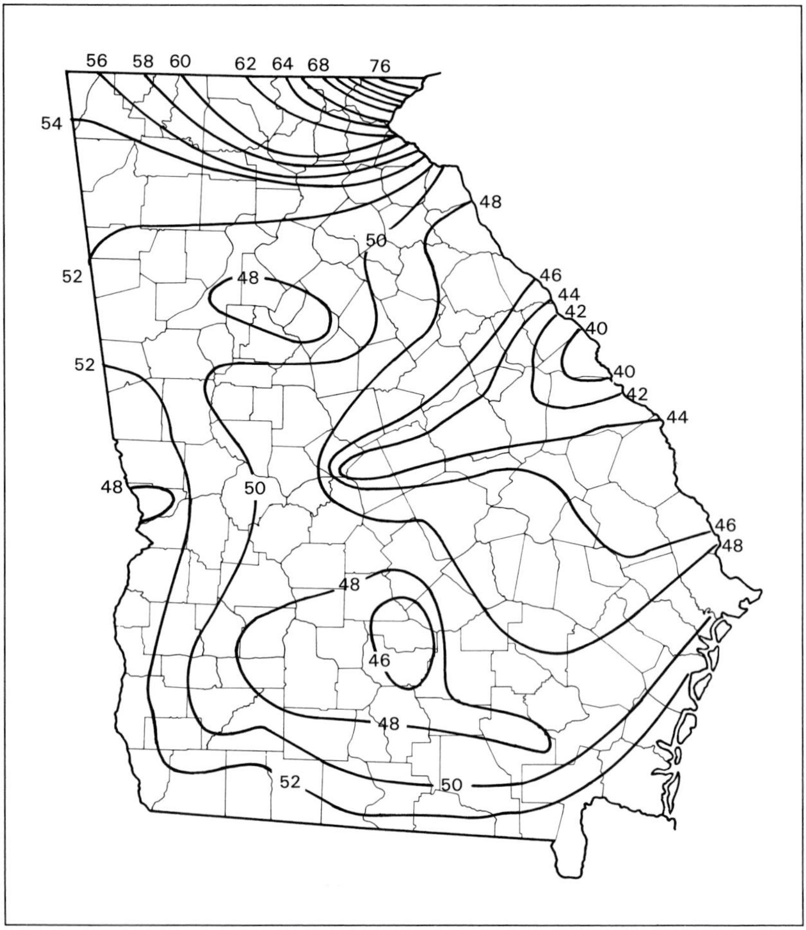

1. Because of the type of bedrock in the area, little groundwater is available.
2. Because Atlanta is located near their headwaters, the streams and rivers are relatively small.
3. Because Atlanta is located on a major watershed divide, water tends to flow from Atlanta (water falling to the north and west of the divide will flow to the Gulf of Mexico, while water falling to the south and east will flow to the Atlantic).
4. Because the area is geologically old, natural barriers have long been eroded away, resulting in a lack of natural lakes.

Figure 3: Major Rivers and Reservoirs in Georgia

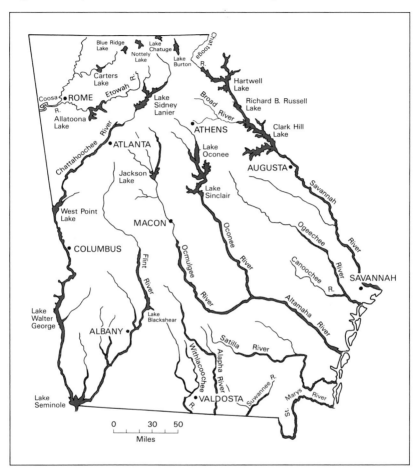

As a result of these four factors, water is limited in the Piedmont. Consequently, the region is dependent on high levels of precipitation and is vulnerable to water shortages during drought periods.

The rivers of Georgia are used for recreation, fish and wildlife habitat, waste assimilation, water supply, navigation, and hydroelectric power generation. Demands for all of these uses are increasing.

Naturally poor quality water is associated with the swamp-like streams in south Georgia. These streams tend to be warm-water streams with less dissolved oxygen than cool-water streams. Since the amount of dissolved oxygen determines the ability of the stream to assimilate organic waste, these streams are quickly overloaded with natural decaying matter. Organic acids from the decaying vegetation also degrade the water quality. As a result, these streams are naturally below national water quality standards. The water quality of these streams cannot realistically be raised to high standards.

Human activities have the greatest impact on water quality in the metropolitan areas of the state. Water quality is poorest in streams below cities such as Atlanta, Macon, Athens, and Rome. Contamination results from municipal and industrial waste and runoff from streets, lawns, and parking lots.

Major efforts have been focused on upgrading the quality of these streams. Industries have been responsive to water quality laws and have improved the quality of waste discharges. Municipalities have generally been less successful in improving their waste releases.

Lakes. No major natural lakes exist in north Georgia. Natural lakes are most commonly associated with areas in which geologic events of the recent past have formed the lakes. For example, northern North America was covered by glaciers only 12,000 years ago. These glaciers carved out valleys and created barriers which impounded water to form lakes. Since north Georgia is geologically old, the barriers that existed at one time have long since been eroded away.

Nevertheless, lakes can be found in north Georgia today. The U.S. Army Corps of Engineers, Soil Conservation Service, Tennessee Valley Authority, Georgia Power Company, and various other agencies and organizations have created numerous lakes for various purposes such as hydroelectric power generation, flood control, and water supply.

In the southern part of the state, standing water bodies are present in the form of swamps and marshes. These tend to be found in areas with poorly drained soils and high water tables. The largest swamp in the state is the Okefenokee Swamp in southeast Georgia, nearly 400,000 acres of which are included in the Okefenokee National Wildlife Refuge.

Lakes are also associated with sinkholes and Carolina bays. When dissolvable bedrock such as limestone is near the land surface, sinkholes may form. Over a long period of time, the rock material will dissolve in the water, forming caverns or solution channels. During a drought or period of high water usage, the water level may decline, removing the support from the land surface. The land subsides and a sinkhole is formed. When water levels return to normal, a pond is produced. This is how some major springs, such as Radium Springs in Albany (the largest spring in the state), were formed.

Carolina bays are a mystery. These shallow water bodies are found in the coastal plain from New Jersey to Florida. Georgia probably has more Carolina bays than any other state except the Carolinas. Over 1,000 exist in Georgia and comprise some 250,000 acres. Carolina bays are

Lake Sidney Lanier, formed by Buford Dam on the Chattahoochee River northeast of Atlanta, provides much of metropolitan Atlanta with its water supply.

elliptical, oriented parallel to each other, and have sand rims on the east and south sides. There is no apparent pattern to their distribution, and they vary in size from a few hundred feet to more than seven miles. They are probably all about the same age, something less than 40,000 years old. Of all the possible explanations for their existence, probably the most likely is the impact of shattered pieces of a large meteorite. This would explain the similarity in age, spacing, and orientation. The value of Carolina bays, other than for scientific curiosity, is primarily for groundwater recharge, fish and wildlife habitats, and recreation.

Groundwater

Groundwater is a puzzle to most people. In its natural form you are unable to see it, feel it, or smell it; it is only when you turn on the tap and water comes out that you know it exists. When you do turn on the tap, you see that groundwater generally looks, smells, and tastes like it's just water, which it is. It is simply surface water that has seeped down through the soil and rock. Because it has been below the surface in contact with soil and rocks, it may contain more dissolved minerals than surface water, it may contain less oxygen than surface water, it may be at a more constant temperature than surface water—but it is still water. These differences may not be too important to the rural family that gets its water from a well, but they probably are important to that industry which uses the water to conduct a chemical process or one in which "cold-blooded" organisms such as bacteria are utilized in the process. The time involved for chemical reactions and for microorganisms to do their "thing" is greatly dependent on temperature.

Groundwater availability varies from province to province (see Figure 4). Throughout the state, however, water table aquifers exist. This is water that is in contact with the atmosphere—water that simply seeps down between the soil particles. This upper level of the groundwater is called the water table. Shallow wells are able to obtain enough water from the saturated layer to meet the relatively limited needs of rural households and other nonirrigation farm use.

In the Blue Ridge and Piedmont provinces, groundwater is limited to water table aquifers. The water may be either in the soil layer above the bedrock or in cracks and fissures in the bedrock. In either case, groundwater is limited in these regions. The Ridge and Valley Province is underlain by aquifer-forming sedimentary layers. This area, however, is geologically complex, and groundwater availability varies considerably from place to place.

The Coastal Plain is the major groundwater region of the state, for it is underlain by a number of water-bearing layers. These layers may be confined between less permeable formations and thus are referred to as confined aquifers. There are three major aquifer systems in the Coastal Plain (see Figure 4).

Groundwater Problems. Historically we have treated the surface of the ground as a carpet under which we could sweep all our waste and nobody would know the difference. In recent years, however, this practice has come back to haunt us. Groundwater contaminated with highly toxic substances has been detected across the country. New York's Love Canal, Kentucky's Valley of the Drums, Alabama's Triana, and Missouri's Times Beach are only a few of the sites faced with major groundwater quality problems resulting from improperly disposed of hazardous waste.

Groundwater can be degraded by things other than hazardous waste sites. Septic systems, leaky storage tanks, accidental spills, chemical stockpiles, feedlots, and landfills may all contaminate groundwater. Essentially, anything placed on or in the ground has the potential to

Figure 4: Availability of Ground Water in Georgia

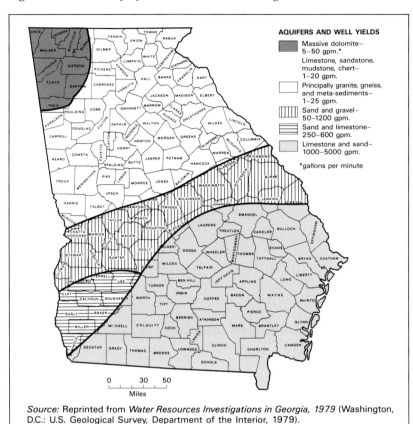

AQUIFERS AND WELL YIELDS

Massive dolomite–
5–50 gpm.*

Limestone, sandstone,
mudstone, chert–
1–20 gpm.

Principally granite, gneiss,
and meta-sediments–
1–25 gpm.

Sand and gravel–
50–1200 gpm.

Sand and limestone–
250–600 gpm.

Limestone and sand–
1000–5000 gpm.

*gallons per minute

0   30   50
Miles

Source: Reprinted from *Water Resources Investigations in Georgia, 1979* (Washington, D.C.: U.S. Geological Survey, Department of the Interior, 1979).

pollute groundwater. For contaminants to infiltrate the ground and move to a well where they might be detected is a long slow process. By the same token, reclaiming a groundwater source once contaminated is almost impossible. Like trying to get soap out of a sponge, no matter how much you squeeze you can't seem to get all the soap out. The only sure way to protect groundwater quality is to prevent contaminants from getting into the groundwater in the first place.

Groundwater quality in Georgia is generally good. The types and amounts of minerals dissolved in groundwater vary from region to region. Throughout the state, iron may be in high enough concentrations to cause staining on sinks and utensils. Groundwater in the Piedmont and Blue Ridge will usually contain fewer minerals (softer water) than water in the Ridge and Valley Province or Coastal Plain. Water in the Floridan aquifer tends to be "harder" (more dissolved minerals) near the coast than it is further west, simply because the water has been in the aquifer longer.

A groundwater quality problem evident in Georgia, as well as many other states, relates to changes in groundwater quantity. When groundwater is pumped from the ground, the area around the well will either be dewatered or, in the case of an artesian aquifer, the water pressure will decrease. In either case, the change induces water to flow toward the well. If this water is of high quality, the system is working properly. If the water moving toward the well is of poor quality, problems result.

In Brunswick, highly mineralized water from a deeper layer has moved upward into what previously was a freshwater zone. As a result, Brunswick has a water quality problem resulting from this change in water pressure. Savannah is faced with a different possibility. Because of the heavy groundwater use in the Savannah area, water from the Atlantic has moved into a previous freshwater zone and moved westward. Currently, Hilton Head Island, South Carolina, is faced with the possibility of this salt water contaminating its wells. In both Brunswick and Savannah, the groundwater quality problems are related to withdrawing a large quantity of water from one area.

Major groundwater contamination resulting from human activities, other than saltwater intrusions, has not been identified as a problem in Georgia. Problems such as groundwater contamination from hazardous waste sites or agrichemicals may appear, but thus far Georgia is in a much better position than more industrialized states in relation to groundwater contamination.

Water Usage Outlook

Each day about seven billion gallons of water are withdrawn from surface and groundwater sources in Georgia. Table 1 presents the breakdown of major water users in the state and how their usage has changed between 1970 and 1980. Not all the water that is withdrawn is consumed. Most of it is returned to the system, possibly in an impaired condition, but where it can be reused. Of the seven billion gallons of water withdrawn daily, about one billion gallons are consumed. This water is not returned to the system; it evaporates, it is transpired by plants, or it is bottled in soft drinks and beer and sent out of the state. Table 2 presents the consumption of water by major water users in Georgia.

Between 1970 and 1980, water usage by all major users except self-supplied industry increased. Some of these large industries have implemented new water-saving procedures or implemented water-saving practices that have reduced their water requirements. For example, indus-

Table 1: Total Water Withdrawal in Georgia, 1970 and 1980 (Million Gallons per Day)

Use	1970	1980	Change (%)
Thermoelectric	3,944	4,437	+ 12.5
Industry	932	818	− 12.5
Public supply	564	773	+ 37.1
Irrigation	40	578	+ 1,345.0
Rural	83	166	+ 100.0
TOTAL	5,563	6,772	+ 21.7

Source: Georgia Geological Survey; U.S. Geological Survey.

Table 2: Total Water Consumption in Georgia, 1970 and 1980 (Million Gallons per Day)

Use	1970	1980	Change (%)
Thermoelectric	0	119	——
Industry	65	59	− 9.2
Public supply	130	180	+ 38.5
Irrigation	40	578	+ 1,345.0
Rural	83	113	+ 36.1
TOTAL	318	1,049	+ 229.9

Source: Georgia Geological Survey; U.S. Geological Survey.

tries in Brunswick have jointly undertaken a multiyear plan to reduce their water requirements. Changes in industrial water use also reflect economic activity. An industry operating at full capacity will use more water than one operating at a lower capacity.

Municipal water use has increased steadily for many years and is expected to do so through the end of the century. As the population of Georgia increases, the demands placed on municipalities to provide water will also increase. Since the center for population growth is the Piedmont, much of this new demand will have to be met from surface water sources.

Thermoelectric use is the major offstream withdrawer of water in the state. Since the bulk of the water is used for cooling purposes, however, only a small percentage is actually consumed (lost through evaporation).

Agricultural irrigation is the major *consumer* of water in Georgia. Since 1975, a phenomenal increase in irrigation has resulted due to below-average rainfall for several years; the development of an infrastructure to sell, install, and service irrigation systems; and active promotion by lending agencies. Currently over one million acres of land in Georgia are under irrigation. The installed capacity of irrigation systems is something over two billion gallons of water per day; consequently, irrigation is potentially the second major *withdrawer* of water in the state.

From a water supply standpoint, two major problems are evident in Georgia; municipal and industrial water supply in north Georgia and agricultural water use in south Georgia. The major urban-industrial region of the state (Piedmont and Ridge and Valley provinces) is an area with limited surface and groundwater resources. Meeting the needs of the expanding population and industry in this area will become more difficult in the future. Both conservation measures and the development of new water supplies will likely be required.

Agricultural water use for irrigation is a concern for a variety of reasons. First, irrigation water use differs from other water uses in that it only occurs for a few days each year, but these tend to be the driest days when the resource is most vulnerable. Second, irrigation is nearly 100 percent consumption. All the water that is withdrawn is lost to the system through evaporation and transpiration from crops; it is not returned to the system to be used over again. Third, irrigation use of water in Georgia has been exempted from the state water management program. All other water users withdrawing over 100,000 gallons per day are required to have a permit to do so issued by the Environmental Protection Division of the Georgia Department of Natural Resources. Irrigation, however, is not required to have a permit. Sound management of the water resources will require developing a mechanism to include all irrigation in the water management program.

Air

Air quality results from the types and amounts of pollutants released into the air and from meteorological conditions. For example, Los Angeles has air quality problems not only because of the release of large quantities of contaminants but also because its location results in weather conditions that tend to hold these contaminants in the Los Angeles basin. To a certain extent this is also true in Georgia. Because of what is generally referred to as the "Bermuda High," a high pressure area in the Caribbean, Georgia experiences more days with temperature inversions and stagnating air masses than other areas east of the Rocky Mountains. When these conditions occur, air contaminants are trapped and not dispersed. This "dead air zone" in north Georgia not only contributes to the creation of poor air quality but also means that wind generation of electricity would probably not be successful in this region.

Although parts of Georgia may have a propensity toward poor air quality conditions, air pollution is not generally a problem. The major air quality concern has related to automobile emissions in the Atlanta metropolitan area. To help alleviate this problem, the state requires autos registered in the Atlanta area to pass an emissions inspection.

Acid precipitation is a concern in many parts of the world. The release of acid-forming compounds and their transport over long distances have resulted in problems in areas such as the Adirondack Mountains and eastern Canada.

Acid rain has also been blamed for the decline in tree growth, particularly at high elevations. Furthermore, a recent survey by the U.S. Forest Service noted a decline in growth of yellow pines throughout the Southeast. Whether this growth decline is a result of acid rain; other air pollutants such as ozone; or other factors such as drought, insects, or the nutrient poor soils of the old "cotton belt" is currently under study.

Consequently, acid precipitation is not known to be a problem in Georgia. The state receives precipitation with a pH as low as 4.0, but no problems have been confirmed in the state as a result of the increasing acidity of precipitation.

Energy Resources

Georgia does not have the vast energy resources found in some states. As a result, Georgia must import much of its energy sources such as coal, oil, natural gas, and uranium. On the other hand, Georgia does have energy resources in the form of hydro- and bioenergy. Since our dependence, however, is currently on fossil and nuclear fuels, Georgia is a net energy importer.

Electricity is the primary form of energy utilized by consumers. Increases in consumption of electricity over time may be attributed to many factors, including increases in population, increases in the number of businesses, changes in technology, higher living standards, and availability of energy alternatives. For whatever reasons, electricity is a commodity that consumers from all sectors increasingly demand. In the residential sector, consumers used 4,469 million kilowatt-hours in 1960. By 1980, residential consumers were using 20,033 million kilowatt-hours a year. The industrial sector also had a fourfold increase in electricity consumption between 1960 and 1980. In 1960 it used 19,195 million kilowatt-hours and in 1980 about 80,000 million kilowatt-hours. In the last two decades, the commercial sector has also increased its consumption of electrical energy dramatically. In 1960 it used 2,788 million kilowatt-hours, and in 1980 its electrical energy consumption was 11,953 million kilowatt-hours. Georgia Power, a unit of the Southern Company, is the biggest distributor of electric power in the state.

Fossil Fuels

Georgia does not have much coal now, nor did it have much coal in the past. But Georgia could have coal in the future. All we have to do is wait a few hundred million years. The conditions under which coal is produced include a warm, moist climate—the type of climate that Georgia has today. Also necessary are swamplike conditions such as those found today in parts of Georgia's Coastal Plain. Vast areas of the Coastal Plain are laying down deposits of plant remains that in time could form coal.

Plants take carbon from the air (in the form of carbon dioxide) and through the process of photosynthesis combine it with water to form sugars. When a plant dies, if it decays in the presence of oxygen, carbon dioxide will be released to the air—a cycle. But, if oxygen is not present because the plant is covered with water with little dissolved oxygen or layers of sediment, carbon dioxide cannot be produced. The carbon builds up, and the formation of peat begins. Currently in Georgia some 450,000 acres of partially decayed organic material or peat reserves exist. Given enough time and the right conditions, this peat will be converted to coal.

Much of the coal consumed in the state is imported from nearby states such as Kentucky and Tennessee. Coal consumption patterns have changed radically since 1960. In both the residential and commercial sectors, consumption of coal in 1980 was only 6 percent of 1960 levels. However, in the industrial sector, consumption of coal in 1980 stood at 143 percent of the 1960 level. Despite the changes in consumption patterns, coal is still an important energy source to Georgia and will likely increase in the future.

Natural gas is formed under conditions similar to those forming coal. Although oxygen might not be present in the partially decayed layers of peat, hydrogen usually is. This hydrogen can unite with the carbon to form natural gas, sometimes referred to as "swamp gas" because it is commonly found bubbling up from swamps. But as with coal, Georgia did not have the necessary conditions when the fossil fuels of the eastern United States were produced, and no recoverable reserves of natural gas have been discovered.

The Atlanta Gas Light Company is the primary distributor of natural gas in the state. The company's pipeline suppliers are Southern Natural Gas Company, Transcontinental Gas Pipe Line Corporation, and South Georgia Natural Gas Company. The natural gas used in the state is from the gulf regions of Texas and Louisiana. Liquefied natural gas was also imported from Algeria for a short time, but changing prices made it more cost effective to buy from U.S. producers. The storage facilities for this foreign natural gas are located off the Savannah coast, so importation is an open option to the Atlanta Gas Light Company.

Consumption patterns of natural gas have vacillated in the post-Arab oil embargo period, particularly for industrial and residential consumers. Only in the commercial sector has natural gas use increased steadily.

According to current theory, petroleum or oil was formed from plankton in the oceans. Through similar processes that formed coal from terrestrial plants, the breakdown of plankton (one-celled floating marine organisms) by bacteria in the absence of oxygen formed crude oil. Petroleum in recoverable quantities has not been found in Georgia, although offshore exploration is under way.

Petroleum usage has decreased in Georgia since the oil embargo. The largest user of petroleum products in the state is the transportation sector, accounting for about 45 percent of the total. Georgia's per capita consumption of petroleum by the transportation sector is about 7 percent higher than the national average because of the demographics of the state (people are dependent on the automobile to transport them greater distances than in most states). Other uses of petroleum in the state include industrial activities, home heating, and commercial uses.

Nuclear Energy

Currently in Georgia, two nuclear generating units are in operation at Plant Hatch near Baxley, Georgia. These units have a capacity of 1,630 megawatts (MW). Another two nuclear generating units are under construction at Plant Vogtle near Augusta. When these units go on line (projected for 1987-88), they will have a generating capacity of 2,320 MW (see Table 3).

Hydroelectricity

About 18 percent of the state's electricity will be generated by current and projected hydro facilities in the state. This does not include the use

Table 3: Current and Projected Electric Generating Capacity in Georgia

Fuel	Number of Units	Total Capacity (MW)	Percentage of Total Capacity
Fossil	49	13,552.7	59.0
Combustion turbines	33	1,305.9	5.7
Nuclear	4	3,950.0	17.2
Hydro	91	4,167.1	18.1
TOTAL	177	22,975.7	100.0

Source: Georgia Power Company.

of small scale hydro facilities which are becoming more popular. It is expected that these plants will produce 1-4 megawatts, or about 0.01 percent of the electricity produced in the state. Major operators of hydro facilities include Georgia Power Company (40 units), U.S. Corps of Engineers (45 units), Tennessee Valley Authority (2 units), and Crisp County Power Commission (4 units).

Bioenergy

The climatic conditions of Georgia make bioenergy (energy derived from plant or animal matter) an attractive alternative to nuclear and fossil fuels. Fast growth of plants and moderate temperatures result in a situation in which burning wood is comparatively inexpensive. A state policy encourages the use of wood for heating and industrial purposes.

Currently some 800,000 cords of wood are used annually for home heating in Georgia. Wood may be burned as the primary fuel for home heating or as a supplemental heat source. A 1980 survey determined that over five percent of the households in Georgia (74,000) depended on wood as their major source of heat. In addition, about 375,000 households depend on wood as a supplemental heat source. This represents about one-third of the households in Georgia (31 percent) which used wood to some extent as a heat source.

Pulp and paper mills have historically used waste wood as an energy source. Recently, however, the Georgia Forestry Commission and the Georgia Institute of Technology have been developing means for public buildings to convert to wood fuel. A notable example is the wood gasification system in operation at the Northwest Georgia Regional Hospital in Rome. The Central State Hospital in Milledgeville and three of the state's prisons are also converting to wood fuel. When all the public wood utilization systems are operational, they will save taxpayers of Georgia an estimated $1.4 million per year in heating costs.

Solar Energy

Because Georgia is located in the South, considerable solar energy is available. Solar energy has been in use in Georgia since the early 1940s, and according to the Governor's Office of Energy Revenues, nearly 400 solar water heaters installed during the 1950s are still operational. Between 1975 and 1980, more than 1,400 active and passive solar energy systems were installed in the state.

Wind Energy

An energy source which has found acceptance in other parts of the country but not to any large extent in Georgia is wind energy. Georgia simply does not receive sufficient wind to consider it as an alternative energy source. Because of the "Bermuda High" which influences our summer weather, wind speeds are frequently insufficient to be a dependable energy source.

Mineral Resources

Because Georgia encompasses parts of five major physiographic provinces which contain rocks formed during different geologic periods and under different conditions, the state has a variety of mineral resources. The igneous and metamorphic rocks of the Blue Ridge and Piedmont provinces contain the greatest diversity of minerals because of their age; complexity of composition; and periods of intrusion, folding, and metamorphism. The Coastal Plain is underlain by sedimentary rocks composed of material transported from the northern part of the state and deposited in the sea that covered the area during the Cretaceous, Tertiary, and more recent times.

The value of nonfuel mineral production in Georgia was estimated at over $700 million in 1982. Clays and crushed stone together account for nearly 90 percent of this total value of production. According to the U.S. Bureau of Mines of the U.S. Department of Interior, in 1979 Georgia led the nation in the production of kaolin, fuller's earth, and dimension stone; was second in the production of kyanite and iron oxide pigments; third in production of bauxite and feldspar, fourth in barite and byproduct gypsum; and fifth in common clays and mica. Some of the rocks, minerals, and clays mined in the state are listed in Table 4.

Plant Resources

Although plant resources encompass a wide variety of forms, the focus of this section will be on the natural forests and associated plant species of the state. From a land use and economic standpoint, forests and forest products are a dominant characterizing factor of the state. Associated with the forests are a number of plant species of notable interest which will be discussed briefly.

Forests

Georgia has the largest commercial forest acreage of any state in the United States. About two-thirds of the land in Georgia, or 23.7 million acres, was classified as commercial forest land in 1982, making the forest products industry one of the state's largest employers. Besides the wood and wood products they yield, these forests are of considerable value for controlling soil erosion and protecting watersheds; providing wildlife habitat; and for recreational, ecological, and aesthetic purposes. Considerable pressure is being placed on these forests by an increased demand

Table 4: *Mineral Resources in Georgia*

Mineral	Location	Use
Barite. Georgia ranks fourth nationally in production.	Cartersville area.	Oil and gas drilling needs; barium chemicals; manufacture of glass.
Bauxite. Georgia is one of three states producing bauxite.	Floyd County and in clay deposits across the state just south of fall line.	Manufacture of aluminum, alum, and abrasives; many industrial applications involving extremely high temperatures.
Feldspar.	Jasper and Greene counties.	Manufacture of glass, pottery, enamels, and abrasives.
Fuller's Earth. Georgia leads nation in production.	Near Florida border in Decatur, Grady, and Thomas counties. In upper Coastal Plain in Jefferson, Houston, and Twiggs counties.	Insecticide carrier; clarifying vegetable and mineral oils; in soap, medicine, kitty litter, and for drilling muds.
Gold. Production in Georgia currently insignificant.	Throughout Piedmont and Blue Ridge area, with Dahlonega being the richest part of the field.	Coins, jewelry, and dentures.
Granite.	Blue Ridge and Piedmont provinces. Even-textured granites are quarried extensively in Elberton area.	Monumental stone, crushed stone, curbstone, and building stone.
Kaolin. Georgia ranks first in nation in production.	In belt extending across state just south of fall line, but primarily in Richmond, Glascock, Washington, Wilkinson, Baldwin, and Twiggs counties.	High-grade white paper; porcelain ware; rubber, paints, and plastics; fine brick mortar; cement; manufacture of aluminum; ingredient in fertilizer, cosmetics, medicines, detergents, and linoleum, in production of alum for paper processing and wastewater treatment.
Kyanite. Georgia ranks second in production.	Minable form in Habersham, Rabun, Dawson, Pickins, Cherokee, Upson and Lincoln counties. Currently mined only in Lincoln County.	Manufacture of refractories for spark plug porcelain; smelting and processing metals.
Limestone.	Northwest Georgia (hard limestone) and Coastal Plain (soft limestone).	Hard limestone: crushed for aggregate and ground for agricultural lime. Soft limestone: manufacture of Portland cement, agricultural lime, numerous chemical and industrial uses.
Marble.	Pickens County; interfolded with other rocks in the Blue Ridge Province.	Dimension stone for buildings, monuments, and interior decorations; mineral extender in paints, plastics, rubber, paper, cosmetics, ink, latex carpet backing; linoleum, phonograph records, glue, and chewing gum.
Mica.	Piedmont and Blue Ridge provinces.	Electronics, roofing mineral, joint cement, well-drilling compounds, rubber, paint, and wallpaper.
Ocher.	Floyd County.	Pigment for paints and mortars; filler for linoleum.

Over the past half century, pine plantations replaced cotton plantations as a characteristic feature of rural Georgia.

for forest products, the conversion of forest lands to nonforest uses, and the demands of an increasing population for recreational purposes.

The virgin forests of the Piedmont and Blue Ridge consisted principally of oaks and hickories associated with other tree species such as yellow poplar (tulip tree, tulip poplar), sourwood, black walnut, beech, sweet and black gum, and scattered shortleaf and loblolly pines. The forests in the Coastal Plain differed from those of the northern part of the state. Drier lands supported yellow pine stands composed primarily of longleaf and slash pine while the wetter areas were covered by hardwood stands composed of oak, gum, and cypress.

In the 50 years, 1780-1830, when settlers moved westward from the Savannah River to the Chattahoochee River, the virgin forest was liquidated. During a 100-year period of cotton growing in the Piedmont, the soils were eroded; the 15-18 inches of topsoil were washed to the streams, exposing the red clay subsoil. Much of the land became too poor to grow cotton, and by the 1920s, with the boll weevil competing with farmers for the fruits of their labor, farmlands were abandoned. Later, these lands reverted to forests. Loblolly and shoftleaf pine generally became established first but over time were replaced by the climax oak-hickory forests. Much of the abandoned land was bought by the wood-producing industries. Although forest products were harvested throughout the history of the state, World War II renewed interest in many of the products. With the war demands, timber, pulp, and naval stores found better markets and production increased.

The types and importance of tree species varies across the state. From a forest standpoint, the state is divided into three major regions: the mountains (including the Blue Ridge and Ridge and Valley provinces), the Piedmont, and the Coastal Plain. Tables 5 and 6 present the distribution of softwood and hardwood species throughout the state. Note that while loblolly pine is the most common in the Piedmont, slash pine is the most common in the Coastal Plain. The control of fire in the Coastal Plain has resulted in an increase in the slash pine acreage and a decrease in the longleaf pine stands. Oak-hickory is the most common hardwood type in the state, while mixed oak-pine stands are most common in the Coastal Plain.

Table 5: Distribution of Pine Types in Georgia, by Geographic Regions (Thousand Acres)

Pine Type	Blue Ridge	Piedmont	Coastal Plain	Total
Loblolly	377.9	4,025.3	611.7	5,014.9
Slash	——	468.0	4,059.6	4,527.6
Shortleaf	287.0	955.1	38.8	1,280.9
Longleaf	6.4	75.6	738.5	820.6
Virginia	325.0	52.7	——	377.7
Pond, spruce and sand	——	16.5	215.2	231.7
White, pitch	44.4	——	——	44.4
Red cedar	4.8	16.8	5.7	27.3
TOTAL	1,045.5	5,610.0	5,669.6	12,325.1

Source: Georgia Forestry Commission.

and 48 species of salamanders. The estimated 111 species and subspecies of reptiles found in Georgia include 2 species of crocodilians, 15 lizards, 60 snakes, and 34 turtles. Nine of the 60 species of snakes are poisonous, including coral snakes, copperheads, cottonmouths, and rattlesnakes. Of the 34 turtle species, 4 are sea turtles, which can be found along the coast. These include the Atlantic Loggerhead, Atlantic Green, Atlantic Ridley, and the Atlantic Leatherback.

Birds. According to the Georgia Ornithological Society, 351 species and 3 subspecies of birds have been identified in Georgia and another 22 species of birds could possibly be found in the state. Among the more noted bird species are mockingbirds, whippoorwills, brown thrashers (state bird of Georgia), and golden and bald eagles.

Mammals. Georgia has 118 species and subspecies of mammals, including 74 nonmarine species and 16 marine species. Common species include white-tailed deer, opossum, rabbit, skunk, fox, raccoon, squirrel, and bobcat. Less common species include manatee, mountain lion, and coyote.

Historic Perspective

Wildlife resources are affected both by natural forces and by the activities of man. Natural forces determine the species able to survive in the state while man changes this natural situation by altering habitat, introducing exotic species, and exploiting native species. All of these can affect the type and extent of wildlife species existing in the state.

The history of Georgia's wildlife parallels the history of wildlife in the rest of the eastern United States. Major changes occurred in the natural environment as humans in greater and greater numbers spread throughout the eastern states. These changes in habitat benefited some species but were harmful to others. When the pioneer philosophy prevailed and many people lived off the land, practically all edible and useful species were taken almost without restrictions of any type. The impact of this laissez faire situation became most evident during the late 1800s and early 1900s. A number of species experienced severe declines in population (white-tailed deer, wild turkey, beaver). Some species disappeared not only from Georgia but from the face of the earth (e.g., passenger pigeon, Carolina parakeet, and probably the ivory-billed woodpecker). Birds such as egrets and herons were hunted fervently for their plumes, which were prized by the Gay Nineties millinery industry for decorating women's hats. It became evident in Georgia, as well as other states, that more species would become extinct unless some preventive action was taken.

Early attempts at wildlife management focused primarily on controlling the hunting of various species. Laws were passed establishing the time of year and day that species could be hunted, the number that could be taken, and the methods that could be used to harvest wildlife. The first game law in Georgia, passed in 1790, prohibited the killing of deer by firelight at night. The penalty for offenders was a $25 fine or 39 lashes "well-laid" to the bare back.

If a species no longer survived in an area, however, game laws would have little effect on its population. Thus, methods for reestablishing species were researched and developed. Trapping animals in one area and transferring them to another area helped repopulate species such as the white-tailed deer and the beaver.

Along with new laws and wildlife research came the creation of federal and state agencies with the responsibilities to implement the laws. At the federal level, the Bureau of Sports Fisheries and Wildlife (now the Fish and Wildlife Service) was created in 1935. Federal wildlife laws apply to certain species of animals, including migratory birds, and to the interstate shipment of wild animals and their products. The states created a wide variety of agencies and commissions to deal with wildlife matters. In Georgia, the 1972 Executive Reorganization Act transferred the responsibilities for wildlife from a number of separate agencies to the Game and Fish Division of the Department of Natural Resources. Besides enforcing the game laws and conducting wildlife management activities, this division manages over 50 Wildlife Management Areas in the state. Special hunts are held on the Wildlife Management Areas including primitive weapons hunts, antlerless deer hunts, trophy hunts, parent/child hunts, and ladies only hunts. The division is also charged with protecting the endangered species of the state. Endangered species are those plants and animals identified by state and federal officials as being in danger of becoming extinct. In Georgia, this includes over 50 species of plants and 20 species of animals.

Coastal Resources

Georgia's coastal resources are varied and interrelated. The merging of freshwater wetlands with tidal salt marshes produces a complex system that supports much of the marine life found along the coast. A system of barrier islands protects these marshes and estuaries from the vagaries of the sea. The ocean floor dips eastward for some 60 miles toward the continental shelf where it drops more rapidly to abysmal depths, providing a wealth of habitats for marine life. This system is influenced by the movement of materials into it and through it, especially from the rivers flowing to it from the mainland and from southward-flowing littoral currents along the barrier islands.

Superimposed on this complex natural system is the human system composed of cities, industries, roads, deepwater ports, recreation facilities, and historic and tourist attractions. These sometimes conflicting uses have varying effects on one another as well as on the natural system.

Barrier Islands

A chain of barrier islands extends along the coast of Georgia. (See Figure 5.) These islands were formed during the past 10,000 years as a result of fluctuations in sea level, movement of sand along the coast, and the action of plants to stabilize this sand. Not all the islands along the coast are barrier islands, however. Some of these islands may be the remnants of old barrier islands, some are parts separated from other islands, some may have been formed from ballast dumped by ships. Most of the marsh islands are alluvial deposits shaped by the estuarine drainage system.

The elevation of barrier islands is typically less than 25 feet above sea level, although dunes may rise to higher elevations. Island topography is typically composed of broad, level areas interspersed with gently sloping ridges. The more recently formed islands may have rather steep, parallel dune ridges.

Although these coastal islands have been used since the earliest days of human habitation of this continent, some are in relatively natural condition. Many of these islands have been preserved through private landowners, industrial holdings, and state and federal government actions.

The major islands along the coast are distinct in their uses. Tybee Island is the northernmost and one of the smallest of the barrier islands in Georgia. It is the location of the city of Savannah Beach, and its 3.4 miles of beach is one of the most accessible beaches for most Georgians. Little Tybee Island, which is somewhat larger than Tybee Island, is privately owned and in a relatively natural state. Wassaw Island is a national wildlife refuge. Ossabaw is the third largest of Georgia's barrier islands and is owned by the state of Georgia, which dedicated the island as a heritage preserve. St. Catherines is a privately owned island used by the American Museum of Natural History to propagate threatened and endangered species of the world. Blackbeard Island, named after the pirate, is a national wildlife refuge.

The fourth largest of Georgia's barrier islands, Sapelo Island, is owned by the state. Part of Sapelo comprises a national estuarine sanctuary and a center for scientific research; the rest of the island is a wildlife management area operated by the Department of Natural Resources.

Little St. Simons Island is privately owned, but reservations can be made by the public to visit the island. The public has ready access to the next three islands. Sea Island, the smallest of Georgia's barrier islands, is a world-renowned resort. The second largest of Georgia's

Figure 5: Georgia Coastal Area

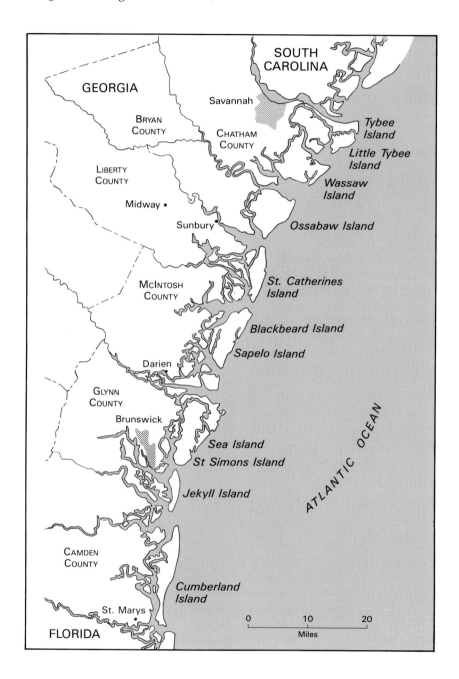

barrier islands, St. Simons, is a mix of residential and resort areas. Jekyll Island is partly residential and partly a state-owned public beach and convention center. Little Cumberland Island is privately owned and under the control of the Little Cumberland Association. The largest of Georgia's barrier islands is Cumberland, comprising some 15,100 acres. This island is now a national seashore under the jurisdiction of the National Park Service and can be reached only by boat or airplane.

The barrier islands of Georgia provide a unique resource for the people of the state. Through historic accident and the hard work of countless individuals, these islands are generally protected for use in various ways for this and future generations.

Of major importance for ensuring the survival of these islands, however, is the maintenance of the sand-sharing system along the beaches. The sand along the coast is constantly shifting and moving, resulting in some areas eroding while other areas accrete or build up with sand. This natural process is a problem only when man places structures too close to the beach, resulting in erosion or causing changes in the movement of sand. Problems of this nature have occurred on Tybee Island and Sea Island. Also, dredging of channels for navigation can intercept the moving sands and alter the erosion and accretion process along the coast. To minimize interference with the sand-sharing system, the Department of Natural Resources has been assigned the responsibility of implementing Georgia's Shore Assistance Act, which requires a permit to build structures that might affect sand movement.

Salt Marshes

Lying behind the barrier islands is a 4- to 6-mile band of marshland comprising about 393,000 acres. About three-fourths of this marshland is covered with one species of plant known as salt marsh or smooth cordgrass *(Spartina alterniflora)*. The remaining acreage consists of several types of saltwater, brackish, and freshwater wetlands.

Research conducted at the University of Georgia by Eugene Odum and associates established that salt marshes are very productive ecosystems. The productivity of these marshes is based on photosynthesis of the marsh vegetation, tidal ebb and flow, abundant supplies of nutrients, and year-round production. The combined effect of these factors produces one of the most naturally fertile systems of the world. The net production of the marshes amounts to about 10 tons (dry weight) of organic material per acre per year. Fifty-five percent of this net production is consumed by the marsh inhabitants, while the remaining 45 percent is exported to the estuarine system. This biological productivity supports much of the shell- and finfish production along the coast.

The value of these salt marshes became the center of controversy in the late 1960s when a private company proposed to mine phosphates along the coast. Phosphates are needed by all living things but are frequently quite limited in the environment. Lack of phosphate may inhibit the growth of plants and animals; thus, phosphates are a major component of synthetic fertilizers. Phosphates are also used to make hard water soft and are therefore found in most detergents. Some states have banned the use of phosphate detergents, not because they didn't get clothes "whiter than white" but because they got the waterways "greener than green." Increasing the phosphate content of wastewater caused algae "blooms" in water bodies. Excessive algae can lead to overpopulation of oxygen-requiring organisms and detritus and the "killing" of the water body.

Mining of phosphates may lead to similar problems. When the proposal was made to mine along the coast, the governor requested the chancellor of the University System of Georgia to appoint a committee of university system personnel to conduct an in-depth study of the impact of phosphate mining on the coast. The committee concluded that the mining operation would have significant impacts on the marshes and, since the phosphates would be mined in Georgia but refined elsewhere, would result in little economic activity of benefit to the state. Consequently, not only was the permit application denied under the state water law but also the then revolutionary Marshland Protection Act was enacted. This law requires a permit for activities that will alter or interfere with the functioning of the salt marshes.

Estuarine and Marine Waters

Estuaries are partially enclosed water bodies having free connection with the open sea and having seawater diluted with fresh water derived from land drainage. The estuaries of Georgia connect with the sea through sounds that separate the barrier islands. As a result, these estuaries serve as the connection between the highly productive marshes and the sea.

The continental shelf along the Georgia coast is 70 to 80 miles wide, sloping at about 2 feet per mile toward the continental slope where it drops more rapidly to the ocean basin. The coastal waters are somewhat more diluted with fresh water from the mainland and are more turbid and productive than seawater farther east.

The Georgia coast is subject to two tides per day of approximately equal height, ranging from about 5½ feet to 7 feet. The tidal movement of salt water into the estuaries and the drainage of fresh water into them causes the complicated hydrologic patterns of the estuaries.

These waters off the coast of Georgia contain a wealth of sea life. Shrimp, crabs, clams, snails, oysters, and scallops are found within the territorial waters. Some 300 species of fish inhabit or visit the waters off Georgia's coast. Among these are shad, flounder, whiting, snapper, grouper, and porgy. The multitude of edible shellfish and finfish provide the commercial fisheries of the state with a wide variety of marketable products.

In recent years, the continental shelf off Georgia has received attention for three other reasons. First, exploratory drilling for petroleum has taken place, but recoverable quantities have not been identified. Second, a section of very productive sea floor known as Gray's Reef has been set aside as a marine sanctuary. The purpose of the sanctuary is to provide an undisturbed marine environment for scientific research into marine processes. Third, this area off the coast of Georgia has been found to be a major calving ground for the right whale, an endangered species.

How Is Environmental Quality Protected?

How a state addresses its environmental concerns depends on a variety of factors, such as the nature of the problems, the state's bureaucratic structure, and the political arena in which the decisions are made. As a result, each state's environmental program has evolved independently of that in other states.

At the same time, however, states have been subjected to common stimuli such as federal mandates, federal funding, and new information and insights obtained through research activities. Also, a wide variety of communication mechanisms exist that enable personnel from different states to interact and to exchange ideas. These common experiences, coupled with a limited number of available alternatives for addressing environmental concerns, have led to considerable similarity in the general environmental protection approach adopted by states. Although no two states protect the environment in exactly the same way, they tend to address similar problems in similar ways.

As in most states, the major components of the environmental protection program in Georgia have been developed since the mid-1960s. As new environmental concerns appeared, the general tendency in most states, including Georgia, was to create new bureaucratic units to deal with each separate problem. By the 1970s, the state bureaucracy of Georgia was composed of a mixture of distinct but functionally related commissions, boards, authorities, agencies, councils, and departments.

During the early 1970s, many states, confronted by the inefficiencies of a jerry-built bureaucracy, reorganized their state agency structure. Then-Governor Jimmy Carter spearheaded this action in Georgia, which resulted in the passage of the 1972 Executive Reorganization Act. This act created a superagency, the Department of Natural Resources

(DNR), and assigned to it functions previously conducted by the Recreation Commission, State Parks Department, Coastal Marshlands Protection Agency, Natural Areas Council, Waterways Commission, Historic Commission, Game and Fish Commission, State Health Department, State Water Quality Control Board, State Department of Mines, and several authorities.

DNR is divided into four major divisions: the Coastal Resources Division which performs the department's functions in the coastal area; the Game and Fish Division, which conducts the fish and wildlife activities of the department; Parks, Recreation and Historic Sites Division, which maintains and operates recreation and historic sites in the state; and the Environmental Protection Division (EPD), which is charged with maintaining the environmental quality of the state.

Georgia has developed a "one-stop-shop" program for environmental permits. Consequently, any industry, municipality, or individual requiring information on any environmental permit need contact only one unit of government, EPD. EPD regional offices in Albany, Atlanta, Brunswick, and Macon perform much of the agency's monitoring activities. The majority of the agency's activities, however, are conducted by the state office in Atlanta.

Not all environmental functions of state government were assigned to DNR in the 1972 reorganization. Four other agencies have duties which relate to environmental quality: the Department of Agriculture regulates the use of chemicals such as pesticides, herbicides, and rodenticides; the Department of Human Resources has authority over small septic and water systems; the Forestry Commission performs state activities associated with forestry; and the Soil and Water Conservation Committee works with Soil and Water Conservation Districts to reduce erosion and sedimentation in the state.

Potentially, the greatest impact on the quality of the environment, however, may come at the local government level. Federal and state laws may require permits to protect air and water quality, but local government decisions determine the overall quality of the environment. Local governments make decisions on land use, solid waste disposal, sewage treatment, recreation areas, aesthetics, noise, litter, and other activities which determine the quality of the environment.

Factors Contributing to Georgia's Environmental Quality

Although Georgia is faced with degradation pressures similar to those of the rest of the industrialized world, its environment is generally of high quality. Georgia's environmental situation results from the interplay of geophysical, biological, economic, social, and political forces. Consider the following:

Kudzu Not Cactus

Georgia's warm temperatures and abundant precipitation produce an environment in which plant growth is rapid. Unlike the desert or tundra, where plant growth is slow, scars of past land abuses in Georgia are hidden under kudzu and pines; recovery is rapid.

Ours Not Theirs

Georgia's water resources are essentially formed within the state or along its boundaries. Because it receives no water from other states, it receives no polluted water from other states. True, the quantity of water in rivers and streams formed in Georgia's mountain and piedmont provinces is low, but the quality is high. Although there are no major natural lakes, reservoirs store water in north Georgia. As with surface water, groundwater resources are formed or recharged within the state, and the quality of this water is generally very good. Problems do occur, however, when people try to take too much water from one place.

Kaolin Not Coal

Environmental impacts associated with the mining of coal and iron, copper, and other metals can be very severe. Impacts from the extraction activities that take place in Georgia—clays, sand, gravel, marble, granite, and mica—are less severe. While the rich fall line deposits of kaolin have been strip-mined in a manner similar to coal in other states, regeneration of plant cover has generally been rapid under Georgia's climatic conditions. Moreover, much of the early research on land reclamation took place in Georgia, and the state was among the first to have passed a mined-land reclamation law (1969).

Pulp Not Steel

Steel mills, smelters, and other primary industries can exert great pressure on the environment. Georgia does not have much heavy industry. The industries concentrated in Georgia are primarily pulp and textile mills. The large quantities of water used by pulp and paper mills may adversely affect water sources and other water users. Pulp mills may also affect air quality. However, water and air quality laws and the installation of new technologies by the industry have decreased environmental impacts in recent years. Textile mills require water for production, cooling, and waste assimilation, but the major environmental problem associated with the industry relates to its location in a relatively water-short area in northwest Georgia.

Now Not Then

Georgia's growth and development were comparatively late in coming. Much of its development has taken place in the postenvironmental awareness period. Georgia has learned from the experience of other states and required new development to be conducted in an environmentally conscious manner. While "growth at any cost" is still a popular motto in some parts of the state, and many local governments shun land use planning and zoning, the amount of information available to local officials for making sound appraisals of the costs and benefits of development and the impetus to use that information continues to grow.

Us Not Them

Georgia lawmakers have long looked askance at federal government involvement in state affairs. This feeling of "being able to do the job better and cheaper than the feds can" has permeated the environmental management field. Georgia is one of the few states that sought and received authority to implement all major federal environmental laws. At the same time, Georgia lawmakers have supported efficient, effective administration of state environmental laws. The result is a centralized, integrated environmental management approach well supported by industries, governments, and environmental interests.

Synergism: The Total Effect

In sum, Georgia's great diversity coupled with the interplay of the forces described in the preceding paragraphs have resulted in a generally high environmental quality. Abuses have occurred but, in most cases, the environment has recovered. As we approach the carrying capacity of our environmental and natural resource base, new problems will appear. And, our alternatives for resolving those problems will become more limited. A sound environmental management program for the future will be one designed to prevent abuses from occurring rather than attempting to correct them after they have occurred.

CHAPTER THREE

Economic Growth and Change

By Charles F. Floyd

An Introduction: Two Outlooks

Don't be surprised to find a job application crammed between your Big Mac and fries at McDonald's.

Retailers and fast-food operators all over Atlanta just can't seem to find enough ways to say they need help.

Winn-Dixie grocery stores are stuffing employment invitations in grocery bags with the milk and eggs.

Rich's Gwinnett Place Mall store has set up an employment booth on the selling floor to hand out applications to browsing shoppers.

"We know that of all the shoppers in the store, not all of them are employed. We want to be out front, to plant the seed in the minds of potential employees," said Gail Nutt, vice-president and general manager of the Gwinnett Place Mall store.

The irony of a bustling metro economy with such extraordinary commercial growth and no workers to support it has grown from a cocktail party joke to a dire concern in retailing circles.

"The pool of employees is getting smaller in Atlanta, especially north of the city. Fast-food restaurants are going up so fast, labor is a growing problem," said John Byrnes, advertising director for McDonald's Atlanta division of 119 stores.

Added Bill McBrayer, president of the Georgia Retail Association, "Competition for employees is so intense here, especially in areas like Gwinnett County. Retail stores are going up so rapidly that the labor force can't keep up with the growth."

Unfortunately, that situation is not likely to change soon.

Some 28,200 people have already found jobs in the retail and service industries since June 1984, according to the Georgia Labor Department.

But 18,000 more jobs will need to be filled in the retail sector by the end of the year, estimated Arnie Dill, chief economist with Citizens & Southern National Bank.

So much hiring is going on in that sector that retail employment in metro Atlanta is exploding at an annual 8.5 percent clip. . . . (*The Atlanta Constitution,* September 3, 1985, p. 1-C.)

In the past two years, Clay County lost more than 100 jobs when the sewing operation moved out and the peanut shelling plant closed. In a county that had only 629 jobs in 1985, the loss was significant. Between 1970 and 1980, Clay was one of only 10 Georgia counties that lost population.

James E. Coleman, an organizer of the Clay County Economic Development Council, can point out changes in local fortunes from the front porch of the Dill House, a forlorn reminder of the days when Ft. Gaines, the county seat, was a regional trade center and steamboat stop on the Chattahoochee River. "This was a hotel, there was a hotel right there, there was a hotel on that corner, there was one down further; the train came in twice a day; there were drummers in; prosperous little place. . . ." The economic slide that began in the Depression slowed in the mid-1950s with construction work on the Walter F. George Lock and Dam. But, with the dam completed and the lake filling up, even the less-used railroad tracks were pulled up. "Buildings get old," Coleman continues, pointing to open spaces between vacant stores. "That building had nobody in it, so they tore it down. That one over there was dangerous, scared the children were going to hurt themselves, so they tore it down." Coleman has bought six or seven big old houses, repaired the leaking roofs, and hopes for the day when people will want to move to Ft. Gaines and fix them up.

Clay County's repeated attempts to attract industry have met with failure. "I could tell tales that would make people want to sit down on the floor and cry," Coleman says. "We have tried. We put our money up, we put our time up. . . . But when people go to Industry and Trade [the state's industrial development agency], nine times out of ten they know where they want to go. Usually it's the metropolitan area of Atlanta or on an interstate. Getting somebody down to the boondocks is practically impossible."

The development council now aims for recreation and retirement rather than industry. Lake Walter F. George is the big lure, but the relaxed small town environment is also touted in promotional literature. Coleman gets around town on a bicycle, which is ironic since he owns the local oil dealership and until recently ran the auto parts store. "I've had more people come up and say

'I'd give anything in the world to be able to make a living in Ft.
Gaines so I could live there or on that lake.' The living is better;
I just wish we could share it with a few people." (Interview,
October 19, 1985.)

The Georgia economy has made immense strides during the modern
era, being transformed from a poor, primarily agrarian society on the
eve of the Great Depression into the present strong and diversified
economic leader of the Southeast. But many areas of Georgia outside
the Atlanta metropolitan region are not sharing in the state's rapid rate
of economic growth and prosperity, and Georgia remains relatively poor
in comparison with the United States as a whole, particularly in many
of its rural areas. Unless these lagging areas are brought into the
economic mainstream, the problem of two Georgias—one prosperous
and one poor—will become even more acute. In addition, the state's low
relative position in education does not bode well for growth in the high
technology industries that promise much of the nation's employment
growth during the remainder of this century.

Georgia's Recent Economic Growth

Until recently, economic underdevelopment forced most Georgians to
either endure a tradition of genteel, and not so genteel, poverty or leave
the state to find adequate economic opportunity. Georgia had all the
characteristics of an underdeveloped economy, including relatively limited
manufacturing activity and an over-reliance on the agricultural sector.

In 1929, for example, the average resident of Georgia had an income
approximately half that of his national counterpart. Various factors,
including rapid national economic expansion during World War II and
improved transportation, greatly accelerated the state's economic growth,
however. As shown in Table 1, by 1950 the per capita income level had
risen to 71 percent of the United States average. Since that time, the
Georgia economy has experienced several periods of fluctuating growth
relative to the national economy.

Following a period of rapid expansion during World War II and
the early postwar period, Georgia's rate of economic growth slowed in
the 1950s, primarily due to a considerable loss in agricultural employment. Relative per capita income, however, continued to increase, to 75
percent of the national average by 1960. During the 1960s the pace of
economic activity in Georgia again accelerated, further closing the
relative income gap, so that by 1970 the average Georgian received an
income equal to 84 percent of the national average.

Employment and population grew at greater than national average
rates during the decade of the 1970s, but Georgia's relative per capita

Table 1: Per Capita Income, Selected Years

| | Per Capita Income | | Georgia Income as a Percentage of U.S. Income |
	United States	Georgia	
1929	$ 697	$ 345	49
1940	589	334	57
1950	1,492	1,054	71
1960	2,216	1,658	75
1965	2,772	2,202	79
1970	3,945	3,323	84
1975	5,842	4,972	85
1980	9,494	8,021	84
1983	11,687	10,389	89
1984	12,789	11,548	90
1985	13,867	12,543	90

Source: U.S. Department of Commerce, Bureau of Economic Analysis.

income failed to increase. The state's relative economic performance during the current decade has been much better, per capita income rising to 90 percent of the national average by 1985. As we will see, however, this overall state average masks the state's economic problem areas.

Exodus from Agriculture

The demand for agricultural products did not rise as rapidly as the demand for other goods and services during the 1950s, and this, combined with increasing productivity per agricultural worker, led to a large reduction in national agricultural employment. The relative impact of the decreased demand for agricultural manpower was more severe in Georgia than in the nation because of the relatively large percentage of total employment concentrated in the agricultural sector. Not only did Georgia's agricultural employment decline at a more rapid rate than in the nation as a whole, but the absolute loss was much greater in relation to total employment.

Exodus from agriculture was the primary reason for the extensive out-migration from Georgia that occurred during the 1950s, and this exodus from the agricultural areas of Georgia continued in the 1960s. By 1980, Georgia's rural-farm population had fallen to 121,000, from 967,000 only 30 years earlier. The percentage of gross state product generated by the agricultural sector had fallen from 7.0 percent in 1950 to 2.4 percent in 1983.

Growth of the Nonagricultural Sector

In contrast to the agricultural sector, Georgia's nonagricultural employment grew faster than the national average during this period. Partially reflecting the state's large supply of labor in rural areas willing to work for relatively low wages, apparel manufacturing expanded rapidly, and the textile and food processing industries experienced sizable growth. Employment in the higher wage industries also increased, particularly in automobile and aircraft manufacturing, fabricated metals, and paper manufacturing. Overall, manufacturing employment in the state between 1950 and 1980 grew at twice the national average rate.

Of late, this favorable growth rate for manufacturing employment in Georgia has begun to slow, largely because of the state's heavy concentration in the hard-pressed textile and apparel industries. Between July 1984 and July 1985, for example, Georgia manufacturing employment declined by 7,400 workers; increases in durable goods, particularly automobile manufacturing and wood products, were not large enough to offset declines of 6,500 in textiles and 4,300 in apparel.

Impact of Transportation

One of the chief reasons for the nonagricultural employment and population growth in the nation's and Georgia's nonmetropolitan counties was transportation improvement, particularly the interstate highway system. The construction of this multilane freeway system was especially important to the southeastern United States, which had long suffered a transportation disadvantage when compared to other areas of the nation. The spreading of good transportation services to more rural communities enabled them to attract manufacturing and other nonagricultural jobs, and, hence, to achieve economic vitality. In some cases, improved highways made it possible for workers to commute longer distances to places of employment, thus enabling communities to be attractive as places to live even though they were not employment centers.

The Two Georgias

Georgia's recent economic and population growth has by no means been uniform. The population statistics presented elsewhere in this book clearly show that although nonagricultural employment growth has brought renewed population growth to most of the state's rural counties, the bulk of Georgia's population growth has been concentrated in the Atlanta region. That area, which had 37 percent of Georgia's population in 1970, gained 52 percent of the state's total population increase during the 1970s, and 63 percent of its net in-migration.

Personal Income

Per capita income, that is, average income per person, is computed by dividing total personal income by total population; it is perhaps the best single measure of the economic well-being of an area. The U.S. Department of Commerce's estimates of personal income in Georgia for 1984 are shown in Table 2 and Figure 1.

Although Georgia has enjoyed considerable economic development during the past two decades, these income data clearly show that the state's citizens remain relatively poor when compared to the United States as a whole. As noted earlier, the state's per capita income in 1984, $11,548, stood at only 90 percent of the national average, 34th among

Table 2: Georgia Personal Income, 1984

Area	Total Personal Income (Millions of Dollars)	Population (1984 Est.)	Per Capita Income (Dollars)	Percentage of U.S. Average
Georgia	67,402.8	5,836.0	11,548	90
Total Georgia MSAs	46,994.6	3,682.8	12,760	100
Atlanta MSA	32,958.1	2,380.0	13,848	108
Total non-Atlanta MSAs	14,036.5	1,302.8	10,774	84
Albany MSA	1,172.5	116.7	10,050	79
Athens MSA	1,482.2	136.6	10,851	85
Augusta MSA (Ga. counties only)	2,630.4	237.1	11,094	87
Chattanooga MSA (Ga. counties only)	976.9	105.4	9,269	73
Columbus MSA (Ga. counties only)	2,054.7	196.2	10,472	82
Macon-Warner Robins MSA	3,060.8	277.9	11,014	86
Savannah MSA	2,659.0	232.9	11,415	89
Non-MSA counties	20,408.2	2,153.2	9,478	74

Source: U.S. Department of Commerce, Bureau of Economic Analysis.
Note: MSA is an abbreviation for Metropolitan Statistical Area.

the states. Of the designated metropolitan areas, only the Atlanta region had a level of per capita income above the national average in 1984, and no other Georgia MSA was above even the *state* average. Per capita income in the nonmetropolitan counties stood at only 74 percent of the national average.

Figure 1: Georgia per Capita Income as Percentage of U.S. Income, 1984

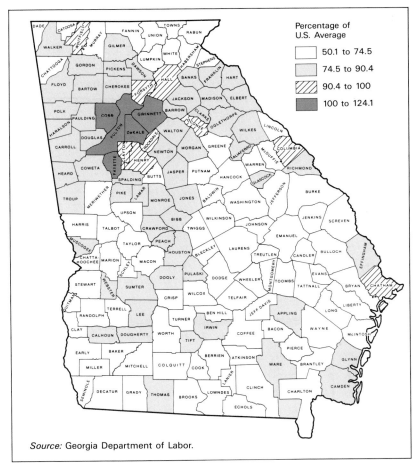

Source: Georgia Department of Labor.

Personal income in Georgia counties is highly concentrated in a few areas. Only five of the state's counties had per capita incomes equal or greater than the national average in 1984—Cobb, DeKalb, Fayette, Fulton, and Gwinnett. Only nine others (Chatham, Clayton, Columbia, Forsyth, Hall, Henry, Oconee, Rockdale, and Whitfield) had per capita incomes above the state average. This means that the citizens of 145 Georgia counties had average incomes below the *state* average; 92 counties, more than half, had average incomes less than 75 percent of the national average, and 19 had per capita incomes less than 60 percent of the national average.

What conclusions can be drawn from these income data? First, despite its record of economic progress in recent years, Georgia is still a relatively poor state. Outside of a few metropolitan areas, average incomes are below that of the average citizen of the United States as a whole. Second, average incomes in almost all of Georgia's rural counties are very low.

Some observers contend that the Department of Commerce's income statistics overstate the low relative income of Georgians because the cost of living is also lower in the state. This argument has some validity; many items such as services which require relatively large inputs of labor *are* cheaper in Georgia because Georgia workers receive lower average wages than workers in most other states. Certain other items, notably housing, are also cheaper in the state. However, most items, and particularly manufactured goods, are sold in national markets where prices vary little from state to state. The somewhat lower cost of living in Georgia, then, means that average living standards in the state are not quite as low as the unadjusted per capita income figures would indicate, but they are definitely considerably below the national average.

Comparisons between the "Two Georgias"

The data in Table 3 give key economic variables for selected regions and counties that are representative of the "two Georgias." Not only do they clearly indicate the economic contrast between developed and underdeveloped economies, but also they show some of the dimensions of poverty. Generally, MSAs have higher average incomes than non-MSAs. Clayton County, Gwinnett County, (both in the Atlanta MSA) and Hall County all have levels of per capita income above the state average. Coffee County, while still a relatively low income area, is a good example of a rapidly developing one. Randolph, Quitman, and Clay counties are among Georgia's poorest and most underdeveloped counties.

As we would expect, the poorer counties have a relatively low percentage of their populations employed, a definite indication of economic underdevelopment. This factor is reflected in the high percentage of total personal income coming from net transfer payments (social security payments, public assistance, government pensions, etc., less social security taxes). For example, in high income Gwinnett County, net transfer payments accounted for only 1.5 percent of total income; in low income Quitman County these payments accounted for 25.8 percent of all income.

The economic status of many of the citizens in low income areas is also reflected in housing data. For example, in Quitman County, which had a per capita income only 57 percent of the national average in 1984, 21.8 percent of the homes did not have inside plumbing, and 14.2 per-

Table 3: Selected Economic Indicators, Georgia Areas and Counties, 1980 and 1984

	Georgia	Georgia MSAs	Georgia non-MSA	Atlanta MSA	Clayton County	Gwinnett County	Hall County	Coffee County	Randolph County	Quitman County	Clay County
1984											
Per capita income (dollars)	11,548	12,760	9,478	13,848	11,937	14,704	12,183	8,254	7,328	7,314	6,861
Percent of U.S. per capita income	90	100	74	108	94	115	95	65	57	57	54
Net transfer payments as percent of total income	7.7	5.8	12.1	3.8	3.7	1.5	7.2	13.3	19.5	25.8	20.7
1980 Population (000)	5,642.0	3,540.0	2,102.0	2,243.1	155.6	199.2	78.1	27.5	9.6	2.3	3.5
Population change 1970-1980 (%)	19.0	21.3	16.0	27.0	76.9	509.5	27.3	17.8	9.9	8.1	-2.3
Black, 1980 (%)	26.8	26.8	26.9	24.6	7.0	2.5	9.0	25.4	56.0	56.7	62.1
In labor force, 1980 (%)											
Male	75.8	78.1	72.2	79.4	86.2	86.3	78.4	71.7	62.3	61.0	60.2
Female	52.3	54.6	48.8	57.0	58.6	60.1	53.7	46.2	40.7	38.8	36.6
Earnings as percent of total earnings:											
Farm	2.2	.6	6.5	.5	0	.3	6.5	12.8	18.7	39.3	26.8
Manufacturing	22.1	17.9	34.1	16.0	8.3	29.4	34.9	35.3	26.0	4.6	13.8
Trade	19.3	21.4	13.2	24.0	21.1	26.4	16.3	16.9	12.7	12.6	13.5
Finance, insurance, real estate	6.0	7.1	2.8	7.9	1.7	4.7	4.5	3.4	3.7	3.2	1.8
Government	17.6	17.5	17.9	12.9	10.9	8.9	14.0	16.1	20.2	27.2	17.0
1980 Housing characteristics:											
Without plumbing (%)	3.8	1.7	6.9	1.5	.7	1.2	2.5	3.8	15.8	21.8	19.1
With more than 1.01 persons per room (%)	5.3	4.2	7.0	4.7	2.9	2.0	4.4	7.7	11.7	14.2	10.7

Source: U.S. Department of Commerce, Bureau of Economic Analysis and Bureau of the Census.

cent of the homes had an average of more than one occupant per room, a definite indication of overcrowding; in Clayton County less than one percent of the homes lacked indoor plumbing, and only 2.9 percent had an average of more than one occupant per room.

The characteristics that economists associate with a relatively poor and underdeveloped economy are (1) a low percentage of the population in the labor force; (2) a high percentage of employment and income in the agricultural sector; and (3) a low percentage of employment and income in the trade, finance, and business services industries. Conversely, we would expect a relatively wealthy and developed economy to have (1) a high percentage of the population in the labor force; (2) a low percentage of employment in the agricultural sector; and (3) a high percentage of employment in the trade, finance, and business services sectors. These are the characteristics exhibited by our sample areas. The higher income areas have a large portion of their total earnings coming from the trade, finance, and business services areas. (In Clayton County, which contains the Atlanta airport, the transportation sector accounts for almost half of total earnings.) Conversely, as we would expect, agriculture accounts for a large portion of earning in the underdeveloped economies.

Coffee County offers a good example of a developing area. Although it still has a per capita income slightly less than two-thirds the national average, is dependent on the agricultural sector for a relatively large portion of earnings, and relies on net transfer payments for a relatively large portion of its total income, it has "turned its economy around" in recent years. The community has experienced rapid expansion in the manufacturing sector, which has increased the percentage of the population employed to levels nearing the state average and significantly above those found in less developed counties.

Industrial Structure

As we have previously noted, not only has the Georgia economy expanded rapidly during the past three decades, its industrial structure has shifted, the most dramatic change being the declining relative importance of agriculture. Let's examine this growth record and some of these structure changes.

Gross State Product—Change: 1950-1983

Gross national product is the dollar value of all goods and services produced in the nation in a particular year. The comparable measure at the state level is gross state product. Table 4 shows Georgia gross state product for selected years between 1950 and 1983 by source and by major sector. The figures are stated in 1972 dollars, that is, they are adjusted to eliminate the impact of inflation and supposedly measure "real" increases in production.

Table 4: Real Gross State Product, by Sector, 1950-1983
(Millions of 1972 Dollars)

| Sector | 1950 | 1960 | 1970 | 1980 | 1983 | Percent of Total | | |
						1950	1970	1983
Farm	546.5	662.5	736.2	683.3	820.5	7.0	3.5	2.4
Mining	29.6	57.9	111.3	112.3	98.6	0.4	0.5	0.3
Construction	514.2	678.2	866.5	1,061.1	1,183.3	6.5	4.1	3.5
Manufacturing	1,763.6	2,589.5	4,785.7	7,660.2	7,477.0	22.5	22.8	22.0
Whsle. and retail trade	1,368.5	2,040.8	3,904.5	6,157.2	6,756.1	17.4	18.5	19.9
Trans., comm., and utilities	578.3	939.2	2,048.6	4,007.6	4,104.3	7.4	9.7	12.1
Finance, insurance, and real estate	886.1	1,648.3	2,923.6	4,883.7	5,215.5	11.3	13.9	15.3
Services	771.0	1,397.8	2,197.0	3,311.9	4,311.1	9.7	10.5	12.6
Government	1,396.3	2,154.0	3,446.5	4,382.5	4,041.3	17.8	16.5	11.9
TOTAL	7,854.1	12,168.2	21,019.9	32,259.8	34,007.7	100.0	100.0	100.0

Source: College of Business Administration, University of Georgia.

Georgia real gross state product more than quadrupled during the period, from $7.9 billion in 1950 to $34.0 billion in 1983. This represented an annual growth rate of 4.8 percent, compared to a 4.4 percent annual growth rate for the entire Southeast and 3.4 percent for the United States as a whole.

The leading sectors in terms of their contribution to Georgia's economy are (1) manufacturing ($7.5 billion); (2) wholesale and retail trade ($6.8 billion); (3) finance, insurance, and real estate ($5.2 billion); (4) services ($4.3 billion); (5) transportation, communications, and utilities ($4.1 billion); and (6) government ($4.0 billion). The contributions of construction ($1.2 billion), agriculture ($.8 billion), and mining (less than $.01 billion) were relatively minor.

During the 33-year period, several major structural shifts occurred in the Georgia economy, and some of these are shown in Figure 2. The relative shares of construction, agriculture, and government declined sharply. On the other hand, those of transportation, communications,

Figure 2: Georgia Gross State Product, 1950, 1970, 1983 (Percentage of Total)

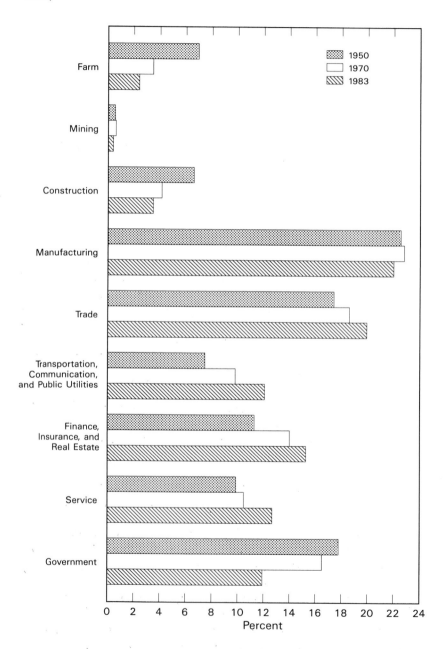

and public utilities; services; finance, insurance, and real estate; and wholesale and retail trade have increased substantially. This latter group of industries accounted for 45.8 percent of Georgia's gross state product in 1950; by 1983 their contribution had risen to 59.9 percent.

These changes in Georgia's industrial structure are similar to those experienced by the United States economy as a whole. The data in Table 5 show that both the national and southeastern economies were becoming more service oriented, with the percentage of product generated by the agriculture sector falling greatly.

Table 5: Distribution of Real Gross Product, by Major Industry, 1950 and 1983 (Percent)

Sector	Georgia		Southeast		United States	
	1950	1983	1950	1983	1950	1983
Agriculture	7.0	2.4	7.5	2.6	5.5	2.8
Mining	0.4	0.3	3.0	3.3	2.2	1.4
Construction	6.5	3.5	6.7	4.3	5.6	3.4
Manufacturing	22.5	22.0	21.6	22.3	24.9	23.7
Trade	17.4	19.9	15.3	18.0	16.6	17.3
Transportation, communication, and public utilities	7.4	12.1	7.0	9.8	7.5	9.2
Finance, insurance, and real estate	11.3	15.3	9.7	14.5	12.2	16.9
Services	9.7	12.6	11.3	13.8	11.2	13.7
Government	17.8	11.9	17.9	11.4	14.3	11.6

Source: College of Business Administration, The University of Georgia.

Employment

As we would expect, shifts in the relative contribution to gross state product by the various sectors have roughly paralleled relative changes in industry employment. One rather dramatic exception is agriculture, where large increases in productivity have led to large employment declines. The data in Table 6 show that the number of agricultural workers in Georgia fell from around 280,000 in 1950 to approximately 76,000 in 1980. The only other decline occurred in personal services, a consequence of a developing economy which offered more remunerative jobs in other industries. Another factor influencing the employment decline in agriculture and personal services has been the increasing availability of job opportunities for blacks, whose employment traditionally has been concentrated in these sectors.

Table 6: Georgia Employment, by Industry, 1950-1980

Industry	1950		1960		1970		1980	
	Number	Percent	Number	Percent	Number	Percent	Number	Percent
Agriculture, forestry, fishing, and mining	282,093	22.49	132,366	9.56	83,348	4.77	76,713	3.28
Construction	71,863	5.73	86,557	6.25	118,660	6.79	150,041	6.42
Manufacturing	288,150	22.97	364,692	26.33	474,961	27.19	562,023	24.06
Trans., comm., and public utilities	75,947	6.05	86,760	6.26	122,262	7.00	188,676	8.08
Whsle. and retail trade	201,862	16.09	244,826	17.68	341,000	19.52	472,049	20.21
Finance, insurance, and real estate	30,165	2.40	49,918	3.60	79,891	4.57	130,329	5.58
Business and repair services	23,391	1.86	28,057	2.03	46,973	2.69	90,702	3.88
Personal, entertainment, and rec. services	131,886	10.51	145,540	10.51	123,312	7.06	104,742	4.48
Prof. and related services	82,058	6.54	134,534	9.71	254,482	14.57	425,186	18.20
Public administration	48,414	3.86	71,988	5.20	101,880	5.83	135,374	5.80
Not reported	18,473	1.47	39,809	2.87	——	——	——	——

Source: U.S. Bureau of the Census.

During the same period, large absolute and relative employment gains were experienced in a number of industries, including transportation, communications, and public utilities; wholesale and retail trade; finance, insurance, and real estate; and business and professional services.

Agriculture

The relative decline of Georgia agriculture has been one of the most significant developments in the state's economy during the past three decades. Nevertheless, for many Georgians agriculture still commands a strong emotional attachment far beyond its current economic significance, and many still regard Georgia as primarily an agricultural state. This view is long outdated; although agriculture still has an important role in providing income to many areas of the state and to many families, the portion of Georgia income and employment generated by the agricultural sector is small.

As recently as 1950, agriculture accounted for 7.0 percent of Georgia's gross state product. Almost a million Georgians lived on 226,000 farms, which represented 69 percent of the state's available land.

A sign of the times in rural south Georgia. A troubled farm economy in the early 1980s brought many farms to the auction block.

By 1983 the number of Georgia farms had declined to 59,000, the farm population had fallen to only 121,000, and farms utilized only 37 percent of the state's land area. In 1983 the portion of gross state product generated directly by the agricultural sector had declined to 2.4 percent. It is certainly a tribute to the agricultural sector that with somewhat less than one-fourth the number of farmers working the land, and with land in farms reduced by almost half, Georgia agriculture still generates a larger real product than it did in 1950.

Since agriculture is a "basic" industry, its overall current contribution to the Georgia economy is greater than these rather minuscule figures would indicate, since many workers are employed in agriculture-related industries. For example, of the state's 175,000 manufacturing workers in 1984, about 20,200 worked in food processing, 3,700 were employed in lumber and wood products manufacturing, and 8,200 worked in paper products manufacturing. By including all activity that has even a remote connection with agriculture, some agricultural boosters even claim that "agribusiness" accounts for as much as 10 percent of Georgia's output, but most economists consider this figure to be grossly inflated.

Principal Crops

Ask the casual observer what Georgia's principal crops are, and you would probably hear mention of peaches, peanuts, and maybe cotton. As we see in Figure 3, peanuts definitely are an important Georgia crop, accounting for almost 14 percent of cash receipts. However, cotton—"king cotton"—now generates only about 2.5 percent of agricultural cash receipts, while peaches produce slightly more than 1 percent of Georgia farm income.

Figure 3: Georgia Farm Receipts, 1984 (Percentage of Total)

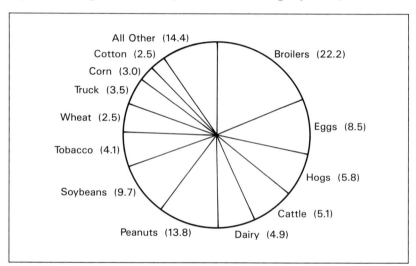

Chickens are Georgia's leading farm commodity—yes, chickens. Broilers account for over one-fifth of farm income, while egg production generates another 9 percent. Other important commodities are soybeans (10 percent), hogs (6 percent), cattle (5 percent), dairy (5 percent), tobacco (4 percent), and wheat (3 percent).

The production of broilers and eggs is centered in northeast Georgia, but most Georgia crops are produced largely in the portion of the state south of the fall line. This is true of almost all peanuts, tobacco, and corn, and most wheat and soybeans. Cattle farms are scattered throughout the state, with dairy farms located primarily in the Piedmont region closer to urban consumers.

Another agricultural development that has had tremendous impact on Georgia is the rise of "tree farming." A large portion of the land removed from the production of row crops was planted in pine trees, with much of the acreage owned by large paper companies. While this development has placed thousands of acres of Georgia farmland in a productive use and provided a source of raw materials for the paper and wood products manufacturing industries, it has also been a significant factor in "depopulating" many Georgia counties. Tree farming provides relatively little employment compared to conventional agriculture.

Manufacturing

The largest single sector of the Georgia economy is manufacturing, accounting for approximately 24 percent of both gross state product and employment. The data of Table 7 show that a large portion of these manufacturing jobs are in relatively low wage industries—textiles, apparel, food products, lumber and wood products, and furniture. Some of these industries, as well as others such as paper and paper products, and stone, clay, and glass products (primarily brick products), depend on the state's natural resources. Figure 4 illustrates change, 1950-84,

Table 7: Georgia Wage and Manufacturing Employment, 1982 (Thousands)

Industry	Employment	Percent of Total	Average Hourly Wage
Manufacturing total	500.3	100.0	$ 6.75
Durable goods	178.6	35.7	7.56
Lumber and wood products	27.8	5.6	5.45
Furniture and fixtures	9.5	1.9	5.04
Stone, clay, and glass	16.3	3.3	7.47
Primary metals	16.1	3.2	8.72
Fabricated metals	18.1	3.6	6.89
Machinery except electrical	20.8	4.2	n/a
Electrical and electronics	23.4	4.7	7.49
Transportation equipment	34.9	7.0	11.09
Other durable	11.6	2.3	n/a
Nondurable goods	321.7	64.3	6.31
Food products	58.3	11.7	6.24
Textiles	102.2	20.4	5.82
Apparel	69.1	13.8	4.60
Paper products	27.7	5.5	10.11
Printing and publishing	25.4	5.1	n/a
Chemicals	17.4	3.5	8.21
Leather products	2.2	.4	4.31
Other nondurable	19.4	3.9	n/a

Source: Georgia Department of Labor.

Figure 4: Georgia Manufacturing Employment Percentage Distribution, 1950, 1970, 1984

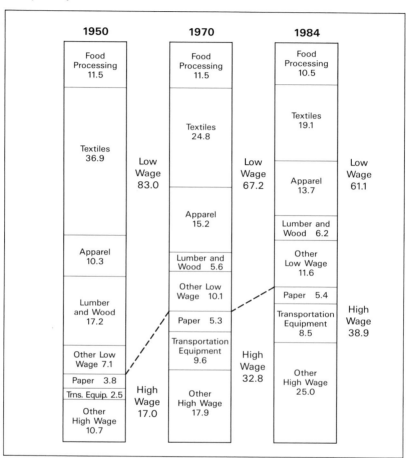

in the proportional distribution of manufacturing employment by major sectors.

Abundant natural resources and attractive wage rates and labor conditions appear to have been Georgia's principal comparative advantages in attracting manufacturing employment in recent years. High technology factors have played only a minor role. For example, less than 5 percent of the state's manufacturing workers are employed in electrical machinery, electronic equipment, instruments, or other technical equipment manufacturing industries. Since the bulk of the nation's future manufacturing employment growth is projected to be in the high technology industries, Georgia faces a decisive challenge to become competitive in this important sector.

The Service Sector

As opposed to the production of goods, the production of services has been capturing an ever-increasing share of the United States economy, and this trend is almost certain to continue. The Georgia economy has followed this national trend. Wholesale and retail trade; transportation, communications, and utilities; finance, insurance, and real estate; and services have all gained in their shares of gross state product and employment. Particularly significant has been the growth of business and repair services, and professional and related services. Together, this part of the service sector now employs almost as many Georgians as does manufacturing. These sectors are also projected to be rapid growth industries during the coming years, primarily in high technology industries. Here again, Georgia will face difficulties in continuing its recent record of rapid economic growth unless it can compete for these jobs.

Government and Military

Although most governmental activity is "population serving" in nature, major facilities can have a great impact on local areas. In particular, educational facilities and military installations often are the foundation of local economies.

The location of major military installations is shown in Figure 5, with employment data given in Table 8. Military earnings alone totalled over $1.4 billion in 1984, considerably greater than total farm earnings. To this must be added the earnings of civilian employees, which total almost $1 billion annually; civilian earnings at Warner Robins Air Force Base alone are in excess of $500 million. When employment in related activities is considered, defense is obviously one of the state's largest economic sectors. Even manufacturing is greatly influenced by the military. For example, at its facility in Marietta, Lockheed-Georgia employs approximately 17,000 workers making the C-5B and C-130 transport aircraft.

Like military installations, large-scale colleges and universities or other large governmental facilities can have a heavy local economic impact. For example, the University of Georgia is by far the largest employer in Athens, state government wages and salaries constituting almost one-third of total county earnings. If related jobs throughout the economy are considered, the university accounts for a dominant share of both income and employment in the area.

International Trade

A factor of rapidly increasing importance to the Georgia economy is international trade and investment. Traditionally, most of Georgia's international trade has been in natural resources products such as agricultural

Figure 5: Major Educational Institutions and Military Installations in Georgia

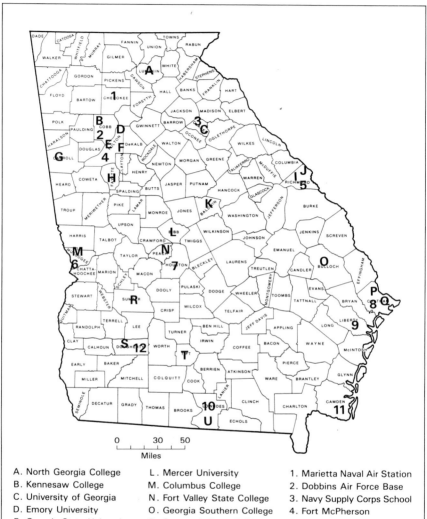

A. North Georgia College	L. Mercer University	1. Marietta Naval Air Station
B. Kennesaw College	M. Columbus College	2. Dobbins Air Force Base
C. University of Georgia	N. Fort Valley State College	3. Navy Supply Corps School
D. Emory University	O. Georgia Southern College	4. Fort McPherson
E. Georgia State University	P. Savannah State College	5. Fort Gordon
F. Georgia Institute of Technology	Q. Armstrong State College	6. Fort Benning
G. West Georgia College	R. Georgia Southwestern College	7. Robins Air Force Base
H. Clayton State College	S. Albany State College	8. Hunter Army Airfield
I. Augusta College	T. Abraham Baldwin Agricultural College	9. Fort Stewart
J. Medical College of Georgia	U. Valdosta State College	10. Moody Air Force Base
K. Georgia College		11. Kings Bay Submarine Base
		12. Marine Corps Logistics Base

commodities, timber, pulpwood, and kaolin (a clay used in paper manufacture). Although trade in these products is still very important, there has been a very rapid increase during the past 10 years in container shipments. Table 9 shows the growing tonnage shipped from the state-owned Georgia Ports Authority facilities at Savannah and Brunswick. A very large portion of the Savannah tonnage is in containers, which are used primarily to ship high-value freight.

With the initiation of direct international flights to Europe and Central and South America, the Atlanta airport assumed a significant

Table 8: Major Military Installations in Georgia

Installation	Approximate Employment (Thousands)	
	Military	Civilian
Naval Air Station, Marietta	3.5	.3
Dobbins AFB, Marietta	1.5	.6
Ft. McPherson, Atlanta	3.0	8.0
Navy Supply Corps School, Athens	.4	.2
Ft. Gordon, Augusta	15.8	3.7
Robins Air Force Base, Warner Robins	5.0	14.0
Ft. Benning, Columbus	28.0	8.2
Hunter Army Airfield, Savannah	3.5	.5
Ft. Stewart, Hinesville	13.7	.5
Marine Corps Logistics Base, Albany	1.2	2.5
Moody Air Force Base, Valdosta	3.5	.5
Kings Bay Submarine Base, St. Marys	Under construction	
TOTAL	79.1	39.0

Source: Department of Defense.

Table 9: Georgia Ports Authority Facilities Tonnage, Savannah and Brunswick, Selected Years

Year	Savannah	Brunswick
1962	1,190,086	34,980
1967	1,725,347	64,960
1972	2,394,338	115,872
1977	2,918,372	101,193
1980	4,458,444	265,753
1982	5,493,591	406,828
1984	5,971,808	419,639
1986	6,783,616	447,309

Source: Georgia Ports Authority.

role in Georgia international trade. Not only have these flights promoted the growth in shipments of high value international freight to and from Georgia, they have been a very important factor in more closely linking the Georgia economy with the international economy.

Challenges for the Future

The state has indeed made tremendous progress during recent years, but the continuation of this record of growth and improvement in the relative economic well-being of Georgians is by no means assured.

The current relatively low average level of income for Georgia citizens hardly gives reason for complacency regarding the state's economic future. Just for Georgia to stay in the same relative economic position it now occupies, the number and quality of new jobs will have to grow rapidly; if Georgia is to advance and improve the economic well-being of its citizens, the quality and quantity of new jobs must grow much more rapidly than in the past.

The "Two" Georgias

Clearly, analyzing the Georgia economy as a single unit gives a distorted view that tends to hide the problems of the state's lagging areas. There

The Georgia Ports Authority, created by the legislature in 1945 to improve the state's deepwater ports, operates this containerized cargo facility at Savannah.

are two major Georgia sub-economies—the Atlanta metropolitan region and the remainder of Georgia. Figures 6 and 7 summarize much of the data on the two Georgias. The first shows that the 18 counties of the Atlanta MSA had 41 percent of the state's population in 1984, 46 percent of its employment, and 49 percent of its personal income. In other words, the residents of the Atlanta region enjoyed a higher rate of employment and higher average earnings than residents of the remainder of Georgia. These higher average earnings were largely a result of employment being concentrated in the higher wage industries, as shown in Figure 7. The Atlanta region has much greater shares of its employment in the high technology, and higher paid service, trade, and finance areas. Since these industries are projected to experience greater than average employment growth, the Atlanta region's industrial structure will help it to continue expanding rapidly. Also, more than half of all Atlanta manufacturing employment is in the higher-wage durable goods industries, with approximately one-fourth in transportation equipment and electrical and electronic machinery.

In contrast, the growth record of much of the portion of Georgia outside the Atlanta metropolitan region has exhibited many of the characteristics common to economically underdeveloped regions. These

Figure 6: Atlanta Metropolitan Region's Population, Employment, and Personal Income as Percentage of Georgia's, Selected Years

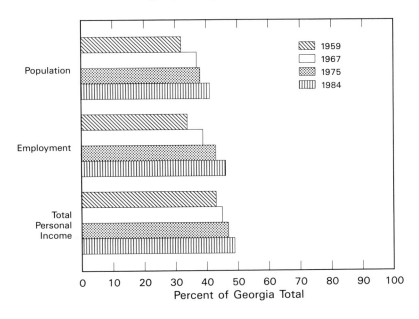

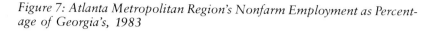

Figure 7: Atlanta Metropolitan Region's Nonfarm Employment as Percentage of Georgia's, 1983

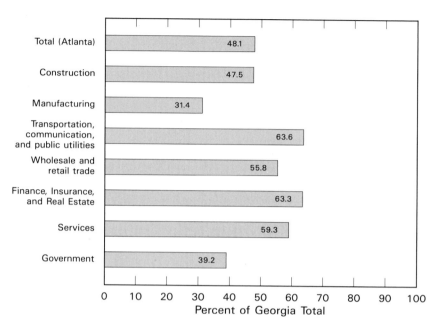

characteristics have included heavy losses in agricultural employment, relatively rapid employment gains in the nonagricultural sector (particularly in the low-wage manufacturing industries), low rates of population growth due to out-migration, and a convergence of per capita incomes toward the national average. The question now is whether these areas will move forward in their economic development and improve the relative economic welfare of their citizens, or whether they will languish as economic backwaters, thereby slowing down the economic progress of the entire state.

Education

Georgia enjoys many competitive advantages in economic development, including favorable labor costs and conditions, natural resources, climate, and taxes. These factors should continue to give Georgia an advantage in attracting the traditional manufacturing and other industries which have paced the state's growth in the modern era. But with the changing structure of the national and world economies, these traditional industries will be less important in the future. Rapid growth and further relative improvement in levels of per capita income depend on the state being a leader in high technology industries, and it is highly trained labor

that is of major competitive importance in attracting these industries—
not cheap labor, abundant natural resources, or low taxes.

Unfortunately, Georgia does not have the stock of highly trained
individuals these industries require, particularly in many of the rural
areas of the state. Georgia's expenditures for education per pupil have
been among the very lowest in the nation, and unless the state vigorously
continues its recent initiative to greatly raise the level of education and
training of its workers, Georgia will be at a severe disadvantage in this
vital area.

Transportation

Another vital need is to improve the state's multilane highway system
to enable the many communities that are not adequately served by good
transportation facilities to be competitive in attracting economic growth
and development. Completion of such a developmental highway system
will not enable these communities to achieve economic development in
the absence of other important growth elements, but without adequate
transportation facilities, development is unlikely.

Georgia has an excellent interstate highway system, but the state's
multilane highways off the interstate system are totally inadequate to
meet critical growth objectives. In fact, it takes only a momentary study
of a southeastern road map to see that Georgia has the most inadequate
four-lane system in the region. The data in Table 10 give another simple
comparison, showing the number of communities of over 10,000 population in the states of the Southeast that are served by divided four-lane
highways.

*Table 10: Multilane Highway Access for Communities over 10,000 Popula-
tion, Southeastern States, 1984*

| | Communities | | | Percent | | |
State	Total	On Inter-state	On 4-lane	Not on 4-lane	On Inter-state	On 4-lane	Not on 4-lane
Georgia	38	20	6	12	52%	16%	32%
Alabama	38	22	14	2	58%	37%	5%
Florida	88	66	21	1	75%	24%	1%
Kentucky	29	18	11	0	62%	38%	0%
Mississippi	25	15	9	1	60%	36%	4%
North Carolina	40	20	19	1	50%	48%	2%
South Carolina	23	12	9	2	52%	39%	9%
Tennessee	32	18	8	6	56%	25%	19%
Virginia	27	17	10	0	63%	37%	0%

Source: Derived from *Gousha North American Road Atlas, 1985.*

The reason for this inadequate system of four-lane highways off the interstate system is quite simple. State financial support for highways is very low, by some measures the *lowest* in the nation. The motor fuel tax rate is among the nation's lowest, but this is only part of the story. Other states provide large portions of highway financing from motor vehicle registration fees, special truck taxes, minerals severance taxes, and general funds. A recent Federal Highway Administration study found that Georgia state highway revenue based on levels of travel (per 1,000 vehicle miles) was the lowest of any state, slightly over half the national average. If Georgia is to have adequate highways to be competitive for economic development in many of the lagging areas of the state, it must spend more money for transportation improvements. Critical among these highway needs is a system of developmental highways to connect more Georgia communities with the interstate highway system to enable them to be economically competitive.

Summary

This brief survey has shown that although the Georgia economy has made tremendous strides in recent years and has become an economic leader of the Southeast, it faces great challenges for the future. Average incomes are still relatively low when compared to those in the nation as a whole, particularly outside the Atlanta metropolitan region. Raising this level of income and bringing the state's lagging areas into the economic mainstream will require an enlightened economic policy, including significantly expanded investments in education and transportation.

CHAPTER FOUR

Population Patterns

By K. Imogene Dean and Lawrence R. Hepburn

From both counties nearly 60 percent of the migrants were males. Unattached males between twenty and thirty moved off first; then the younger couples with few or no children; next the unattached females; and then the families, the wife and children frequently remaining behind until the husband could find work and living quarters; many wives soon joined their husbands. In both counties there were deserted wives who had little hope or no hope of their husbands either sending for them or returning to aid in rearing the children. Left behind, too, were most of the aged and handicapped people. Old men and cripples and children leave home when taken. Frequently the migrants were scarcely able to pay passage for themselves and their immediate families, to say nothing of invalids and defectives who could be sent for later—or never. (Arthur F. Raper, *Preface to Peasantry,* Chapel Hill: The University of North Carolina Press, 1936.)

In such words was the 1920s exodus of farmers from Georgia's Greene and Macon counties described. In some rural districts, hardest hit by the boll weevil, the drought, and the depression, over 50 percent of the population left.

Some of Georgia's rural migrants went no farther than Athens, Augusta, or Atlanta, the first stations on the line and as far as their train ticket would take them. Others made it up to Chicago, Detroit, and Gary, Indiana, to seek factory jobs or down to Tampa and Miami, where the Florida "boom" was on. The 1930 census showed that Georgia's population increased in the 1920s by only 12,674, a mere 0.4 percent—the lowest rate among the 48 states except for Montana.

Fifty years later, population statistics told an entirely different story. In 1980, Georgia registered a 19.1 percent increase for the decade. And,

50.5 percent of that increase was attributable to migration. Since then, estimates for 1980-84 of an increase of 373,000 residents placed Georgia as the fourth fastest-growing state in the nation in absolute numbers for the period.

A population grows by natural increase (births minus deaths) and migration, variables influenced by culture, and a host of environmental conditions. War, pestilence, religious persecution, political oppression, economic depression, and, in the positive aspect, the absence of such things influence population change. The push of economic depression and the pull of economic opportunity account especially for the migration of people into and among the states. Through the years the vagaries of economic life inside and outside Georgia have helped determine the size and shape of its population.

In Georgia's early decades of statehood, each decennial census recorded tremendous increases. Drawn by the promise of economic opportunity, especially the promise of free land and the growing demand for cotton, migrants swarmed down the valleys of Virginia and the Carolinas to populate middle Georgia. During the years 1800-1840, the United States recorded a spectacular population increase of 222 percent. In Georgia, the population increased by 325 percent.

Since 1840, the growth rate of Georgia's population sometimes resembled that of the national population, but often it did not as the fortunes of Georgia diverged from those of the other states. By 1860, Georgia's population reached the one-million mark, but the rate of increase was already falling behind that of the nation as a whole. In the late nineteenth century, Georgia's growth was attributable mostly to natural increase whereas other state populations swelled with immigrants from Europe. Then and into the twentieth century, Georgia supplied more people to other states than it received. The out-migration became an exodus in the 1920s. In the 1930s, the growth rates of Georgia and the United States as a whole were about the same, as Americans chose to have fewer babies amidst the hard times and many out-of-work native Georgians came home from depressed industrial states. Immediately after World War II, the nation grew at a faster rate than Georgia as out-migration, especially by blacks, continued. Since 1960, Georgia's rate of growth has surpassed that of the nation as a whole, with the state's population topping four million in 1970 and five million just 10 years later (see Table 1).

Georgia's rate of growth since the 1940s is part of a larger national trend, the movement of population from north to south. Still, there is and likely will remain a distinctiveness in the patterns of Georgia's growth. For example, in the decade 1970-80, in the United States, the metropolitan areas grew more slowly than nonmetropolitan areas. But in Georgia, the metropolitan areas grew faster than the nonmetropolitan. Also, the movement of blacks to the central cities of metropolitan areas—a movement which occurred earlier for cities in other parts of the country—is still occurring in Georgia. In other ways, too—age, sex, mobility, distribution, race, and ethnicity—Georgia's population differs from others. And, by examining those differences not only can the present conditions of the state be understood, but also the problems and opportunities of the future can be perceived.

Table 1: Population Increases, Georgia and the United States, 1790-1980

Census Year	Georgia Population	Increase (%)	United States Population	Increase (%)
1790	82,548	—	3,929,214	—
1800	162,686	97.1	5,308,483	35.1
1810	252,433	55.2	7,239,881	36.4
1820	340,989	35.1	9,638,453	33.1
1830	516,823	51.6	12,866,020	33.5
1840	691,392	33.8	17,069,453	32.7
1850	906,185	31.1	23,191,876	35.9
1860	1,057,286	16.7	31,443,321	35.6
1870	1,184,109[a]	12.0	38,558,371[a]	22.6
1880	1,542,180	30.2	50,189,209	30.2
1890	1,837,353	19.1	62,797,766	25.5
1900	2,216,331	20.6	76,212,168	20.7
1910	2,609,121	17.7	92,228,496	21.0
1920	2,895,832	11.0	106,021,537	15.0
1930	2,908,506	0.4	123,202,624	16.2
1940	3,123,723	7.4	132,164,569	7.3
1950	3,444,578	10.3	151,325,798	14.5
1960	3,943,116	14.5	179,323,175	18.5
1970	4,587,930	16.4	203,302,031	13.4
1980	5,463,105	19.1	226,545,805	11.4

Source: U.S. Bureau of the Census, *1980 Census of Population, Number of Inhabitants, U.S. Summary;* for discussion of the 1870 revisions see *Eleventh Census of the United States: 1890.*

[a] The figures for 1870 reflect an underenumeration in the southern states. On the basis of the Census Bureau's revision figure of 39,818,449 for the nation, the U.S. population increased by 26.6 percent between 1860 and 1870 and by 26.1 percent between 1870 and 1880. A revised figure for Georgia was not published, but the actual rate of increase was probably about 21 percent for 1860-1870 and 1870-1880.

The Shape of Georgia's Population

While the total size of a population is of prime importance to the condition of the society, the "shape" of the population, in terms of age and sex composition, influences levels of dependency on family and public institutions, demands for goods and services, labor supply and economic productivity, and political issues and government policy.

The double-bar graphs (Figures 1 and 2) demonstrate how the shape of Georgia's population changed from 1930 to 1980. The graphs, based upon the total population at the decade, display the percentage of population by sex in 5-year age intervals and in a 75-year and above category.

A cursory examination of the age-sex pyramids reveals notable changes during the 50-year period. First, the percentage of males and females in each age category upwards from age 55 was significantly greater in 1980 than in 1930. Conversely, the percentage of males and females in each category under age 15 was significantly less in 1980. These changes indicate a more aged population in 1980 than in 1930. The relatively large proportion in the 15-19 and 20-24 age categories in 1980 reflects the higher birth rates of the 1950s and 1960s. Also, the sex ratio differs for the two years. Birth and death rates in 1930 and birth rates in 1980 were about the same for males and females. But, in 1930 females outnumbered males in the 20-24 through 45-49 age categories, then dropped back. An important factor here was differential migration for males and females. In 1980, the high ratio of females to males in the older age categories reflects the differential in death rates for the sexes.

In general, from 1930 to 1980 the shape of Georgia's population pyramid has changed from one having a broad base tapered to a narrow top (reflecting a large percentage of youngsters and a low percentage of elderly people) to one more narrowly based and broader in older age categories. This change is characteristic of a population with declining fertility and mortality.

Fertility and Mortality

Fertility and mortality can be described by a population's birth rate and death rate. Figure 3 shows birth and death rates for Georgia and the whole United States, 1930 to 1980.

In general, while similar curves describe increasing and then decreasing birth rates for both populations, note especially the post-World War II peaks and how the rates have converged since 1950, with Georgians maintaining a higher rate. Similar curves likewise describe decreasing death rates for both populations, with Georgians maintaining a lower rate since 1939.

Figure 1: Age-Sex Pyramid for Georgia, 1930

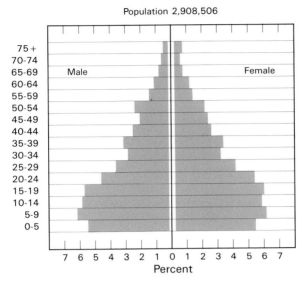

Population 2,908,506

Source: U.S. Bureau of the Census, *1980 Census of Population, General Population Characteristics, Georgia.*

Figure 2: Age-Sex Pyramid for Georgia, 1980

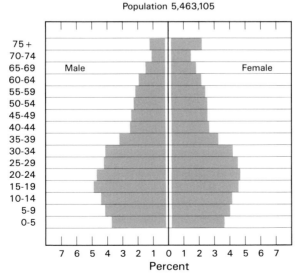

Population 5,463,105

Source: U.S. Bureau of the Census, *1980 Census of Population, General Population Characteristics, Georgia.*

Certain differentials help determine the fertility and mortality of a population. They include, in the main, age, sex, and race; and also education, religion, occupation, wealth, and urban or rural residence. However, taken together, Georgia's crude birth and death rates clearly reflect an aging population.

A Rising Median Age

One of the indicators of the age of a people is the median age—the midpoint in the age distribution, or the age below which and above which there is an equal number of individuals. Higher birth rates, higher death rates, or an out-migration of adults would be reflected in a lowering of the median age. Lower birth rates, lower death rates, and an in-migration of adults is reflected in a rising median age.

Figure 3: Crude Birth and Death Rates, Georgia and the United States, 1930 to 1980

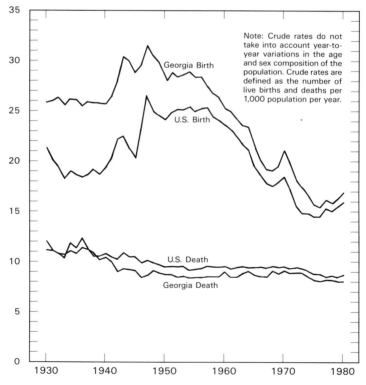

Note: Crude rates do not take into account year-to-year variations in the age and sex composition of the population. Crude rates are defined as the number of live births and deaths per 1,000 population per year.

Source: National Center for Health Statistics, *Vital Statistics of the United States, Natality, Mortality,* 1980, 1971, 1961, 1950, 1940.

The changes in Georgia's median age, from 1930 to 1980, are shown in Table 2. The median age is consistently lower for males than for females; it is lower, also, for blacks than for whites. For the whole population of Georgia, the median age rose by seven years between 1930 and 1980. In addition to lower fertility and lower mortality, since World War II, in-migration has been an important factor in Georgia's changing population. The net effect was to make Georgia's population in 1980 more like the U.S. population in terms of age.

Table 2: Median Age, Georgia and the United States, 1930-1980

Census Year	Georgia Total	M	F	Black	White	U.S. Total
1930	21.9	21.6	22.1	20.9	22.6	26.5
1940	24.5	24.2	24.8	22.8	25.6	29.0
1950	26.2	25.5	26.8	23.2	27.4	30.2
1960	25.9	24.6	27.2	20.9	27.8	29.5
1970	25.9	24.6	27.3	21.3	27.5	28.1
1980	28.6	27.3	29.9	24.2	30.5	30.0

Source: U.S. Bureau of the Census, *1980 Census of Population, General Population Characteristics, United States Summary, Georgia.*

Of course, the 1980 median age of 28.6 years was not uniform across the state. The range in median age—from 21.3 years in Chattahoochee County to 35.3 years in Taliaferro County—reflects differentials within the state in birth and death rates and migration. Figure 4 shows the counties with the highest and lowest median ages. In general, the highest are found above the fall line and the lowest below the fall line. In some cases, low median age is explained by the presence of military facilities, e.g., Chattahoochee County; or educational facilities, e.g., Clarke County. In others, race is a factor in high median age: there are relatively few black residents in north Georgia counties. Above all, differentials in economic opportunity and in-migration for different age groups can account for variance in median age.

Migration

Between 1970 and 1980, Georgia's population grew by 875,175 people, the greatest numerical increase of any 10-year period in its history and the highest growth rate (19.1 percent) since 1900. Most remarkably, by Bureau of the Census estimates, migration from other states accounted for 441,645, or 50.5 percent, of the new Georgians. For the first time

Figure 4: Median Age in Georgia, by County, 1980

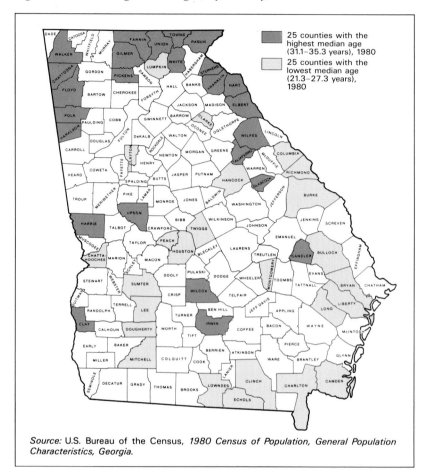

Source: U.S. Bureau of the Census, *1980 Census of Population, General Population Characteristics, Georgia.*

in the twentieth century, in-migration counted for more than natural increase in the growth of Georgia's population.

In the 100 years following the Civil War, Georgia lost more people through out-migration than it gained through in-migration. That the state population grew at all during those years was due primarily to natural increase. Economic opportunities outside Georgia outweighed incentives to remain in or come to Georgia.

Regularly, public and private agencies in the state promoted in-migration. However, as the following excerpt from an 1892 State Department of Agriculture publication evidences, great obstacles (real and perceived) stood in the way of in-migration from other states.

. . .we are looked upon by the outside world as half-civilized ruf-
fians. The idea very largely prevails that it is not safe to come
among us. We are not known as a high-toned Christian people—
civilized, refined and cultured. . . .

There is a prevailing impression that our clime is inhospitable:
that Georgia is largely a sickly marsh; that miasmas and microbes
find here a congenial home—in short, that our climate is too hot
for comfort or health. We need to let the world of home seekers
know that this is emphatically a mistake. . . .

Into the first half of the twentieth century, Georgia continued to
lose far more people to other states than it gained from them. The biggest
surge of out-migration came in the 1920s as the boll weevil worked its
depredations on Georgia and industrial production jobs beckoned
Georgians to the Northeast and Midwest. Between 1920 and 1930, the
state grew by only 12,674 people, or 0.4 percent. By comparison, the
South grew by 14.3 percent and the whole United States by 16.2 percent.[1] In the 1930s, Georgia did not lose people relative to the nation
as a whole. Apparently, the nationwide depression sent many natives
home and discouraged others from leaving Georgia. Since World War
II, however, the rate of in-migration has gradually increased.

One indicator of interstate migration is the percentage of a state's
population born out of state. In 1930, only 10.4 percent of Georgia's
American-born population were not born in Georgia. By comparison,
23.4 percent of all native Americans were born outside the state in which
they were counted in 1930. Figure 5 shows what has happened since
then. In terms of in-migrants as a percentage of its population, Georgia
has become in the years 1930-80 more like the nation as a whole. In
1980, 26.8 percent of Georgia's American-born residents were born in
other states while the average for the 50 states was 30.8 percent.

A second indication of interstate mobility is derived from responses
to census questions about place of residence. Table 3 shows the number
of persons residing in Georgia in 1980 who lived in other states in 1975
and the number residing in other states in 1980 who lived in Georgia
in 1975. (In both cases, only the 10 leading states are shown.)

Georgia's patterns of in-migration and out-migration show a
remarkable consistency. Between 1975 and 1980, Georgia received
581,553 persons (five years old and over) from other states. In the same
period, 450,430 left to take up residence in other states. (Georgia also
had 54,602 in-migrants from overseas, including U.S. military personnel transferred to bases in the state, and an unknown number of out-

---

1. Georgia's loss relative to the rest of the country meant a drop from 12 to 10 in its membership in the U.S. House of Representatives.

Figure 5: Percentage of American-born Persons Born outside Their State of Residence, Georgia and United States Average, 1930-1980

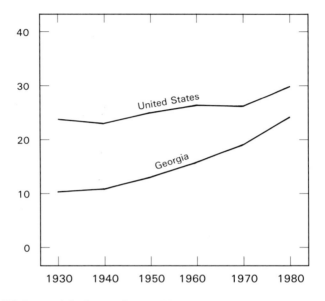

Source: U.S. Bureau of the Census, *Census of Population: 1960; 1980 Census of Population, General Social and Economic Characteristics, U.S. Summary, Georgia.*

Table 3: Leading Suppliers and Receivers of Georgia's Population, 1975-1980

State In-migrants from—		State Out-migrants to—	
Florida	103,782	Florida	75,596
New York	38,498	Alabama	43,433
Alabama	35,641	Texas	32,842
North Carolina	34,695	Tennessee	32,711
South Carolina	32,887	South Carolina	30,549
Tennessee	31,516	North Carolina	29,905
Ohio	25,600	California	22,415
Texas	24,103	Virginia	18,675
California	24,007	New York	11,722
Virginia	22,448	Ohio	10,690

Source: U.S. Bureau of the Census, *1980 Census of Population, Geographic Mobility for States and the Nation.*

migrants overseas.) As Table 3 shows, 10 states supplied more than 60 percent of all newcomers. The same 10 led the list of states receiving persons from Georgia. Clearly there is much back and forth movement between Georgia and those states.

More persons left Georgia for Alabama, Texas, and Tennessee than came from those states to Georgia, reversing in three cases the general pattern of in-migration over out-migration.

Another notable aspect of in-migration to Georgia is that it originates mainly in the South, 58 percent, with only 16 percent from the Northeast and 17 percent from the North Central regions, the so-called Snowbelt, and 9 percent from the West. By contrast, during the same period, 69 percent of the in-migration to Florida (about three times greater than in-migration to Georgia) came from the two Snowbelt regions. Clearly, in-migration and North to South population movement patterns are not the same for Georgia and Florida.

Distribution of Population

For most of Georgia's history, the majority of Georgia's people lived in rural areas, not urban places. In 1860, 92.9 percent of the state population was rural and the largest city, Savannah, had a population of 22,292. In the whole United States, 80.2 percent of the population was rural and only nine cities had populations of 100,000 or more. By 1900, both Georgia and the United States as a whole had doubled the percentage of population living in urban places—to 15.6 percent and 39.6 percent respectively. In that year Atlanta was the largest city in the state with 89,872 residents. Five other Georgia places had 10,000 or more people: Savannah, Augusta, Macon, Columbus, and Athens.

Urbanization came later to Georgia than to most of the United States (see Figure 6). Between 1860 and 1920, after which Georgia farmers began migrating heavily to the cities, the percentage of urban population in Georgia was less than half the U.S. average. (Table 5 on page 119 shows the population for Georgia's largest cities in 1930 and 1980.)

The dominant trend in the distribution of Georgia's people in recent decades has been *suburbanization*. One indicator of this trend is the increase in the number of counties defined as metropolitan by the U.S. Bureau of the Census.[2] In 1950, Georgia had 10 metropolitan coun-

---

2. A metropolitan county is contained within a Metropolitan Statistical Area (MSA). An MSA is defined as a geographic area with a large population center (a city or urbanized area of at least 50,000 people) together with adjacent communities which have a high degree of economic and social integration with that center. Factors such as work commuting patterns and population density patterns are used to define MSAs.

Figure 6: Percentage of Population Classified as Urban, Georgia and the United States, 1790-1980

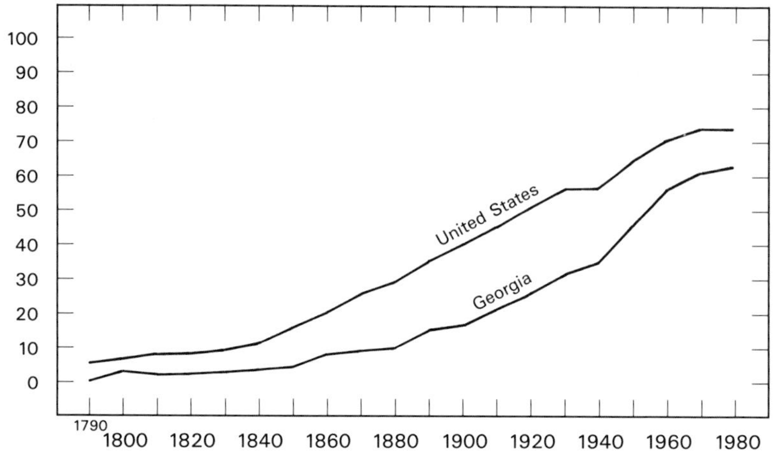

Source: U.S. Bureau of the Census, *1980 Census of Population, Number of Inhabitants, U.S. Summary, Georgia.*

ties containing about 27 percent of its whole population. In 1980, Georgia had 38 metropolitan counties containing about 60 percent of its population. Figure 7 shows the increase of Metropolitan Statistical Area counties in Georgia, 1950-83.[3]

A further indication of suburbanization is that while the population of MSAs increased by an average 21 percent over the decade 1970-80, the central cities (Athens, Atlanta, Augusta, Macon) of four of the seven MSAs lying wholly within Georgia actually lost population and two (Columbus and Savannah) registered an increase by consolidating with a county, in the former case, and by annexation, in the latter case. In 1970, about 40 percent of metropolitan residents lived in the central cities, but in 1980 only about 30 percent lived in the central cities. The rest were living in the suburbs.

The Atlanta MSA obviously dwarfs the others. In 1980, it included 18 of the state's 38 metropolitan counties and held about 39 percent of the state population. Between 1970 and 1980, it grew by 27 percent, the highest rate for any Georgia metropolitan area.

The move to metropolitan areas in the 1970s was a continuation of a trend begun in previous decades, but another trend of those decades,

---

3. In 1983, the Census Bureau revised its 1980 designation of MSA counties. The 1983 revised designations are used here.

Figure 7: Georgia MSAs, 1950 and 1983

Source: U.S. Bureau of the Census.

the flow of population from rural areas, dwindled to a trickle. In the 1950s, 91 of Georgia's 159 counties lost population. All were nonmetropolitan counties. In the 1960s, the number of counties losing people fell to 66; all but one of them (Chatham) were nonmetropolitan. But, in the 1970s, only 10 counties lost population and two of those (Fulton and Chattahoochee) were in MSAs. In the 1950s and 1960s, Georgia's metropolitan areas were growing at the expense of its rural areas as agricultural workers left the farms seeking jobs in industries located in urban counties. By the 1970s, nonmetropolitan population stabilized and even grew by more than 300,000 people, or about one-third of the population increase of the decade. That the eight MSAs accounted for two-thirds of that growth is further evidence that in-migration from other states is now a more significant factor in Georgia's growth than in earlier decades.

What was the destination of migrants from within Georgia and from outside Georgia? Figure 8 shows (1) the 10 counties receiving the highest in-migration (as a percentage of own population) from other Georgia counties, 1975-80, and (2) the 10 counties receiving the highest in-migration from other states, 1975-80. The map also shows (3) the 10 counties that grew the most (in actual numbers) between 1970 and 1980.

Figure 8: Leading Counties in Georgia: In-Migration, 1975-1980; Growth, 1970-1980

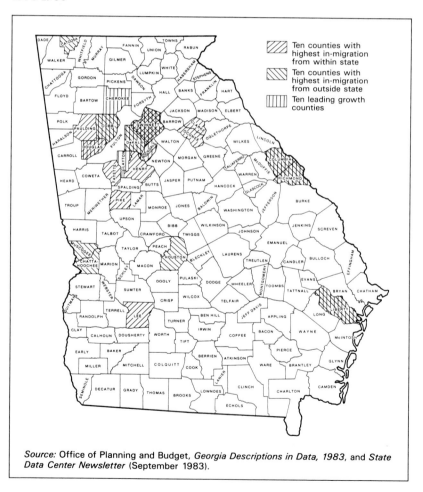

Source: Office of Planning and Budget, *Georgia Descriptions in Data, 1983*, and *State Data Center Newsletter* (September 1983).

The area of highest in-migration and growth is the suburban ring around Atlanta. Gwinnett County is the star—the only county in the top 10 in all three categories shown in Figure 8.

The veritable population explosion of the Atlanta metropolitan region, the overall statewide increase of 19.1 percent between 1970 and 1980, and the fact that only 10 counties lost population in the last decade combine to mask the long-term population decline of wide areas of the state. Just as explosive growth can bring problems in the delivery of utilities, transportation, police protection, education, and other services, so can precipitous decline. In 1980, 58 Georgia counties had fewer people than they had in 1930. Thirty-four counties had declined by more than 20 percent in the five decades and, in 1980, 10 counties had fewer than 5,000 people. The middle part of the state, the old "black belt" running northeast to southwest, had suffered the greatest population loss in the preceding 50 years (see Figure 9).

Race and Ancestry

> Georgia's people are 99½ per cent American-born. Two-thirds of the people are white, preponderantly descended from Anglo-Saxon pioneer ancestors. . . . Georgia's people speak no polyglot of languages. Their language is English, the mother tongue. (State Department of Agriculture, *Georgia and Her Resources,* 1932.)

For most of Georgia's history, at least since the removal of the Indians, the state's population has consisted of two large undifferentiated racial groups, one black and one white. While the affairs of other states have been greatly influenced by the immigration and assimilation in the last 100 years of huge numbers of people from Germany, Scandinavia, Italy, Poland, Russia, and Mexico, the affairs of this state have not.

Race

In 1980, Georgia's black people totalled 1,465,457—the greatest number recorded since the previous all-time high of 1,206,365 in 1920. In numbers, Georgia's 1980 black population ranked fifth in the nation behind those of New York, California, Texas, and Illinois. But, at each census from 1870 to 1950, Georgia had the largest black population in the United States. For the 1980 census, 72.2 percent of the state's residents classified themselves as white and 26.8 percent as black (giving Georgia's black population a fourth place percentage ranking, behind Mississippi, South Carolina, and Louisiana). Only 1 percent classified themselves as "other." Because so few Georgians have classified themselves (or been classified) as any "other" race, the racial composition of the state population is easily illustrated (see Figure 10).

Figure 9: Georgia Population Decline, 1930-1980, and Low Population, 1980

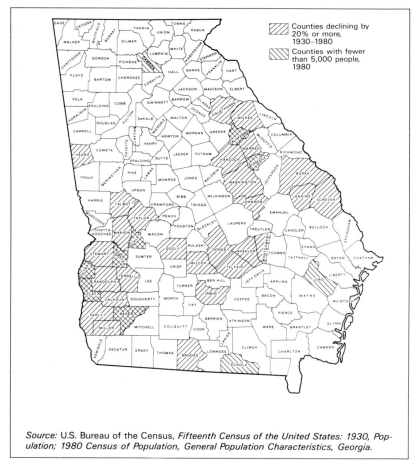

Source: U.S. Bureau of the Census, *Fifteenth Census of the United States: 1930, Population; 1980 Census of Population, General Population Characteristics, Georgia.*

Georgia blacks increased in number to nearly half the state total at the end of the nineteenth century, then declined as a percentage of the population. In the two decades immediately following the Civil War, whites migrated out of Georgia (especially to the West) at a greater rate than blacks did. However, by the 1890s black out-migration grew, corresponding with the general south-to-north migration of blacks leaving a worsening racial climate and seeking economic opportunity in the industrialized regions. Although the percentage of black Georgians began declining at that time, black numbers continued to grow to a peak in 1920. The decrease of blacks was especially steep from 1920 to 1930 and from 1940 to 1950. In the 1920s, the number of blacks decreased

Figure 10: Percentage of Blacks in Georgia Population, 1790-1980

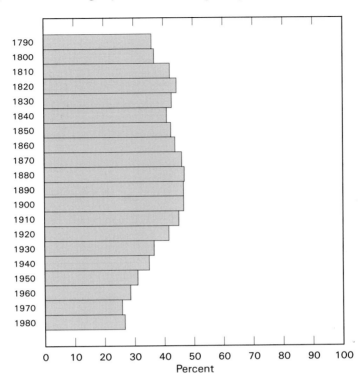

Source: U.S. Bureau of the Census, *Historical Statistics of the United States, Colonial Times to 1970; 1980 Census of the Population, General Population Characteristics.*

by 11.2 percent as whites increased by 8.7 percent (which resulted in a total increase for the decade of 0.4 percent; see Table 1). Although, in the wake of the boll weevil both blacks and whites left the state looking for jobs in more prosperous regions, blacks left at a greater rate. Likewise, in the 1940s the black population decreased by 2.0 percent as the white population grew by 16.8 percent. Although both black and white farmers were deserting rural areas for the cities after World War II, more blacks were migrating out of the state and whites from other states were moving in.

With a moderated racial climate and increased economic opportunities, Georgia experienced, in the 1970s, a reversal of the black migration pattern. For the first time since 1880, the percentage of black Georgians grew, from 25.9 percent to 26.8 percent; for the first time in 100 years Georgia's black population grew at a greater rate, 23.8 percent, than did the white population, 16.4 percent.

For the period 1975-80, in-migration of black persons was 1.6 times greater than out-migration. For whites, in-migration was 1.3 times greater. However, the in-migration of persons of Spanish origin was 2.2 times greater than out-migration (see Table 4).

Distribution by Race

In the half century, 1930-80, the redistribution of Georgians from rural to urban areas was the dominant population trend within the state. This shift was especially dramatic for the black population. For the better part of two centuries, Georgia's black people were concentrated in farming areas. (They had been brought to Georgia to be agricultural workers.) Long after the Civil War, black farm labor remained in high demand. Opportunities for blacks in Georgia industry, however, were strictly limited to less desirable work in turpentine distilleries, cotton-seed oil refineries, fertilizer plants, and the like. And blacks were not welcomed as residents in most Georgia cities.

The heaviest concentrations of black people were in the old cotton belt counties comprising a northeasterly to southwesterly band across the midsection of the state. Even after the boll weevil devastation in the 1920s forced thousands of black sharecroppers to abandon the cotton fields, most of these black belt counties—and a few others—still had black majorities. In 1930, populations in 48 of 161 counties were 50 percent or more black (see Figure 11). All were rural counties: only one, Dougherty, had a city (Albany) of more than 10,000. That same year, 22 counties, all in the northern part of the state, had fewer than 10 percent blacks.

By 1980, only 19 counties had black majorities (see Figure 12). Of the old black belt counties, 18 still had black majorities, and Fulton County had gained a black majority. From 1930 to 1980, Fulton's black population grew from 31.9 percent to 51.5 percent of its total. During those same years, the number of counties having fewer than 10 percent black population increased from 22 to 30; all but one of them were in the northern part of the state.

Table 4: Net Migration in Georgia, by Major Group, 1975-1980

	Total	White	Black	Spanish Origin
In-migration	636,155	504,292	107,435	16,877
Out-migration	450,430	373,692	68,889	7,714
Net migration	185,725	130,600	38,546	9,163

Source: U.S. Bureau of the Census, 1980 Census of Population, General Social and Economic Characteristics, Georgia; Geographic Mobility for States and the Nation.

Figure 11: Population Distribution in Georgia, by Race, 1930

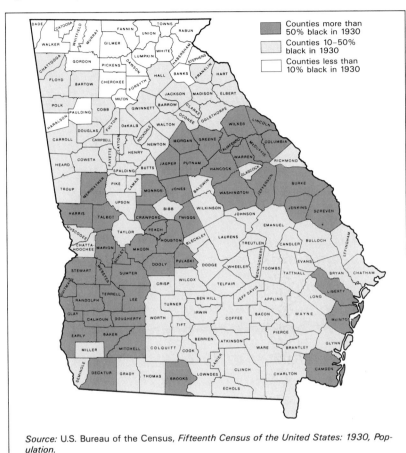

Source: U.S. Bureau of the Census, *Fifteenth Census of the United States: 1930, Population.*

The relative proportions of black and white people in Georgia's major cities are presented in Table 5. Of the seven central cities of MSAs lying within Georgia, only Atlanta recorded a substantial increase both in total population and in percentage of black residents between 1930 and 1980.

Ancestry

Compared to Americans as a whole, the people of Georgia are more likely to find their ancestral roots in the British Isles than anywhere else. In 1909, and using schedules from the first population count, the Bureau of the Census estimated that the 1790 distribution of white Georgians

Figure 12: Population Distribution in Georgia, by Race, 1980

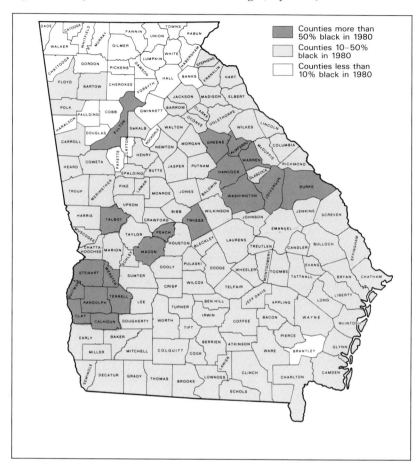

according to nationality was 83 percent English, 11 percent Scottish, 2 percent Irish, and 3 percent German. The bureau held that were it feasible to make an analysis of the population of the southern states in 1900 similar to that made from the 1790 schedules, "it is probable that little change would be noted in proportions shown in 1790." Even the most casual observer in 1909 would have noticed that while the populations of most of the states had undergone great changes in ethnicity since the Civil War, those of the southern states had not.

In the four decades following the Civil War, two great changes that swept the nation left Georgia largely untouched. First was the great switch from agriculture to industry. Second was the shift from north-western European emigration to southern and eastern European emigra-

Table 5: Total Population and Percentage Black of MSA Central Cities in Georgia, 1930 and 1980

	1930 Total Population	Black (%)	1980 Total Population	Black (%)
Atlanta	270,366	33.3	425,022	66.6
Savannah	85,024	45.7	141,390	49.0
Augusta	60,342	40.1	47,532	53.5
Macon	53,829	43.0	116,896	44.5
Columbus	43,131	32.8	169,441	34.2
Athens	18,192	35.1	42,549	27.4
Albany	14,507	51.0	74,059	47.7

Source: U.S. Bureau of the Census, *Fifteenth Census of the United States: 1930, Population; 1980 Census of Population, General Population Characteristics, Georgia.*

tion. In the immediate postwar years, Germans and Scandinavians took advantage of the Homestead Act and went west to farm the prairies. By the 1880s, the newly arriving Italians and Poles found the frontier closed and though most of them had been farmers, they settled in northeastern and midwestern cities to supply the labor for American industry.

From the late 1860s through the 1880s, Georgia made a halfhearted effort to recruit immigrants. The state government published handbooks for immigrant settlers and campaigned to attract Europeans (and northerners) to come south. The railroads pushing into the coastal plain in the 1880s offered their own inducements: land for less than $1 per acre and free sidings to farmers who would grow fruit.

These public relations attempts attracted to Georgia only a tiny fraction of the thousands of Europeans that the advocates of emigration expected. The presence in the South of a black underclass which reportedly worked for the lowest wages and under the poorest conditions likely dissuaded immigrants from heading south. Also, free land in the West and industrial jobs in the North were probably more attractive than Georgia's offerings. Of the few who did come, many left complaining of heat, insects, poor land, bad roads, and unfriendly natives. In the end, probably no more than 1 percent of the immigrants who landed in New York settled in the South. The census of 1910 shows the sharp contrast between the percentage of foreign-born population in Georgia and the most popular immigrant destinations:

Massachusetts	31.5	Minnesota	26.1
New York	30.2	Georgia	0.6
North Dakota	27.1		

With the federal government's enactment of immigration restrictions in 1921, the percentage of foreign-born in the U.S. population gradually decreased. By 1950, the percentage for the whole nation was 6.7 percent; for Georgia it was 0.5 percent.

In 1980, Georgia's 91,480 foreign-born residents represented 1.7 percent of the population, about three times the average percentage for the previous 100 years. Although still well below the national average of 6.2 percent, the 1980 figure marks an increasing variety of people in the state and supports the claim that Georgia is entering the mainstream.

Yet regarding ancestry (or ethnicity), Georgia's population retains a distinctiveness vis-à-vis the whole nation. In 1980, for the first time the census collected ancestry data on persons regardless of the number of generations removed from their country of origin.[4] Table 6 shows

---

4. The data were derived from a general ancestry question based on self-identification. Ancestry refers to person's nationality group or country in which the person or parents or ancestors were born before their arrival in the United States. Reponses reflected the ethnic group(s) with which persons identified but not degree of attachment. As self-identifications they reflect not only actual ancestry but also perceptions of who one is and who one would like to be.

Table 6: Ancestry of Georgia Residents, 1980

	United States		Georgia	
	Number	Percentage of Total	Number	Percentage of Total
Total population	226,545,805	100.0	5,463,105	100.0
Persons/single group ancestry	118,564,678	52.3	3,009,484	55.1
English	23,748,772	10.5	1,132,184	20.7
Afro-American	20,524,020	9.1	1,144,020	20.9
German	17,943,485	7.9	152,464	2.8
Irish	10,337,353	4.6	282,108	5.2
Mexican	6,992,476	3.1	6,832	0.1
Italian	6,883,320	3.0	21,143	0.4
Polish	3,805,740	1.7	13,496	0.2
French	3,062,077	1.4	31,769	0.6
Persons/mult. group ancestry	69,737,760	30.8	985,333	18.0
Ancestry not specified	38,243,367	16.9	1,468,288	26.9
American or United States	13,298,761	5.9	633,522	11.6

Source: U.S. Bureau of the Census. *1980 Census of Population, Ancestry of the Population by State* (Supplementary Report, April 1983).

Note: Also among the 10 largest single ancestry groups in Georgia in 1980 were the following: Scottish, 26,975; Dutch, 15,844; and Russian, 9,214. Another 9,209 Georgia residents reported "Spanish-Hispanic," a general type of response which may encompass several ancestry groups.

ancestry groups that were identified by at least 1 percent of the U.S. population as their ancestry groups, and the corresponding percentage by Georgia residents.

The largest self-identified single ancestry group among Georgia residents is Afro-American. A slightly smaller number of Georgians identified their ancestry as English, but they did so at almost twice the percentage as do Americans as a whole. While similar percentages of Georgians and all Americans identify with a single ancestry group, far more outside than inside the state indicate multiple ancestry, e.g., "German-Italian" or "English-Irish." Likewise, Georgians are more likely not to specify an ancestry group or to identify their ancestry as "U.S." or "American" than are Americans as a whole.

Religion

Just as Georgia's population per se was little changed by the arrival of "new Americans" in the late nineteenth and early twentieth centuries, so too was the religious identification of the population little changed from that established in the antebellum years. In the colonial period, Georgia had Anglicans, Presbyterians, Lutherans, and Jews among its people, but between the Revolutionary and Civil wars two religious traditions, the Baptist and the Methodist, using the camp meeting and revival to greatest effect in the frontier society, grew to preeminence. That preeminence remains unchallenged: in 1980, about three-fourths of all church adherents in Georgia were Baptists or Methodists.

Statistics regarding religious affiliation, church membership, or religious practice are elusive. The Bureau of the Census discontinued questions about religion in 1936; some religious bodies do not publish membership information; and definitions as to what constitutes membership vary among the bodies. However, in the United States three related studies have been conducted regarding church membership; data were obtained from more than 100 identifiable church bodies. (Independent churches having no connection with a denomination were not included in these studies.) These studies, sponsored by the National Council of Churches of Christ in the U.S.A. and reported in 1952, 1970, and 1980, enumerated "adherents" rather than members or communicants in the attempt to obtain information with most comparability.

Fifty-nine denominations with churches and members in Georgia participated in the 1980 study.[5] The study estimated almost 2.6 million Georgians (or 47 percent of the total state population) to be adherents of some denomination.

---

5. Several large predominantly black denominations did not participate, thus the data are not complete.

Figure 13 shows the 10 largest denominations or denominational families in the United States and their percentages of total United States and Georgia adherents in 1980. From a quick perusal of the graph, it is evident that religion in Georgia remains largely a Protestant affair. Clearly, the size of the Baptist community exceeds all other denominations in Georgia. In fact, one denomination, the Southern Baptist Convention, accounts for 53.5 percent of all adherents in the state. On the other hand, the Catholic Church, which leads in the United States with over 42 percent of all adherents, accounts for only 5.5 percent of all adherents in Georgia. However, as the following passage suggests, even that small percentage indicates a growing heterogeneity in Georgia's religious makeup.

> . . . at the beginning of the twentieth century there were 17,500 Catholics among three million people in Georgia. Approximately 15,000 of this number lived in five counties, which meant that the majority of non-Catholics in the state knew little or nothing of Catholic beliefs and practices. Such ignorance was responsible in part for the campaigns of vilification directed against the Catholic Church. . . . (Robert H. Ayers, "The Role of Organized Religion," in *Georgia Today,* John C. Belcher and K. Imogene Dean, eds., Athens: University of Georgia Press, 1960, pp. 157-58.)

Not shown in Figure 13, but composing .07 percent of the U.S. and .04 percent of Georgia totals in 1980 are adherents of Conservative and Reform Judaism. (No data for Orthodox synagogues were available.)

Households

> "Livin' by yourself ain't all roses—and it ain't all thorns." (Aunt Arie Carpenter, in *Aunt Arie, A Foxfire Portrait,* Linda Garland Page and Eliot Wigginton, eds., New York: E.P. Dutton, Inc., 1983.)

In 1980, 97.4 percent of all Georgians lived in some type of household.[6] And of all the households in the state, about 76 percent were family households and 24 percent nonfamily households.[7] Table 7 shows the breakdown of household types for Georgia and the nation. In Georgia, family households are somewhat more popular and nonfamily households somewhat less popular than in the nation as a whole.

---

6. In 1980, there were 142,344 persons, or about 2.6 percent of the population, living in homes for the aged, hospitals, college dormitories, prisons, and other group quarters.

7. A family household is maintained by a man or woman living with at least one relative; a nonfamily household is maintained by a man or woman living alone or with one or more others to whom he or she is not related.

Figure 13: Percentage of Total Adherents, United States and Georgia, 1980

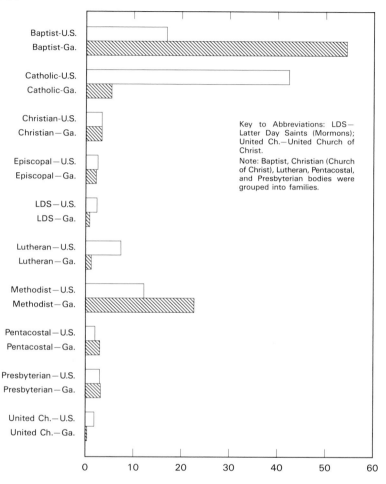

Key to Abbreviations: LDS—Latter Day Saints (Mormons); United Ch.—United Church of Christ.

Note: Baptist, Christian (Church of Christ), Lutheran, Pentecostal, and Presbyterian bodies were grouped into families.

Source: Bernard Quinn et al. *Churches and Church Membership in the United States, 1980.* Atlanta: Glenmary Research Center, 1982.

In 1980, about 11 percent of all *individuals* in the United States and 10 percent of all individuals in Georgia living in households were in the nonfamily type. In both Georgia and the United States, nonfamily households are more often headed by women than by men. (In Georgia, women head family households at a greater rate than do women in the nation as a whole.)

From 1970 to 1980, nonfamily households increased from less than 18 percent of the total households to almost 27 percent in the United

States and from 16 percent to almost 24 percent in Georgia. The increased popularity of nonfamily households coupled with a decline in the average size of family households has resulted in a striking decrease in the size of households in Georgia and the United States. From 1970 to 1980, the average number of persons per household dropped from 3.14 to 2.76 nationwide and from 3.25 to 2.84 in Georgia. Table 8 shows the distribution of households by size, Georgia and the United States, for 1970 and 1980. Only households of three or four persons remained about the same. Those having fewer than three persons increased from 46 percent to 54 percent of all U.S. households and from 43 percent to a little over 50 percent of all Georgia households. During the same decade, households of more than four persons dropped from about 21 percent to around 13 percent of the total nationwide and from 21 percent to 14 percent of the households in Georgia.

Table 7: Household Types in Georgia, 1980

Type Household	United States		Georgia	
	Number	Percentage of Total	Number	Percentage of Total
Total households	80,389,673	100.0	1,871,652	100.0
Family households	58,882,153	73.2	1,426,645	76.2
Male head	48,675,827	60.5	1,132,573	60.5
Female head	10,206,326	12.7	294,072	15.7
Nonfamily households	21,507,520	26.8	445,007	23.8
Male head	9,187,093	11.4	180,683	9.7
Female head	12,320,427	15.3	264,324	14.1

Source: U.S. Bureau of the Census. *1980 Census of Population, General Population Characteristics, United States Summary, Georgia.*

Table 8: Persons per Household, Georgia and the United States, 1970 and 1980

	1970		1980	
	Georgia	United States	Georgia	United States
One person	14.3	17.1	20.5	22.7
Two persons	28.5	28.9	29.7	31.4
Three persons	19.0	17.3	19.1	17.5
Four persons	16.8	15.8	16.7	15.7
Five persons	10.1	10.3	8.2	7.5
Six or more persons	11.3	10.6	5.8	5.3

Source: U.S. Bureau of the Census. *1980 Census of Population, General Social and Economic Characteristics, United States Summary, Georgia.*

Although more than three-fourths of the Georgia households in 1980 consisted of families, the number of nonfamily households had increased by 98 percent in 10 years. The deferral of marriage among young adults, the high incidence of divorce and separation, and the ability of elderly individuals to maintain their own homes alone are among the reasons for the increase in nonfamily households.

Of all the *households* in Georgia in 1980, 383,806, or 20.5 percent, were one-person households. In other words, 7 percent of all *individuals* in households lived alone. In 1940, only 1.8 percent of Georgians were alone in households. There is wide variety among one-person households; persons 65 and over make up 37 percent of them (elderly widows compose the largest group), but 38 percent are male and many young singles—male and female—establish their own households.

The rapid growth of one-person households and the decreasing average size of households are attributable to numerous factors, but a primary factor is certainly the widening of choice among many possible living arrangements that have evolved in the past few decades. And the choice to live in a one-person household—which has been made by one in every five householders in Georgia—must have, as one of its consequences, the situation described in the 1983 *Foxfire* portrait: ". . .*every* community, no matter how small, has its own Aunt Arie Carpenters, sitting alone, largely unrecognized, waiting for company."

Families

Though the number of families is enumerated and reported as 1,426,645 for Georgia in 1980, and though the family is accepted as the basic unit of society, the concept of "family" has become increasingly difficult to characterize. A new definition of family is in the process of creation in American society. In the country as a whole, one-fifth of all children live with a single parent. Between 1970 and 1980, in the United States, the number of unmarried couples living together as "families" increased from around 520,000 to 1,763,960, thereby introducing a new categorical name, POSSLQ (Persons of the Opposite Sex Sharing Living Quarters). The Bureau of Census reports for Georgia 29,331 unmarried couples living together in 1980.

The range of structures which may be considered as families include married couples with one or more children; male or female single parent (divorced, widowed, or never married) with one or more children; husband and wife with no children; the POSSLQ; a previously married couple and their children from former marriage(s) and, perhaps, offspring of the couple; and groups of related individuals including aunts, uncles, cousins, and grandparents. In sum, family forms have multiplied.

Between 1970 and 1980, the average number of persons in family households dropped from 3.61 to 3.31 nationwide and from 3.64 to 3.33 in Georgia. Fewer children per marriage, a higher average age at death, and more one-parent families are among the reasons for this drop in average family size.

Whatever importance a particular change in family is assigned by society depends upon the values that society holds in consensus and the likely implications of that change on other aspects of the socio-cultural system. Perhaps of most concern to observers of family changes are the effects of those changes on children and child rearing. In 1980, about 12.5 million American children lived with only one parent; this represents an increase of more than 50 percent since 1970. In Georgia in 1980, 312,451 children lived with only one parent, an increase of 41 percent over 1970. Table 9 shows the incidence of women with no husband present heading families with one or more children under 18 years of age. Compared to the country as a whole, Georgia has slightly higher percentages of families with children under 18 and families with children under 18 headed by women. Within Georgia, the most significant differences are between white and black families. Almost one-fourth of all black families with children under 18 are headed by women with no husband present whereas about 6 percent of white families are. Also, this type of one-parent family is more likely to be found inside an MSA than outside an MSA.

The stability or quality of families, or marriage, may only be inferred from quantitative measures. Figure 14 allows comparison of crude marriage rates (no./1,000 population/yr.) and crude divorce and annulment

Table 9: Families with Children under 18, Headed by Women; Georgia and the United States, 1980

	Number of Families	With Own Children under 18		Headed by Female Householders/No Husband Present	
		Number	Percentage of Col. 1	Number	Percentage of Col. 1
United States	58,882,153	30,136,510	51.2	5,062,180	8.6
Georgia	1,426,645	766,306	53.7	144,833	10.2
White	1,085,652	558,454	51.4	63,099	5.8
Black	330,895	201,128	60.8	80,831	24.4
Inside MSAs	850,263	466,019	54.8	94,520	11.1
Outside MSAs	576,382	300,287	52.1	50,313	8.7

Source: U.S. Bureau of the Census. *1980 Census of Population, General Population Characteristics, United States Summary, Georgia.*

Figure 14: Marriage and Divorce Rates, Georgia and the United States, 1955-1980

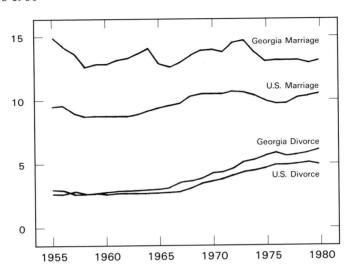

Source: National Center for Health Statistics, *Vital Statistics of the United States, Marriage and Divorce,* 1980, 1976, 1971, 1966, 1956.

rates (no./1,000/population/yr.) for Georgia and the United States. This data should be viewed cautiously, with the knowledge that a population base changes over time and that a crude rate does not reflect such changes. Nevertheless, the Georgia rates for the years 1955-80 indicate that the popularity of marriage has remained rather stable while the rate of divorce and annulment has more than tripled during the 25-year period.

Housing

The extraordinary increase in households in Georgia during the 1970s resulted in a similar increase in housing. From 1970 to 1980, the number of housing units in Georgia grew by 38 percent. Within that gross figure were wide differentials in location of new housing, occupancy by tenure and race, and structural type.

Reflecting the population growth patterns of the state, housing units increased in MSAs by 42 percent, in nonmetro areas by 32 percent. In general, the highest rates of increase in housing were in suburban metro counties. Six counties—Columbia, Douglas, Fayette, Gwinnett, Liberty, and Rockdale—increased in housing units by 100 percent or more during the 1970s. Only Liberty County, whose increase was the result of military activity, was not in an MSA. High rates of increase in housing also occurred in mountain counties where second-home development boomed. Figure 15 shows the distribution of new housing activity around the state.

Owner-occupied housing increased by a greater rate between 1970 and 1980 than did renter-occupied housing, and black-occupied housing increased at a greater rate than did white-occupied housing. Figure 16 shows the increase in housing by tenure and race.

Whether housing is owner- or renter-occupied is related to location in the state as well as to racial identification of the occupants. In 1980, of all households in Georgia, about 75 percent were identified as white,

Figure 15: Percentage Increase of Housing Units in Georgia, by County, 1970-1980

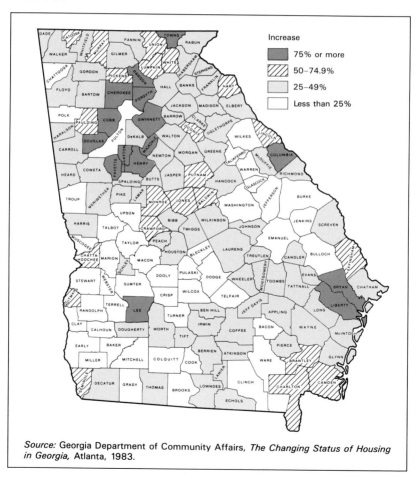

Source: Georgia Department of Community Affairs, *The Changing Status of Housing in Georgia,* Atlanta, 1983.

Figure 16: Increase in Housing in Georgia, by Tenure and Race, 1970-1980

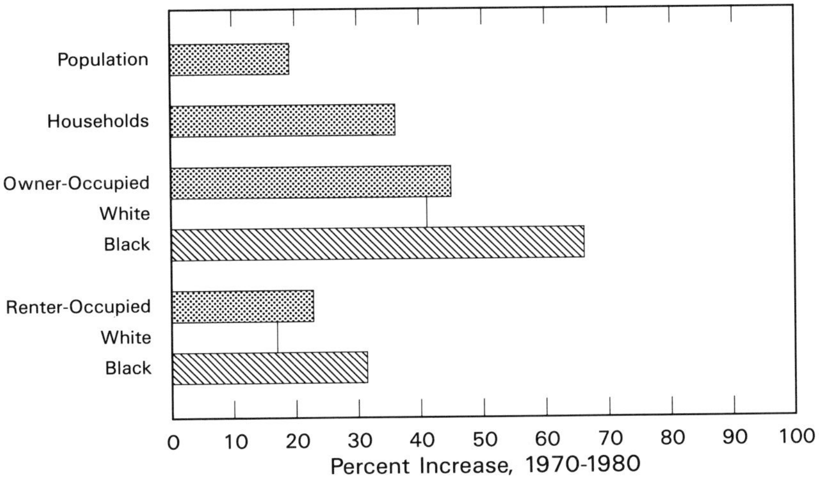

Source: Georgia Department of Community Affairs, *The Changing Status of Housing In Georgia,* Atlanta, 1983.

almost 25 percent black, and under 1 percent other racial groups. Table 10 shows occupancy by tenure and race for MSAs and non-MSAs. Clearly, the preponderance of owner-occupied to renter-occupied housing is greater outside than inside the MSAs. Although the rate of increase in black owner-occupied housing was much greater than the white rate during the 1970s, blacks are still less likely to own their own homes than are whites.

In both 1970 and 1980, detached single-family houses accounted for three-fourths of all housing units in Georgia and accounted for the greatest number of new units built during the decade—418,190 of a total

Table 10: Occupancy by Tenure and Race, MSAs and Non-MSAs, Georgia, 1980

Location/Race	Owner-Occupied (%)	Renter-Occupied (%)
MSA	61.6	38.4
White	67.8	32.2
Black	43.2	56.8
Non-MSA	70.2	29.8
White	75.1	24.9
Black	53.7	46.3

Source: U.S. Bureau of the Census, *1980 Census of Housing, General Housing Characteristics Georgia.*

546,376 new units. However, more spectacular rates of increase were recorded by mobile homes and condominiums. Between 1970 and 1980, while the number of single-family houses grew by 38 percent, mobile homes increased in number by 127 percent and condominiums by more than 1,000 percent. (Of course, condos accounted for a mere one-tenth of 1 percent of all Georgia housing in 1970.) Multifamily rental units grew by less than 8 percent in the 1970s. Table 11 shows the percentage of all housing units in the state for each housing type. While the single-family dwelling is the clear choice of Georgians inside and outside MSAs, alternate housing forms geared to urban or to rural environments are important considerations to many people.

Over one-fifth of all MSA housing units are multifamily. While rental units far outnumber owner-occupied units in this category, the 1970s saw many rental units converted to condominiums. Condos are overwhelmingly an urban phenomenon. In 1980, 82 percent of all condos in Georgia were found in seven MSA counties: Clayton, Cobb, DeKalb, Fulton, and Gwinnett in the Atlanta MSA; plus Chatham and Richmond.

Mobile homes, on the other hand, are more a rural phenomenon and serve for many households as a lower-cost alternative to the traditional single-family detached house. In 1980, mobile homes accounted for more than 20 percent of the housing units in 15 counties: Bryan, Camden, Charlton, Crawford, Echols, Effingham, Forsyth, Jones, Lee, Liberty, Long, McIntosh, Madison, Murray, and Towns.

The Future

What will be the size and shape of Georgia's population in the years to come? Because it is impossible to know the precise future course of the variables that determine population size—fertility, mortality, and migration—predicting the size and shape of any population is "educated guessing." However, population projections are vitally needed by

Table 11: Housing Units in Georgia, by Type and Location, 1980

Type Housing Unit	State (%)	MSA (%)	Non-MSA (%)
Single family	75.8	73.7	79.0
Multifamily	16.6	21.7	8.8
Rental	15.5	20.1	8.8
Condominium	1.1	1.6	0.2
Mobile homes	7.6	4.6	12.2

Source: U.S. Bureau of the Census, 1980 Census of Housing, General Housing Characteristics, Georgia.

government—in planning roads, schools, health care, water and sewage systems, and other services—and by businesses in planning for product development, marketing, capital investments, and other endeavors. Population projections are based on reasonable assumptions about present trends in fertility, mortality, and migration.

Georgia's population is projected to reach 6,462,313 in 1990 and 7,422,594 in 2000. These projections produce growth rates of 18.3 percent for the 1980s and 14.9 percent for the 1990s, rates below the 19.1 percent increase of the 1970s. Yet, if the projection for the year 2000 is reached, Georgia will have more than doubled its population in the half century 1950-2000.

A trend begun in the decade 1970-80 will likely continue. That is, about 56 percent of the predicted increase—or 1.1 million of the almost 2 million new Georgians—will result from net in-migration, only 44 percent from natural increase. Thus, the population will have a higher percentage of non-natives. The nonwhite percentage is projected to increase from 27.8 percent in 1980 to 30.9 percent in 2000.

Most significantly, Georgia's population will—like the national population—be much older. Figure 17 shows Georgia's actual population distribution by age for 1980 and projections for 1990 and 2000. Note that the percentage of persons to age 44 is projected to increase

Maxeys, Georgia (1980, Population 619). John and Belle Griffith, Raleigh George, and Lee Vinson joke that "mostly old people are left in Maxeys." Rural populations in particular are growing older.

Figure 17: Population Distribution in Georgia, by Age, 1980, Projected 1990, 2000

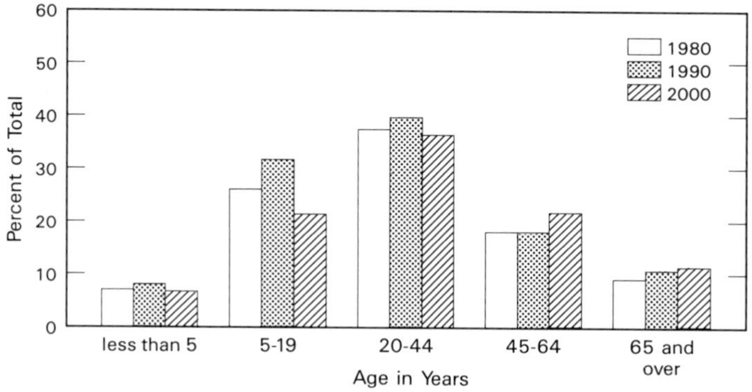

Source: U.S. Bureau of the Census, Atlanta Office.

through the 1980s, then decline in the 1990s, while persons 45 and over increase through the period.

Projections regarding the *distribution* of Georgia's future population might be characterized as "more of the same." Since the mid-nineteenth century, Georgia's population has concentrated in the Piedmont region and is projected to become even more concentrated there. Ten counties are projected to increase their population more than 50,000 by the year 2000. All 10 are in the Piedmont and all but one, Richmond, are in the Atlanta MSA (see Table 12).

In 2000, two counties will share top honors: Gwinnett for total growth, 274,777, and Fayette for percentage increase, 309 percent.

Table 12: Projected Leading Growth Counties in Georgia: 50,000+ increase, for the Year 2000

County	Increase 1980-2000 (No.)	(%)	Population 1980	Population 2000
Gwinnett	274,777	165	166,903	441,680
Cobb	120,586	41	297,718	418,304
Fulton	103,418	18	589,904	693,322
Fayette	89,674	309	29,043	118,717
DeKalb	88,658	18	483,024	571,682
Clayton	69,447	46	150,357	219,804
Douglas	61,687	113	54,573	116,260
Richmond	55,531	31	181,629	237,160
Rockdale	50,833	138	36,747	87,580
Cherokee	50,713	98	51,699	102,412

Source: Office of Planning and Budget, *State Data Center Newsletter* (September 1983), Atlanta, Ga.

Figure 18: Georgia Population, by Region, 1980, Projected 1990, 2000

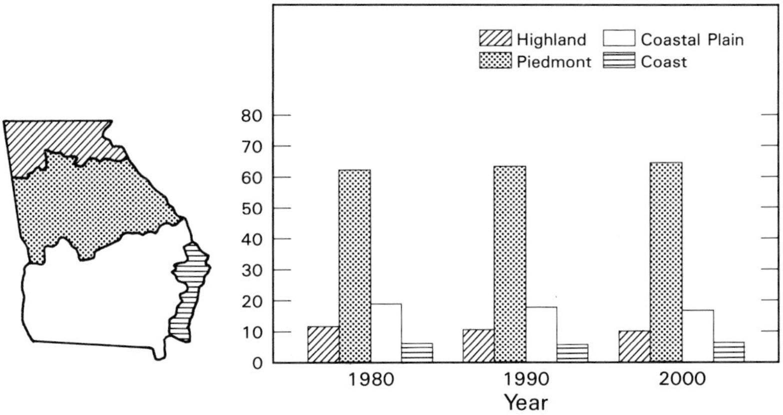

Source: State Data Center, Office of Planning and Budget, Atlanta, Ga. (unpublished data).

The Atlanta MSA, which comprised 37.2 percent of Georgia's people in 1980, is projected to have 42.2 percent of the state population in 2000.

A notable feature of Georgia's population distribution is projected to continue into the next century: the distribution of people along Georgia's 125-mile coastline is unlike that of the United States as a whole. Whereas 55 percent of the national population live within 50 miles of the coast, in Georgia less than 10 percent do. Figure 18 shows Georgia population by region. Note that to avoid dividing any county populations, the regions are defined here by county lines, not natural features. The coastal counties have been treated as distinct from the rest of the coastal plain.

And what of Greene and Macon counties, whose farmers began leaving in the 1920s? Through the 1960s, both counties continued to lose population, with Greene dropping from 18,972 in 1920 to 10,212 in 1970 and Macon dropping from 17,667 to 12,933. Since then, both have turned around: Greene grew to 11,391 in 1980, Macon to 14,003. Projections for 2000 put Greene at 14,703 and Macon at 17,313, increases of 14 percent and 11 percent respectively per decade. The "push" of depression has been replaced by the "pull" of opportunity in both counties.

CHAPTER FIVE

Politics and Government

By Lawrence R. Hepburn

> The way to keep a government good, and to keep its citizens pros-
> perous, is to have a poor government.
> —Gov. Eugene Talmadge, 1935

Georgians themselves (at least those with more than a casual familiar-
ity with the state's history), would readily admit that while the state
has been long on politics, it has been short on government. Historically, in Georgia and in the South generally, government provided
fewer services and levied lower taxes than governments of most northern and western states. Today government in Georgia is less likely to
intervene in daily life and to promote social change than government
in Massachusetts or Minnesota. Why? Because that's what a majority
of Georgians, at least a majority of those who participate in politics,
prefer.

　　This majority reflects the dominant attitudes and values in the state
regarding such things as the legitimacy of political authority, the proper
role of government, the importance of citizen participation, and the need
for political parties. These attitudes and values are products of Georgia's
unique patterns of population growth, composition, and distribution;
land-use and economic activities; social organization; and even religious
affiliations. The intrusion of such major events as the Civil War and
Reconstruction, the Great Depression, and World War II are also sources
of contemporary attitudes and values.

Finding the Common Thread

Of course, the political attitudes and values of Georgians vary with place
of birth and residence, education, economic status, age, sex, and race.
How politics is carried on and the quality of local government varies

from place to place. Differences in such things as the level of police protection, quality of schools, and the handling of elections reflect what people value and what they can afford.

However, across the whole state some common ideas about politics and government are discernible in the expectations Georgians voice about government officials; in politicians' campaign style and style of doing public business; in citizens' explanations for voting or not voting; and in citizen support or nonsupport for government initiatives in social and economic matters. Two features stand out: little government and consensus politics.

Little Government

Traditionally, Georgians expect to get little from government and to pay as little as possible for what they get. This preference for little government traces to the view of limited government propounded by the bourbon Democrats who gained control of the state government in the 1870s. In reaction to the social engineering, economic development schemes, and other excesses of the state reconstruction government, the bourbons denied any role to government other than maintaining the existing social order. In 1877, they wrote a state constitution to guarantee that Georgia's government would be minimal. Whatever social and economic progress evolved would be by the natural order of things, not by government effort.

Public schooling, sanitation, health, criminal justice, resource development—all were retarded in Georgia by the bourbons' constitution. Said Georgia's Judge Orville Park in 1938, the constitution is

> shot through and through with distrust, fear, and suspicion. It restricts government actions almost to the point of strangulation. . . . In an effort to prevent an abuse of power, it conferred none, and it hedged about legislative and executive so as to deny them power essential to the proper discharge of their functions.

The restrictions of 1877 meant that only through the difficult process of amendment (and therefore belatedly if at all) could Georgians obtain the kinds of public services readily adopted in other states.

Under the bourbon formula, politics, too, was limited—limited to men who stood at the top of the social order and who saw themselves as custodians of that order. Their relationship with Georgians black and white who stood lower down in the social order was paternalistic. However, as long as they faced Republican and later Populist opposition, the bourbons sought the votes of these people.

The bourbon formula for limited government was supported by three elements in Georgia's heritage: (1) rural-agrarian culture, (2) biracial society, and (3) economic depression.

The *rural-agrarian culture* of Georgia did not support the expansion of government. Usually miles from their neighbors, farm families depended on individual enterprise, not community effort, and what public life the small farmer had was centered on the church, not the town hall. Geographic isolation and economic self-sufficiency bred independence in some small farmers: they avoided elections, taxes, and public affairs in general. For others, the black and white tenants of big landowners, plantation paternalism substituted for government. Farm-to-market roads were about the only public service of use to the majority of Georgians.

Industrial and urban development came late to Georgia: until the mid-1950s, the state's population was still 50 percent rural. And, as the bulk of Georgia's population increase until the 1970s was due to natural increase, not immigration, traditional rural-agrarian values remained embedded in a large portion of the population even after urbanization.

Georgia's *biracial society* underpinned the little government tradition. The bourbon Democrats regularly faced "the Negro question," that is, what would be the place of blacks in the scheme of things? Would blacks receive the same public services as whites? Would whites be taxed to support those services going to blacks? For 20 years, the bourbons, with their Confederate identification, managed to accommodate black interests such as voting and schools without alienating the mass of whites.

By the 1890s, however, the threat of black social equality implied in the success of the new People's Party (Populists) in bringing together black and white farmers, and the coming to Democratic leadership of a new generation of whites, brought the end of bourbon-era accommodation. The Democrats now adopted a doctrine of "white supremacy" that defined the blacks' place in society. New laws strictly regulated the social and economic relations of blacks and whites and eliminated blacks from politics. In white supremacy the Democratic Party found political supremacy as Republican and Populist opposition withered and died.

Until the 1960s, white supremacy was a fixed consideration against which Georgia government officials made policy. Progressive measures such as compulsory school attendance; regulation of child labor; public health, welfare, and housing; and other tax-supported social services were rejected because they threatened to undermine a social structure that kept blacks in their place and dependent upon the private paternalism of whites.

Finally, the *economic-depression* that Georgians suffered for 75 years following the Civil War also militated against the growth of government. By any measure of income or wealth, Georgia was one of the poorest states in the nation. Until the 1930s, when the Great Depression dragged the rest of the nation down, Georgians' per capita income was less than half the U.S. average. Not surprisingly, Georgia's per capita expenditures from the 1880s to the 1930s for most government services were also less than half the U.S. average.

The New Deal, World War II, the decline of agriculture, the civil rights movement, urban growth, economic boom, and Sunbelt migration have all contributed to a dilution of the little government ideal. But the attitudes and values of the past continue to influence Georgia politics and government. They can be observed in the operation of "consensus politics"—a second feature that distinguishes Georgia from most other states.

Consensus Politics

A preference for consensual politics over conflict politics emerged in the 1960s as a response to the civil rights movement. Georgians learned to bargain, compromise, and accommodate as many political interests as possible so that everyone would get something.

Into the early 1960s, the response of Georgia's political leadership to the push for civil rights had been one of intransigence. Campaigns featured vows to maintain white supremacy, and legislators threw up new legal barriers to social equality for blacks. During the sixties, however, attitudes of the state's business leadership became increasingly predicated on the need to keep Georgia on its economic roll. In white backlash and politicians' strident calls for defiance lay the spoilage organism that threatened the economic harvest to come.

Business leadership in Atlanta took the initiative in avoiding conflict through accommodation. The chiefs of Georgia's biggest commercial and financial institutions (the so-called "downtown establishment"), the moderate politicians, the influential members of the black community, plus the reasoned arguments of Ralph McGill, editor of the *Atlanta Constitution,* all contributed to developing a process that could later be called "consensus politics." The process worked; conflict was defused and business grew even faster. Atlanta became "the city too busy to hate."

Throughout the 1960s, as sit-ins, boycotts, marches, and other civil rights activities became more widespread and as the Civil Rights Act of 1964 went into effect, Atlanta's consensual model of politics gradually spread to other, but certainly not all, communities. Not only civil rights organizations and ad hoc community associations, but also other groups with some self-interest in the resolution of race issues were drawn in: merchants, farmers, unionized laborers, manufacturers, educators, preachers, bankers, managers, and public officials and employees. There were accommodations in voting and officeholding, jobs and schooling, housing and recreation, police and social services, and other areas of public and private interest. These arrangements became policies that did not please everyone, but they were policies with which most groups could live. By the mid-1970s, civil rights issues were no longer center stage. But, the consensus techniques developed to resolve those issues prevailed as a dominant feature of Georgia politics.

In other states, politics between the elections may feature well-defined conflicts between a majority and a minority, a government and an opposition, or Democrats and Republicans, but Georgia politics features an ill-defined negotiation among multiple interest groups. There is no majority, no minority, no opposition; only a loose alliance of disparate interest groups—blacks, courthouse politicians, corporate executives, organized labor, farmers, urban liberals, bankers, educators, other public employees—who share no ideology or party principles, but only a feeling that government should do something for each of them.

The bargaining and compromising of consensus politics not only aggregates the interests of all participant groups, but also diffuses conflict. The bargains struck are in effect handed over to officeholders for policymaking. The general result is middle-of-the-road policy: relatively conservative in fiscal matters, mildly progressive in social matters.

No norms of little government or consensus politics are written down for Georgia politicians and public servants to follow. Yet one finds, in greater or lesser degree, throughout the state, a reluctance to initiate, to spend, to substitute public for private interest, and (between elections) to do battle. These habits give Georgia politics and government their special flavor and distinguish them from their counterparts in other states.

Governments in Georgia

In 1982, Georgia had 1,269 governments, as follows:

    1 state government
  158 county governments
  533 municipal governments[1]
  187 school district governments
  390 special district governments[2]

All the so-called general purpose governments—state, county, and city governments—have legislative, executive, and judicial functions. They

---

1. This includes one consolidated county-municipal government.

2. Examples of special districts are Metropolitan Atlanta Rapid Transit Authority (MARTA), Georgia Ports Authority, Stone Mountain Park Authority, and Georgia Building Authority.

make laws, raise and spend money, deliver services to the public, and handle disputes between citizens, and between the citizen and the government. School district and special district governments are created by the legislature for specific purposes (usually a single purpose) and authorized by it to raise and spend money. The general purpose governments will be the focus of this section.

Local Government

Because Georgia was until recently a predominantly rural state, the county—the local government form most associated with rural America—was more important in Georgia politics and government than the municipality. Georgia had a penchant for creating counties; there are 159, more than in any other state except Texas. One explanation for this number is that the legislature wanted to enable farmers to travel (by horse or mule) to their county seat, do their business, and get home by sundown. But, from the Civil War to 1924 when the last county was created, new counties were born of politics. Towns aspired to be county seats because such status would offer at least a dozen jobs plus extra business for merchants, especially on court days. Local squabbles over roads, tax assessments, or representation in the legislature (every county had at least one representative in the old days) also led to cutting a county in two. Moreover, and most importantly, with the creation of a new county, the local power structure gained clout at the state capital. The source of this clout was the county unit vote.

Until 1962, each Georgia county had two, four, or six votes in state-wide Democratic primaries. These county votes were analogous to the states' electoral votes in United States presidential elections. Under this unique system, nomination in the Democratic primary (which meant election in a one-party state) was based on a candidate's receiving a majority of county unit votes, not popular votes. To win the unit vote of a county a candidate had to gain only a plurality of the votes cast.

The unit vote gave tiny rural counties inordinate power in state politics. In 1960, Echols, Quitman, and Glascock counties, with a combined population of 6,980, cast a total of six unit votes. Fulton County (Atlanta) also had six unit votes, but its population was 556,326. A popular vote in the smallest county carried one hundred times the weight of a vote in the largest county.

Candidates for the governorship and other state offices played to the interests of the rural people and curried the favor of the so-called "courthouse gangs"—the county machines—who could deliver the county's unit vote. So unimportant were the urban areas in this scheme of things that Eugene Talmadge, elected governor four times, publicly wrote off "any county that had streetcars." Sometimes, as was the case in

Talmadge's 1946 primary win, candidates would win a majority of the unit votes while trailing in popular votes.

The county unit system, ruled unconstitutional by the federal courts in 1962, in *Sanders v. Gray*, had a lasting effect on the state: after the court decision, rural dominance quickly began to fade, but the influence of the system is apparent even today. Counties, not cities, have the strong ties to the legislature; voter turnouts are low (the courthouse gangs needed only a manageable turnout); and county officials guard prerogatives (real or imagined) against encroachment by state-level bureaucrats. In most cases, Georgia's two main state police agencies, the Georgia State Patrol and the Georgia Bureau of Investigation, may provide assistance to county sheriffs or county police only upon request by local authorities, not on their own initiative. Proposals for statewide grand juries to investigate organized crime have come to nothing.

Consolidation is a touchy subject. Proposals to decrease the number of counties are met with hostility in most places. Efforts to merge city and county governments are almost surely doomed to failure. From 1969 to 1984, there were 13 city-county consolidation referenda in Georgia. Only one, merging the city of Columbus and the county of Muscogee, passed.

County Government

Under provisions of the state constitution and statutes passed by the legislature, the governing authority of the county is the board of commissioners. Beyond that, there is little uniformity. As Table 1 shows, the size of county commissions varies widely. Individual acts of the legislature establishing the commission form of government in a given

Table 1: Size of Boards of Commissioners in Georgia

Number of County Commissioners on Boards	Number of Counties with This Size Board
1	24
3	33
4	3
5	81
6	7
7	7
8	2
9	1
11	1

Source: Georgia County Government Yearbook, 1986. Association County Commissioners of Georgia.

county set the size, usually unrelated to population or other quantifiable considerations. Such acts also change the commission size, upon local request, from time to time. Most commissioners are elected to a four-year term, but in some counties they have two-, three-, or six-year terms. Most commissioners are part-time county officials, holding regular jobs outside government.

Selection of the chairman of multimember boards differs from county to county. In Fulton County, for example, the board elects its own chairman; in Chatham County the electorate chooses the chairman; and in Emanuel County the chairmanship rotates at four-month intervals. Franklin County has an advisory board in addition to a sole commissioner.

In the commission form of government, legislative and executive functions are combined. As legislators, commissioners enact county ordinances and set policies regarding services, taxes, and expenditures. As executives, they carry out those policies themselves or oversee the work of employees.

The powers of commissions vary somewhat from county to county as provided by acts of the legislature. In the years following World War

Especially in urbanizing counties, the style and substance of government are far removed from that of the unit vote days.

II, as the population grew outward from Georgia's larger cities, county governments that had formerly limited themselves to the old rural services such as scraping roads, recording deeds, and collecting property taxes took on functions associated with municipalities. Urban sprawl in Georgia involved somewhat different local government adjustments than in other parts of the country because Georgia's large cities were generally surrounded by unincorporated rural areas, not small municipalities. Rather than incorporate new suburban municipalities to provide water, sewerage, garbage collection, full-time fire protection, and other urban services, suburbanites more often opted to expand the role of existing county governments—thus creating the "urban county." One effect of suburbanization was to increase the diversity among county governments in the state. While the smallest counties haven't gone much beyond the road-scraping and deed-recording of the last century, the metropolitan counties provide their citizens with swimming pools, airports, hospitals, animal control, and emergency medical assistance.

A notable feature in the large county organization is the position of county administrator or county manager. As county government services grew in scope and complexity, some commissions appointed full-time professional administrators to handle day-to-day operations, in effect splitting the legislative and executive functions of the commission.

So diverse are local needs and provisions for services that even the functions of a particular office are difficult to generalize. For example, all counties have a sheriff—a constitutional requirement—but in some counties the sheriff retains all responsibility for police protection, including traffic regulation and criminal investigation, running the county jail, and serving court papers. In others, the sheriff has surrendered all but the jail and court functions to a county police force hired by the board of commissioners.

One generalization may be made for all counties, however. They all serve three masters: the state government, the federal government, and the local population. Originally, counties served as administrative arms of state government—collecting taxes, holding elections, and such. In the last few decades, they have also become local administrative units for federal health and welfare programs. Today, they must respond to local initiatives for whatever services the county population wants. It is in this third realm that most of the controversy in county government erupts.

As rural counties become suburbanized, their politics frequently takes on a new stridency as the disparate interests of old residents and new residents clash head-on. From animal control to zoning, urban-type services are often the subject of controversy between the newcomers who want them and are willing to pay for them, and natives, who can't see why anyone would want to be taxed for such things. Gradually, more counties are assuming the style of municipalities, providing urban-type services demanded by local residents.

In the past two decades, the legislature has given the counties more "home rule" authority, but at the same time has acted to bring uniformity to county operations. Predictably, the imposition of uniform tax assessment procedures and hiring and purchasing practices have met with opposition in the local press and at public meetings (although county officials may be relieved to have the onus of change hung on state officials). Some counties have only recently instituted bid-letting, written contracts, formal budgeting, and record-keeping practices.

Municipal Government

In 1982, Georgia had 533 municipalities. About 62 percent of the state population was urbanized, yet only 45 percent of the people actually lived in areas with municipal government. These seemingly contradictory figures are easily explained: municipalities in Georgia tend to be small, and three-quarters of them are located outside metropolitan areas. In 1980, only one Georgia city, Atlanta, had more than 200,000 people; only three—Columbus, Savannah, and Macon—had more than 100,000; and only one other, Albany, had more than 50,000. Of Georgia's 533 municipalities, 282 had fewer than 1,000 residents.

Regardless of their population size, all municipalities in Georgia, whether they call themselves cities or towns, have essentially the same legal status. (There are no classes of cities, towns, townships, as in other states.) Each operates under a charter of incorporation granted by the legislature. Since 1963, to become incorporated, a community must meet certain requirements, including

  a. a minimum population of 200;
  b. a proposed boundary of at least three miles from the boundary of any existing Georgia municipality; and
  c. at least 60 percent of the proposed area developed and divided into tracts of land for either residential, industrial, commercial, institutional, or governmental purposes.

Most Georgia municipalities are part of only one county, but a municipality may extend across county lines. For example, Atlanta lies partly in Fulton County, partly in DeKalb County. Bogart straddles the boundary of Clarke and Oconee counties. And, tiny Allentown (1980 population: 321) spreads itself into four counties: Bleckley, Laurens, Twiggs, and Wilkinson.

Although Georgia's population grew notably in the past three decades, the number of new cities did not. Table 2 shows the change in the number of municipalities between 1962 and 1982.

Table 2: Number of Municipalities within and outside Georgia Metropolitan Statistical Areas (MSAs), 1962-1982

Year	Total Municipalities	Within MSAs	Outside MSAs
1962	561	68	493
1967	512	66	446
1972	530	66	464
1977	530	116	414
1982	533	135	398

Source: U.S. Bureau of the Census, *Census of Governments, Vol. 1, Governmental Organization,* 1962, 1967, 1972, 1977, 1982.

As population declined in the rural areas in the early 1960s, a number of small cities went out of business. Since then, the number of cities created, or recreated, does not reflect the population increase of urbanized areas. Metropolitan Statistical Areas (MSAs) have spread out to engulf existing municipalities, and the unincorporated areas among them receive municipal-type services either through expanded county governments or by arrangement with the existing municipalities.

The structure and powers of Georgia municipalities are set forth in each municipality's charter of incorporation. In Georgia, each municipality follows one of two basic forms of city government—mayor-council or council-manager (or some variation on these forms). None uses the commission form that is found in other parts of the country.

The mayor-council form is the more popular form in Georgia. In general, a strong mayor-council form is found in larger cities, the weak mayor-council form in smaller cities. As small cities expand services in response to growing population, they often move to the council-manager form, thus gaining a full-time administrator of day-to-day governmental operations.

Atlanta: A Special Case

Once upon a time Atlanta was merely the state's political capital and largest municipality. The political culture of Atlanta wasn't much different from that of the rest of Georgia. A large part of the city population, which had immigrated from the countryside in the 1920s after the ravages of the boll weevil and again after World War II and the demise of tenant farming, maintained a decidedly rural outlook in social and political matters. However, the city population also included cosmopolitan elements since it was the center for finance and commerce and black higher education in the South.

After World War II, Atlanta's leadership became distinctly more tolerant of black claims to political and economic rights than did local

Atlanta's Political and Civic League

Big Mass Meeting!

Tuesday, April 16, 1946, 8 P. M.

Greater Mt. Calvary Baptist Church

Rev. B. Joseph Johnson, Pastor

Two Negroes within 3 weeks have been shot by Street Car operators. Your boy, brother or husband may be next.

We want Negro Policemen!

We want better Schools!

We want equal protection by the Law!

See and hear Hon. John Wesley Dobbs, Pres. Civic League.

Reverends: D. A. Dixon, Gilead, Jones, L. M. Terrill, R. H. Porter, B. J. Johnson, W. H. Borders, Mr. Chas. Greenlea.

Have you Registered? If not---Do it now!

Music will be furnished by outstanding quartets.

Free to All Negro Citizens!!

A fair share of local government services was an immediate interest of blacks in post-World War II Atlanta politics.

power structures elsewhere in Georgia. Of course, Atlanta's black population was also swelling with migrants from rural counties. The city's moderate white politicians, led by Mayor William B. Hartsfield, established a coalition with the leaders of the black community to maintain control of city hall. Through the 1950s and 1960s, including the administrations of Mayor Ivan Allen, Jr., city politics became more liberal, city government more progressive. The direction behind this moderately liberal-progressive course originated largely with Atlanta's "downtown establishment," the commercial and financial elite of the city.

Meanwhile, in state politics, Atlanta was practically impotent, despite its bourgeoning population, because of the county unit system and a grossly malapportioned legislature. The legislature, dominated by those with rural white supremacist views, was not inclined to help a city with an increasing black population find ways to handle its problems. Then, as blacks moved into formerly all-white neighborhoods, gained access to public jobs, and in 1961 integrated the first public schools in the state, Atlanta suffered attacks by racist demagogues.

By the end of the 1960s, federal court rulings establishing the "one person, one vote" principle in legislative apportionment, and federal civil rights laws guaranteeing economic and political opportunity for blacks gave Atlanta new clout in state politics and blacks new influence in city politics. From the mid-1960s to the mid-1970s, Atlanta's black citizens moved from being junior partners in a coalition with white moderates to domination in city politics. The first break in the order of things came in 1969 when white Vice-Mayor Sam Massell, not the candidate of the downtown establishment but the favorite of black voters, won the mayorship. Subsequently, black voters with the support of a minority of white voters put black men—first Maynard Jackson then Andrew Young—into the mayor's chair.

Today, instead of little government, Atlanta has big government; instead of the status quo and small clique control, it has change and broad participation. On its own, in concert with several metropolitan county governments, and through public authorities, Atlanta engages in a myriad of services. Operation of enterprises ranging from the airport to the zoo are regularly the focus of interest group politics. Neighborhood associations, unions, business groups, state legislators, corporations, welfare organizations, churches, and other entities involve themselves in Atlanta politics. The stresses of white flight and retail business flight to the suburbs, of school resegregation and job desegregation, of expressway development and downtown redevelopment—all symptoms of a city undergoing change—have been relieved within the arena of political consensus-making. Even as the cast of city officials changed from predominantly white to predominantly black and the business leadership remained mostly white, the dynamics of consensus politics have continued. Into the mid-1980s, race continues to be an important political factor in city government—especially in the operation of police and fire services. But, as race issues in general diminish across the state and as suburbanization of an 18-county ring around the city blurs geographical distinctions, tensions between Atlanta and the rest of Georgia are subsiding.

State Government

Beyond guaranteeing that the people in every state shall have a republican form of government, the United States Constitution leaves to the states the authority to structure their governments. Accordingly, while all follow the practice of dividing government by function into three branches— executive, legislative, and judicial—the states vary widely in the way they organize and carry out those functions, especially in the executive branch.

At the Capitol: The Office of Governor

The office of the governor carries great prestige in Georgia, and its occupant can have wide influence in state affairs. The Georgia Constitution gives the governor a term of four years and, since 1976, the opportunity to serve two successive terms. In earlier times, popular distrust of executive authority was embodied in constitutional limits to one-year terms, then two-year terms, then a single four-year term. Even today, the state constitution limits the office's formal powers to the extent that Georgia appears to have on paper a moderately weak chief executive, compared to the heads of other state governments.

Most significantly, the governor lacks extensive appointment power. The heads of several major state agencies, whose counterparts in "strong governor" states are appointed by the chief executive, are elected independently of the Georgia governor. Consequently, instead of functioning as the chief executive's "cabinet" accountable to the governor, these elected heads function as a plural executive accountable to their own constituencies. These "constitutional officers," as they are collectively known (noted in Figure 1), may have no ties or loyalty to the governor. They make all appointments within their agencies and formulate their own policies (within limits to be discussed later). They enjoy the support of interest groups and legislative allies. (The lieutenant governor, whose primary duty is to preside over the state Senate, is also elected independently of the governor.) With extremely limited authority to remove as well as appoint officeholders, the Georgia governor lacks a measure of control over the executive branch of government.

However, with one exception, Georgia governors since 1931 have been strong executives (see Table 3 for a list of governors). A few completely dominated state government by force of personality, political skill, and sometimes by extralegal measures; most have exerted strength by controlling the state budget.

Before 1931, the Georgia governor had very limited influence on state government. The legislature controlled all state finances and even dominated executive agencies, except for those headed by elected officials. By 1930, amidst the worsening depression, the legislature lost track of state finances. State government was broke, and public employees were owed millions of dollars in back pay.

Promising "a complete and thorough overhauling" of the state

Figure 1: Georgia State Government

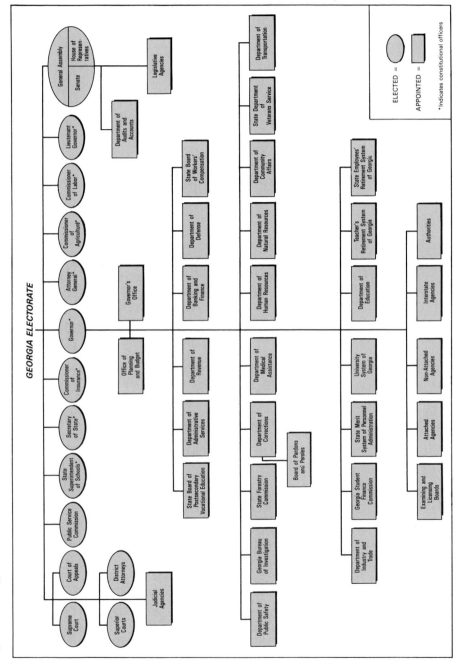

Table 3: Georgia Governors, 1931-1983

Richard B. Russell, Jr.	1931-1933
Eugene Talmadge	1933-1937
Eurith D. Rivers	1937-1941
Eugene Talmadge	1941-1943
Ellis G. Arnall	1943-1947
M. E. Thompson	1947-1948*
Herman Talmadge	1948-1955*
S. Marvin Griffin	1955-1959
S. Ernest Vandiver, Jr.	1959-1963
Carl E. Sanders	1963-1967
Lester G. Maddox	1967-1971
Jimmy Carter	1971-1975
Georgia D. Busbee	1975-1983
Joe Frank Harris	1983-

*In 1946, Eugene Talmadge was elected to a fourth term, but died before taking office. Lt. Governor M. E. Thompson was acting governor until the next election, which was won by Herman Talmadge.

government, Richard B. Russell, Jr., was elected governor in 1930. The next year, he persuaded the legislature to prune the executive branch to a mere 19 departments and, more importantly, to centralize budget management in the office of the governor.

The Budget Act of 1931 made the governor ex officio director of the budget with the authority not only to set budget limits for all state agencies within one executive budget but also to approve or deny requisitions for expenditures, including purchases and salaries. The Appropriations Act passed by the legislature became more a recommendation than law. The governor had an item veto, authority to choose which programs in an agency would get funds, a large discretionary fund, and (until 1943) the right to strike names from the state payroll. Between 1931 and 1962, by many accounts, "the governor literally ran the state out of his hip pocket."

Since 1962, the governor has been required by law to comply with specifics of the Appropriations Act passed by the legislature at its annual sessions. However, that act regularly contains only minor revisions in the budget proposal submitted by the governor to the legislature each January. Actual shaping of the budget is done in behind-the-scenes negotiations between the governor's staff and key legislators, not during the legislature's public debate.

The budget authority is the governor's primary mechanism of control over agencies. (By his own admission, George Busbee, 1975-1983, spent the largest block of his time in office preparing and writing the annual budget.) By September 15th of each year, agency heads must submit detailed budget requests to the governor. The Office of Planning and Budget analyzes, alters, and approves or disapproves these requests in light of the governor's own policies and within limits of estimated revenue for the next fiscal year. The revenue estimate is all important because by law Georgia's state government (like 48 others) may not spend more than it takes in each year. The budget has to be balanced. If revenue collections fall below estimates, the governor has the power to reduce expenditures already authorized by law. The budget authority goes a long way toward ensuring the governor the support of the other elected executives and influence over policy formulation in their agencies.

In addition, an unusual custom attached to the office of governor gives its occupant another measure of influence within the plural executive. Regularly, but not always, elected constitutional officers (and elected supreme court justices and court of appeals judges) resign before the expiration of their term in office. This practice allows the governor to choose an appointee to a nominally elective office. This "incumbent," enjoying the backing of the governor, then runs for reelection, usually without opposition. The outstanding example of this process is the office of state superintendent of schools: not since 1932 has the superintendent been initially elected to office on his own. (The 1986 election of an appointed incumbent followed the death of the state superintendent, not his resignation.) The effect of this custom is, of course, to bind these officeholders to the governor who appoints them.

Legislative Relations. In relations with the legislature, the governor once employed several customary but informal powers to great advantage. Through the tenure of Carl Sanders, 1963-1967, the governor actually named the Speaker of the House of Representatives, Speaker pro tem, and committee chairmen, as well as designating floor leaders to ensure passage of administration bills. The governor had similar influence in the state Senate, even though it was presided over by the independently elected lieutenant governor. Administration bills were almost always passed. Bills the governor opposed were assigned to "killer" committees for a quick death. The governor rarely had need for the veto. During the floor debate, if needed, the governor could use a direct phone line to the Speaker's rostrum to call the shots.

Federally mandated legislative reapportionment in the early 1960s brought an influx of urban, black, and Republican legislators. The old ties established among county courthouse rings, rural legislators, and a governor elected by unit votes began to weaken. The clear opportunity for the legislature to assert its independence, however, was the election of Lester Maddox, 1967-1971.

Political cartoonists enjoyed a field day during the Maddox years, caricaturing the governor as bewildered or clownish.

When the ballots were counted after the 1966 general election for governor, no candidate had a clear majority. Republican nominee Howard "Bo" Callaway had a plurality; Lester Maddox, winner of the Democratic Party's primary, trailed by some 3,000 votes; but over 50,000 write-in votes had been cast for Democratic ex-governor, Ellis Arnall. The state constitution provided that in such a situation the legislature would elect a governor from the top two candidates (the constitution was later amended to provide for a run-off election). In January 1967, the heavily Democratic legislature chose Maddox. Before doing so, however, the legislators had, without direction from a governor, chosen their own officers and established their own legislative agenda for the upcoming session. The new governor, who owed his election to the legislature and had little grasp of the legislative prerogatives of his office, allowed the lawmakers to go their own way. In doing so, he lost for the chief executive much of its informal power.

Jimmy Carter, 1971-1975, struggled to reassert gubernatorial authority, but Lester Maddox who had been elected lieutenant governor, fought him tooth and nail as presiding officer of the state Senate. The current balance of power between the governor and the legislature may be credited to Carter's successor, George Busbee. Himself a veteran representative of 18 years, Busbee used his mastery of budget matters plus a low-keyed diplomacy to retrieve for his office more influence, but not renewed dominance, in lawmaking.

Changes in Style and Expectations. For the past half century, most Georgia governors have been conservatives who espoused little government. However, popular expectations of the office and the leadership style of its occupants have changed with the time. Eugene Talmadge's campaign promises reflected circumstances of the depression years: a $3 auto tag for all, reduced property taxes, lower utility rates, and decreased government spending. Blocked by the General Assembly in his attempts to meet his campaign promises, the governor determined to rule by executive fiat and used control of the budget and even martial law to run executive departments his way. At the same time, Talmadge vehemently opposed most of the New Deal as well as locally initiated social measures. On the occasion of his 1935 veto of a pension bill, he reiterated his basic belief that "it is not the purpose of the State to support its people." Talmadge's advocacy of as few services and low taxes as possible was pure bourbonism, and earned him strong support by business leaders. But, Talmadge's arguments for little government had a populist tone: "Whenever you have rich government . . . you usually have a poor citizenry." And, "The way to keep a government good and to keep its citizens prosperous is to have a poor government." In his opposition to progressive measures, such as state-provided textbooks for the public schools, Talmadge made more difficult the material advancement of the very people who most consistently supported him at the polls—low-income rural whites. It was left to E.D. Rivers, 1937-1941, to bring Georgia its own "little new deal," expanding social services and the size of government.

In 1976, George Busbee, presiding over a state government establishment 30 times larger than that of the Talmadge era, was to echo the desire for little government: "I hope we have no more employees when I leave office than we had when I took office." Ironically, Busbee voiced his hope at a time when American government was decentralizing. State and local governments were assuming more responsibilities and hiring employees at a greater rate than was the national government. Bucking that tide, in 1978 Busbee reiterated, "The dominant responsibility of those of us who hold positions of public trust is to practice what we preach, and that is respect for the taxpayer, commitment to efficiency, and determination to put the brakes on growth in government."

Among Georgia's modern governors, the most aggressive advocate of both social and political reform was Ellis Arnall, 1943-1947. A confirmed New Deal liberal, Arnall was elected on a wave of popular resentment against Gov. Eugene Talmadge's attacks on the University of Georgia. (It was the only election for the governorship that Talmadge would lose.) Holding to his campaign promise to eliminate the "dictator" (an effective slogan in a war year, 1942), Arnall obtained legislation eliminating the governor's pardon power, control of the state board of education and board of regents, and authority to suspend state officials or strike the names of state employees from the payroll. He also obtained the vote for 18-year-olds—the nation's first—abolition of the chain gang, repeal of the poll tax, and a new state constitution.

The election campaigns and subsequent administrations of Herman Talmadge, 1948-1955; Marvin Griffin, 1955-1959; and Ernest Vandiver,

Worker in Office of the Georgia Secretary of State, Elections Division, is swamped with soldiers' ballots in the nation's first 18-year-old vote in 1944.

1959-1963; were dominated by race issues. Yet, Talmadge and Vandiver formulated mildly progressive policies in education and health. Georgia's 3 percent sales tax was initiated under Talmadge, and Georgia's schools began a relatively peaceful desegregation under Vandiver.

The administration of Carl Sanders, 1963-1967, was hailed at the time as a new chapter in Georgia politics. The 1962 election of the youthful urbane Sanders (who was often compared in the media with John Kennedy) over the white supremacist ex-governor, Marvin Griffin, was based on the popular vote, not the county unit vote outlawed that year by the federal court. Sanders sought to shift state politics from race to substantive issues, especially education and economic development. A spectacular expansion of the university system and greatly increased outlays for public schools earned Sanders acclaim as Georgia's "education governor." While he pursued policies of racial moderation and accommodation with federal desegregation mandates, his term was marked by white backlash following passage of the Civil Rights Act of 1964 and the Voting Rights Act of 1965.

That backlash brought the election of avowed segregationist Lester Maddox, 1967-1971. The governor's actions provided good copy for the media which featured his clowning, denouncing of socialists and communists in Washington, and fulminating over school desegregation orders. However, more than his predecessors, Maddox showed real concern for the condition of the state's prisoners and, ironically, appointed more blacks to state positions than earlier governors had. He put forth little in the way of new programs and had little impact on legislation. At the end of his term, one Atlanta newsman commented that Maddox had proven that "Georgia doesn't need a governor."

With Jimmy Carter, 1971-1975, a trend obvious in the Sanders years was renewed: a shift from a governorship characterized by personalized politics devoted to preservation of the status quo to bureaucratized politics directed at economic development. Perhaps the best-remembered feature of the Carter years was his reorganization of the state bureaucracy.

Along with their propensity to create counties, Georgians have traditionally liked to create state agencies. As the state government took on new functions early in this century, instead of assigning a new function to an existing agency, the legislature would create a new bureau, board, commission, or department to carry it out. Like new counties, new bureaus provided jobs for officeholders' family, friends, and political supporters. By 1930, there were over 90 of them, often duplicating services and wasting money. In his short administration, Gov. Richard B. Russell, Jr., pruned the rambling structure down to 19 agencies. But immediately afterward, and stimulated by New Deal programs from Washington as well as local patronage opportunities, the bureaus began to proliferate again. Into the 1960s, the bureaucratic units grew, each with its special interest constituency, corps of employees, and legislative appropriation.

In 1971, newly inaugurated Gov. Jimmy Carter told the legislature, "During my campaign I stated that there were 140 agencies in our state government. Now I find that in the executive branch alone, we have more than 200 agencies. . . . It has gotten so that every time I open the closet door in my office, I fear that a new state agency will fall out."

Obtaining a coherent state bureaucracy wasn't easy. Carter's plan for reorganization faced stiff opposition from heads of agencies marked for the axe, the special interests those agencies served, and legislators led by Lt. Gov. Lester Maddox. Compromises were made with powerful interests. For example, a comprehensive Department of Natural Resources was proposed to administer all the functions its title implies, but Georgia's forest resources remained the province of a separate State Forestry Commission through the power of the forest products industry. In the end, the Carter reorganization left the state with two dozen major agencies.

Besides being essentially conservative in fiscal and social policy, the most recent Georgia governors have been conservative in style. George Busbee's business-manager style earned the media's observation that the governor was somewhat dull. Busbee replied, "I must plead guilty to dullness, as dullness means doing the job I was elected to do and having an impact on how your tax dollars are spent."

After eight years of relative calm in state government, the voters in 1982 opted for what promised to be more of the same. They elected Joe Frank Harris, like Busbee a veteran legislator widely acknowledged as an expert in fiscal matters—a work-a-day businessman who promised stability, not change. Harris was reelected in 1986. Other than keeping the machinery of government running smoothly, staying free of scandal, and promoting economic development, Georgia's most recent governors haven't been asked by the people to do much else.

The new business-managerial style in the office of governor is reflected throughout state government. Down through the bureaucracy the operational style is shifting from political to managerial. The "good ole boy" political appointees are being replaced by professionals whose style is middle-level management and whose aim is better labelled "efficient government" than "little government."

At the Capitol: The General Assembly

The lawmaking power of state government resides in the legislature, known officially in Georgia as the General Assembly. It makes two basic kinds of laws: general and local. General laws apply throughout the

Gov. George Busbee greets a trade delegation. By the mid-1970s, economic promotion was a characteristic function of Georgia governors.

state; local laws apply only to specified cities or counties. The General Assembly may not pass local laws which contravene laws of general application.

In addition to making laws, the legislature also passes resolutions (such as for making its will known on proposed amendments to the Georgia or United States constitutions); appoints a limited number of executive officers (such as members of the State Transportation Board); and may conduct impeachments.

The Georgia General Assembly is made up mainly of "citizen legislators" who divide their energies between politics and such occupations as law, farming, and business. There are only a handful who regard themselves as full-time "professional legislators." Annually, starting the second week in January, the legislature meets for 40 days. Upon occasion, the legislature is also called into special session to consider specific agenda items (such as budget revision, reapportionment, or constitutional revision). Between sessions, individual members of the legislature may work in an official capacity on study committees, housekeeping chores, and in the service of constituents.

The General Assembly is a bicameral legislature composed of a Senate and a House of Representatives. Each chamber conducts its business separately according to rules of its own making. Each utilizes standing committees composed of only its own members to study, hold public hearings on, and make recommendations on bills. The House and Senate have no joint-standing committees, and joint sessions are rare—held mainly on ceremonial occasions. However, for a bill to become law it must be passed in exactly the same form by both houses. Therefore, conference committees including both senators and representatives are utilized to resolve any differences between versions of bills passed by each body. The ongoing rivalry between the two bodies has at times delayed passage of crucial legislation. Most legislation requires only a simple majority in each house to pass. Constitutional amendments, overrides of gubernatorial vetoes, and other specified cases do require more than a simple majority.

Georgia has one of the largest state legislatures, currently 56 senators and 180 representatives. Senators and representatives have the same two-year term, the same salary, and basically the same duties and prerogatives. The Senate's special duties are to ratify specific executive appointments; the House initiates appropriations legislation. Apportionment of seats in each house is based strictly on population, so that each senator represents approximately the same number of residents as any other senator, and each representative the same as any other.

Unlike the Senate-House relationship in Congress, the Georgia Senate is not more powerful or prestigious than the Georgia House. In fact, the converse is the case. At one time, before federal court "one person, one vote" rulings invalidated the practice, Senate seats were rotated among the counties comprised in Senate election districts. As a result, senators generally lacked opportunity for reelection. With few exceptions, they could not accumulate the expertise and the influence that accrues with seniority. Even though the original cause has disappeared, the Senate has remained in the shadow of the House. Accordingly, the most powerful state official, right behind the governor, is the Speaker of the House. Elected by vote of the House members, the Speaker not only rules over floor debate but also controls committee appointments, the assignment of bills to committee, and (to a great extent) if and when a bill comes up for a vote. From 1967 through 1986, two especially skillful politicians, George L. Smith and Thomas B. Murphy, enhanced the power of the Speakership by virtue of their ability. Their support for major legislation was crucial for its passage; their opposition was almost always fatal.

The lieutenant governor, the Speaker's counterpart in the Senate, is elected by popular vote to a four-year term, which runs concurrently with the governor's. No limit is placed on the number of terms one person can serve. In 1975, a reform-minded lieutenant governor, Zell Miller, delivered on his campaign promise to make the state Senate more accountable to the people by opening Senate committee proceedings to the public. (Later, the House followed suit.) In 1987, Miller started his fourth term in office.

Although individual legislators generally enjoy the respect and support of the public, the collective membership is frequently criticized in the press. Criticism is occasioned by the passage of faulty (sometimes unconstitutional) legislation and legislation patently beneficial to special interests, or by the failure of commendable legislation for reasons of self-interest on the part of legislators themselves. Some of the General Assembly's problems can be pinned on its minimal staff and material resources. (They are especially meagre compared to those of the governor's Office of Planning and Budget.) Until 1983, legislators (except for the leadership) had no office space at the capitol. They had no assigned staff (except student interns) to take care of constituents or do research on bills. With low salaries and expense allowances, few legislators could hire their own aides. As a result, Georgia's part-time citizen-legislators have had to depend heavily on lobbyists (as well as on one another) for information and advice regarding complex legislation.

In recent years, the General Assembly has tried to strengthen itself, but Georgians traditionally oppose any bill that seems to increase the power of government. Thus, attempts to give legislators longer terms, longer sessions, and greater ease in overriding a gubernatorial veto were defeated.

In terms of the rank and file membership, power in the legislature may be characterized as thinly diffused among individuals whose common interests bring them together into coalitions of but little cohesion and short endurance. As a result, the concentrations of power that do exist reside with the Speaker, the lieutenant governor, and their immediate circles of pro tems, majority leaders, and major committee chairs. Aside from the General Assembly's "management," only the black caucus sticks together with any degree of consistency.

Consensus politics, played in the General Assembly as elsewhere in Georgia, focuses almost exclusively on economic and fiscal issues. The force behind resolution of those issues is pragmatism, not ideology. Sometimes *ends* as well as *means* are debated. But the most important end in consensus politics is allocating some satisfaction to everyone concerned—especially industry, agribusiness, utilities, and banks, but also to public employees and minorities—so that no one goes home angry.

Consensus politics is not only nonideological; it is also nonpartisan. Except for patently partisan issues, such as legislative and congressional redistricting, voting in the General Assembly is seldom influenced by party identification or the stated policies of Democratic and Republican organizations.[3] Voting is influenced, however, by legislators' own connections with, or the lobbying efforts of, special interest groups.

Each year, some 500 registered lobbyists work the 40-day session of the General Assembly. "Grass-roots" organizations may mobilize hundreds of one-day lobbyists to descend on the state capitol to sway lawmakers' thinking on social or environmental issues. Another category of lobbyists are those representing the interests of organized occupation groups. Especially active are groups who enjoy the benefits of state licensure—from pharmacists and funeral directors to plumbers and private detectives—and whose livelihood is directly influenced by legislation. Only a small percentage of Georgia's workforce is unionized, so the labor lobby is not notably effective. Consistently more influential are the so-called "corporate lobbies." Private corporations and business and trade associations mobilize professional, financial, and information resources to influence legislation. To legislators short on their own information resources, lobby-supplied information is especially welcome.

The influence of business and industry on state government has long been a fiercely debated issue in Georgia. In the 1880s, Tom Watson, then a fiery young lawyer in east Georgia, inveighed against banking interests who obtained legislation that kept farmers in perpetual debt. Fifty years later, Gov. Eugene Talmadge castigated the big utilities and forced some lowering of rates. In 1945, Gov. Ellis Arnall personally argued in federal court the state's case against discriminatory railroad freight rates. In 1974, Gov. Jimmy Carter asked legislators to consider their noninfluential constituents: the consumer, the borrower, the client; as well as the producer, the lender, the practitioner.

Georgia media have also criticized the corporate lobbies' relationship with the General Assembly. The repeated targets of media attacks are the big utilities, major banking corporations, and trade associations representing certain segments of the economy, such as the mobile home industry, trucking firms, and auto dealers. One focus of criticism is the state's minimal regulation of lobbying. Lobbyists are required merely to register by name and organization and to wear a badge at the capitol. They need not report their lobbying expenditures or activities.

The legislature and state government in general remained relatively free of major scandal between the end of Marvin Griffin's administration, 1959, and 1983. Then between 1983 and 1986, an appointed legislative officer's conviction brought sloppy fiscal practices to light, the head of the State Department of Labor was convicted of misusing

---

3. The success with which the overwhelming Democratic majority (in the state as well as in the General Assembly) achieves consensus to the satisfaction of many interest groups means there is little discontent upon which viable Republican opposition might be based.

his office, and the State Patrol was rocked by a ticket-fixing controversy. But despite these events and the frequent criticism of the ties of legislators and other officials to special interests, state government has in no way suffered the problems that local government has in staying both clean and fair.

The Court System

As much as recent changes in any other area of government, recent changes in Georgia's court system reflect the general shift from highly politicized and localized government to more centralized and professionalized government. Until recently, Georgia had a confusing hodgepodge of tribunals that were established piecemeal over the years—often by legislation tailored to the interests of this or that county—and which featured overlapping jurisdictions, an absence of state-level administrative controls, and a multiplicity of court rules and record-keeping practices. There was little provision for ensuring the qualifications of judges (who were elected in partisan elections), and many courts were served by part-time judges. In such a system there was much room for inefficiency and abuse.

In 1971, the following observation was made in a report to Gov. Jimmy Carter:

> Georgia has an unorganized court structure substantially the same as that in existence almost a century ago. The structure is fragmented and complex. . . .There is no system for central administration. . . .In short, there is little "system" in our system. (*Report of the Governor's Commission on Judicial Processes,* Atlanta, 1971, p. 2.)

Since 1971, the judicial branch of Georgia government has undergone a reformation. In addition to the Commission on Judicial Processes, the 1970s saw establishment of a Judicial Nominating Commission and a Judicial Qualifications Commission, both of which addressed the need to have better-qualified persons on the bench. Change culminated with the adoption of the Constitution of 1983: there emerged a true system of courts consisting of seven classes of courts, two appellate and five trial courts. The administration, jurisdiction, and procedure of the five trial courts are far more uniform in each class than was possible to achieve before 1983. The present court system is shown in Figure 2.

Superior Court

The superior court is Georgia's court of general jurisdiction. The superior court is the highest ranking court in Georgia with original jurisdiction and has exclusive jurisdiction over trials in felony cases

Figure 2: Georgia Court System

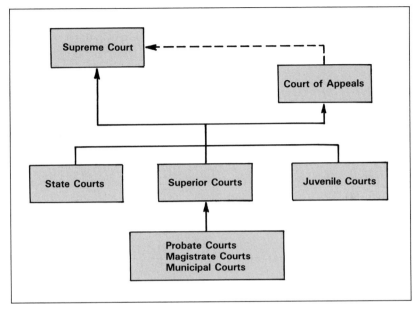

(except in cases of juvenile offenders) and in cases involving divorce, equity, and questions of land title. The superior court also has appellate jurisdiction: it can review and correct errors in decisions of courts with limited jurisdiction.

The superior court is located in each of the 159 counties and is organized by judicial circuits or groups of counties. In earlier days, judges had to "ride circuit" to hold court in each of many counties at least twice a year. In 1986, there were 45 circuits of one to eight counties each. Serving these circuits were 131 judges elected on a nonpartisan basis within their circuits for a term of four years.

Supreme Court

The Georgia Supreme Court is the state's highest court of review, exercising exclusive appellate jurisdiction over cases involving the construction of the Georgia or U.S. constitutions, all cases in which the constitutionality of a law or ordinance has been drawn into question, and all cases of election contest. The court also has general appellate jurisdiction in cases involving title to land, equity, wills, habeas corpus, extraordinary remedies, divorce and alimony, questions certified by the Georgia Court of Appeals, and the conviction of capital felony. It may also review, by certiorari, court of appeals cases deemed to have great public import.

The seven justices of the supreme court are elected to six-year terms in statewide, nonpartisan elections. Vacancies on the court are filled by appointment of the governor. The court elects a chief justice, who is the administrative head of the court and presides at oral arguments, and a presiding justice, who acts in the place of the chief justice when necessary.

Court of Appeals

The Georgia Court of Appeals exercises appellate jurisdiction in all cases where exclusive jursidiction is not reserved to the supreme court or conferred on other courts. The court may also certify questions to the supreme court for instruction.

The court of appeals consists of nine judges elected in statewide, nonpartisan elections. Vacancies may be filled by gubernatorial appointment.

Other Courts

The *state court* is a county-level court of limited jurisdiction. It is usually established to ease the workload of the superior court. State courts exercise jurisdiction over trials of nonfelony criminal cases and general civil actions except where exclusive jurisdiction is vested in the superior courts.

In 1986 there were 63 state courts. State court judges may be full-time or part-time, are elected in nonpartisan elections by the voters of their respective counties, and serve terms of four years.

The *juvenile court* has exclusive jurisdiction in cases involving delinquent children alleged to have committed noncapital offenses, unruly children under the age of 17, deprived children under the age of 18, and juvenile traffic offenders under the age of 16. The juvenile court also has jurisdiction in custody proceedings referred from the superior court and in cases involving termination of parental rights.

Although there is a juvenile court for each county, in the majority of counties the superior court judge sits as the juvenile court judge. In the counties with independent juvenile courts, the superior court judge (or judges) of the circuit appoints one or more juvenile court judges to serve terms of four years.

The *probate court* exercises jurisdiction in the probate of wills, the administration of estates, the appointment of guardians, and the involuntary hospitalization of incapacitated and dependent persons. In some counties, probate courts also hear traffic cases and try violations of state fish and game laws.

There are 159 probate judges, each serving a single county, elected in a partisan election by the voters of the county to serve a term of four years.

The *magistrate court* has jurisdiction to issue search and arrest warrants, preside in actions concerning bonds for good behavior and bonds to keep the peace, hold criminal commitment hearings, try county ordinance violations, try civil claims up to $2,500 where jurisdiction is not vested exclusively in the superior court, and preside over dispossessory actions and issue distress warrants.

There is a magistrate court located in each county, with one chief magistrate and one or more additional magistrates. The term of office of magistrates is four years; the chief magistrate, who is elected in partisan elections, appoints the additional magistrates with the approval of the superior court judges. In some counties, probate judges also serve as chief magistrates.

Along with the seven classes of courts in the state judicial system, there are approximately 350 municipal courts which try local traffic offenses and violations of municipal ordinances.

Politics around the State

Consensus politics around the state, as in the legislature, is characterized by the interaction of interest groups, not by competition between Democrats and Republicans. The vast majority of those Georgians who profess a party identification call themselves Democrats, and this century-old tradition has led to Georgia being called a "one-party" state. More accurately, it has been a "no-party" state.

Political Organization

Georgia politicians' overwhelming preference for the Democratic label can be traced to native white Georgians' resentment of the activities of "carpetbagger" and "scalawag" Republicans during Reconstruction. Even after the national Republican Party ceased to champion the rights of southern blacks, the Democrats' white supremacy ideology plus the power they were amassing within the national Democratic Party precluded Republican success in recruiting white members in Georgia. (From 1861 to the present, however, tiny Republican strongholds have been maintained in the Georgia mountains.) In the 1890s, the Populists—led in Georgia by Tom Watson—mounted a strong challenge to the established Democrats. The Democrats then espoused the small farmers' causes that originally gave rise to the Populists. They were able to counteract any serious opposition by the Populists, whose incorporation of black support made them an easy target for racist invective. For 60 years after 1900, the Democratic establishment stood virtually unopposed in Georgia politics.

From time to time, factions of Georgia Democrats have provided some semblance of party competition. The only long-lived factions were the Talmadge and anti-Talmadge factions. From the mid-1930s to the mid-1950s, the two factions competed for the governorship, congressional seats, and other offices; they opposed each other on issues ranging from participation in the New Deal to black participation in politics. The anti-Talmadge faction, led successively by governors E.D. Rivers, Ellis Arnall, and M.E. Thompson, usually had the financial support of the Atlanta establishment and the editorial backing of the *Atlanta Constitution* and *Journal*. It disintegrated with the growth of "massive resistance" sentiment following the *Brown v. Board of Education* school desegregation ruling. After Herman Talmadge's departure for the U.S. Senate in 1957, the Talmadge faction slowly dissolved.

Structure and Strength

Until the mid-1960s, only the Democrats had an officially sanctioned state party. Only the Democratic Party held a statewide primary. With no organized opposition, Georgia Democrats had no impetus to build a strong organization of their own. Events of 1964 gave the state's Democratic establishment its first inkling of the need to have a functioning party apparatus. In that year, for the first time since Reconstruction, a Republican presidential candidate took the state's electoral vote. In fact, Barry Goldwater took it with the announced support of many of the Democratic Party's county executives. A post mortem ordered by the party's titular head, Gov. Carl Sanders, revealed that only Fulton and DeKalb counties actually had permanent working party machinery. Sanders, who had already tried to broaden the party's base by adding black members to the Georgia delegation to the 1964 Democratic National Convention, pushed the state party to create responsible units in all 159 counties.

Twenty years later, the Democratic Party was organized on paper in all counties, with an elected county committee in each. Still, the apparatus functions meaningfully in only the larger counties where there is Republican strength; in smaller counties, party positions frequently remain vacant. As in the past, Democratic dominance rests on the personal ties of local and state leaders—in and out of government—not on the formal party structure.

Although the 1960s witnessed an auspicious reemergence of a Republican Party in Georgia, GOP strength has not gained in predicted measure. Modern Georgia Republicanism was born amidst white backlash to the civil rights push of the Johnson Administration. The Goldwater majority and the election the same year of Howard "Bo" Callaway as Georgia's first modern Republican congressman was in

Albany, 1940. Eugene Talmadge, with trademark suspenders, exhorts a typically huge crowd to return him to the governor's office.

essence reactionary. As long as state Democrats suffered by association with their national party leaders, Republicans made headway. Callaway, as mentioned earlier, had the popular vote, but lost the governorship in the General Assembly. In 1968, several top Georgia Democrats switched to the GOP after their National Convention seated delegates led by black legislator Julian Bond. In 1970, a Republican political novice, TV newscaster Hal Suit, gained 41 percent of the gubernatorial vote versus Jimmy Carter. By 1972, Republicans held 37 legislative seats (up from four seats in 1962) and two seats in Congress. In 1980, Republican Mack Mattingly won a U.S. Senate seat. In 1984 and 1986, Republicans scored victories in local and legislative races in the suburban ring around Atlanta. Generally, however, Republicans have contested only scattered legislative seats and practically no statewide offices—except the race for the governorship in which they were unsuccessful in 1982 and 1986.

In sum, based on primary turnouts and officeholding, Republican numbers are less than 10 percent of the Democratic. Outside suburban areas with heavy concentrations of newcomers, Republicans have yet to establish a broad base of popular support.

Citizen Participation

Democratic primaries in the 1930s and 1940s generated great excitement throughout Georgia. Politics was entertaining and there was usually a barbecue or fish fry for the faithful. But the crowds jammed into the courthouse square to hear Talmadge or Russell or Rivers or Arnall did not reflect the true level of popular participation in politics. Tenant farmers didn't normally vote. Neither did the cotton mill workers. Ignorance and apathy, plus the poll tax, literacy tests, residency requirements, and intimidation, (and of course the white primary) kept registration and voting levels the lowest in the nation. Politics was the preserve of the white farmer who owned his own land and paid property taxes, the small town merchant, the lawyer, and the banker. The courthouse establishment decided who would run in the Democratic primary for local offices and the legislature. Without two-party competition, incumbents tended to stay in office a long time. Lack of turnover in public office discouraged citizen participation in elections. Only in the governor's office, with its term limited by law, was there regular turnover.

Although voter registration in Georgia increased greatly after the federal Voting Rights Act of 1965, it remains low by national standards, and voter turnout is dismally low. When Jimmy Carter ran for the presidency in 1976, 75 percent of the eligible black Georgians could vote, 66 percent of the eligible whites could. However, only 43 percent of all those eligible turned out to cast a presidential ballot. By comparison 54 percent voted nationwide. Four years later, again only 43 percent turned out to vote in the presidential election. In 1982, the turnout for a well-contested governor's race was only 28 percent. That year, Georgia had the lowest general election turnout in the nation. In the presidential election of 1984, Georgia's turnout was again among the lowest in the nation.

Black Participation

Until the 1960s, black citizens had no real voice in Georgia politics and government. At the turn of the century, the state's political establishment began using several legal devices to disfranchise blacks, the most effective of which was the white primary. The white primary was based on the legalistic argument that a political party was a private organization and therefore might name by whatever means it so desired its candidates for public office. In 1917, the General Assembly passed a primary act which required any party nominating candidates to use the primary method, thus involving the state in conducting these white primaries. Some 20,000 black Georgians were registered to vote in Atlanta and a few other communities, but they could do so only in the uncontested general election (and special elections). The election that really mattered, the primary, was off-limits to blacks.

In 1946, after the federal courts had ruled unconstitutional the white primary laws of several southern states, Georgia blacks reentered politics. Blacks immediately registered in substantial numbers (though many were just as quickly purged from the rolls in some 30 counties). With the 1946 gubernatorial election—and Eugene Talmadge's campaign to restore the white primary—race became the dominant issue in Georgia politics. It would remain so for 20 years. In the late 1940s and 1950s, white supremacists used voter list purges and a new literacy test to keep blacks from voting. (The literacy test was suspended because many whites couldn't pass it.)

The growing urban vote, particularly in and around Atlanta, was also alarming to a strongly segregationist and rural-dominated legislature. (In the 1946 gubernatorial primary, James Carmichael, candidate of the anti-Talmadge faction, won the gubernatorial primary popular vote largely on the strength of huge urban majorities of blacks and moderate white voters, only to lose the unit vote.) In 1952, the General

DeKalb County, 1946. After the white primary was outlawed, black citizens voted in substantial numbers for the first time in four decades.

Assembly passed a constitutional amendment to apply the unit vote system to general elections. It was not ratified due to a heavy urban vote against it.

Black participation in Atlanta politics increased as steadily as the black percentage of its population. In 1972, with both black and white support, civil rights leader Andrew Young was elected Georgia's first black congressman since the 1870s. A year later, city voters chose Maynard Jackson as Atlanta's first black mayor. In 1981, Young succeeded Jackson in the mayor's office.

Across the state, black Georgians now enjoy a measure of political opportunity, but in some rural counties racial discrimination still blocks participation. After passage of the Voting Rights Act of 1965 and a subsequent rise in black registration, the election of blacks to public office rose significantly. From 1968 to 1979, the number of elected black officials in local government rose from 10 to 214. Black membership in the General Assembly increased from 11 to 23 during the same period. However, only one black, Georgia Court of Appeals Judge Robert Benham, had been elected to statewide public office by 1984.

Participation by Women

Women have not been prominent in state government. In 1986, Court of Appeals Judge Dorothy T. Beasley was the only woman in statewide office, and only 23 women held seats in the legislature. In local government, however, women held hundreds of positions on city councils, county commissions, school boards; and as mayors, judges, school superintendents, and court clerks.

Winning Public Office in Georgia

Although Georgia politicians are no longer exclusively middle-aged white males, they belong to a relatively homogeneous group whose members are often characterized by some form of business background or affiliation. The homogeneity is not so remarkable given that recruitment into Georgia politics is typically by association with a community's business-commercial establishment—or power structure—not by membership and work in a political party.

The membership of the General Assembly provides a good example of this homogeneity. In 1986, about 47 percent of the members were regularly occupied in business-industry, 10 percent in farming, and 17 percent as lawyers. Other indicators of homogeneity: the membership was 90 percent male; 89 percent white; 82 percent college-educated; 85 percent Democratic; 73 percent aged 36-65; and 64 percent Baptist or Methodist.

The sameness among officeholders is somewhat paradoxical in light of the broad opportunity (except in a few closed counties) to run for office in Georgia. The requirements are simple: (1) pick out an office to run for, (2) decide which primary to run in, and (3) pay the qualifying fee set for that office. One has only to be a registered voter to qualify for most offices. No party membership is required. By custom, the Democratic label is preferred (and is more likely to get you elected except in Cobb, DeKalb, Gwinnett, and north Fulton counties) and the Democratic primary draws about 10 times the voters (and 30 times the candidates) as does the Republican. Party officers have no control over who runs, so "unknowns" frequently become party nominees.

Actually, Georgia politicians normally campaign as if there were no party considerations. They run as independents, seldom stressing party affiliation and often omitting it in campaign advertising. In Georgia the person, not the party, moves the electorate to action. But informal ties to local and state-level Democrats can be critical in organizing campaigns locally and in getting out the vote.

The typical successful candidate must not only ascribe to the political values of the majority—little (read: "cost efficient" sometimes) government and low taxes, but also conform to popular norms: individualism, social conformity, material success, personal morality, and educated intelligence tempered by practicality. In addition, candidates must not be too unlike their neighbors in manner of speaking, dress, and behavior.

In general, in most parts of the state (Atlanta is the notable exception), candidates jockey for the "real conservative" position. Being seen by the voters as more conservative than an opponent is almost always an advantage. Being seen as liberal almost always means defeat. Toward that end, candidates seek the endorsement of conservative interest groups, not those advocating change or spending.

Georgia and the Nation

Of course, what happens in state politics is influenced by what happens in national politics, and vice versa. To a great extent from the mid-1930s to the mid-1960s, and to a lesser extent since then, the political culture of Georgia included a rather negative—sometimes hostile—orientation toward national politics and government. Georgia politicians regularly gave voice to popular frustrations with the federal authority's "intrusion," not only into state politics but also into Georgia social and economic life.

Federal intrusions beginning under President Franklin D. Roosevelt were particularly vexing to some Georgia Democrats after years of "solid South" loyalty to the national Democratic Party during Republican control in Washington. By adding labor, blacks, and professionals to their southern base, the Democrats had become the majority party. Eventually, national party policy could be formulated with little regard for southern views. With that change, the votes of Georgia Democrats and nonsouthern Democrats in Congress increasingly diverged on social and economic matters.

At the same time, however, the federal government—again starting with Roosevelt and the New Deal—provided the state with money for roads, welfare, health and educational facilities, and social services. With World War II, the federal military establishment was in good part responsible for the start-up of Georgia's economic prosperity.

Much of the credit for the federal presence in the state may be attributed to the extraordinary effectiveness of Georgia politicians in Washington. In the House, Georgia congressman Carl Vinson became in the 1930s Roosevelt's strongest ally in the long struggle, against congressional isolationist sentiment, to build a navy second to none. Vinson, whose 50-year service in the House, 1914-1965, is the longest in the nation's history, is universally credited with preparing the U.S. Navy adequately to fight World War II and with moving the military establishment into the missile age. Vinson's partner in the Senate, Richard B. Russell, Jr., 1933-1971, was for many years that body's architect of military preparedness. The Vinson-Russell duo, in concert with equally heavyweight politicians in the other Senate seat, Walter F. George, 1922-1957, and Herman Talmadge, 1957-1981, gave Georgia prolonged power in national politics matched by the politicians of few other states.

More recently, U.S. Senator Sam Nunn has assumed Russell's mantle as Senate military expert. However, the more open politics of contemporary Georgia likely precludes the kind of extended incumbency and longterm influence enjoyed by Georgia's earlier representatives. Senator Talmadge himself was upset in his 1980 reelection bid by Mack Mattingly, an unknown Republican from Indiana who had never held elective office in Georgia. In turn, Mattingly was upset in 1986 by Wyche Fowler, a Democratic congressman from Atlanta. Congressional districts now change hands among Democrats, a few of them between Democrats and Republicans, to the degree that in 1986 no U.S. House member from Georgia had accumulated more than 12 years seniority.

The presidency of Jimmy Carter, 1977-1981, catapulted Georgia into the national limelight. Myriad aspects of Georgia society and culture, from church attendance to habits of speech, were examined and expounded upon repeatedly in news magazines and Sunday supplements. Television commentators and op-ed journalists discovered cultural elements to support their fuzzy explanations for the president's policies or personal behavior. The Carter presidency begat television spoofs and boosted tourism in Georgia. Though his election in 1976 was a source of state pride, Carter's performance was not applauded in his home state any more than elsewhere. Indeed, some of his policies found less favor in Georgia than in more liberal regions of the North and West. His loss in 1980 was a disappointment to many Georgians but a relief to others. Jimmy carried his home state, but Ronald Reagan, whose campaign rhetoric was more in tune with the political climate of Georgia than was Carter's, gained support both deep and wide.

The 1984 election found Georgia voters returned to a position first taken in 1964: embracing state Democrats while rejecting national Democrats. Except for native-son Jimmy Carter, no Democrat since John Kennedy has won Georgia's electoral vote. At the same time, no Republican has won a statewide office in Georgia government. So great was the desire of state Democratic leaders to disassociate themselves from the national party that they, including the governor, kept their distance from the Mondale-Ferraro ticket.

At this writing, there are no clear trends to indicate what the future will bring in Georgia politics and government. What is clear is that politics will be different. Georgia has changed. The social and economic underpinnings of traditional Georgia politics are gone from the places where most Georgians now live. The old dominant political values are today blended not only with those of thousands of non-natives but also those emerging from a new set of circumstances: prosperity not depression within the state, assimilation not isolation in relation to the mainstream of the nation. The preference for little government is not likely to fade—indeed arguments for the same have won acceptance across the nation since 1980—but consensus politics may, in the emergence of a true two-party system in Georgia, become a thing of the past.

CHAPTER SIX

Public Education

By Lawrence R. Hepburn

Reporters gathered early at the Capitol on the morning of April 28, 1960. At 10 a.m., the General Assembly's Committee on Schools would make public its eagerly awaited report. Speculation ran high on the answer to the important question of the day: Would Georgia's public schools stay open? For several weeks, newspapers throughout the state had featured the committee's progress. Travelling to each congressional district in Georgia, 19 legislators, laypersons, and professionals, headed by Atlanta banker-lawyer John A. Sibley, had taken the testimony of some 1,800 citizens—1,600 white and 200 black. There were reports of packed hearings and charges of coercion and intimidation.

In the face of a pending suit in federal court to desegregate Atlanta's schools, the legislature had created the Sibley Commission—as it was popularly called. Its charge was simple: to determine the opinion of the people on whether or not to maintain the public schools "notwithstanding that the school system of Atlanta and even others yet to come may be integrated."

But the people's opinion was not so simple to determine. An overall majority of witnesses favored segregation, but they also wanted public schools. In southwest Georgia, a clear majority of whites at the hearings preferred to abandon the state's public schools rather than accept integration. In the mountains, other Georgians were not willing to give up their public schools for the sake of preserving segregation anywhere in the state. The pattern of reaction to the proposal to do away with public schools seemed related to the geographic distribution of blacks.

The Sibley Commission, itself, harbored disagreement on what it had heard and how to proceed. Most members leaned toward some kind of local option and pupil assignment plan; that is, keeping the schools open at the cost of a little integration on a local basis. The majority opined, ". . . it will be impractical to develop a system of private schools."

Chairman Sibley subsequently recommended that the state repeal its "massive resistance" laws. From public schools advocates, there was a collective sigh of relief.

Since the 1954 Supreme Court decision in *Brown v. Board of Education,* massive resistance had dominated state politics. Three successive governors had promised to maintain segregation. Elections were won by "outsegging" the opponent. The General Assembly piled up legislation to thwart any move toward integration: school systems would lose their funds, and school officials their jobs, if they participated in any integrated schooling. But by 1960, legal barriers to school desegregation in other southern states had already fallen before suits in federal court. The election of John F. Kennedy promised a more pro-civil rights posture in the White House. Some Georgia politicians saw only one simple choice remaining: public schools or no public schools. With the Sibley report in hand, and federal court rulings at hand, the legislature abandoned massive resistance. The public schools had been saved.

What was saved? In 1960, 97 percent of Georgia children enrolled in school were in public schools, only 3 percent in nonpublic schools. Of the fifty states, only four showed a greater preference for public over private schooling. Compared to other states, however, Georgia's ranking in education was very low. Relative to the other states, Georgia ranked 46th in per pupil school expenditures (the same ranking as in 1939-40 and 1949-50).

In 1960, Georgia's public school system was just 90 years old. Founded when the state was in the throes of Reconstruction, the schools suffered in their infancy a special stigma of association with that period. Throughout their formative years the schools would be retarded by forces associated with the agrarian, economically depressed, and biracial character of society in Georgia.

Making firm the provision for public education in Georgia was a struggle. In this chapter, as the story of public education in Georgia unfolds, that ongoing struggle emerges as a principal theme.

The Early Years (1777-1866)

Before the Civil War, the schools in Georgia were mostly private. The Constitution of 1777 said: "Schools shall be erected in each county and supported at the general expense of the State as the Legislature shall hereafter point out." This Revolutionary War ideal gave way, however, to the rough and tumble realities of frontier life: the provision for schools was never put into effect. The ideal was also in the 1785 Charter of the University of Georgia. Its framers envisioned a system of public education from primary to collegiate. The system did not materialize and the University of Georgia, which enrolled its first students at Athens in 1801, remained a small liberal arts institution, popularly called Franklin College, through the antebellum years.

Children of families who could pay the tuition could attend private schools and colleges. In and about Georgia's cities, 106 academies were chartered by 1832. In the 1830s, the various church bodies were notably active in founding schools, some of which grew into colleges and universities.

College	Date	Affiliation	Location
LaGrange	1831	Methodist	LaGrange
Mercer	1833	Baptist	Penfield
Oglethorpe	1835	Presbyterian	Milledgeville
Emory	1836	Methodist	Oxford
Wesleyan (women)	1836	Methodist	Macon

For most white children dispersed in the countryside, schooling was catch-as-catch-can. Farmers in a rural district might throw up a schoolhouse and obtain whomever they could to teach the three Rs. These schools, typically built on worn out land, were dubbed "old field schools." After 1820, repeated attempts were made to found a system of free schools, but the most the legislature did was to create a "poor school fund" from which counties could draw to support schools for the children of paupers. The onus of the pauper label probably kept many farmers from sending their children to such schools.

On the eve of the Civil War, Gov. Joseph E. Brown led an effort to establish public schools. A state school fund was set up and counties were authorized to levy additional taxes for instruction in the "elementary branches." Georgia's confederate state constitution of 1861 included a provision for legislative appropriations for "the education of the people."

All the colleges and schools, public and private, were meant only for whites. State law forbade teaching blacks to read and write. But, on some plantations and at clandestine schools in Savannah and Augusta, a handful of blacks were taught.

The meagre educational opportunities that Georgia had established were devastated by the Civil War, but immediately after the war, movements began both inside and outside the state to educate Georgia's people. In 1865, a convention of native white Georgians put the education provision of 1861 into a new state constitution. A December 1866 act of the legislature called for a system of Georgia schools for any white inhabitant between the ages of 6 and 21 and any disabled soldier of the state. Although this system never materialized, schools for black Georgians did.

After the war, efforts began to provide education for Georgia's former slaves. In March 1865, Congress set up the Freedmen's Bureau; one of its tasks was to organize schools in the South for children and adults. In concert with the bureau, and on their own, northern philanthropies joined the effort to educate black southerners. Church associations—mainly Congregationalist, Methodist, and Baptist—sent resources and teachers. Schools operated in churches, houses, barns, barracks, and abandoned structures of all sorts, even old box cars. Not only the three Rs, but also the virtues of hard work and republican government were taught. Sometimes local whites, suffering the ravages of war and resenting the favor shown former slaves, drove out the teachers and burned the school buildings. But the teachers kept coming: from 1865 to 1873, the missionary organizations sent 367 teachers—80 percent of them women—to Georgia.

Post-Civil War (1867-1900)

The Common Schools

The genesis of Georgia's public school system dates from 1867. Early in the year, philanthropist George Peabody set up a $1 million fund to establish common schools in the southern states. Word of the Peabody Fund brought immediate action. In August 1867, 25 Georgia educators met in Atlanta and founded the Georgia Teachers Association. With Peabody support, the Association worked for two years devising a plan for a Georgia school system. Meanwhile, in 1868, another state constitution was adopted that provided for schools "free to all children of the state."

The fight for a school system wasn't easy. Georgia had no common school tradition and the value of such schools was largely unknown to the people. Coming in the wake of the Freedmen's Bureau and the "Yankee schoolmarms," the school proposal was viewed by many white Georgians as part of a design to impose northern ways on southern society. Gustavus John Orr, a founder of the Georgia Teachers Association, later recalled that the common school system was seen as "a badge of our subjection to another part of the Union." The common school was, suggested the editor of the Covington *Georgia Enterprise* in 1869, an attempt at "socialism." He predicted that the people's first notice of the establishment of a state system would be

> the discovery that the control of education of their own children has been taken out of the hands of parents, and transferred to strangers whose interest only leads them to train the rising generation to be subservient to the directions of a central oligarchy. A

State religion is scarcely more at variance with free government than a state educational system.

In 1870, the General Assembly passed "An Act to Establish a System of Public Instruction." It provided for a State School Commissioner, State Board of Education, 136 county boards of education, and 1,291 sub-districts drawn to include at least 30 residents between the ages of 6 and 21 and to have at least one school. The law gave Georgia a common school system initiated and funded at the state level but almost completely localized in its organization and administration. The counties, directed by the state to have schools, were largely left up to their own devices to carry out that direction. The local boards were given limited power to levy taxes for building and furnishing schoolhouses but not for teacher salaries or general purposes. A State Common School Fund was set up to finance the latter for a term of three months a year.

The new schools got off to a shaky start in 1871. Suffering from underfunding and low enrollment, the state system was suspended for 1872.

In the meantime, the founding by special legislation of municipal systems in Atlanta, Savannah, and Columbus foreshadowed a pattern that would be firmly established over the next half century: alongside the state common school system created in the law of October 1870, there would be independent local systems. Usually established by the simple device of having the legislature approve in a city's charter of incorporation the authority to maintain and levy taxes for public schools, municipal systems would enjoy not only a share of the state school fund but also a privilege of local self-support denied the common schools. With the wealth of cities behind them, the municipal systems would have longer school terms, finer facilities, more progressive leadership, and better-trained teachers than the common schools that enrolled the bulk of Georgia's children.

In 1873, the common schools began again under the direction of State School Commissioner Gustavus John Orr. Until his death in 1887, Orr struggled to secure the fledgling schools against popular indifference, economic distress, and political and religious opposition.

Orr realized that public sentiment had to be changed. Opponents of public schools argued that, as in business, the supply of education in Georgia would best come from the demand of those interested in having it. Orr replied in 1874, "It is painfully evident to all observers in every ignorant community, that in respect to that immaterial commodity represented by the word education, the rule is, the less the supply the less the demand."

Orr argued that popular support depended on the people perceiving they had a direct stake in the education of their children and pointed out that the states with well-established common schools, in New England and the Midwest, depended mostly on local taxation. Equipped with passes from the railroads and expenses from the Peabody Fund, Orr travelled the state exhorting the people to tax themselves for schools. In Atlanta, he lobbied the General Assembly to amend the school law to allow a general local school tax.

Then, in 1877, a reactionary constitutional convention practically closed the door on local taxation. Furthermore, the new constitution that emerged restricted public funds to the university and the "elementary branches of an English education only." That meant there would be no high schools in the state system. The prohibition against high schools was construed as not applying to incorporated municipalities. So, cities could have high schools, and for the most part that's where they remained until just before World War I.

Hovering over all in the 1870s was the "Negro question." The idea of "taxing the white man to teach the children of the black man" was anathema to many white Georgians. If there had to be schools for the blacks, then, according to a notion popular among whites, let only the taxes directly paid by blacks be used to support black schools. Although the legislature in 1874 did enact a law requiring county officials to make separate tax returns for blacks and whites, the State Common School Fund was not so divided. County school authorities could divide whatever state funds they received among white and black schools as they saw fit. Orr stressed the need for the white race to bring about the "elevation of the colored race" and even advocated the employment of white teachers to instruct black children, an idea that gained little acceptance.

One Georgian who did support that idea, and was perhaps Orr's strongest ally in the fight for common schools for blacks as well as whites, was Atticus G. Haygood. The sermons and writings of Haygood, a former chaplain in the Confederate Army, leader in the Southern Methodist Church, and president of the denomination's Emory College in Oxford, Georgia, had won Methodist preachers to the public school cause. In 1881, Haygood published a book, *Our Brother in Black*, in which he argued that with education blacks would become a positive force in the community. Later, he headed the Slater fund, a philanthropy dedicated to the education of blacks in the South.

One of the biggest obstacles to having good schools, for blacks and for whites, was the paucity of qualified teachers. Of some 6,000 teachers in the state in 1882, Orr estimated that only a few hundred had college educations. Sometimes, the local preacher or doctor, being the only educated person in a district, doubled as schoolteacher. In sum, the vast majority of teachers were, said Orr, "persons of limited education."

Teacher education in Georgia remained hit or miss through Commissioner Orr's tenure. The legislature was unresponsive to his repeated pleas to establish normal schools[1] such as those found in the northern states. In 1882, he used money from the Peabody Fund to inaugurate summer teacher institutes. Through 1887, 2,177 teachers, about two-thirds of them white, received a few weeks of instruction in teaching methods and subject matter at these Peabody institutes. Unfortunately, during the summer, when the city teachers could attend, most rural teachers had to hold school. In 1892, the first state-financed summer institutes began, and in 1895 a State Normal School commenced at Athens.

The public school enterprise had grown measurably under Orr's hand. The state appropriation had risen from $250,000 in 1873 to $489,000 in 1887. During the same period, school enrollment had increased from 83,677 to 342,294. But in the latter year, Georgia's school age population was 560,281 and average attendance was only 226,290 or 40 percent.

Low attendance was a function of several factors. In farming districts not only the need for children to work but also the sparsity of population, the primitive roads, the abysmal conditions of schoolhouses, and even the camp meetings and revivals militated against attendance.

Above all, low attendance was a function of economics. In the late nineteenth century, children were economic assets to the family and in chronically depressed Georgia their work, whether on farms or in mills, was no small contribution to family well-being.

By the turn of the century, the nonattendance of mill children had become a vexing problem for school officials. "It is not the factory owners that stand in the way," reported Superintendent Jere Pound of Bibb County, "but the parents themselves, who want their children to begin earning money just as quickly as possible. . . ." In Polk County, where children eight years old and up were employed by one factory, Superintendent J.E. Houseal suggested, "the only way to get them into the schools is to talk to the management in the absence of a child labor law, and get them to refuse to employ these children. I think the only way over the problem finally is to enact a child labor law. . . ."

In the 1890s, the weakness of the common school system and the wretchedness of rural schools came under attack. The Farmer's Alliance, a political force 100,000 strong in Georgia, saw the common schools as important to improving the small farmer's lot and, in concert with the Georgia Teachers Association, obtained from the General Assembly

---

1. After the *Ecole Normale* in France, a model school for training teachers. Massachusetts established the first U.S. version in 1839.

Tifton, 1909. This widow and all but her four youngest children worked for a total $9.00 a week in the cotton mill.

an increased state property tax. At mid-decade, the state school fund topped $1 million, newspapers in Atlanta and other cities joined the crusade for better rural schools, and the state-funded term reached five months.

Yet, gross inequalities between the rural schools and the city schools remained. For each common school pupil there was $2.79 of state funds in 1896; for each pupil enrolled in one of the "independent" systems (31 cities and 4 counties by then) there was $12.79 in state and local funds. By the end of the century, however, a new movement called consolidation was upon Georgia; it promised rural schools as good as those in the cities. Consolidation depended upon transportation, and transportation depended upon good roads. A good roads movement, just beginning in Georgia, would accelerate with the coming of the automobile.

Growth of Higher Education

After the Civil War, the State University and Emory, Mercer, Wesleyan and other private colleges reopened. In 1867, Atlanta University, the first such institution in the state for black students, was chartered by the American Missionary Association. Like that of the common schools, the growth of higher education in Georgia would suffer the influences of protracted economic depression, popular indifference, and racism. At the same time, agricultural, commercial, industrial, and common school interests helped initiate a type of higher education that departed from the narrow liberal arts curricula of the antebellum period.

In 1872, the state government took advantage of the Morrill Act, the federal land-grant college act of 1862, to establish a Georgia State College of Agriculture and Mechanic Arts at Athens as part of the university. In the same year, the state acquired the Medical College of Augusta, privately chartered in 1828, and in 1874 made it a department of the university. In 1873, an agricultural college was opened at Dahlonega, to be followed in a few years by others in south Georgia. Thus did Georgia take the first tentative steps toward a system of higher education.

Given the prohibitory language of the Constitution of 1877, if the state were to expand public higher education, it would have to do so under the provision for one state university. And, because the educationally conservative university at Athens, also known as Franklin College, did not readily respond to the state's need for persons with professional and vocational training, over the next half century several varieties of branch institutions that tried to meet the educational needs of industrialization would be grafted onto the University of Georgia. Some of the branch colleges were of little consequence, withered, and died. But, others established new directions of growth in Georgia higher education.

In 1885, the General Assembly, prodded by commercial and industrial interests, established the Georgia School of Technology (later Georgia Institute of Technology). Atlanta was chosen for its site, and in 1888 "Tech" began offering a curriculum oriented toward practical subjects in science, technology, and industry. In a few years this "branch" had virtually a separate identity.

One year later, 1889, the legislature created another branch institution of vocational nature—and the first state college for women, at Milledgeville. The Georgia Normal and Industrial School (later Georgia State College for Women) was to prepare young women for industrial occupations "consistent with feminine refinement and modesty" and for teaching school.

The great need for trained school teachers resulted in a third major addition to the university, the State Normal School at Athens. Operated as summer institutes only in 1892-1894, the Normal School commenced full-time operations in 1895. Although planned primarily for men (in light of the Milledgeville school's existence), the Athens normal school was immediately dominated by female students. For its first 15 years, it offered a two-year program, some of it at the high-school level.

The need for teachers counted greatly in the founding of higher education for blacks. When the American Missionary Association chartered Atlanta University in 1867, the title "university" was more a vision than a reality: the school began in 1869 with normal and preparatory departments and added a college department in 1872. In 1876, six Atlanta University students received the first bachelor's degrees ever awarded to blacks in Georgia.

Atlanta became home to other black institutions that would grow from preparatory and normal school beginnings into true colleges. Like Atlanta University, they were sustained mainly by private philanthropy.

Clark College	1869	Freedmen's Aid Society of the Methodist Episcopal Church (North)
Morehouse College	1879	American Baptist Home Mission Society
Spelman College (women)	1881	American Baptist Home Mission Society
Morris Brown College	1885	African Methodist Episcopal Church

Over the next half century, these colleges and Atlanta University would move closer together and establish Atlanta as the leading center of black higher education in the United States.

Until 1890, the state government almost completely ignored the higher education of blacks. To prevent the state from losing its claim on the federal land-grant fund, the General Assembly transferred $8,000 of it each year between 1874-87 to Atlanta University. This practice ended when several white students were discovered to be enrolled there.

In 1890, Congress passed a second Morrill Act which made available proceeds from the sale of federal lands. It provided that the states had to use Morrill funds for the higher education of blacks as well as whites. As Georgia's existing state colleges admitted no black students, an institution for blacks had to be established. In 1891, the Georgia State Industrial College for Colored Youths (later Savannah State College) was opened as a branch of the university and the designated land-grant college for blacks. By the turn of the century, it had departments for normal, agricultural, and industrial training.

Through the 1880s and 1890s the university at Athens found itself under regular attack from agricultural and church interests in the state. Franklin College had maintained its classical orientation and given only perfunctory attention to the "agricultural and mechanic arts," even though almost two-thirds of its annual income came from land-grant funds. Its alleged mismanagement of those funds to support the liberal arts curriculum, and not the state agriculture college on its campus, led to proposals to take the agriculture college and thus the land-grant funds away from Athens.

Meanwhile, legislation of 1881 that provided for free tuition at the university and its branches, and proposals for an annual maintenance appropriation from the legislature roused the state's denominational colleges who feared prospective students would be siphoned off by the university. The leading spokesman for the church colleges was Warren A. Candler, president of Emory College. Like his predecessor, Atticus G. Haygood, Candler espoused public schools for universal education and denominational schools for higher education. He suggested that the state should spend its funds exclusively to put the common schools on their feet and that "the University is old enough to stand alone." Candler also argued the superiority of Christian higher education over the variety dispensed by the university at Athens where "now a Mussulman or an agnostic may be a professor." Denominational detractors also depicted the university as an unchristian place where students were given to "hugging" (dancing) and "social wine drinking."

Until the turn of the century, these attacks kept the university at bay, but in 1899 it found its own champion in Walter B. Hill, elected chancellor in that year. Hill was an outspoken progressive who publicly campaigned for better common schools for blacks and whites. He was also a Methodist and prohibitionist and managed to quell the sectarian attacks against the university. Hill obtained from the legislature an appropriation of $300,000 (double the amount received during the entire nineteenth century) and secured the annual maintenance allowance that had eluded his predecessors. Hill died in 1905, but with money from the state and from philanthropist George Foster Peabody, he had launched the university's first large-scale building program. He had set in motion the founding of schools of pharmacy, forestry, and education that in addition to a restructured agriculture school would move the Athens institution from small college status (enrollment in 1899-1900 was 129) to that of a true university. By 1918, schools of commerce and journalism were added, and female students were admitted.

About the same time, another university was rising in Atlanta. Under the auspices of the Methodist Episcopal Church, South, and with a $1 million gift from Coca-Cola magnate Asa G. Candler, brother of Warren Candler, Emory College of Oxford, Georgia, became Emory University of Atlanta, Georgia. By 1919, the new university was fully operating with professional schools of theology, law, medicine, and business administration, as well as undergraduate and graduate schools. Emory quickly rivalled the University of Georgia for preeminence in the state.

The half century following the Civil War also saw the establishment or reestablishment of more than a dozen private colleges. In 1871, Mercer University commenced operations at a new campus in Macon and eventually became the leading Baptist institution in the state. Shortly afterward, Oglethorpe University moved to Atlanta, floundered, only to be revived in the same city in 1913. Most of the new schools began as less than collegiate institutions. A good example is Agnes Scott College. Founded in 1889 as Decatur Female Seminary by local Presbyterians, Scott graduated its first college class in 1906. In 1907 it became the first higher education institution in Georgia to be accredited as a college by the Southern Association of Colleges and Preparatory Schools.

The Progressive Era (1900-1920)

In the history of the United States, the years from the turn of the century to the United States entry into World War I are usually called the "Progressive Era." With a general aim of making a more just, more moral, and more democratic society, progressives attacked a myriad of social abuses and problems and brought reform to business, politics and government, and other institutions. For some reformers inside and outside the South, the condition of children and education in the South were special concerns. Fortuitously for Georgia, the progressive spirit sweeping the nation coincided with a period of relative prosperity within the state; the years 1900-1920 brought notable developments in local and state school taxation, public high schools, compulsory attendance, adult literacy, vocational education, and state government regulation of teachers and schools.

The improvement of education in Georgia had antecedents in the state's own populist movement of the 1890s and was supported by a rising economy. Most of all, it traced to a new phase of philanthropic activity dating from the first meeting in 1898 of the Conference for Education in the South, an association composed of educators, clergymen, businessmen, and industrialists from the North and South. At its fifth annual meeting, Hoke Smith, perhaps Georgia's leading progressive and in a few years to be governor and later U.S. senator, addressed in familiar terms the problem in bringing universal education to the southern states: a sparse rural population, relative poverty compared to the North, and a biracial society.

> . . .the rural school question is the great problem. Between eight-ninths and nine-tenths of our people live in the country. . . .
>
> The sparsity of the population, bringing with it an enormous increase of expense, is the most serious problem connected with our rural schools. Let me illustrate our difficulties as compared

to those of Massachusetts by calling attention to the difference of our conditions in this regard. Massachusetts has eight thousand square miles of territory. . .Georgia has fifty-eight thousand square miles. The people of Massachusetts are worth five times as much per capita as the people of Georgia. The population of Massachusetts is four hundred thousand larger than Georgia, yet we have two hundred thousand more children. . . . Massachusetts can build a school to every square mile and have sixty-five children to put in it. Georgia to every square mile has eleven children, and of these six are white and five are black. This requires two separate schools. Yes, separate schools for whites and blacks, and this question with us is settled. . . .

From the Conference for Education in the South emerged the General Education Board (GEB), arguably the most influential nongovernment agency for education change in the South. For over a half century, the GEB directly nourished the growth of education as it disbursed the munificence of John D. Rockefeller. By 1932, Rockefeller would give the GEB over $129 million for schools and colleges outside as well as inside the South.

GEB grants were intended to help people help themselves and supported practically any kind of educational project. One of its first grants went to Hancock County, Georgia, to extend the school term. The county superintendent, M.L. Duggan, faced with the constitutional restriction on local taxation, had devised a subscription plan based on voluntary contributions that extended to 6½ months the term of every school in the county for every child of both races. Wanting a full eight-month term for his schools, Duggan applied to the GEB saying, "We have done all that we can; now will you help us?"

Money went to state agencies as well. For example, when in 1911 the Georgia Department of Education set up its Division of Negro Education, it did so with GEB's promise to finance the division with an annual appropriation of $3,500. The GEB made grants for school and college buildings; it subsidized college faculty salaries in order to inaugurate new curricula; it gave scholarships for advanced study; and it underwrote public campaigns for educational improvement.

GEB's contribution of private money to government agencies to provide public services followed a pattern established in the previous century by the Peabody and Slater funds. It was not uncommon for local schools to be financed by a mix of public revenue and private money. For example, in 1915 the Ben Hill County Training School (for black children) had an income of $1,775 that included $750 from the state and county, $500 from the Slater Fund, and $475 from the Baptist Association.

In addition to the GEB, other educational philanthropies were founded during the Progressive Era. Especially influential in Georgia were the Anna T. Jeanes Fund and the Julius Rosenwald Fund. The former provided specially trained supervising teachers to help black teachers overcome their deficiencies in general education and preparation to teach. In 1910, 70 percent of Georgia's approximately 4,000 black teachers had less than an eighth-grade education. The "Jeanes Teachers" also helped secure the attendance of black children, support of local white officials, start of health programs, and better maintenance of school buildings. Better buildings for black schools were the special legacy of the Rosenwald Fund. In 1912, schools for black children were most often held in churches, lodge halls, and tenant shacks. To remedy this situation, the Rosenwald Fund provided matching money to build modern schoolhouses for blacks in rural areas. In Georgia alone, in the 10 years from 1917 to 1927, 261 Rosenwald schools were constructed.

Local Taxation Obtained

One of the GEB's initial priorities was to help southern educators obtain local school taxation. Explaining to the National Education Associa-

Into the 1940s, schools for black children depended on private contributions of labor, materials, and money to augment meagre public funds.

tion the board's formation, board secretary Wallace Buttrick noted that one of the hindrances to universal education peculiar to the South was "a dislike of direct or local taxation." Dependence on a state fund, as in Georgia, resulted in very poor schools and short terms—certainly from the lack of money but even more from the attitude that "what we don't pay for we don't care for."

In 1903, the push for local taxation began in earnest in Georgia. The General Assembly passed a constitutional amendment that eased the prohibitory procedure by which a local population might be permitted to tax itself for schools. Then with funds from the GEB, Chancellor Hill, bishop and ex-president of Emory College Warren A. Candler, Hoke Smith, and other influentials led a statewide campaign for voter ratification. The amendment was ratified in 1904 and implemented by law in 1905.

Reaction to the new law was varied. By the end of 1905, people in Hancock, Fulton, and Monroe counties voted to tax themselves in order to have better schools and longer terms throughout their counties. By 1909, 21 counties had countywide local taxation. In many other counties, the peculiar dislike for local taxes came to the fore and no taxes were voted. Tax elections were hard fought, as the school commissioner for Warren County attested: "We are anxious to put our county in the local tax column, but while we were agitating the matter our courthouse was burned and our people became very much disturbed on the high tax question." In a third group of counties, people only in sections of each county—several hundred subdistricts—voted in favor of local taxation.

The new law was flawed. It provided for subcounty tax districts so that residents of this district might vote to tax themselves while residents of that district did not. In many cases, local officials gerrymandered tax district boundaries in order to isolate the taxable wealth of certain sections of a county at the expense of other sections. The law also encouraged the proliferation of municipal systems, again to fence off taxable wealth—especially railroad, utility, and other corporate wealth—from poor rural sections. By 1909, Georgia had a miscellany of about 150 independent and semi-independent local systems as well as a system of common schools supported by state and local revenues in some places but only by state funds in those districts unwilling to vote local taxes.

In sum, the move to local taxation meant better schools and longer terms in many communities in Georgia. But it also furthered the inequalities that already existed between the schools of the cities and towns and the schools of the rural areas.

The High School Established

When the Progressive Era began, state law provided for public elementary schools and a public university, but no public high schools. For white children there were public high schools in the cities, where only 16 percent of the people lived, and private high schools scattered around the state. For black children there were a few private high schools and, in Athens, one public high school. Thus, for most of Georgia's children the opportunity for schooling ended after seven years, about when they reached age 13.

Only a handful of the institutions called high schools measured up to the term. Some consisted of one teacher offering high school subjects to a few advanced pupils. There were no standards for high school work and no standards upon which to admit college freshmen. As a result, most Georgia colleges had preparatory departments to get students ready to do college work.

In 1903, Chancellor Hill moved to eliminate the four-year gap in public education. He employed Joseph S. Stewart to devise a plan for accrediting high schools and to supervise the founding of public high schools accredited for college preparation. In 1904-5 Stewart surveyed the existing high schools and found only 11 four-year schools worthy of accreditation. These seven public and four private schools graduated a total of 94 students that term. Stewart also accredited 39 three-year public high schools. Thus began the University of Georgia's program for accrediting high schools, the first of its kind in the South. In 1929, the function was assumed by the Georgia Department of Education.

To build a system of public high schools required that several barriers be overcome: no state revenue (or local revenue outside the cities) was appropriated for high schools; few qualified high school teachers were employed; little popular support for public secondary education existed. While the state constitution's restriction against local taxation for elementary schooling had been eased, the ban against county and state funds for high schools remained. Stewart hit the road campaigning for high schools, urging people in towns and cities to tax themselves for them, and calling for state funding. From 1905 to 1909, about 60 high school buildings were erected in municipalities at a cost of $1,870,000. A constitutional amendment in 1910 lifted the ban on county taxes for high schools and another in 1912 made the high school a part of the state school system. In the latter year, the legislature enacted a bill to require high school teachers to hold a state license.

From the outset, few qualified teachers were available for the high schools. (Many common school teachers didn't have even a high school education.) In 1903, with philanthropic help, Chancellor Hill organized the first university summer school expressly for teachers. Stewart was its director for many years. Five years later the university made elementary and high school teaching a major focus with the opening of its Peabody School of Education. Hand-in-hand with teacher education came higher standards for licensure. In 1912, the State Board of Education instituted state licensure based on examination and completion of normal school or college work.

Stewart worked single-mindedly (until his death in 1934), to establish high schools in the hearts and minds of the people as well as in the law. He guided local school boards in setting up the schools; he helped them hire teachers, organize courses of study, and choose textbooks. He set up high school associations of teachers, administrators, school board members, and lay citizens which, under his guidance, sponsored all manner of exhibitions, festivals, and contests. Thousands of boys and girls competed at school, district, and state meets for books, medals, and other prizes. Ten years after his initial appointment, Stewart enthusiastically reported:

> The associations have developed track athletics throughout the state, have revived declamation training, improved the piano instruction, cultivated essay writing, improved the spelling, organized statewide debates, and created a loyal school spirit that is a pleasure to experience. It is remarkable how in many towns the annual meets have enlisted the interest of the business men of the community in the high school. They encourage the students while training and accompany them to the district meets.

By 1920, the high school was already becoming a center of social life in rural communities and the support it engendered spread to the elementary schools. Although Stewart's original charge was to establish high schools for college preparation, from the outset he pushed school boards to include manual training; and the district associations made cooking, sewing, and shopwork exhibitions part of their programs, too. After passage of federal legislation providing funds for secondary vocational education, high schools became even more attractive to rural Georgians.

Far-reaching was the effect of two acts cosponsored by Georgia's U.S. Senator, Hoke Smith: the 1914 Smith-Lever Act and the 1917 Smith-Hughes Act. The former aimed to increase farm efficiency and improve rural life by extending to country people the best information in agriculture and home management. Through demonstrations, short courses, and printed materials a teaching corps of agricultural specialists and home economists established in effect an out-of-school system of education. The extension service, organized cooperatively among the federal government, the state colleges, and the local community, helped to break down traditional rural apathy toward education by revealing its practical benefits.

The Smith-Hughes Act of 1917 provided for teaching vocations— agriculture, trades, industries, and home economics—in secondary schools. This marked the first important federal aid to secondary education. The act authorized money for college training of vocational teachers and reimbursements to the state for the salaries they were paid. In Georgia's rural high schools, where few teachers were adequately trained or paid, the "Smith-Hughes teachers" were often the schools' best teachers and naturally rose to prominence in school adminstration. (After Smith left the Senate, Georgia's Walter F. George took up the vocational education cause, sponsoring between 1929 and 1946 four major acts which greatly expanded the federal role in vocational education and, incidentally, helped to solidify the vocational emphasis in Georgia public education.)

Compulsory Attendance Stumbles

One of the most controversial school issues was compulsory attendance. As early as 1852, Massachusetts had required parents to send their

Agricultural education, 1950. A county extension agent with two boys enrolled in a calf-raising program.

children to school. Most other states had fallen into line around the turn of the century. By 1912, only Georgia and Mississippi did not compel school attendance. Neither did they have child labor laws.

Nationally, the impetus for compulsion came from three sources:

1. the need to train youth for industrial society (and protect youth against industrial society, i.e., child labor)
2. the need to instill in youth traditional values, habits, and outlooks of the community, especially in an increasingly multicultural society
3. the need to Americanize immigrant youth

Georgia, however, had little industry for which to train. Georgia's rural youth, who were rather isolated from the main currents of American life, weren't likely to have their values challenged by competing cultures. And, the state had practically no immigrant children to Americanize.

Moreover, advocates of compulsory schooling faced the same old "Negro question." In 1910, only 43 percent of Georgia's black children went to school; 62 percent of the white children did. Compulsion, said its opponents, would bring hoards of black youngsters into the system, a burden white taxpayers could not possibly bear. (In 1910, 45 percent of the state's population was black.) Also, the labor of black children was a concern not only to black families but also to white landowners. In 1913, Joseph Stewart wrote, "The question still remains, shall the whites remain in darkness because bringing them the light lets it shine on the black also? God pity us, if it is so."

In 1914 the General Assembly passed a child labor law and in 1916 a compulsory attendance law. The latter required 8- to 14-year-olds to attend school for four months per year. But it excused children who lived more than three miles from school and those needed for seasonal agricultural work, and as there was no way to enforce the law, many children remained unschooled. (Not until 1945 did Georgia pass a law that effectively compelled school attendance.)

State Control Grows

With the growth of public education during the Progressive Era came a greater measure of state regulation and supervision of local schools. In 1909, in his *Annual Report* to the General Assembly, State School Commissioner Jere M. Pound protested the state's lack of power to organize and systematize public education.

> Atlanta, for instance, or Macon or Savannah, in all school affairs is as independent of the supervision, direction and control of the State Department of Education as is Timbuctoo. Millions of dollars are disbursed annually through this department and, at times, its

agency is not even recognized by so much as the courtesy of a receipt or a reply.

In 1911, the General Assembly passed legislation giving the State Board of Education broader authority for supervising all public schools in the state. School facilities, courses of study, textbook selection, teacher education and certification, and the qualifications and responsibilities of county school superintendents[2] would be subject to rules and regulations made by the board and carried out by the Department of Education. That same year, the state employed its first three school supervisors "to aid generally in supervising, systematizing and improving the schools of the State under the direction of the State Superintendent of Schools." The superintendent, M.L. Brittain, and his supervisors established standards against which a school's teachers, building, equipment, grounds, teacher's salary, length of term, and associated activities were measured. Schools that measured up were designated "Standard Schools" by the state and honored with a diploma and publication of their status. Those that didn't measure up were shown how they could.

Liberalizing amendments to the state constitution, successful local tax elections, incorporation of public high schools into the common school system, and other advances were carried out during the period, 1900-1920, that reflected a progressive spirit nationwide and relatively good times in Georgia. A booming cotton economy enabled many rural Georgians to have better houses, better roads, and better schools. In this heady atmosphere, education reformers were able to make solid the public school foundation in the state.

In 1919, a package of education reform legislation enacted by the General Assembly resolved a jumble of often-conflicting laws into a school code and brought some uniformity to finances and operations. It authorized local spending for pupil transportation, state bonuses for consolidation of one- and two-teacher schools, and local bond issues for schoolhouse construction. Most significantly, the law required for the first time that all counties levy taxes for schools. In short, by 1920 the system was in place.

Post-War and Depression Years (1921-1945)

The relative prosperity of the Progressive Era and World War I years was brief. With the war over, the worldwide demand for cotton disappeared. Worse yet, the boll weevil spread across the state. As thousands of farms were abandoned, the taxable wealth in rural school districts dwindled.

---

2. The 1911 law uniformly changed the title "commissioner" to "superintendent."

By the mid-1920s, the disparity among rich and poor districts widened. Approximately 50 percent of Georgia's taxable wealth was concentrated in 10 counties. The move to local taxation heightened this disparity and average teacher salaries, set by local school boards, ranged from $292 to $1,418 annually.

Determining the state and local share of public school financing was (and remains) a vexing problem. In the first two decades of the century, "localization" of funding was advocated by many educators as the key to building local commitment to public schools. And, in Georgia, where the schools had originally been imposed from the top down, from Atlanta, the state-local split was reversed by 1930. By then, however, the state had already moved in a small way to shore up the poorest districts. As Figure 1 shows, the state government would eventually reassume the lion's share of school funding.

In the mid-1920s, the Georgia Education Association led a campaign for equalization. Based on the progressive idea that even the poorest districts should have basic facilities and length-of-term equal to those of better-off districts, equalization in some form was already a feature in the financing of schools in other states. In 1926, the General Assembly passed an equalization act which earmarked a tax on motor fuels for distribution to local districts on the basis of need. With this act, the state's apportionment of school funds was determined at least partly by local tax valuations, not just numbers of children in the districts. By 1928, the new tax realized $1 million.

In that year, State Superintendent M.L. Duggan observed that in addition to the new tax, the county schools, wherein 66 percent of the

Figure 1: Georgia School Support from State, 1900-1960 (Percentage)

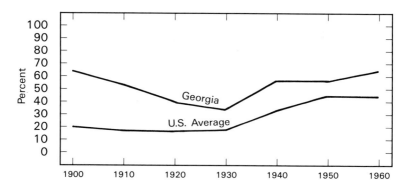

Source: National Education Association, *Education in the States: Nationwide Development Since 1900,* 1969.

state's children were enrolled, had three sources of support "supposed to guarantee state protection, county pride and local interest." They were as follows: a direct apportionment from the state fund, about $5 per child; the required county levy; and a permissive district levy "wherever public demand for education is strong enough to influence the required number of voters." The yield from these three sources was from $10 to $40 per child enrolled. In 1928, Georgia's per capita expenditure for education was $2.77—behind every one of its neighbors including Mississippi and South Carolina and compared to the United States average of $4.37.

By 1930, the rest of the nation was slipping into depression. The rural areas continued to be among the hardest hit. Georgia, with a farm population of 1,418,000—only Texas and North Carolina had more farmers—stood at the bottom of most measures of economic status. The farmers' schools suffered the most. As farmers, merchants, and country banks failed in order, local levies failed and school districts went into the red. It meant premature closing of thousands of rural elementary schools. Some districts paid teachers in scrip redeemable with local merchants, but many teachers taught for months without any pay.

Though school conditions in general were lamentable, they were especially so for black children. By 1933, the enrollment of the school-age population reached 94 percent for whites and 84 percent for blacks. Of those enrolled, average daily attendance was 76 percent for whites and 74 percent for blacks. In the elementary grades, the average pupil/teacher ratio was 38:1 in white schools and 50:1 in black schools. For the school year, 1933-34, black teachers were paid an average $278 or just 40 percent of the average white teacher salary of $695.

The depression brought a reversal to the trend to localization in school funding and a greater role for state government in school operations. Already by 1930, the State Department of Education had overseers for rural schools, black schools, high schools, vocational education, teacher certification, and schoolhouse construction. Gradually, control over public school was moving from the cities and counties to the state. The gross inequities in teacher salaries and school facilities, and the inability of poor districts to operate more than six months brought local school officials, teachers, and civic leaders together to pressure the legislature to shift the tax burden back to the state and provide state minimums in school terms and teacher salaries. After protracted political battles during the regime of Gov. Eugene Talmadge, the school legislation was finally passed in 1937 with the support of Gov. E.D. Rivers. The landmark "Seven Months School Law" not only guaranteed state funding for a minimum seven-month term in all counties and a minimum state teacher salary, but also free textbooks for all students and state

By 1940, increased public school support allowed some rural children to enjoy such things as rhythm bands and hot lunches.

funds for pupil transportation. From 1930 to 1940, the state's share of school costs increased from 36 percent to 57 percent. Naturally, these developments brought a greater penetration by the state Department of Education into local school affairs. With state money came new state standards and enforcement procedures regarding teacher qualifications, textbook adoption, and school buses and bus drivers.

Higher Education Gets Organized

During the depths of the depression, the situation in public higher education had also been chaotic. The University of Georgia, Georgia School of Technology, and 24 other institutions, all nominally branches of the university, but some of them no more than boarding high schools for rural youth, competed willy-nilly for appropriations from the legislature. To remedy the situation, a single higher education agency, the Board of Regents of the University System of Georgia, was created as part of the 1931 reorganization of state government by Gov. Richard B. Russell, Jr. The Board of Regents was empowered to create, operate, and allocate funds to public colleges from a lump sum appropriation from the General Assembly. By 1933, a pared-down system of 12 white colleges (including one university) and 3 black colleges enrolled 8,035 students.

Like the public schools, the public colleges continued to suffer underfinancing. In 1939-40, Georgia's per capita appropriation for higher education was $3.83, the lowest in the nation.

Moreover, public higher education was plunged into crisis upon Eugene Talmadge's return to the governorship, 1941-43. Vowing to rid the university system of anyone advocating "communism or racial equality," Talmadge demanded that the Board of Regents, of which the governor was then an ex officio member, fire certain educators. When the board refused, Talmadge replaced several members and obtained the removal of 10 educators.

Governor Talmadge's repression of academic freedom brought an upheaval in state politics and government. In December 1941—four days before Pearl Harbor—the Southern Association of Colleges and Schools voted to end the accreditation of Georgia's 10 public colleges for whites. In 1942, comparing Talmadge to the dictators America was fighting overseas, Georgia Attorney General Ellis Arnall trounced the governor in his re-election bid after a campaign that focused on the higher education crisis. In 1943, under Arnall, the governor was removed from membership on the Board of Regents and its legal structure was changed to minimize political interference in its operations. Changes made in the university system plus a doubling of the average income of Georgians during the war years promised better public higher education in the postwar years.

After World War II (1945-1963)

The immediate postwar years saw major changes in the organization and financing of the state's public schools. In 1945, a new state constitution eliminated the 1,257 sub-county tax districts which fostered inequalities *within* counties. The county school board was made the sole education agency (except in certain municipalities), with all fiscal and management authority for elementary and secondary schools. The existing independent municipal systems were allowed to continue, but no new ones could be created. The new constitution also opened the way to a 12-grade system.

After the war, the state continued to finance only seven elementary and four high school grades. Some city and county systems had used local taxes in the 1930s to add a 12th grade. In 1947, the General Assembly authorized counties to spend state funds and use the free textbook program in a 12th grade. However, as it appropriated no state money for the additional teachers and classrooms required by the expansion, only the wealthier counties could begin the transition to a 12-grade system immediately.

The plan for a 12th grade, the impending enrollment of postwar "baby boomers," a state survey that publicized deplorable conditions in rural school districts, and the first rumblings of the civil rights movement provided impetus for a greater leap forward in state funding for schools. The 1947 *Survey of Public Education of Less Than College Grade in Georgia* found that there were too many schools, especially small ones; rural schoolhouses were often dilapidated; equipment was obsolete and supplies were missing. Moreover, most local systems did not have the financial capacity to construct new facilities.

Separate but unequal was still the rule: the survey found that conditions were worse in black schools than white schools. In 1947-48, of 2,647 black schools 1,566 were one-teacher schools, while only 192 one-teacher white schools remained. Average costs per pupil in average daily attendance for that year were $126 for whites and $55 for blacks. Proposals to spend more money on the education of black children would soon gain politicians' support; in some cases for the wrong reason: to head off challenge to the notion that separate schools were equal schools.

In 1949, the General Assembly enacted "The Georgia Minimum Foundation Program for Education Act." The Minimum Foundation Program for Education (MFPE) guaranteed the school term at nine months and raised standards for buildings, equipment, transportation, curriculum, and instruction. It included a new equalization scheme for allocating state funds to local districts based on each district's ability to support itself. Such factors as local retail sales, property income, utilities, and effective buying power went into determining what a local district's fair share of school costs should be.

To finance the state share of the MFPE, a 3 percent sales tax was enacted in 1951. This measure had been proposed since the early 1930s, but couldn't get passed until the relatively prosperous years following World War II and support came forth from the state's dominant political faction led by Herman Talmadge. With the new tax in hand and the Georgia economy on the move, the state appropriation jumped from $50 million in 1950-51 to $87 million in 1951-52. Average teacher salaries were boosted by $500 the first year as the state's contribution for teacher salaries was equalized for black teachers and white teachers.

Also in 1951, the General Assembly created the State School Building Authority to issue revenue bonds for school building construction. By this device, the state constitution's prohibition against the state government issuing bonds was side-stepped. The building program made possible by this new source of funds, plus increased pupil transportation outlays under the MFPE, brought further consolidation and all but the elimination of the one-room country school during the 1950s. In 10 years, the state system was handling 200,000 more pupils, most of them bused, with 10,000 more teachers in 2,000 fewer schools (see Table 1). New consolidated schools featured not only well-heated and well-lit classrooms, and sanitary facilities, but also cafeterias, libraries, laboratories, and sometimes gymnasiums—rare luxuries in the 1940s.

By 1960, the state's share of school financing, vis-'a-vis the local share, was reinstated to its 1900 level: 64 percent. The MFPE required, on the average, only a 15 percent local share, but even that amount was avoided by some counties. The problem was not merely low taxable wealth but local indifference, and even opposition to school improvement. Lack of uniformity in assessing property taxes, which were the main source of local revenue, and the law's lack of penalties for not paying the prescribed local share, hampered operation of the MFPE. Following the 1954 Supreme Court ruling, *Brown v. Board of Education,* the politics of "massive resistance" further impeded progress, but nevertheless the MFPE helped close the gap between rich and poor districts, black and white schools.

The New Imperative (1964-1984)

The publication of the Sibley Commission report in April 1960, the admission of the first black students, Charlayne Hunter and Hamilton Holmes, to the University of Georgia in January 1961, and the enrollment of black pupils in formerly white Atlanta schools in August 1961, signalled the end of "massive resistance" but not the end of the dual system of education. Through the 1960s, the pace of school desegregation was agonizingly slow and resulted in only small numbers of blacks in classrooms with whites. But the biracial feature of Georgia society was beginning to change.

The traditional Georgia society was changing in other ways that held vast implications for public education. The census of 1960 showed

Table 1: School Growth and Consolidation in Georgia, 1949-1950 through 1959-1960

School Year	Average Daily Attendance	Pupils Transported	Schools	Teachers
1949-50	619,846	246,903	3,906	23,766
1951-52	637,529	290,537	3,290	26,153
1953-54	705,712	336,205	2,998	28,081
1955-56	747,012	374,933	2,480	29,687
1957-58	770,959	408,701	2,119	31,326
1959-60	820,995	436,079	1,930	33,302

Source: Georgia Department of Education, *Georgia Education: Past, Present, Future, 1972.*

1985. *At its bicentennial, the University of Georgia honors its first black students, Charlayne Hunter-Gault and Hamilton Holmes (with University President Fred Davison). They were admitted in 1961.*

that the population shift renewed after World War II had resulted for the first time in the number of urban Georgians equalling the number of rural Georgians. Also, the state's traditional low-level manufacturing- and agriculture-oriented economy was shifting toward a complex service-oriented economy. What is more, the nation was entering the "space age," and Americans were looking to the South and West for economic opportunity. The state's provision for public education that had scarcely served the needs of a largely agrarian-rural society appeared even less adequate in the new order of things.

As it slowly freed itself from the burden of maintaining a dual school system, Georgia embarked on an expansion of education that would require tripling expenditures. The imperative for the expansion was clear. In their ability to hold students from the 8th through the 12th grade, Georgia schools ranked 50th in the nation. And, according to the 1960 census, while some 22 percent of the people in the United States had fewer than eight years of schooling, in Georgia 41 percent had fewer than eight years. In the percentage of its college-age population (18-21 years) enrolled in college, Georgia ranked next to last among the states.

Concerted action to improve Georgia's educational standing began with the election of Carl Sanders to the governorship in 1962. Sanders had campaigned on educational improvement and in 1963 obtained from the legislature authorization for the most comprehensive study of public education—kindergarten through graduate school—ever undertaken in the state.

The report of the Governor's Commission to Improve Education, *Educating Georgia's People: Investment in the Future,* stressed the tie between economic opportunity and educational opportunity. It noted that Georgia's per capita income ranked among the lowest in the nation and opined that Georgians were being robbed of the chance to compete in the national marketplace for good jobs. "This is due to lack of enough years of school for many—but for many others it is the poor quality of schooling they do get." The commission said the state was hurt by not being able to attract well-paying jobs. Indeed, through the 1950s, the bulk of nonagricultural jobs developed in Georgia were in low-wage, low-skill manufacturing. If Georgians were to have a shot at the high-paying jobs of "space-age industries," they would first have to have a higher level of educational attainment. The cost? Financial support for education in the coming decade would have to increase threefold.

Deficiencies in elementary and secondary financing remained despite improvements obtained through the MFPE of 1949. The General Assembly responded in 1964 with a revised MFPE that included a new cost-sharing formula and requirements for uniform property assessments. There were also new taxes on alcohol and tobacco. Money was targeted for more teachers, higher salaries, instructional materials, a statewide educational television network, and a Governor's Honors Program for talented students. Between 1963 and 1967, appropriations for county school systems rose by 80 percent. By 1967, capital outlays provided for 22 new vocational schools and some 6,000 new classrooms. By 1968, public high schools graduated 17,111 more students than they had in 1963, the 11th best increase in the nation. Also by 1968, about 14 percent of Georgia's black pupils were enrolled in predominantly white schools.

Ending the Dual System

Desegregation had proceeded slowly, almost imperceptibly at first, since August 1961 when under court order Atlanta enrolled the first black pupils in formerly white schools. Three years later, Atlanta began teacher desegregation. In 1964, 10 years after *Brown v. Board of Education,* only 12 Georgia districts had token integration and only 0.4 percent of black pupils were in school with white pupils. For those 10 years, the federal courts had shouldered the responsibility for desegregation.

Congress and the federal executive branch became meaningfully involved in school desegregation with passage of the Civil Rights Act of 1964. It provided for witholding federal funds from segregated schools, charged the Department of Health, Education, and Welfare (HEW) with enforcing that provision, and authorized the U.S. Attorney General to file desegregation suits where there was a private complaint. With passage of the Elementary and Secondary Education Act of 1965, which made huge outlays of federal funds available to local districts, the threat of "withdrawal of funds" became a more serious matter to local school officials. A district not in compliance stood to lose substantial money. In 1967, 151 of Georgia's 195 districts (only 189 of which had black and white pupils) had desegregation proposals approved by HEW. But in that year only about 9 percent of black pupils were actually enrolled in desegregated schools, a figure that increased to 14 percent by 1968.

Resistance to desegregation in Georgia was stiffened somewhat by the General Assembly's election of Lester Maddox to the governorship in 1967. An avowed segregationist, Maddox publicly decried the federal government's desegregation-related activities, counseled defiance of federal orders, and resurrected "massive resistance" era proposals for state aid to private schools.

The "gradual phase" in school desegregation ended with federal court rulings in *Alexander v. Holmes* (1969) and *Swan v. Charlotte-Mecklenburg County* (1971). *De jure* segregation had collapsed, but *de facto* segregation, based on residential patterns, school building locations, attendance zones, and other local district practices, continued. To this point, the burden of desegregation was placed on black pupils. The *Holmes* ruling transferred the burden to the local district authorities: dual systems had to be terminated immediately, using the best means toward that end. The *Swan* ruling said in effect that busing could be the means required to eliminate racially identifiable schools within a district.

Busing became the desegregation issue of the 1970s. Across Georgia parents were furious over having their children bused past neighborhood schools to attend schools perhaps miles away. In Clarke County, Supt. Charles P. McDaniel (later to become state superintendent) put things in perspective: "For half a century we have been busing black students past white schools and vice versa to maintain segregation. Now we are busing to eliminate segregation." By 1980, about 40 percent of black pupils were in predominantly white schools.

As the dual systems were eliminated, new problems emerged. Black principals were often "demoted" to assistant principal or classroom teacher. Black teachers were not rehired at the end of the year. And within school buildings there was often segregation into racially identifiable classes.

Advancement in Higher Education

Real as the elementary and secondary improvement was, the most visible advance was in higher education. In 1960-61, the University System of Georgia enrolled 25,129 full-time students. The college attendance rate of Georgians was about one-half the national average. The Governor's Commission urged expansion of the University System to provide equal and universal opportunity for education beyond high school and to meet the enrollment of the first of the "baby boomers" who would reach age 18 in 1964. A specific goal was to locate at least a junior college within 35 miles of 98 percent of the population. By 1976, 12 new junior colleges were added to the system, and with the enlargement of existing institutions, 94,488 full-time students were enrolled. Figure 2 shows the distribution of system institutions 10 years later.

The Governor's Commission was as concerned with the "apex" of higher education as with its base. It noted that as recently as 1960-61, the University System of Georgia awarded only 24 doctorates (not counting M.D.s and D.V.M.s). "The development of graduate education and research," said the commission report, "should be given high priority in the years ahead." Underfinanced, understaffed, ill-equipped, and poorly housed, the state's public research institutions—the University of Georgia, Georgia Institute of Technology, and Medical College of Georgia—were by most accounts definitely not first class.

Sanders lined up the active support of the state's business and political elite for money for high-quality graduate education, a task far easier than getting support for public schools. The state's investment in higher education rose spectacularly in the 1960s and 1970s (concurrently with a rise in federal money for higher education). Most spectacular of all was the growth of graduate and research programs (see Table 2). With money in hand, the University System of Georgia could offer salaries and facilities to lure top research and teaching faculty from other states. As Georgia's standing in higher education improved, research monies and graduate students were increasingly drawn to Georgia.

Table 2: University System Growth in Georgia, Selected Years

	State Appropriation	Research Expenditures	Fulltime Enrollment	Doctorates Awarded
1960-61	$ 30,201,667	$ 9,858,429	25,129	24
1975-76	$263,979,493	$ 50,446,159	94,488	445
1984-85	$608,796,690	$143,180,763	113,085	469

Source: University System of Georgia, *Annual Report,* 1960-61, 1975-76, 1984-85.
Note: Includes research sponsored by federal and other public and private agencies.

Figure 2: The University System of Georgia, 1986

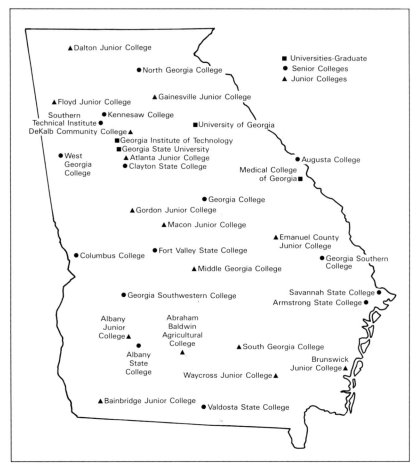

The visible payoff of the investment in higher education has continued to mean more ready funding of public colleges and universities than public schools in Georgia. Twenty years after Governor Sanders' commission made its recommendations, Georgia ranked 20th among the states in per student expenditures for higher education, but in expenditures per pupil for elementary and secondary schools, it ranked 44th in the nation.

The Struggle Continues

The struggle for the public schools continued through the 1970s and into the 1980s. Gov. Jimmy Carter, who as a freshman legislator had served on the Sanders Commission, pushed through the General Assembly yet another comprehensive education package, entitled Adequate Program for Education in Georgia (APEG). The APEG legislation, as its title implies, aimed to take Georgia public schools beyond the "minimum" of the 1964 MFPE law to a certain level of adequacy spelled out in specific areas. There were provisions for kindergartens; special and compensatory education; libraries; instructional media; laboratory equipment; and specialists in health, fine arts, counseling and testing.

By 1983, enrollments in public kindergarten had increased from 13 percent in 1970 to 83 percent, pupil-teacher ratios had dropped from 24 to 1 to 19 to 1, and performance on standardized tests drew closer to national norms. However, in the face of economic recession; popular demands for property tax relief; and the competing dollar demands of roads, prisons, health, and other public service areas; spending for schools declined as a percentage of state expenditures. In 1965, 46 percent of the state budget had gone to elementary and secondary schools, and in 1984 only 37 percent did so.

In 1983, another Georgia governor, Joe Frank Harris, appointed another commission to determine what needed to be done to improve the schools. This time the problems that the Governor's Education Review Commission wrestled with were not unlike those with which similar groups in other states wrestled: teacher education and pay, curriculum standards, and funding resources. But, the flurry of state-by-state rankings that appeared in the media gave the commission's work a special urgency because they indicated that Georgia was still near the bottom in most measures of educational quality. Georgia had made progress since 1964, but its progress barely kept pace with the progress of other states, most of which enjoyed higher standards of education at an earlier point in time.

Comparative Evaluation

Comparing one state's public schools with those of other states is fraught with problems. With no national curriculum, no uniform standards, and no mandatory tests administered nationwide to all students, the available measures of educational results are at best unsatisfactory. Moreover, the size of the educational task, the resources available to support public education, and expenditures for education vary widely from state to state.

Essentially, the educational task of a state is indicated by the size of the school-age population, age 5-17. The size of this group in relation to the adult population that must bear the burden of public schooling, characteristics of the school-age group, and the proportion of children enrolled in private as opposed to public schools are pertinent factors. In 1980, Georgia ranked 10th among the states in number of school-age children per 1,000 adults age 21 and over: Georgia had 323 children per 1,000 adults while the U.S. average was 291. Minority public school enrollment composed about 34 percent of total public school enrollment in Georgia and 27 percent in the nation. As a percentage of total school enrollment, private school enrollment was about 7 percent in Georgia and 11 percent in the United States as a whole.

In sum, Georgia's educational task is relatively heavy compared to other states. Not only is the proportion of children to adults high in Georgia, but the proportion of minority children, who often require extra educational effort to compensate for past discrimination and current social and economic disadvantage, is the ninth largest in the nation. Finally, private schools, which under certain circumstances can lighten the burden on public schools, are less common in Georgia than in the nation as a whole.

Financial support for public education comes in the main from taxes paid from income derived from salaries, wages, and business profits. In 1981, Georgia's per capita personal income was about 85 percent of the national average of $10,491. In per capita income, Georgia ranked 38th in the nation. However, in personal income *per school-age child,* Georgia ranked 42nd in the nation: $41,846 for the state compared to $52,995 for the nation. Georgia's personal income per child of school age was less than 80 percent of the national average.

The effort expended to support public education may be viewed in absolute and relative terms. In *absolute amount,* Georgia's current expenditure per pupil in average daily attendance for public elementary and secondary schools in 1981-82 was $2,111 or about 78 percent of the U.S. average of $2,721. By this measure, Georgia ranked 43rd among the states and the District of Columbia. However, if the differences in financial resources available in each state to support education are taken into consideration, a measure of *relative effort* is obtained. Georgia's expenditure as a percent of personal income was 4.15 percent compared to a national average of 4.20 percent. Thus, Georgia's effort relative to its resources was about 99 percent of the average effort in all states. By this measure, Georgia ranked 30th among the states. In sum, Georgia's school expenditure amounts to slightly more than three-fourths of the average state school expenditure. Relative to personal income, Georgia's educational effort is only slightly below the average for the nation.

The biggest single item of expenditure is teacher salaries. In 1982-83, the average salary of public school teachers in Georgia was $17,412 or about 85 percent of the national average, $20,603. In teacher salaries,

Georgia ranked 42nd in the nation. Over the 10-year period, 1972-73 to 1982-83, salaries increased by 100 percent in Georgia and 102 percent nationwide.

The results obtained from a state's efforts in public education are especially difficult to measure. None of several commonly used indicators of achievement are adequate to specify the relationship between inputs and outputs or to make wholly valid comparisons among the states.

Attendance, while not an "end product" of education, is an *en route* objective: children cannot be taught unless they come to school. In Georgia, where average daily attendance (ADA) determined the amount of money local schools received from the state, local authorities placed a premium on increasing school attendance. In 1971-72, ADA as a percentage of enrollment was 88 percent in Georgia and 90 percent in the nation. By 1982-83, the figure was 93 percent for Georgia and 92 percent for the nation. In the latter year, Georgia ranked 23rd in this measure.

The proportion of population of 17- to 18-year-olds graduating from high school is another measure of results. In 1980 in Georgia, high school graduates were 63 percent of the 17-18 age group; the U.S. average was 72 percent. In this measure Georgia ranked 47th in the nation.

A state population's level of educational attainment also reflects on its provision for public education. In 1970, of Georgians 25 years old and over, 59 percent had fewer than 12 years of school completed. By 1980, that figure was reduced to 44 percent. During the same period, the percentage of all persons in the United States 25 years old and over with fewer than 12 years of school completed dropped from 48 percent to 34 percent. In 1970, Georgia had ranked 47th in this measure; in 1980 it ranked 44th.

Statewide score averages on the Scholastic Aptitude Test (SAT), a test designed for college admissions purposes, are frequently cited in the media in comparing the states' achievements in public education. The SAT is taken by some percentage of high school students in all states, and average scores are published. In 1983-84, Georgia's SAT average scores were the lowest among the states excepting those for South Carolina. However, performance scores of any kind cannot be used to make valid comparisons among states unless all students take the test. This is not the case with the SAT. In fact, the number of students taking the SAT varied from 3 percent in Mississippi, Iowa, and the Dakotas to 69 percent in Connecticut; with 49 percent taking it in Georgia (only nine states had a higher percentage participating). The group taking the test in a state almost never approximates the total student population of the state, and the greater number of students taking the test in a state, the lower the scores in that state. From 1972 to 1984, Georgia SAT average scores increased from about 89 percent of the national average to about 92 percent of the national average.

The statewide averages, which suggest a Georgia population somewhat "disadvantaged" in education, mask the real picture. Great differences remain from one part of the state to another. A closer look at educational attainment illustrates the point.

In 1980, 44 percent of Georgians 25 years old and over had fewer than 12 years of school completed. But among the 159 counties, the range was from under 25 percent to almost 75 percent. Figure 3 shows educational attainment by county in 1980. Higher levels of educational attainment are concentrated in a few metropolitan counties.

Figure 3: Educational Attainment in Georgia, 1980

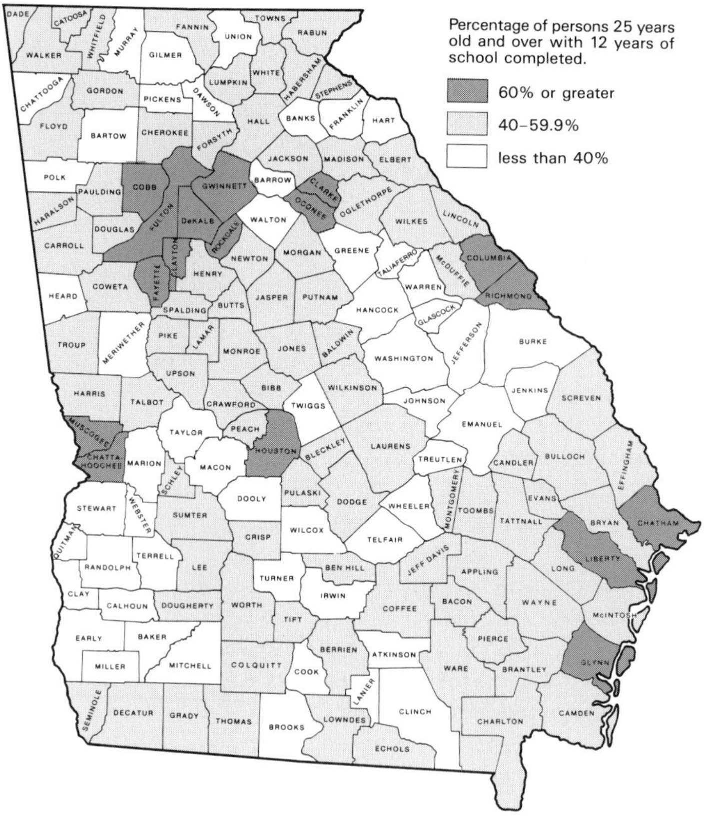

Source: U.S. Bureau of the Census, *1980 Census of Population, General Population Characteristics, Georgia.*

Variables Affecting Education

Numerous social and economic variables, as well as the local provision for education, may influence educational attainment. Together with political factors they can influence that provision for education. Three variables to be considered are the apparatus, the capacity, and the commitment for maintaining public schools.

The School Apparatus

As the biggest single responsibility of state government—public schools and the university system costs combined account for about 50 percent of the annual state budget—education requires a sprawling administrative apparatus. Since 1933, this structure has been divided into two separate parts: one for the elementary and secondary schools and one for the public colleges and universities.

The higher education apparatus is tightly structured with clear lines of accountability and control running from the Board of Regents through administrators of 34 colleges and universities to more than 30,000 faculty and other personnel (see Figure 4). Policies and procedures are essentially uniform for all units of the system. All personnel in the system are employed by state government and are paid through one budget authority, the Board of Regents. Financing derives from state authority only.

In contrast, the elementary and secondary school apparatus is not tightly structured (see Figure 5). Lines of accountability and authority cross among layers of appointed and elected state and local officials. State Department of Education personnel are employed by the state government; but principals, teachers, and other personnel in some 2,000 public schools are employed by county and city governments. Policies and procedures for 186 school districts[3] are set at both levels of government—and while state policies are uniform, local policies are not. Likewise, school financing derives from a blend of state and local budget authority.

The control executed by the State Board of Education and the state superintendent over the public schools is less than that enjoyed by the Board of Regents and its chancellor over the public colleges. Local school board members, superintendents, principals, teachers, other employees, parents, minorities, and other taxpayers may each have their own agenda for the schools. Given the existing apparatus, it is easier to expedite change in public higher education than in elementary and secondary education. And, of course the former is more manageable in size.

---

3. One independent city system was merged with a county system in 1986; the number of districts decreased from 187 to 186.

Figure 4: Georgia University System Apparatus

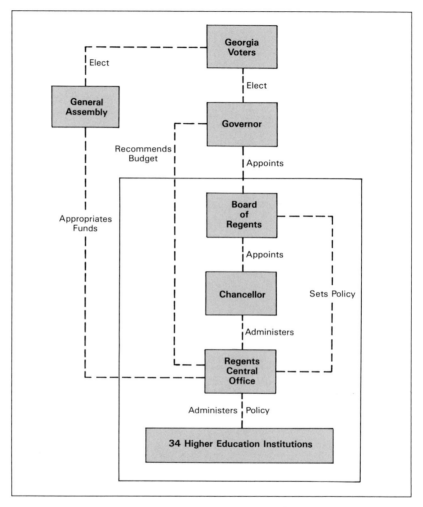

Local Capacity

In 1984, wide disparities remained in providing for education among the state's 187 school districts. For example, local supplements to the state teacher salary allotment ranged from $0 to more than $1,500. And, some districts featured personal computers for students while others barely supplied adequate textbooks and paper.

In a state in which average per capita income in the 159 counties ranged in 1980 from less than 60 percent to more than 100 percent of the national average and in which local dollars accounted for about 36

Figure 5: *Georgia Public School System Apparatus*

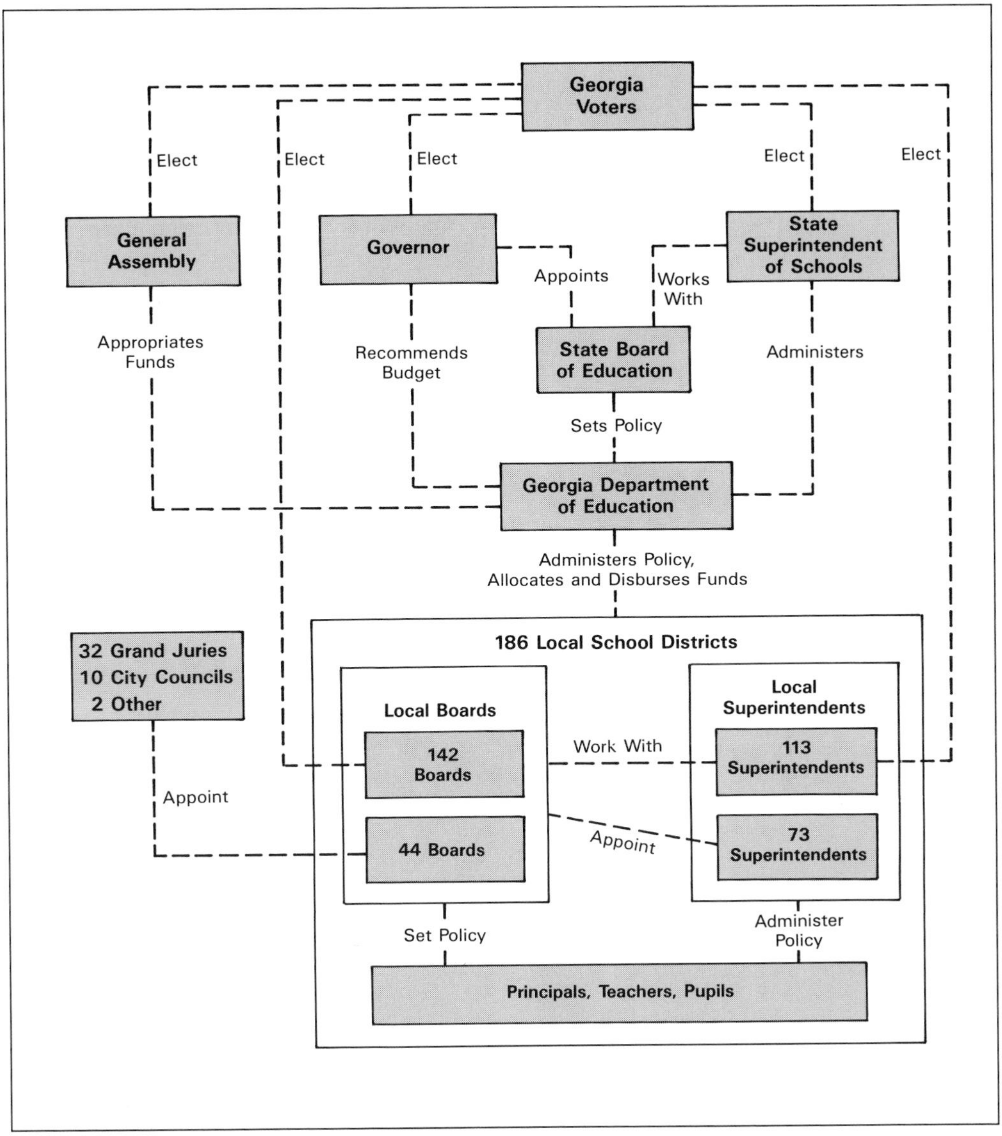

percent of school costs, local capacity remains a factor in such disparities. Local capacity has influenced the quality of public education since the formation of the independent local systems alongside the common school system in the nineteenth century. The move to local taxation in the early twentieth century only magnified the disparities. Since 1919, state law has *required* local districts to foot a share of the bill, and historically the local share has derived from a levy on property. In the 1980s, in districts with high tax valuations, such as those of the sub-urban counties around Atlanta, a local tax rate of one mill (a mill is one-tenth of one percent of assessed property value) could yield six times the money generated by one mill in a poor south Georgia district. In other words, to realize a given amount of local revenue equal to that of a wealthy district, the poor district needed a tax rate six times greater than the wealthy district. Of course, two districts might reasonably have different millage rates not only because they have unequal tax digests but also if the size of their pupil populations differ.

Recognizing the inequalities in local tax valuations, the legislature passed several equalization schemes over the years. These schemes were designed to give poor districts more per pupil state money than rich districts. By freeing up more state money for poor districts, the required local effort of rich districts effectively subsidized poor districts to a certain extent.

In 1972, in the face of demands for property tax relief, the General Assembly froze at $78.5 million the total amount required from local effort. At that time, that amount accounted for some 18 percent of the state's elementary and secondary school costs. But, after 12 years of rising costs, $78.5 million represented only 5.3 percent of the total. The freeze undid Georgia's existing equalization scheme.

In 1974, a lawsuit challenging the legal basis for local dependence on the property tax to fund schools was filed by Whitfield County citizens. The suit was based on the difference in local funding of the Dalton city schools, which raised $77 per pupil with each mill of local property taxes levied, and surrounding Whitfield County schools, which raised only $25 per pupil with each mill levied. Although in 1981 the Georgia Supreme Court, in *McDaniel v. Thomas,* agreed that the state's system of financing was "flawed," it was not found unconstitutional.

Local Commitment

More than 100 years ago, Gustavus John Orr argued repeatedly that the common schools would be secured only when the people developed the commitment to educate not only their own children but all the children. In the past, that kind of commitment was rejected by the tax-payers and politicians who walled off the wealth of municipal districts, educated their own children, and left the children in poor rural districts to suffer. Gradually, the horizons of commitment expanded in Georgia, eliminating most of the inequalities within counties. Yet, commitment often stops at the county line. In 1984, Georgia's 187 school districts raised over 10 times the required local effort frozen in 1972 at $78.5

million. But the bulk of that money was raised by local choice in the prosperous districts to enhance their own educational offering beyond that provided by state funds.

While there might be room to criticize residents of one part of the state who are unwilling to subsidize the education of children in another part—and there certainly isn't reason to criticize their effort to make their own schools the best possible—there is also reason to criticize the "leading citizens" of some poor districts. In 1984, an *Atlanta Journal-Constitution* survey found that local tax support for schools was related to the racial composition of local school populations. Among the 50 poorest counties, majority-white systems, according to the survey, received an average $3.50 per $1,000 valuation of local property. But, majority-black systems got only $2.68 per $1,000. One problem: of 187 local systems (45 of them with majority-black student populations), only three were governed by majority-black school boards.

Related is the problem of the so-called "segregation academies." In 1960, when the Sibley Commission made its report, only 3 percent of Georgia's children were enrolled in private schools. By 1980, over 7 percent were in private schools. While that was still below the national average of 11 percent, private schools had a significant impact in rural districts where many were located.

1986. At the Greene-Taliaferro Comprehensive High School, a rare example of multicounty school cooperation.

Private schools can take some of the educational burden off public schools. Such is the case in Massachusetts where parochial schools have traditionally enrolled about 10 percent of the state's children. But those schools enroll poor as well as wealthy pupils, and do not undermine community political and financial support for the public schools. Conversely, in Georgia, the post-1960 private schools enroll students from the highest socioeconomic levels of the local community and do siphon off support for the public schools.

In 1982, there were 524 private schools in Georgia (certainly not all of them segregation-inspired). In some counties, the financially and politically influential families have no interest in the public schools because their children are in the private schools. The result is another dual system of education: a white private school system and a predominately black public school system.

Withdrawal of white community support can have a devastating effect on the public schools. First, the loss of white students reduces the local district's Average Daily Attendance (ADA) and therefore the state funds it receives. Second, local school boards frequently dominated by the local white community are committed to keeping public school expenditures and operations to a bare minimum. Third, the public school diminishes as a center of social life: extracurricular activities dwindle, the organized enthusiasm of PTAs and booster clubs is transferred to the private academy or church-sponsored activities, and local business looks elsewhere for worthy causes to support. If tuition tax credits, vouchers, or some other inducement to private school enrollment should come to pass, the problems of some of Georgia's rural districts could be greatly compounded.

Quality Basic Education (QBE)

In March 1985, the General Assembly passed a package of legislation that promised to mitigate the foregoing negative factors and move Georgia out of the cellar in national rankings. For the preceding two years, public education had been a hot issue from Maine to California, and state after state jumped into line to improve their schools. Not since the Soviet launching of Sputnik in 1957 had so much attention focused on the nation's schools. Public awareness that something was wrong— an awareness advanced by the media—helped create a climate for reform in Georgia as well as in most other states. In Georgia, economic competition was even more than 20 years earlier the winning argument for better schools—with "high tech" replacing "space age" as the buzzword for that competition—and the business community lined up in support of better schools.

The Governor's Education Review Commission had made its report in late 1984, and in January 1985, Gov. Joe Frank Harris had proposed to a joint session of the General Assembly an education reform program that was estimated to cost $1 billion over then-current expenditures. By March, the legislature had unanimously passed the program with only minor changes. The state's new basic education law—entitled "Quality Basic Education Act"—ran to 127 pages and had 201 separate provisions. From a "minimum" education in 1949 and 1964 and an "adequate" education in 1974, the state government had moved to guarantee its children a "quality" education by the late 1980s.

The Quality Basic Education Act (QBE) substantially changed the formula for allocating state funds to local systems by basing allocations on the number of pupils enrolled in each of 12 instructional categories rather than on the number of pupils in average daily attendance (ADA). Costs vary with different instructional settings. For example, instruction in self-contained classrooms for handicapped children that require lower pupil-teacher ratios and special facilities can cost four times as much as instruction in a regular ninth-grade English class. Under a new weighted formula for allocating state money, local districts enrolling proportionately more pupils in high-cost categories—such as handicapped, remedial, gifted, and laboratory programs—would get proportionately more money. The act also contains provisions requiring districts to raise a "local fair share" of funds equivalent to a school property tax of at least five mills and requiring the funneling of more dollars to poor districts under a new equalization formula.

The General Assembly's intentions, stated in the act, included the following:

> a substantial reduction in the number of teachers who leave the teaching profession for reasons of job dissatisfaction;
>
> a decrease in the percentage of students who enter high school but do not graduate;
>
> an increase in the number of students mastering each skill in reading, mathematics, or other subject test areas; and
>
> a significant increase in the test scores of Georgia students who take the Scholastic Aptitude Test (SAT).

In order to attract and keep good teachers, the act contained provisions to make starting salaries in public school teaching competitive with starting salaries in other fields and to enable teachers to make more money for outstanding performance and for taking on more curricular responsibilities in the school. The act also required teachers, and other school personnel, to pass tests on subject matter and professional knowledge and demonstrate satisfactory on-the-job performance.

The QBE law addressed the lack of rigor and uniformity in the school curriculum. The act directed the State Board of Education to "establish competencies that each student is expected to master prior to completion of his public school education." To develop these competencies, the state board was to "adopt a uniformly sequenced core curriculum for grades Kindergarten through 12" and to see that all local systems included this core curriculum as the basis for their own curricula. Also required were regular assessments, using standardized tests, of all students' progress. The QBE Act also provided for mandatory full-day (4½ hours) kindergarten; remedial education for pupils achieving below specified levels; programs to decrease student suspensions, expulsions, dropouts, and other negative aspects of the school environment; and programs for pupils with limited English-speaking fluency. To give needed attention to an area that often falls between the cracks, the act established a State Board of Post-Secondary Vocational Education.

The QBE program also provides for an element often missing in public education—accountability. The State Board of Education was directed to oversee the evaluation of each public school and local system regarding the extent to which they implement QBE. Local systems are required annually to inform local citizens of the collective achievement of enrolled students by school and system, costs of providing its program, and the results of evaluations of schools and system conducted by the state board. In cases where local school authorities refuse to take corrective measures when systems received unsatisfactory evaluations from the state board, the board and the superior court can step in to implement such measures.

In sum, QBE requires state government—namely the State Board of Education through the State Department of Education—to shoulder far more responsibility than ever before for ensuring the quality and equality of educational opportunity in Georgia's public schools. The impetus for reform came not from the legislature itself, but from the larger community—especially business and the professions (including teaching). The legislature acted with a blueprint in hand—18 months of work by the Education Review Commission. In dealing with such a complex problem as suggested by Georgia's well-publicized low rankings on various measures of educational quality, the legislature chose not to spell out the details of implementation but to enact a law directing that action be taken to deal with the problem and to turn over the details to an executive agency. QBE is significant not only for education in Georgia but also for government in Georgia: "little government" is becoming bigger government.

CHAPTER SEVEN

Human Services

By Sam Mitchell

> More infants per thousand die in the first year of their lives in Webster, Treutlen, Wheeler, Schley and Hancock counties [in Georgia] than in Russia, Czechoslovakia, Bulgaria, Jamaica, Singapore, and Italy.
>
> —U.S. Sen. Sam Nunn, August 1977

One Million in Need

In 1984, more than one million people, from infants to the aged—many of them poor, some of them mentally or physically disabled—received some direct assistance from the Georgia Department of Human Resources, the state agency responsible for providing a broad range of social services to people in need.[1] Given a state population of some 5.5 million, this means that in 1984 approximately one out of five Georgians or 20 percent of the population had a mental, physical, or financial problem that interfered with their adjustment to family or community life or sense of well-being. If the needed service had not been available, many of these Georgians could conceivably have become permanently impaired. Depending on one's point of view, these people represent either a major liability draining away resources or a potentially enormous asset if the barriers to their development can be removed so they are able to participate more fully in the life of the community.

Who are the people comprised in the one million? The following persons are not real, but their situations, synthesized from actual cases, illustrate the major categories of need.

---

1. Some of these people and thousands of others also used services offered by other public agencies and private religious, volunteer, nonprofit, and for-profit organizations.

The Poor

Loretta

Loretta is 22. She and her three children were evicted from their house following desertion by her husband. They moved in with Loretta's mother, who lives in public housing, until Loretta got a job and found her own place. She now rents a small trailer.

Last year the family's income from Loretta's sporadic earnings amounted to less than $5,000. Loretta has only a ninth-grade education and few job skills. She has not been able to hold a job for more than a few months.

In order to work, Loretta has child care and car expenses. She is usually behind in utility and rent payments. The trailer is sometimes without heat and light. When the rent isn't paid on time, the landlord will padlock the trailer while Loretta is away. Upon occasion she and the children have had to sleep in the car.

Whether or not the conditions under which Loretta and her children live indicate that they are poor depends upon how we define poverty. A commonly used federal government definition: an individual or family is poor by having an income below a specified minimum, the so-called *poverty level*. The dollar amount, or threshold, used to determine poverty level varies according to family size, whether the householder is over age 65, and changes in the consumer price index. In 1959, 1969, and 1979 the average threshold for a family of four was $2,973, $3,743, and $7,412 respectively. For an individual in 1979 the average threshold was $3,686.

The 1980 census reported that in 1979 almost 900,000 persons in Georgia, or 16.6 percent of the population, lived below the poverty level. Georgia ranked eighth among the states in percentage of population below the poverty level.

Economic progress in the South has served to bring the region's poverty statistics closer in line with those of the nation. As Table 1 shows, between 1969 and 1979, in Georgia and the South as a whole the number of people living below the poverty line and the percentage of population below that line decreased. During the same period, the number of poor increased in the United States.

The incidence of poverty in Georgia is not evenly distributed across the state. Figure 1 shows where poor people make up higher percentages of local populations. Rural poverty remains a feature of Georgia life: higher ratios of poor to nonpoor are found in rural counties. However, almost a third of all persons living below the poverty line in

Table 1: Persons Living below Poverty Level: Georgia, South, United States

	Number of Persons (Thousands)			Percentage of Total Population		
Year	Georgia	South	United States	Georgia	South	United States
1969	924	12,388	27,125	20.7	20.3	13.7
1979	882	11,276	27,383	16.6	15.4	12.4

Source: U.S. Bureau of the Census, *Statistical Abstract of the United States, 1982-83.*

Figure 1: Percentage of Population in Georgia Living below the Poverty Level, 1979

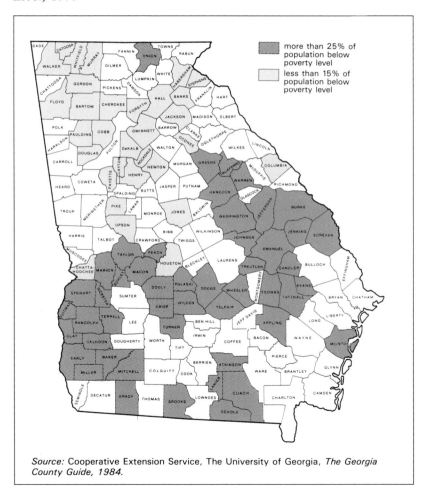

more than 25% of population below poverty level

less than 15% of population below poverty level

Source: Cooperative Extension Service, The University of Georgia, *The Georgia County Guide, 1984.*

1979 were concentrated in six metropolitan counties: Fulton, 121,399; DeKalb, 46,015; Chatham, 36,347; Richmond, 30,618; Muscogee, 29,392; and Bibb, 28,591.

The relative incidence of poverty was concentrated in 1979 in two population groups: blacks, 34.1 percent, and female-headed households, 35.5 percent.

People with Special Needs

The number of people living in poverty is a good indicator of the overall social welfare of the state. Many social ills, such as mental illness, alcoholism, and drug abuse, are directly linked to the stresses associated with living in poverty. Many of the same people represented in the poverty statistics are also represented in the figures describing troubled children, mental retardation, rehabilitation, and public health. The cost of poverty to the state is far greater than the direct financial assistance represented by a welfare grant. Several large portions of the total human services budget, including physical health, mental disability, and related services, address problems which often originate from conditions of poverty.

The Mentally Impaired

Ronnie

Ronnie is 29 years old and a patient at a Georgia regional hospital. His diagnosis is paranoid schizophrenia with a secondary diagnosis of drug and alcohol abuse. Ronnie's parents are elderly, live on social security, and have no other children.

After graduation from high school, Ronnie failed at college and vocational school and drifted from job to job. His initial hospitalization was for drug overdose. Between 1973 and 1984 he had convictions for drug possession and DUI, hospital and outpatient treatment for drug and alcohol abuse, and psychiatric care following an attempted suicide. For much of this period, Ronnie lived with his parents.

Ronnie's latest hospitalization came following an argument with his parents after which he took their car and deliberately wrecked it.

In FY 1985, the Division of Mental Health and Mental Retardation of the State Department of Human Resources served 115,212 clients. They included the mentally ill, the mentally retarded, and people impaired by drug or alcohol abuse.

Although this figure serves to describe a major problem, it does not include large numbers of people with emotional impairments who either go untreated or have the resources to pay for treatment in private hospitals or drug treatment centers.

Juvenile Offenders

Freddie

Freddie is 12 years old. He lives with his mother and father, both of whom work, in metropolitan Atlanta. A sister and two brothers are in their twenties.

Freddie has run away from home several times, once staying away for a week. He is regularly truant from school. His attendance is marked by unruly behavior.

Freddie's runaways and run-ins with security at the shopping malls brought him to the attention of the juvenile court. Freddie's mother told a juvenile probation officer that Freddie was a mistake, that he came along when she was ready to have some time to herself. The officer notes that Freddie seems to enjoy making his parents angry with him.

Each year approximately 20,400 persons between ages 9 and 19 receive some services from DHR's Division of Youth Services. A large number represent such offenses as running away or truancy.

During FY 1984, of 2,200 juveniles committed to the division (that is, placed in state custody), 138 were committed for serious or violent offenses.

Vocationally Handicapped

Henry

Henry is 44 years old, married, with five children. Henry was a machinist employed in the production of scientific instruments when he suffered a severe head injury.

After treatment, Henry tried to resume his job. Headaches and blurred vision impaired his ability to do close work. He had to quit his job.

Henry, his wife, and children had enjoyed a stable and comfortable family life before he was injured. His inability to perform at his old job left him depressed and irritable. The family was under great stress. His wife sought professional help.

A vocational rehabilitation counselor helped Henry enter a new line of work, heavy equipment repair, that does not require close vision.

The best indicator of the number of people who have handicaps that interfere with their ability to be fully competitive in the labor market are those people who are eligible to receive services from the state/federal vocational rehabilitation programs and injured workers receiving rehabilitation services through the State Board of Workers' Compensation. The programs are designed for different purposes, but individuals served by both programs have two characteristics in common: (1) all have some physical or mental impairment which represents a significant handicap to employment, and (2) a determination has been made that with rehabilitative services and training, the person has potential to be gainfully employed. About 26,000 people are receiving services through the Division of Vocational Rehabilitation of the state Department of Human Resources, and approximately 4,500 injured workers are receiving rehabilitation services under supervision of the Rehabilitation Section of the State Board of Workers' Compensation.

The Aged

Angus

Angus is 81 years old, widowed for 10 years, and has no family. He lives alone in a house he and his wife owned for 50 years.

Angus is reclusive and antisocial. After his house was burglarized in 1981, he rarely ventured out. He keeps doors and windows locked year round and lights burning in all rooms day and night.

For three years Angus entrusted a neighbor woman to do grocery shopping and errands for him. Recently he has become abusive, accusing the woman of stealing from him. Two weeks after the neighbor last saw Angus, she called the police to check on him. Angus was found near death. There was no food in the house.

Georgians over 60 years of age make up the fastest growing population group in the state. The older population increased by 35 percent between 1970 and 1980, according to the 1980 census. In 1980, 732,600 Georgians were over 60. By 1990 they will number more than 900,000.

By virtue of their increasing numbers and increasing tendency to organize and lobby, older citizens are demanding a reexamination of public policies that affect their welfare. Public policies regarding employment, medical services, housing, and retirement programs all have a direct bearing on the elderly. In 1980, about a fourth of Georgians over 65 had incomes below poverty level. In 1984, about 17,900 older Georgians sought admission to nursing homes.

Mandatory retirement policies, social security regulations, and age discrimination in hiring prevent many from working who are otherwise able and willing to continue participating in the workforce.

Infants

Stacy

Stacy is 14 and lives with both parents and three younger brothers in a rural community. The family income is below the poverty line.

Stacy is of low normal intelligence and often sleeps during school. Health screenings showed she has badly decayed teeth, has an upper respiratory tract infection, and is anemic. A caseworker found that neither Stacy nor her parents seem to understand her need for dental and medical treatment.

Stacy has told her physical education teacher that she thinks she is pregnant and must quit school. Her boyfriend is 15.

The caseworker contacted Stacy's parents. A medical examination confirmed Stacy is four months pregnant.

One-fifth of all Georgia's babies are born to teenagers. Between 1983 and the year 2003, 1.8 million babies will be born in Georgia. It is estimated, based on current trends, that about 55,000 of those babies will have major physical handicaps, 72,000 will be mentally retarded, and 180,000 will develop mental illness. In spite of decades of progress, Georgia still ranks 43rd among the 50 states in the rate of infant mortality. Major problems that contribute to these statistics include unprepared parenting, ignorance of the importance of prenatal care, and inaccessible health care.

Historical Development of Social Welfare Programs

The quality of services provided to people in need depends on three factors: the attitudes and values of the culture, the resources available, and the knowledge and skills of the people who deliver the services. Economics, politics, education, and the social environment all bear on the resources and services available to people.

The traditional agrarian culture of Georgia rested on values of individualism and self-reliance. It included acceptance of a dual social order of "haves" and "have nots." Within the traditional value system, the state incurs no responsibility to minister to people with special needs. The state protects the rights of people to work and achieve but leaves it up to the charitable interest in family and community to assist those in need. The traditional culture also included racial attitudes that gave rise to a kind of plantation paternalism, which defined the obligations of white haves and black have-nots.

The traditional values, reinforced by Georgia's long experience with economic distress following the Civil War, relate directly to the historical reluctance to expend state financial resources for human services. It took the Great Depression of the 1930s to generate sufficient political pressure to pass human service legislation and to levy taxes for human service programs. Not until the late 1930s did recognition of the need for skilled social welfare professionals become widespread. Before professionalization, the necessary credentials for providing services involved little more than a sensitivity to human need, patience, and a sacrificial spirit.

This section sketches the historical development of Georgia's social welfare programs and the influence of several factors on that development.

Family and Community Responsibility

No society has been able to avoid accommodation for those unable to care for themselves. From the ancient codes of Hammurabi and Moses to the current struggle for human rights and equal opportunity, all governments are ultimately judged by the value they come to place on the welfare of people.

The welfare of people was central to the founding of Georgia. At least part of the motivation for establishing the colony was philanthropic: the worthy poor were to be given the opportunity to earn a living and be self-supporting. The colonists themselves brought a strong sense of responsibility for the needy and as early as 1737 at Ebenezer and 1740 at Savannah they established orphanages for children of settlers who perished.

Local responsibility was the basic principle in caring for the poor during colonial times and remained a prevailing influence for the first 200 years of Georgia's history. This principle, not fundamentally altered until the social security legislation of the mid-1930s, had its legal origin in the Elizabethan Poor Law of 1601, which made parishes responsible for the poor. This English law required parishes to repress begging, provide work relief for the able-bodied poor, provide direct relief for those unable to work, apprentice children, and establish workhouses.

Early laws of the state of Georgia made the county the administrative unit for public welfare. County authorities could establish pauper farms and levy a tax to purchase the farm and finance services. A county could establish an almshouse, later called the "county home," for the poor, aged, and otherwise needy. Georgia law also provided that the county could recover the cost of services from relatives of the poor. The levels of responsibility were clearly established beginning with the individual and progressing to the immediate family, the relatives, and finally the local unit of government.

The First State Institutions

In the early 1800s, the rapid growth of the United States in population and material wealth was accompanied by an optimism that America could be made even better through common action. Reformers, many of them clerics, launched crusades for measures to improve society and rehabilitate individuals. Many Americans joined the causes of temperance, abolition of slavery, humane treatment of the insane, and public schools. Some even joined utopian communities.

In Georgia, the reform spirit plus population increases that rendered counties incapable of providing adequate care led to the establishment of state institutions. In 1817, one year after adopting the nation's first comprehensive criminal code, Georgia opened a penitentiary for the humane treatment of prisoners. Innovations radical for that time were instituted: a system of rewards and punishments, Sunday school, yard privileges, and industrial activities thought to have a rehabilitative effect. The Georgia Lunatic Asylum was opened in 1842, the School for the Deaf and Dumb in 1845, and the School for the Blind in 1852.

In the beginning, the institutions were small. (The penitentiary had only 160 prisoners in 1841.) Their purpose was to remove part of the burden from the counties and provide specialized care. In the early years, judging by standards of the time, they served both purposes well.

No institution was opened without opposition. Dissenters organized their objections around two themes. In the first place, they argued, state-

REWARD!

Escaped from our Camp, on the
A. & H. Railway,

JOE KELLEY,

From Fulton County.
Color, Mulatto; Age, 24 years;
Weight, 165 pounds; Height, 5
feet nine and one half inches;
has lost the second and third
fingers of left hand.

We will pay a Reward of ONE
HUNDRED DOLLARS for his delivery to
us at Atlanta, Ga.

CHATTAHOOCHEE BRICK CO.

Oct. 13, 1887.

From 1868 to 1908, the state leased its convicted felons to private enterprises to work on "chain gangs."

supported institutions violated the principle of local responsibility, a precedent they feared would lead to the eventual loss of local control. The other frequent objection to state institutions stemmed from prejudice against specific classes of needy people—the age-old belief that mentally ill, retarded, and epileptic persons were possessed by demons. Little wonder that it was difficult to gain the needed financial support for adequate facilities and care.

That difficulty was compounded in the economic and political climate of the decades following the Civil War and Reconstruction in Georgia. Lack of money was a compelling reason for abandoning the state penitentiary and inaugurating a penal system based on convict labor—the chain gangs. Furthermore, the 1877 Constitution was written with the expressed intent to restrain government intervention in economic and social matters. Inadequate financing forced most state institutions to abandon virtually any attention to treatment. Facilities for the mentally ill and elderly became dumping grounds: people by the thousands were simply "put away" and often forgotten by family and the community. The characteristic overcrowding and understaffing of Georgia's state institutions fostered abuses that would continue far into the twentieth century.

Influence of Attitudes and Values

The influence of cultural values and the frustration in developing public services for the needy are illustrated in the case of public health.

The General Assembly created a State Board of Health in 1875. It appropriated only $1,500 for the board's first year expenditures, but the board was active in encouraging the establishment of county health boards and in publishing information on such subjects as yellow fever and mental illness. However, in 1877, the legislature voted not to continue funding the Board of Health. The vote was in line with the adoption that year of a new state constitution that severely restricted the role of state government over matters considered to be of local concern. Not until 1903, and then despite political opposition and public apathy, was the board recreated. Its appropriation was $3,000 per year.

A published report of the first 10 years of the Board's operation, by Dr. H. F. Harris of Atlanta, conveys conditions of trial and tribulation:

No greater indictment could be lodged against the effectiveness of our boasted free institutions than a simple statement of the deaths annually caused by preventable disease in the United States. But this leaves the story only half told, for when we call to mind the frightful sufferings produced by the same causes in at least ten times as many others who recover, and when we add still to this the anguish and sorrow of those who are near and dear to the victims and the poverty and misery which in many instances ensues, the horror grows beyond all bounds, and would excite to pity the most hardened of mankind. But who knows about it, and who cares?

The subject is an unpleasant one as is always pain and suffering and death, and when by chance any reference to it occurs in the newspapers we are in no mood to read it, and naturally prefer the gruesome but not wholly uninteresting details of the latest murder, or the still more satisfying and delectable details of the marital troubles of our next door neighbor. Besides, we do not look upon it as any of our business. Herein really lies the crux of the situation for if in a republic the most vital of all questions, the life and happiness of its citizens, is not the business of each and every voter, in Heaven's name to whom shall the burden be assigned? The truth of the matter in the subject is one which is highly special, and can only be dealt with intelligently by men who have made it their life study, and even where mildly interested the average man feels this, and naturally shifts the burden to other shoulders—with the result that nobody does anything. (Thomas F. Abercrombie, *History of Public Health in Georgia, 1733-1950*, Atlanta: Georgia Department of Public Health, n.d., pp. 55-56.)

In this document, and in the one presented below, the attitude that the health of others was "not any of our business" is clearly a greater barrier to progress than any lack of scientific knowledge and skills.

While Dr. Harris's report deals with frustrations of those in top leadership positions, the following report describes the situation from the perspective of a public health nurse. It originated in the May 1929 issue of *Georgia Health,* published by the Department of Public Health.

ONE DAY WITH AN
ITINERANT NURSE IN GEORGIA
Her Diary

By Valeria Shell, R.N.

7:00 A.M. Breakfast—good strong coffee, fresh ham, scrambled eggs, biscuits.

8:00 A.M. On the road, with a list of the people to see. . . .

The various roads necessitated several inquiries before I finally reached Mrs. Evans (midwife). A strong aroma of cooking turnip greens greeted me along with the appearance of Mrs. Evans, and she waited, with a puzzled expression, for me to speak.

"Mrs. Evans," I began, "this is Miss Shell, from the State Board of Health. I guess you had a letter about my coming."

A midwife going on call in the vicinity of Siloam, 1941. The midwife was a very important health care provider in rural Georgia.

"Yessum," she replied; "I did that, I sho did; but I just couldn't get in to meet you'uns at that courthouse. My old man and me talked about it when we got dat letter, but we ain't got but one mule, and times is so hard we needs to work every putty day we kin to ever git de work done. I was pickin' cotton, too, and I jest couldn't get thar. I hopes you'll excuse 'er old lady, Miss."

I assured her that she was excusable, and added: "I am very anxious to explain my work to you, and I think it will be a help to you. I am having classes for the good ladies who are midwives, and am trying to give them some new ideas which will be of value, and possibly serve to save lives. To attend these classes will help you, and when you have done so, if you are willing to follow our advice, and understand your work as a midwife, you will be given a certificate which will be of great help to you."

"I know it's de truth," she replied; "yessum, that's all so. I will be there if I live and nothing happens. When is the next one?"

Seeing that she was now pleased, I said: "Tomorrow afternoon at two o'clock: Bring me some old cloths, nice and clean. I want to show you how to make some things that you may keep ready for use."

And then a question:

"What is this here license going to cost me?"

Assured that there was no charge for the work of the State Board of Health and none for the certificate, she said: "Thank you, ma'am; I sho' will be there."

On my way again, having learned that the "jestice," Mr. Henry Jones, a local registrar, lives in the third house on the right along the same way. Reaching the home, I stopped, got out, and told the lady of the house my name and business. She went through the house, called her husband, and returned to visit with me till "Henry" could come. . . .

Mr. Jones then came up and I told him who I was. Then he explained:

"Yes, Mr. Toombs wrote me to meet you at the courthouse, and I made sure I would be there; but some of the hands were sick with the flu and I couldn't."

"Well, Mr. Jones, I'm sorry you couldn't come. Since I'm here we will talk over the work and see if I can help you."

"Miss Shell, I'll tell you the most good you can do me. I want you to help me with the doctors. Some of them are mightly slow about turning in births and deaths, and that's the reason I don't make my reports like I ought."

"Yes, Mr. Jones, I visit all the doctors, and they tell me that they do not intend to break the law about reports, but just forget. I will be glad to go over a birth and death certificate with you to be sure you know just how the Board of Health wishes them to be prepared."

It is all gone over, and he is glad.

. . . .

The Mt. Pleasant school is in sight. Arriving, I ask for the superintendent. As he approaches, I introduce myself:

"This is Miss Shell, from the State Board of Health."

"Gaines is my name, Madam," he replied; "And what is yo' business?"

"I wanted to talk with you, Mr. Gaines, about the work of the State Board of Health in the schools, and arrange with you to organize classes composed of the girls over ten years of age. This work we call "The Little Mother's League," and we teach the girls the important things about child care. Most girls in school need constantly to aid their mothers with the other children of the family.

The death rate of babies in Georgia is very high, and we undertake to help the girls to properly care for little brothers and sisters as one means of saving the little ones. I would like you to suggest one of your teachers who could take charge of this work in your school. I will aid her to organize, and leave all necessary literature with her. There is no charge for our work."

Judging by the personal appearance of Prof. Gaines, and his apparent lack of interest in my statement, I felt I had made very little impression. Then he parried:

"Well now, I don't guess any of my teachers have time to teach anything but what they are already teaching, and they don't hardly have time to do what they are doing. If you want the girls taught anything new, and it's a good thing, why don't you teach 'em yourself? Besides, the children have all they can do already."

"Mr. Gaines, I'm very sorry; but I have the entire county to cover in two weeks. It is impossible for me to remain at any one school, and do the teaching. Any one of your faculty could do it, and, really, without loss of time. The girls would be intensely interested."

And his reply was positive and final: "We just haven't got time to do any more than we are doing and can't do it. I don't see that it would do much good anyway. You see, we haven't got time to take up all these new notions. But we thank you ma'am for coming around."

"Thank you and good-day, Mr. Gaines."

The afternoon is almost spent, and no lunch yet.

. . . .

Returning to town I stopped to see Dr. Payne. After explaining my business, he replied:

"Yes, I know the State Board of Health. They are always trying to help somebody."

"Dr. Payne, midwives do a class of work that is not very desirable, nearly all of it being charity, and you cannot afford to keep going to these people who cannot pay you; then, too, there are times in bad weather when, in the remote country sections, a doctor cannot be had. These women are a great help in such communities. They are a necessity. The State Board of Health has been requested by the State Medical Society to instruct them. They need it and we ask your assistance."

"You are right. When they learn to be clean and when to stop, they could be some help to me."

"Thank you, doctor; let me give you a few ampoules of our silver nitrate solution to use in baby cases. It is so convenient, and we are glad to furnish it free of charge."

The diary expresses in clear, human terms the difficulties in gaining acceptance in a rural community. During this typical day the nurse experienced the deep appreciation of some, was received with suspicion by others, and on at least one occasion had her services completely, albeit politely, rejected. These three reactions typify the major segments of community culture during the early 1900s. In general, there were those who were ready to move beyond the post-Reconstruction era and eager to learn new ways; those who were weary of poverty and disease but suspicious of outsiders; and those committed to the status quo (usually in positions of local authority and influence) who viewed new thinking and change as a threat to their authority and esteem in the community.

That threat was heightened with the Great Depression of the 1930s and the advent of the national government's intervention in social and economic matters. Georgia government was slow in responding (on its own and in cooperation with the national government) to the social and economic realities represented by the hard times of the depression. The political leaders of the time were not insensitive to human need. But, their traditional value system rejected the notion that government has a legitimate role as guardian of its citizens' welfare and progress. What is more, when the national government offered help, many state and local officials turned it down. In their view, they were defending individual and states' rights which, to them, were essential for preserving individual freedom. However, the real problem for them was not the acceptance of federal funds per se; it was the new source of influence they expected would follow (and of course did!) that was the problem. They saw it as a threat to their own influence and power in the established order.

New Resources for Public Welfare

As Georgia's population moved from rural to urban settings and as the Great Depression wrought changes in the social fabric of the people, the resources available for welfare services began to improve.

In the early 1900s, the need grew for a state system of welfare. County and state facilities, created piecemeal under a variety of legislative acts, operated under their own governing bodies with no uniformity and little coordination. Between 1900 and 1919, the General Assembly authorized a Confederate Veterans Home, Reformatory, Tuberculosis Sanitarium, Training School for Girls, and Training School for Mental Defectives; giving Georgia nine state eleemosynary institutions plus 70 county almshouses.

Georgia was among the last states to establish a central welfare authority. In 1919, primarily in response to reports of abuse in child care institutions, the legislature created an unpaid lay Board of Public

Camden County. The state's mobile clinic, known as "the blood wagon," was a nationally recognized innovation in the 1930s.

Welfare. Its duties were visitorial and advisory: visit charitable and correctional institutions; gather information on the "dependent, defective and delinquent classes"; and submit reports of conditions to the governor. The board had no authority to mandate changes.

In 1931, under Gov. Richard B. Russell, Jr., state government was reorganized. Centralization and coordination of state level welfare activities were accomplished to some extent by abolishing most of the separate governing bodies of state institutions and creating a Board of Control of Eleemosynary Institutions with responsibility for general policies. However, all direct welfare services continued to be provided by counties and municipalities.

The state contributed nothing to the direct relief of the indigent, sponsored no general welfare service, and took no part in general relief activities except to encourage counties to establish adequate welfare departments. However, as late as 1935, only 15 of the 159 counties had an organized public welfare department, as did five of the largest cities: Augusta, Savannah, Macon, Atlanta, and Columbus. In the remainder of the counties, relief funds were under the direction of the county commission or ordinary (now called probate judge) who functioned in some counties as a sole commissioner. Even after welfare departments were organized, county commissioners in some counties retained control over expenditures of "pauper funds" and maintained pauper lists. Commenting on the "pauper fund" method of relief, a report of the state welfare department said:

> From a long list of applicants, the Board of County Commissioners or Ordinary selects those who are deemed most needy, and the eligible ones are placed on the pauper list. The amount of a monthly pension might depend on the financial condition of the county *or upon the standing of the citizen who assisted the pensioner in getting on the list.* County officials generally know the applicants and do not deem further investigations necessary. Many of these cases could be kept off the pauper list by the help of case work with relatives and friends. But once placed on the list, they usually stay until death.

Changed Conditions Bring New Institutions

Across the nation, the depression of the 1930s created social conditions unlike any that existed previously. These conditions brought forth the New Deal politics of the 1930s and generated grassroots support for those politics. The national government under Franklin D. Roosevelt assumed the responsibility for direct relief via social security and work relief to train and employ idled workers. The latter included programs of the Public Works Administration, the Works Progress Administration, and the Civilian Conservation Corps.

Even in the face of changed conditions, many leaders of Georgia government continued to cling to the principle of local responsibility in public welfare. Thousands of Georgians from industrial and agricultural areas of the state were without means of support. They did not fit the traditional notion of "paupers" indigenous to a particular county or city. They were the unemployed and the families of the unemployed—mostly responsible, hard-working people. Many had no ties to local communities, having left hometowns and relatives to look for jobs, and were still on the road.

Generally, these unemployed masses had two urgent needs that the state was totally unprepared to meet. They needed funds to survive and they needed opportunities to work. As their numbers grew and the resources of private agencies, churches, and local government proved totally inadequate, state government began the process of assuming a major role in providing services to people.

That process featured a fierce debate between the leading political

After the 1937 reform, prisoners in this public work camp could eat their meals without being chained.

factions of the day: the Talmadge and anti-Talmadge factions. Generally, the faction led by Gov. Eugene Talmadge opposed federal and state initiatives in public welfare. In 1935, Talmadge vetoed amendments to the state constitution that would have enabled Georgia to participate in social security. Georgia's joining the New Deal was a major issue in the 1936 races for governor and U.S. senator.

A new role for the state began in 1937 under newly elected Gov. E. D. Rivers. Legislation was passed enabling Georgians to participate in social security and authorizing the state and counties to levy taxes to provide the matching funds required to receive federal public assistance money for the aged, the blind, disabled, and for dependent children.

Also in 1937, prison reforms began. The chain gangs were renamed "public work camps" and placed nominally under state control. In reality, the chains came off in some camps and the state instituted a plan for the classification and segregation of prisoners. In 1938, a new penitentiary was opened at Reidsville.

Georgia became a full participant in federal relief programs when Governor Rivers signed the 1937 Welfare Reorganization Act, (often referred to as Georgia's "Little New Deal"), establishing the State Department of Public Welfare. This benchmark legislation established two principles which formed the basis for future development. First, the law set forth the state's responsibility to provide services to people in cooperation with federal and local government. In financing the cost of old age assistance and aid to the blind, the counties were responsible for 10 percent of benefits paid, the state for 40 percent, and the federal government for 50 percent. In aid to dependent children, counties likewise paid 10 percent, the federal government one-third, and the state the balance. Furthermore, the law required the establishment of a properly constituted welfare department in each of the 159 counties in order to meet federal guidelines that all benefit programs be administered through a uniform administrative structure and using uniform eligibility criteria in all counties.

The new State Department of Public Welfare assumed all welfare functions formerly assumed by the county governments and several state agencies. Through the 159 new county welfare departments, this new agency supervised all forms of public assistance. The new department also took over operations of all state institutions for the care of children, the aged, and mentally and physically disabled persons. In its first year, the department provided services to 96,638 families of the state, or 14 percent of the 652,793 families recorded in the 1930 census.

Reform continued at a slower pace in the 1940s and 1950s. In 1943, Gov. Ellis Arnall obtained the establishment of a Department of Corrections which assumed control over all prisoners. Shackles, whippings, sweatboxes, and other forms of corporal punishment were outlawed in all county and state facilities, and a program of rehabilitation was begun at the state prison. A Board of Pardons and Paroles was also created to eliminate another abuse—the selling of pardons—in the prison system. In 1951, all activities involving crippled children were transferred to the State Department of Health, as was the largest institution, Milledgeville State Hospital, in April 1959.

During the period from the depression up to the resurgence of social legislation in the 1960s, Georgia had a properly constituted state agency or institution responsible for addressing almost any human problem. The issue during the past four decades has not been the existence of services but rather the *adequacy* of services related to changing needs and expectations on the part of Georgia citizens.

People-Helping Professions

The expansion of public social services in the 1930s gave impetus to the development of a professionalized service industry of "people-helpers" in the United States. Not surprisingly in a state that had no real welfare system until 1937, Georgia lagged behind in the preparation of social workers. The first school of social work had been established in New York in 1898. Thirty years later, there were some 40 schools of social work in the United States and Canada. In Georgia, the only school of social work in the 1930s was for black students at private Atlanta University. The first annual report of the Georgia Department of Public Welfare acknowledged the state's need for professionally trained workers:

> Special courses in social work were arranged at two units of the State University System soon after the Welfare Department was organized due to the fact that a shortage of qualified welfare workers impended to hamper full and quick development of the new system. Financed largely by the Works Progress Administration and supervised by the State Department, the special courses have become a regular part of the University of Georgia Summer School Curriculum. . . .

In 1939, the University of Georgia organized a Department of Social Work.

Not until 1964, just as the demand for social workers was increasing, was the first full-fledged school of social work in the public university system established—at the University of Georgia. Responding to a demand emanating from "War on Poverty" and "Great Society" programs, by 1973 eleven colleges in Georgia offered some kind of social work program.

The 1960s had brought the second great wave of federal initiatives in social welfare. As in the 1930s, Georgia received massive infusions of money and in the process was required to adjust to sweeping reforms directed by the national government. Legislation such as the Civil Rights Act of 1964; poverty programs that expanded services to the economically disadvantaged; and major amendments to social security, including medical services for the poor (Medicaid) and the aged (Medicare), required changes in the delivery of services through state and local welfare agencies to make sure that client groups, including minorities, were served effectively and equitably. Federal money came with strings attached to assure those changes.

The nation's situation in the 1960s was, however, different from that in the 1930s, and assumptions underlying the social legislation of the 1960s were fundamentally different from those of the 1930s. In the 1930s, reformers assumed that the *economy* needed to be changed and the thrust of legislation was financial assistance, jobs, and economic reform. In the 1960s, they assumed that some *people* needed to be changed and myriad services were offered to help them overcome disadvantages and find their rightful place in the opportunity structure.

To provide all these services, an industry of professional helpers has developed.[2] Between 1953 and 1982, the number of public welfare workers in state and local governments in the United States increased from 92,000 to 379,000 or from six public welfare workers per 10,000 population to 17 per 10,000 population. The industry is staffed by social workers, guidance counselors, psychologists, mental health therapists, and vocational rehabilitation counselors, among others—all with different approaches, traditions, and training but sharing a faith in technologies for changing attitudes and behavior. Whether this legion of professional helpers has permanently improved the quality of life for the groups they serve may be a matter of debate; nonetheless, it has been a major force in shaping priorities in social policy and in determining how social services have been delivered to people during the past two decades. Together, the helping professions have proven to be an effective lobby for the interests of needy people. However, differences in professional standards and goals among the various specialities in the helping professions have created barriers to a unified system for delivering services.

An Integrated System for Human Services

In 1972, Gov. Jimmy Carter presented to the General Assembly a plan to reorganize state government. The most expansive and controversial proposal in the plan was to consolidate all state human service activities into one large agency under a single policymaking board. The rationale for a single agency was that by eliminating eight separate agencies and 50 district programs, people in need of services would be relieved of a "frustrating maze of referrals and eligibility disputes." As an alternative, the proposal promised to "create a single force in government which will efficiently deliver comprehensive programs and services for the physical, mental, and social well-being of Georgia's citizens."

The proposal met with intense opposition. For example, the medical lobby, fearful of losing control over public health policy, waged political war to maintain the Health Department as a separate agency. The debate

---

2. This industry's organizations include not only public agencies like DHR but also nonprofit United Way-type agencies and for-profit organizations. In addition to services within the scope of DHR's program, the industry's services include public housing, unemployment and job training programs, legal services for the poor, day care, and corrections-related services.

"Golden Olympics," recreation for the elderly sponsored by DHR in cooperation with Department of Natural Resources, University of Georgia, and other agencies.

was so polarized that a bill to abolish the existing Health Board in favor of a Board of Human Resources passed by only one vote.

In July 1972, the functions of the state departments of Family and Children Services (welfare), Public Health (including mental health), Vocational Rehabilitation, Youth Services (juvenile offenders), and the Commission on Aging became divisions of a unified Department of Human Resources (DHR), governed by a 15-person board. The board shortly thereafter set policies to bring about an integrated service delivery system.

After more than a decade of operation, DHR is still working to achieve the goal of integration. The size of DHR (28,000 employees in 1985), the complexity of its programs, and the conflicts naturally arising among the professional groups who deliver services and the client groups who receive services are hindrances to the functional integration of services that planners envisioned in 1972. Yet, effective coordination has been accomplished. For example, in 159 counties the Division of Public Health and the Division of Family and Children Services (DFCS) cooperate in providing periodic health screening tests and treatments to Medicaid-eligible persons. DFCS caseworkers often begin the process by informing clients of the availability of screenings to determine health defects; visual, hearing, and dental problems; and needed immunizations; and how to obtain medical and dental care.

The ways in which agencies, not only DHR divisions but also other public agencies such as the juvenile court, and private agencies such as hospitals and nursing homes, come together to provide integrated services vary from case to case. The case of "Stacy," the pregnant teenager (see page 221), can be used to illustrate how the services of several agencies might come into play. Had the story of Stacy been carried further, a DFCS caseworker likely would have set in motion a series of events to help Stacy and her baby. The paths in Figure 2 show the points at which help from several agencies could be received. Not all the thousands of pregnant teenagers in Georgia would follow the same path.

Current Issues

Reviewing the past four decades, Georgians can note with pride great improvements in the care of their less able neighbors. The mentally ill are no longer warehoused and forgotten; children are not detained in adult jails; the poor are not demeaned and segregated in pauper farms or almshouses; modern health care education and facilities are available to all Georgians; nursing homes are designed to provide care for the infirm elderly rather than lonely detention while waiting for the relief of death. These and other improvements mark real progress in the continuing struggle to provide adequate services to people unable to care for themselves.

Since the late 1930s, the state has accepted the responsibility for providing a net of security to protect the health and well-being of Georgia citizens. The issue 40 years ago and still current today remains: Are the available services adequate? To illustrate the present debate regarding the adequacy of human services in Georgia, we will review in some detail the issue of care for the mentally ill and we will briefly look at issues regarding the poor and health care.

The Mentally Ill

The public human service institutions that have received the most media attention, both in Georgia and the nation, are facilities and programs for the public offender and the mentally ill. The recent history of public care of Georgia's mentally ill serves as a good example of the kind of struggle required to bring about reforms in all areas of human services.

A facility for the mentally ill opened at Milledgeville in 1842, and a facility for the mentally retarded opened near Augusta in 1921. Until 1965, those were the only two state mental institutions to serve a population grown to over four million. Public knowledge of these institutions, except for occasional widely publicized scandals, was almost non-

Figure 2: "Stacy's Case" and Agency Coordination

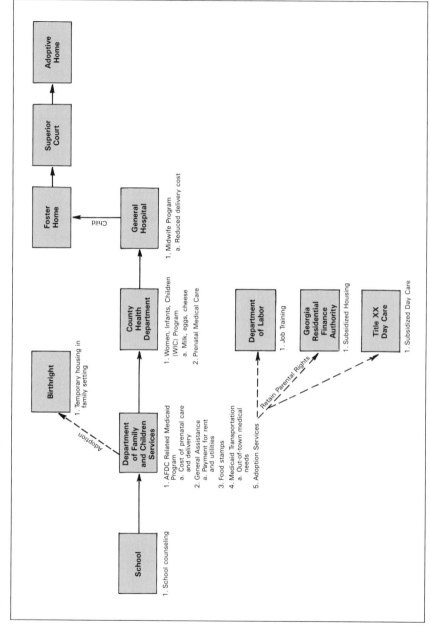

existent. In 1960, Georgia had the second largest mental hospital in the world, with 12,000 patients. (Only the infamous Pilgram State Hospital in New York, with 16,000 patients, was larger). For 12,000 patients, Georgia's hospital at Milledgeville had fewer than 50 physicians—less than half of whom were psychiatrists. The nursing staff numbered 78. The total operating budget for the hospital divided by the number of patients equaled $2.76 per patient per day.

As late as the mid-1950s, the huge hospital was considered a custody institution—a place to dispose of people with mental illness. The average length of stay for a patient was three years, one month, and one day. The pathetically small treatment staff was testament to a meagre faith in treatment and restoration. For the 1954-55 fiscal year, the total cost of all medical personnel, supplies, and equipment was a mere 4 percent of total expenditures!

The reform climate of the 1950s differed from earlier times in that for the first time three prominent sources of influence came together in support of change. The first source of influence was within the medical community with the discovery and use of amazingly effective psychotropic drugs of the phenothiazine and reserpoid classes. These and subsequent derivatives proved effective in controlling the symptoms of psychotic and depressive behavior to the extent that restoration to community living was a reasonable treatment goal for thousands of formerly unreachable patients. The second influence was public awareness. The Association of Mental Health was established in 1951. Mental health advocacy was a prominent goal for a variety of influential civic and religious groups, such as the Georgia Federation of Women's Clubs, United Church Women of Georgia, and the Georgia Junior Chamber of Commerce.

Professionals and civic leaders charted a direction for change based on enlightened attitudes toward mental illness and faith in new treatment technologies. However, it took a third influence, a well-publicized scandal, to generate the pressure required to shake loose the state dollars required to finance a treatment-oriented health care system for the mentally ill.

The scandal broke on March 5, 1959, with a front-page story in *The Atlanta Constitution* with the headline, "Unapproved Drugs Given Mental Cases." The first paragraph read—

> A Milledgeville State Hospital doctor has been using experimental, unapproved drugs on mental patients here under research programs financed by drug firms.

Subsequent articles during the next few days alleged that several staff physicians were observed performing their duties under the influence of alcohol. One of the more shocking disclosures was a March 7 article headlined "Nurse Did Key Surgery, Aides Swear." The article went on to quote a hospital technician alleging "an unnamed nurse had performed major surgery with no qualified physician present." The media painted a picture of decadent conditions in Georgia while pointing out the advances in other states such as Kansas, Kentucky, and California.

During the public furor, Gov. Ernest Vandiver asked that the Medical Association of Georgia appoint a committee to investigate the situation and make recommendations. A committee headed by a prominent Georgia physician, Dr. Bruce Shaeffer of Toccoa, Georgia, made an investigation that resulted in numerous recommendations. The report was similar to earlier investigations done by the U.S. Department of Health in 1945 and a prestigious joint legislative study committee headed by Peyton Hawes of Elberton, Georgia, completed just one year before the Shaeffer Report. The difference in 1959 was a political and social climate conducive to reform.

Reaction to the Shaeffer Report was swift and far-reaching. Shortly after the report was released in the spring of 1959, Milledgeville State Hospital was transferred from the Welfare Department to the Health Department. Within a few months, a nationally prominent expert in mental health was appointed to head the hospital. Shortly thereafter, plans were announced to redirect mental health care from custodial "warehousing" of the mentally impaired to treatment and the restoration of the mentally ill to community, work, and family living. It required all three influences—the proven fact of effective treatment technologies, public awareness, and a well-publicized scandal to create a climate of support sufficient to bring about needed reforms.

Thirty years ago the phrase "sent to Milledgeville" represented the ultimate horror of being rejected by family and friends and literally being "put away." To say simply that things have changed is an understatement. The community-based and treatment-oriented mental health system that was planned in the early 1960s has been, for the most part, accomplished. As Table 2 shows, the vast majority of mentally disabled persons in Georgia are served in communities, not state institutions.

Today, mental health services are available through eight consortia linking eight state hospitals, four retardation facilities, and 31 community mental health centers. Local mental health centers provide evaluation, counseling, and treatment services for the mentally ill, the mentally retarded, and people impaired by alcohol and drug abuse. Because services are available close to where people live, hospitalization has been cut by 56 percent in the last 10 years. A person entering a regional mental hospital may expect to stay about 38 days. The person then returns to

Table 2: Clients Served by the Division of Mental Health and Mental Retardation, Georgia Department of Human Resources, FY 1985

	Mental Health Clients	Mental Retardation Clients	Substance Abuse Clients	Total
State hospitals	13,820	2,722	8,846	25,388
Community programs	65,481	11,369	27,401	104,251
*Total clients served (statewide)	70,595	13,588	31,029	115,212

Source: Communication, Division of Mental Health and Mental Retardation, Department of Human Resources, October 18, 1985.

*Total clients served (statewide) does not equal the number served in the hospital added to the number served in the community because some clients were served in both locations. This total is an unduplicated count regardless of where the client was served.

the local community for follow-up counseling and treatment in the local community mental health center.

The goal of treatment in the "least restrictive environment" has been achieved. Legislation protecting the rights of the mentally impaired has been enacted. However, the achievements of the past three decades have created new problems. The central issue is the difference between the level of adjustment which qualifies a patient to be discharged from institutional care and the level of adjustment that is required to function responsibly in the community. This is a difficult problem because after release from the hospital, patients may choose not to participate in follow-up services in the community and soon require rehospitalization.

Another problem is that standards of care and treatment are more difficult to monitor in the community than in an institution. Community group homes for the mentally impaired serve as a good example. According to DHR's Office of Regulatory Services, of approximately 2,500 personal care homes in Georgia, only 250 have been inspected and licensed by the state. With no system for establishing and monitoring minimum standards, conditions exist such as those described in *The Atlanta Constitution* in 1983:

PERSONAL CARE HOMES ARE OFTEN SUBSTANDARD

(When Georgia released thousands of mental patients from Central State Hospital a decade ago, officials looked for them to prosper—thanks to new drugs that controlled the symptoms of their diseases and ambitious plans for community treatment centers. Many have prospered. Thousands more have not. They have gone from hospital wards to lives of poverty and illness, in boarding houses and prisons, with overburdened families, or alone. . . .)

By Gregg Jones, Staff Writer

Meals were served twice a day in the brown brick personal-care home in southwest Atlanta: a breakfast of grits and eggs at 11 a.m. and a dinner at 5:30 p.m. that typically consisted of pigs' ears, rice and peas.

On a sultry day last July, Michele McClave inspected the house, where 14 mentally ill men paid $225 each month to live. Outside, its green and white awning cast an inviting blanket of cool shade over the front porch.

Inside, there were no sheets on the beds, no soap or toilet paper in the bathrooms, and no lights—because the power had been shut off, she noted in her report. She added that there was no one supervising the home and that there was no phone.

In the back yard, spotted with clumps of high, scraggly grass, several mentally ill men sat in rusting metal chairs, Ms. McClave recalled.

One old man—with eyes yellowed and bloodshot and hands that looked as if they had been burned and not given care—caught her eye.

"The residents at this home all seemed to have serious mental problems which appeared to need some intensive help," she wrote. "One 21-year-old resident. . .was constantly laughing loudly, and followed us around the facility interrupting our conversations with other residents. . . ." (*The Atlanta Constitution,* April 7, 1983)

There are great problems to be overcome if we are to provide a measure of care and support in the community that recognizes the difference between being stabilized within a hospital setting and being adjusted to community living. But, improving community care provides the only long-term hope of avoiding the temptation once again to dispose of the mentally ill by confining them to institutions.

The Poor

Of the approximately 900,000 Georgians who are officially poor, about two-thirds are poor enough to be eligible for some direct financial assistance from tax-supported state/federal programs. In fiscal year (FY) 1985, 239,007 individuals (average per month) received Aid to Families with Dependent Children (AFDC) direct money payments and 570,027 individuals (average per month) received food stamps. Discounting the 70 percent of AFDC recipients who also received food stamps, the average number of Georgians receiving assistance in FY 1985 was 641,889.

Of the Georgia *families* eligible to receive aid to families with dependent children (AFDC), 80.3 percent are black, 19.2 percent are white,

*What is poverty? Consistent and directed public policy regarding the
poor is elusive in the absence of an accepted definition of poverty.*

and 0.5 percent are other races (Hispanics, Asians, etc.). Ninety-one
percent of all AFDC cases are families of four or fewer people. Families
of two (generally two children or a mother and one child) make up 40
percent, the largest single group. Families of three (generally a mother
and two children) account for 26 percent, and single child recipients
account for 6 percent.

State/federal assistance to the poor is mainly delivered through local
government. To determine eligibility for public assistance, county departments of family and children services employ some 1,650 eligibility
benefits caseworkers. In addition, in FY 1985, some 1,100 social services caseworkers handled 31,985 child protective cases (including neglect
and abuse) and 8,123 adult protective cases (including neglect and abuse
of the elderly). In general, caseworkers are hampered by huge caseloads
and frustrated by inadequate resources. The *1982 Census of Governments* showed that while there were 17 public welfare workers per 10,000
population employed by state and local governments in the United States,
Georgia had only 12 per 10,000.

The frustrations of caseworkers mirror the more basic issue of
ambivalent public policy. Consistent and directed public policy regarding the poor is elusive in the absence of an accepted definition of poverty,
and in the presence of considerable disagreement on the level of support
the government should provide people who qualify for public assistance.

The public tends to vascillate between guilt over providing too little and concern that providing more may lead to dependency and discourage self-sufficiency. Politicians exploit these competing emotions and our priorities swing between "wars on poverty," marked by massive buildups of programs to serve the poor, and "wars on impoverished people," marked by drastic cuts in public monies that finance public assistance programs.

As Table 3 shows, per capita expenditures by state and local governments for public welfare increased in Georgia and in the United States as a whole between 1962 and 1981-82. But, as a percentage of the average expenditure for all states, expenditures by Georgia governments decreased from 89.1 percent to 68.4 percent.

Georgia lags far below the national average in the amount of public assistance granted to the poor. In calendar year 1984, approximately 3.7 million American families (average per month) received an average AFDC monthly payment of $325.46. In the same year, 88,523 Georgia families (average per month) received an average AFDC monthly payment of $186.36. Among the 50 states and District of Columbia, Georgia ranked 44th in average AFDC monthly payment.

Health Care and the Poor

The quality of health care for the poor and disadvantaged remains a major public policy issue. Unlike the situation in public assistance, the situation in health care cannot be explained simply as a lack of public funding. Georgia consistently ranks second or third in the nation in the proportion of state and local expenditures committed to health and hospitals. Table 4 compares per capita state and local spending for health and hospitals in Georgia and in the nation as a whole. From 1962 to 1981-82, expenditures for health and hospitals in Georgia rose from 122

Table 3: State and Local Government per Capita Expenditures for Public Welfare, Georgia and the United States, 1962 to 1981-1982

	1981-82	1976-77	1971-72	1966-67	1962
U.S. average	$248.14	$159.57	$101.41	$41.53	$27.36
Georgia	169.70	102.34	84.44	30.73	24.39
Georgia as percentage of U.S.	68.4%	64.1%	83.3%	74.0%	89.1%

Source: U.S. Bureau of the Census: *Historical Statistics on Governmental Finances and Employment, 1982 Census of Governments,* 1985.

percent to 172 percent of the national average. As a percentage of all direct general expenditures of state and local government, health and hospital spending in 1981-82 accounted for 18.4 percent of the total in Georgia and 9.5 percent in the United States as a whole. Unlike welfare spending, health and hospital spending is not focused on serving the poor but on serving whole communities. However, the burden of health care for the poor falls mainly on tax-supported facilities.

Table 4: Per Capita Direct Expenditures by State and Local Governments for Health and Hospitals, Georgia and the United States, 1962 to 1981-1982

	1981-82	**1976-77**	**1971-72**	**1966-67**	**1962**
U.S. average	$180.46	$106.48	$ 62.54	$ 33.56	$ 23.37
Georgia	309.92	168.86	90.71	40.13	28.48
Georgia as percentage of U.S.	171.7%	158.6%	145.0%	119.6%	121.9%

Source: U.S. Bureau of the Census: *Historical Statistics on Governmental Finances and Employment, 1982 Census of Governments,* 1985.

Georgia's relatively high level of expenditure reflects the predominance of public over private health care facilities in the state. In 1983, Georgia ranked second in the nation in the number of beds in public community hospitals. About two-thirds of Georgia's hospitals, holding 60 percent of the state bed capacity, were publicly owned.

The predominance of public facilities is related to Georgia's late start in developing an adequate system of health care facilities. That start was coincident with federal and state funds becoming available in the post-World War II years for hospital construction. In 1946, Congress passed the Hill-Burton Act which provided federal funds for hospital construction, and in 1949 the General Assembly provided for state aid to construction projects. A 1947 survey showed 50 percent of Georgia's need for general hospital facilities was unmet: of 159 counties, 60 had no such facility and another 23 had no acceptable facility. Georgia communities took full advantage of the federal and state funds made available, and in 1951 the state ranked fourth in the nation in new hospital and health center construction. Most of these facilities were in rural areas. By 1966, the 20th year of the Hill-Burton program, Georgia had built 93 new general hospitals, 47 health centers, and 106 auxiliary health centers. From 1953 to 1983, the number of general hospital beds in public and private hospitals increased from 10,677 to 25,943. At the same time, the number of nursing home beds increased from a mere 843 to 37,034!

A major portion of the state's commitment to health care is for Medicaid. In FY 1971, Georgia Medicaid expenditures—about one-third state-appropriated funds and two-thirds federal appropriation—totalled almost $120.8 million. In FY 1986, total Medicaid expenditures in Georgia were $785.5 million. In the latter year, about 26.5 percent of the total was spent on AFDC recipients; the rest covered aged, blind, and disabled recipients. About 27.6 percent of total Medicaid expenditures went to nursing home care for the elderly.

In spite of the substantial growth in health care expenditures, major problems in both the cost and accessibility of health care remain for needy Georgians. As health care costs spiral upward and as the operations of publicly owned hospitals are turned over to for-profit companies, the quality of health care for the poor is affected disproportionately. The dilemma some small communities face in providing health care to the poor, especially those who "fall between the cracks" in government programs, is illustrated in the following article from a publication directed to Georgia's county commissioners.

PUT SANITY BACK INTO THE HEALTH CARE SYSTEM

"The reason your hospital bill is so high is that there are so few paying patients," a hospital administrator candidly told a Candler County man recently. The same statement could have been made in almost any community of the state, for it demonstrates the plight of health care providers and that of responsible people who expect to pay their own way.

A citizen had brought his complaint to the Candler County Board of Commissioners: his wife had gone to the local hospital as an out-patient, had spent about three hours there and received a bill for $1,083. The facility averages about 15 patients in its care unit daily, and costs over $5-million to operate annually.

The board explained to the citizen that they had no way, as elected officials, to address the problem of his wife's bill; he was told to talk with the hospital clerk, administrator, hospital board and finally the Grand Jury.

This the citizen did, and reported polite treatment at every point, but he came back to the board of commissioners with what he believes is their problem too: paying patients can't bear the whole cost of hospital care for indigent patients, yet the billing structure was, indeed, trying to absorb indigents' costs by passing them on to paying patients.

. . . it has long been the practice for many physicians and most hospitals to extend free care to those who cannot pay. When medical costs were moderate, it was not so much of a burden. But medical costs have raced ahead of the rest of the economy. . . .

It was comfortable for us to assume a decade or two ago that the doctors and the hospitals would take care of that small group of people who needed care and couldn't pay. But that group isn't small any more. . . .

Public health and medical care programs have definitely improved care for millions and have doubtless extended life. But we still have people who "fall through those cracks," as Washington is fond of terming its program gaps. When they do, it is county government that is left to decide who will pick up the bill.

We don't argue that they should not get the care they need. The debate is over who pays. Someone always does.

If, like the community I mentioned at the start of this column, we have a small town and a small community hospital with no direct subsidy from the county, paying patients can pay double for hospital services because they have to subsidize those who can't pay. The only alternative available to us now is to pass those costs on to the whole community—small though it may be—through higher property taxes.

Are we going to have to go to our small hospitals and say, "We can't afford you. Shut your doors?" At the same time we would be telling the paying patients as well as indigents who have even greater difficulty traveling to distant hospitals that they can't have a local hospital any more.

For so massive a problem, there is no single answer. We have repeatedly asked for more state involvement in indigent health care. Seems like the state determines who is indigent and what kind of care they should get, so the state should back up its judgment with money. Yet that isn't the only answer.

In almost any public health or welfare situation, county government is the court of last resort. We don't have anyone to make the hand-off to. County commissioners and local taxpayers are not inhumane when it comes to indigent care, but we would all like to see some sanity in the system. It's sadly lacking now. (Charles Roberts, "Put Sanity Back into the Health Care System," *Georgia County Government,* November 1985.)

No statistic is more indicative of the need for health care improvement than Georgia's infant mortality rate. In 1983, the state ranked 43rd in infant mortality with a rate of 13.7 deaths per 1,000 births. The rate for the United States as a whole was 10.9 per 1,000. High infant mortality rates are generally associated with poverty: the mortality rate for black babies is about 20 per 1,000, about 10 per 1,000 for white babies.

Inaccessibility of care for the poor is a function of both geography and cost. Only 58 percent of all active physicians in Georgia participate in the Medicaid program. In 1985, *The Atlanta Constitution* reported:

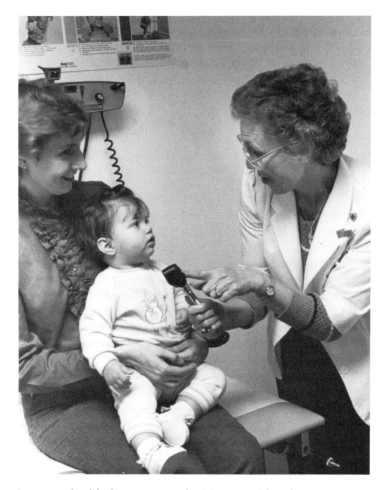

At county health departments, physicians provide a large measure of health care to the state's youngest residents.

. . .In 56 of Georgia's 159 counties there is no obstetrician, and in 18 there are no obstetricians who accept Medicaid patients.

In another 26 counties, there are no obstetricians to treat those patients who are too poor to afford health insurance but make too much money to be eligible for Medicaid.

Proposals to solve the dilemma described include increasing state payments to physicians who treat patients not covered by health insurance or Medicaid; developing a midwife service in rural areas without physicians; and expanding prenatal care programs.

The Future a Matter of Priorities

The Great Depression of the 1930s forced us to change our response to people in need. Even those skeptical of government aid came to realize that because of advances in technology and population mobility, permanent shifts in the economic structure, and the rising expectations of a rapidly increasing urban population, a new social order was created that demanded a more responsible role for government. The state and federal social legislation of the 1930s established a permanent role for government in the welfare and progress of people. A dialogue was begun which continues to this present day:

> At what level is the government responsible for providing for the needs of people without endangering the fundamental principle of individual freedom and individual, family, and community responsibility?

This question has been a recurrent theme in all debates on social welfare issues during the past 50 years. Although never without intense debate, on balance, the last 50 years is a record of continuous expansion of the role and responsibility of government in providing services to people. Yet, the issues raised in the examples of the mentally ill and the health and welfare of the poor remind us that available services are still not adequate.

In the introduction to this chapter we mentioned three factors which determine the quality of services to people: (1) the attitudes and values of the culture, (2) the resources available, and (3) the knowledge and skills of the people who deliver the services. Further development in all three areas will be required before the adequacy of services to needy people will be sufficient to ensure that they have a fair chance to achieve their potential for participation in the social and economic life of the community.

How important is the welfare of people? How should we invest our resources? In the final analysis it becomes a question of priorities.

CHAPTER EIGHT

Culture and Arts

By John D. Burke

Culture has many meanings. In its broad sense, culture is that complex whole of habits and capabilities—of doing and thinking—acquired by human beings as members of a society: knowledge and language, ideas and outlooks, values and beliefs, religion and morals, government and laws, education and customs, economy and technology, science and the arts. Every people has a culture. Their culture changes over time by invention and, when they come into contact with the culture of another people, by assimilation. In a narrow sense, culture is synonymous with the arts: literary, visual, plastic, and performing arts. Each of these categories may be identified—according to the standards applied—as popular culture, folk art, ethnic culture, fine art, or high culture; and even as democratic or aristocratic, indigenous, or imported art.

This chapter focuses on contemporary culture in the narrow sense, but from the outset it addresses the relationship of the arts to the larger culture—a relationship inevitably the subject of controversy.

Roots of Contemporary Georgia Culture

Contemporary Georgia culture was conceived in controversy. In 1920, a strident iconoclast from Baltimore, H. L. Mencken, stung the pride of the South with his essay, "The Sahara of the Bozart" (In *Prejudices: Second Series* [New York: Alfred Knopf, Inc.]). A few quotations make the point:

> [The South] is almost as sterile, artistically, intellectually, culturally, as the Sahara Desert. There are single acres in Europe that house more first-rate men than all the states south of the Potomac, . . .
>
> In all that gargantuan paradise of the fourth-rate there is not a single picture gallery worth going into, or a single orchestra

capable of playing the nine symphonies of Beethoven, or a single opera-house, or a single theatre devoted to decent plays, . . .

And when he narrowed his focus to Georgia:

> If one turns to such a commonwealth as Georgia the picture becomes far darker. There the liberated lower orders of whites have borrowed the worst commercial boundarism of the Yankee and superimposed it upon a culture that, at bottom, is but little removed from savagery. . . . in thirty years it has not produced a single idea. Once upon a time a Georgian printed a couple of books that attracted notice, but immediately it turned out that he [Joel Chandler Harris] was little more than an amanuensis for the local blacks. . . . And he is not only the glory of the literature of Georgia; he is, almost literally, the whole of the literature of Georgia—nay, of the entire art of Georgia.

Mencken's diatribe provoked a wide response among southerners. Most were hostile, but the approving reaction that the Sage of Baltimore received from other southerners was of such magnitude that he predicted a southern cultural renascence similar to the one in New England some 80 years before. Two months after the publication of his essay, two literary magazines appeared; and Mencken later took credit for what he considered a revival of southern arts and letters.

Viewing that diatribe today, we see that in making his judgment Mencken applied a standard of value derived from a cultural tradition largely foreign to the southern people. In Mencken's narrow view, there was a superior culture—an extension of European culture—in the Northeast, with its urban population concentrations, industrial wealth, advanced education, leisure time, and large monied class. The South was distinctly different. The region had remained isolated from the main currents of American life in the late nineteenth century—industrialization, urbanization, and immigration by non-British peoples—and its people suffered a local isolation on scattered farms and plantations. If Mencken wanted to transplant his culture to the South, he would in some way have to transplant the northeastern environment, too.

Instead, Mencken held up another environment for southerners of his time to emulate. It was the Old South:

> More, it was a civilization of manifold excellences—perhaps the best that the Western Hemisphere had ever seen—undoubtedly the best that These States have ever seen. . . . But in the south there were men of delicate fancy, urbane instinct and aristocratic manner—in brief, superior men—in brief, gentry. . . . The *Ur*-Confederate had leisure. He liked to toy with ideas. He was hospitable and tolerant. He had the vague thing that we call culture.

Mencken had supplemented his initial misjudgment with another: he reinvigorated the battered myth. In a South that was burdened with the experience of the Civil War and its aftermath, that bitterly resented outside criticism, that was unprepared for critical attention from its own writers, Mencken's essay encouraged the rebirth of the fantasy of southern gentility and plantation aristocracy.

Much of southern literature in the 50 years following the Civil War had been apologetic and sentimental, and the tendency to idealize the Old South continued. As late as 1930, in a collection of essays entitled *I'll Take My Stand,* a group of distinguished southern writers, dubbed the Vanderbilt Agrarians, extolled the virtues of the antebellum South's pre-industrial society, where the values of leisure, grace, tradition, beauty, and religion had not been traded for economic gain. Six years later, Margaret Mitchell, an Atlanta journalist, published *Gone With the Wind,* a novel that contained all the romantic myths of the Old South. It was an immediate sensation and in 1937 won a Pulitzer Prize for Mitchell. Neither the essays nor the novel accurately described or plausibly resolved the difficulties that southerners faced. Instead, their idealization of the Old South suggested that the present was best spent in creating some new version of the past. But because the legendary Old South had never existed, those who looked to it for guidance in the artistic development of the New South would be disappointed, for fact cannot be built upon fiction.

W. J. Cash in his *The Mind of the South* (New York: Alfred A. Knopf, Inc., 1941), recounted the legend: the Old South was peopled with country gentlemen and demure damsels who acted out, in magnificent white-columned plantation mansions, a social life dominated by polished manners, honor, and chivalry—all derived from the late Restoration period of England and all destroyed by the Civil War and the 30 years of brutal social upheaval that followed it.

> These legends bear little relation to reality. There was an Old South to be sure, but it was another thing than this. And there is a New South. Industrialization and commercialization greatly modified the land including its ideology, as we shall see in due course. Nevertheless, the extent of the change and of the break between the Old South that was and the New South of our time has been vastly exaggerated.

There indeed was an Old South, but it was peopled more with individualistic backcountry farmers who had little opportunity for a social life beyond work, family, and church than with country gentlemen and ladies. A small group of successful middle-class planters did send their sons off to college in New England or Britain where they learned something of high culture. "And the sons of these (sons) began to think of themselves as true aristocrats and to be accepted as such by those about them—to set themselves consciously to the elaboration and propagation of a tradition." But even the well-educated plantation owner was more concerned with attaining the social graces than with cultivating the arts. Cash's book described the Old South as it was and showed that the myth was as unlikely a model for the future as it was an unreliable reflection of the past.

When Cash's book came out, the South was already in the midst of rapid change wrought by industrialism, World War I, and the Great Depression. Cultural isolation began to give way to cultural assimilation, and eventually Georgians came to appreciate not only the European culture that Mencken espoused but also African culture. More importantly, the real southern culture began to put out its first flowering. Southern culture emerged from within the region and had little to do with the criticism of Mencken or the Vanderbilt Agrarians. Like the New England literary outburst of the mid-nineteenth century, it was distinctly American. And like the works of those earlier Yankees, the artistic expressions of Southerners emanated from the realities of contemporary life, not from an idealized past.

Literary Contributions

Within a scant two years after the publication of *I'll Take My Stand,* a Georgian from Wrens was to bury the agrarian legend. Writing out of his experience of rural Georgia—the economic deprivation, the sharecropper's existence, the overworked red clay, the heat, the hostility— Erskine Caldwell produced *Tobacco Road* (New York: Charles Scribner's Sons, 1932), a story of Georgians who barely worked the land and whose values mocked those of Mencken and the Vanderbilt Agrarians. The main character of the novel, Jeeter Lester, delivers the following speech after agreeing to help his son-in-law rape his 12-year-old wife (Jeeter's daughter) in exchange for a bag of turnips. Jeeter never goes through with the deal, but obviously, his poverty allows him little dignity.

> By God and by Jesus, Lov, all the damn-blasted turnips I raised this year is wormy. And I ain't had a good turnip since a year ago this spring. . . .What God made turnip-worms for, I can't make out. It appears to me like He just naturally has got it in good and heavy for a poor man. . . . But I ain't complaining, Lov. I say, "The good Lord knows best about turnips. . . ." Some of these days He'll bust loose with a heap of bounty. . . . But we got to stop cussing Him when we ain't got nothing to eat. He'll send a man to hell and the devil for persisting in doing that.

Caldwell's story dealt with the reality of the Georgia sharecropper during the early 1930s. The conniving character of Jeeter Lester, who dominates the story with his wily skulduggery, is a symbol of the social injustices present in the Georgia that Caldwell described in *Call It Experience* (New York: Duell, Sloan and Pearce, 1951).

> Within a few miles from town, families on tenant farms were huddled around fireplaces in drafty hovels. Most of them were despondent. Some were hungry as usual; others were ill and without medical attention. Food and clothing were scarce, and in some instances non-existent; . . .
>
> Day after day, I went into the country, . . . I could not become accustomed to the sight of children's stomachs bloated from hunger and seeing the ill and aged too weak to walk to the fields to search for something to eat. In the evenings I wrote about what I had seen during the day, but nothing I put down on paper succeeded in conveying the full meaning of poverty and hopelessness and degradation as I had observed it.

Tobacco Road was not an outstanding commercial success. But Caldwell's *God's Little Acre* (1933) was, surviving midst its success obscenity charges instituted by the New York Society for the Suppression of Vice. In the same year, Caldwell received the award for fiction from the *Yale Review*. Then, in December of 1933, the stage adaptation of *Tobacco Road* appeared on Broadway. It had a continuous run of seven and a half years, setting a record at that time, and brought Caldwell popular acclaim and financial success.

Some critics have called the period that began with Caldwell's work Georgia's literary renascence. But it was more of a birth than a rebirth, when we consider what preceded Caldwell. Mencken was correct in claiming that Joel Chandler Harris's *Uncle Remus* stories were transcripts of black folktales. Nevertheless, Harris took pains to verify that the tales were genuine, and folklorists respect his devotion to recording plantation tales that otherwise would have perished. He is not exactly a folklorist, however, because he created the fictional framework within which the stories are told. A fictional character, Uncle Remus, tells these traditional tales to "Miss Sally's little boy." The little boy is sometimes arrogant, but Uncle Remus uses wit and the wisdom of his stories to correct the boy's superior attitude. Harris's phonetic spelling, as used in "Mr. Fox Is Again Victimised" (In *Uncle Remus, His Songs and His Sayings* [New York: D. Appleton and Company, 1880]), though probably done with the best intentions, is patronizing and detracts from the tales.

"I ain't tellin' no tales ter bad chilluns," said Uncle Remus curtly.

"But Uncle Remus, I ain't bad," said the little boy plaintively.

"Who dat chunkin' dem chickens dis mawnin'? Who dat knockin' out fokes's eyes wid dat Yallerbammer sling des' fo' dinner? Who dat sickin' dat pinter puppy atter my pig? Who dat scatterin' my ingun sets? Who dat flingin' rocks on top er my house, w'ich a little mo'en one un em would er drap spang on my head?"

"Well, now, Uncle Remus, I didn't go to do it. I won't do so any more. Please, Uncle Remus, if you will tell me [a story], I'll run to the house and bring you some teacakes."

The only other notable literary presence in Georgia prior to the rise of Caldwell was poet Sidney Lanier (1842-81). A Macon native and Civil War veteran, Lanier was in his time considered on a lyrical level with better known contemporaries, including Walt Whitman. Some of Lanier's works reflected his belief in the superiority of the southern agrarian ideal over the northern industrial creed. Several of his poems, "Song of the Chattahoochee" and "The Marshes of Glynn," had southern settings.

For Caldwell, the South provided more than a setting. Many of his contemporaries considered him to be a sensationalist and claimed that his fame resulted from the sexual notoriety of his stories. Few recognized the social protest he intended the work to express. Yet he was the first flowering of a new generation of writers in Georgia—a generation that would include Flannery O'Connor, Carson McCullers, and Lillian Smith who, between 1930 and 1960, emerged as three of Georgia's most talented writers.

Carson McCullers, a native of Columbus, Georgia, began publishing short stories in 1936 at the age of 18. Four years later she completed her first novel, *The Heart Is a Lonely Hunter*. It lifted her to fame and success overnight. McCullers dealt with the contemporary South both in this novel and those that followed. In 1941, *Reflections in a Golden Eye* appeared, but it achieved only meagre success. Then, in 1946, McCullers completed *A Member of the Wedding* (Boston: Houghton Mifflin Co., 1946), considered by some her most sensitive work. The action revolves around 12-year-old Frankie Addams and her search for her own identity. The setting is the South in the dog-days of August. The place is the kitchen of a small home, where the reality of the contemporary South is acted out in the person of Frankie (who wants to be called F. Jasmine) and the housekeeper Berenice. The flavor of rural southern society flows forth easily, and a pattern of sayings and behavior emerges which reveals, with tenderness and humor, the personalities of the leading characters.

The afternoon was like the center of the cake that Berenice had baked last Monday, a cake which failed. The old Frankie had been glad the cake had failed, not out of spite, but because she loved these fallen cakes the best. She enjoyed the damp, gummy richness near the center, and did not understand why grown people thought such cakes a failure. It was a loaf cake, that last Monday, with the edges risen light and high and the middle moist and altogether fallen—after the bright high morning the afternoon was dense and solid as the center of that cake.

"Fool's hill. You have a whole lot less of sense than I was giving you credit for. What makes you think they want to take you along with them? Two is company and three is a crowd. And that is the main thing about a wedding. Two is company and three is a crowd."

F. Jasmine always found it hard to argue with a known saying. She loved to use them in her shows and in her conversation, but they were very hard to argue with, and so she said:

"You wait and see."

"Remember back to the time of the flood? Remember Noah and the ark?"

"And what has that got to do with it?" she asked.

"Remember the way he admitted them creatures."

"Oh, hush up your big old mouth," she said.

"Two by two," said Berenice. "He admitted them creatures two by two."

A Member of the Wedding was adapted by the novelist herself as a very successful drama in 1950. *Ballad of the Sad Cafe* was published in 1951 and dramatized by Edward Albee in 1963. Again, the setting is a dreary small town, and the action is focused in a cafe, a place of talking and reminiscing, a retreat from reality. McCullers completed her last novel, *Clock without Hands,* in 1961. It has as its subject the imminent end of segregation.

Some critics have faulted Carson McCullers with having a predilection for the bizarre, grotesque, and sentimental. Nevertheless, her examinations of the dark, lonely side of life—sometimes physicalized in the character of a dwarf, a deaf mute, or a psychopath—reflect a view of the southern experience that is similar to Caldwell's. They link her with the author who today is considered by many to be Georgia's finest writer of fiction, Flannery O'Connor.

O'Connor, who lived in Milledgeville, expressed the culture of the South in short stories and novels that often have underlying religious themes. Her Bible Belt characters are products of the "Christ-haunted" (her words) region to which they belong and from which they are alienated. A Catholic, O'Connor reveals a love for her characters that some critics say is Christ-centered. Yet, she expresses that love only after the characters have been sacrificed—redeemed, in a sense, by a grace often gained through a grotesque type of suffering. Violence as redemption and sardonic ridicule as comic punishment or penance emanate from her stories with unsentimental brutality. If true art does challenge our myths and fantasies, Flannery O'Connor does more than challenge the myth of the Old South: her harsh irony storms its walls. Yet it is out of such ruins that O'Connor apparently believed the South could be resurrected, leaving behind the ashes of hypocrisy that myth and fantasy engender.

O'Connor's reputation was established by the 1952 publication of *Wise Blood*. Its central character, Haze Motes, is a pathetic, comic figure. The setting of the novel is a southern city, a nothing place, lacking identity, tradition, and order. When Motes arrives there, the emptiness suggests a type of limbo where all people are in need of baptism, and is accentuated by Motes's backwoods and backwards preaching of salvation to its citizens. Of its inhabitants—Hawks, Sabbath Lily, Enoch Emery, Solace Layfield—none is capable of being saved. They meet Motes at different points of his ridiculous but honest pilgrimage downward, where frozen in blindness, and finally in death, he is ministered to by Mrs. Flood, a parody of faded southern femininity. Motes' suffering, however, is a way to grace, and we are moved to pity him at the end.

Violent and shocking events confront the self-satisfied, unsympathetic characters of O'Connor's fiction. In "A Good Man Is Hard to Find" (*Modern Writing*, William Phillips and Philip Rahv, eds. [New York: Avon Publications, 1953]), the grandmother keeps advising The Misfit to pray to Jesus for comfort, but when her son is killed and her own life is threatened, she stops recommending Jesus and, mistaking The Misfit for one of her own children, she tries to comfort him herself. The Misfit has already worked himself up to a state of violence and he shoots her. After this brutality, The Misfit's conversation with his accomplices is mild and full of platitudes, but he cannot confirm that the meanness of his life has brought any pleasure.

> "She would of been a good women," The Misfit said, "if it had been somebody there to shoot her every minute of her life."
> "Some fun!" Bobby Lee said.
> "Shut up, Bobby Lee," The Misfit said. "It's no real pleasure in life."

The Violent Bear It Away appeared in 1960. It is O'Connor's most extended work and perhaps most eccentric vision of God's redeeming mercy. The principal conflict, between the ignorant Tarwater and his educated uncle, is over the baptism of the uncle's idiot child. Tarwater is impelled toward a blasphemous perversion of the sacrament in order to free himself from what he considers the religious spell of his great uncle, half lunatic and half prophet, who had kidnapped Tarwater as a child. The climax occurs when he does baptize the child—by immersing its head under the waters of a lake until it dies. Rayber, the uncle, a distant witness, is, by his complacency, a willing accomplice.

At times, O'Connor's characters tend to vacillate between platitudes and brutality. In "Revelation" (*Sewanee Review* 72, no. 2, 1964), the main character, Mrs. Turpin, has adopted a system of complacencies which allows her to classify everyone else in relation to herself and to deal with them without feeling the compassion that comes of identifying oneself with others.

> Without appearing to, Mrs. Turpin always noticed people's feet. The well-dressed lady had on red and grey suede shoes to match her dress. Mrs. Turpin had on her good black patent leather pumps. The ugly girl had on Girl Scout shoes and heavy socks. The old woman had on tennis shoes and the white-trashy mother had on what appeared to be bedroom slippers, black straw with gold braid threaded through them—exactly what you would have expected her to have on.
>
> Sometimes at night when she couldn't go to sleep, Mrs. Turpin would occupy herself with the question of who she would have chosen to be if she couldn't have been herself. If Jesus had said to her before he made her "There's only two places available for you. You can either be a nigger or white-trash," what would she have said? "Please, Jesus, please," she would have said, "just let me wait until there's another place available,. . ."

Two short story collections compiled during O'Connor's lifetime are *A Good Man Is Hard to Find* (1955), and *Everything That Rises Must Converge* (1964). The latter work was published posthumously.

Three years after O'Connor's death in 1964, Carson McCullers died. Both women's lives had been ones of intense physical suffering. Miss O'Connor was a victim of lupus, a progressively degenerating disease accompanied by tremendous pain. Carson McCullers was paralyzed on her left side at the age of 29 and spent her last years in a wheel-chair, dying at the age of 50.

Lillian Smith was born in Jasper, Florida—on the Georgia line—and lived at Clayton, Georgia, where she directed a girls camp until 1945. She differs from McCullers and O'Connor in that her fiction—while dealing with the problems of southern racism, fundamentalist religion, and narrow economic exploitation—has characters and plots that do not emanate from a genuine experience of the South and could easily have taken place in any environment of the United States. Smith, perhaps more successful as a liberal polemicist than as a writer of fiction, is nevertheless best known for her 1944 novel, *Strange Fruit,* a story, controversial for its time, of the tragic outcome of an interracial love affair. Her best nonfiction work, *Killers of the Dream* (1949), is ostensibly a critique of the double standards existing in the South in regard to racism. Yet much of what she says is applicable to the North as she deals with such topics as exploitation of the poor, the strangulation of the individual, and the failings of the established Christian church.

Smith's death in 1966 was followed shortly by that of McCullers. Lillian Smith has been treated herein out of chronological order, for she is a transitional figure in the state's literature. The South was changing. World War II, the media, urbanism, integration, and the Sunbelt dream were adulterating the southern experience with cosmopolitan values, attitudes, and social mores from outside the South. It is this transition that Smith mirrored.

More recently, three talents from the Georgia environment,—James Dickey, Harry Crews, and Alice Walker—have cast the southern experience in new terms.

James Dickey is Georgia's most renowned poet—at least from a contemporary point of view. Dickey's roots are in Georgia, but not agrarian Georgia. He was born and raised in Atlanta. He attended Clemson University in 1942 but left to join the Army Air Force, an experience that was a primary force in motivating him to write poetry. Upon his return, he enrolled at Vanderbilt University, where he was ingrained with the greatness of the southern literary tradition. There he became aware, he states, of "what it really meant for me to be a Southerner." Emanating from his poetry is a romantic worship of nature, manliness, and family ties.

His first book of poetry, *Into the Stone* (1960), dealt with the family (especially the brother who died before James was born) and his wartime experiences (as a fighter-bomber pilot in World War II). In 1962, *Drowning With Others* appeared. A prolific writer, Dickey has received many awards for his poetry. In 1966, he received the National Book Award for *Buckdancer's Choice* and shortly thereafter was appointed Consultant in Poetry for the Library of Congress.

Dickey was appointed Writer-in-Residence at the University of South Carolina in 1967, and while there he completed the novel *Deliverance* (New York: Dell Publishing Co., 1970). The film version of the book brought him fame (and some stardom, since he appeared in the role of the sheriff). Four friends decide to go white-water rafting down a river in the North Georgia mountains. All four men are approaching middle age and looking for some deliverance from the monotony and superficiality of urban life. The story is told by Ed Gentry, a moderately successful ad-agency owner.

> The feeling of the inconsequence of whatever I would do, of anything I would pick up or think about or turn to see was at that moment being set in the very bone marrow. How does one get through this? I asked myself. By doing something that is at hand to be done was the best answer I could give; that and not saying anything about the feeling to anyone. It was the old mortal, helpless, time-terrified human feeling, just the same. I had had a touch or two before, though it was more likely to come with my family, for I could find ways to keep busy at the studio, or at least to seem busy, which was harder, in some cases, than doing real work. But I was really frightened, this time. It had me for sure, and I knew that if I managed to get up, through the enormous weight of lassitude, I would still move to the water-cooler, or speak to Jack Waskow or Thad, with a sense of being someone else, some poor fool who lives as unobserved and impotent as a ghost, going through the only motions it has.

The wild river current turns out to be less treacherous than the lawless mountain men who hunt along the riverbank. They threaten Gentry and his friends. In order to survive, Gentry must make life-or-death decisions. Gentry is by nature unheroic, yet he rises to the occasion and becomes the hero of the tale.

After the success of *Deliverance*, Dickey's productivity seemed to wane. In 1974, he published *Jericho: The South Beheld;* it was an enormously successful work in terms of sales. Later, in 1976, Dickey wrote *God Images* for Jimmy Carter's inauguration. In 1987, he completed a long-promised second novel, *Alnilam.*

Departing from the literary tradition of Caldwell, McCullers, and O'Connor, who make locality an essential part of their characters' personalities, Dickey creates, in *Deliverance,* principal characters (suburbanites) whose identities are not tied to a particular region. Harry Crews, a contemporary of Dickey, uses regionalism in a traditional way; that is, the place is part of the characters' identity. But unlike Caldwell, McCullers, and O'Connor characters, Crews characters at times seem to be trying to escape from their regional limitations.

Harry Crews was born in Bacon County, by his own words "in the worst hookworm and rickets part of Georgia." The South he grew up in, the rural South of sharecropping, grinding poverty, and brutality is sharply etched in his memoir, *A Childhood: The Biography of a Place* (1978). His novels, however, are set in a South losing its regional identity and traditional values—mainly south Georgia and north Florida in the 1960s and 1970s.

His first novel, *The Gospel Singer*, (1968) is set in Georgia. The titular hero is worshipped as a Jesus healer by the desperate and degraded people of the community. When the gospel singer fails to live up to the town's expectations, they turn on him in violent disillusionment. Crews deals with the hypocrisy of Bible-belt religion, and he points this out in his epigraph to the story, "Men to whom God is dead worship one another." And they will kill to protect the hypocrisy of this illusion.

After *The Gospel Singer*, Crews produced a fairly steady stream of seven novels, heavily peopled with physical freaks and psychological misfits who despair of finding any meaning in their lives.

In *Feast of Snakes* (New York: Atheneum, 1976), Crews's vision is one of hopelessness. It is set in a rural south Georgia town whose annual tradition of rounding up rattlesnakes has degenerated into a tourist attraction. The central character, Joe Lon Mackey, has lost control of *his* life, too. The town's greatest high school football star can't go to college because his teachers never taught him to read and write. The golden boy to whom cheerleaders and majorettes gladly gave their bodies is trapped in a trailer with a wife who has rotting teeth, and two babies. After a humiliating encounter with his old girlfriend and a polished young man she has brought down from the University of Georgia, Joe Lon goes to the trailer.

> . . . he just sat at the little white Formica table, holding on to the edge of his chair, and looking out the window. She was watching him and he could feel the weight of her gaze.
>
> "I'll git the coffee, Joe Lon, honey," she finally said.
>
> He nodded but did not answer. . . .
>
> "Honey, here's some fresh hot."
>
> She set the coffee on the table and waited for him to taste it. He bent his head to the raised cup.
>
> "Is it good?"
>
> "Yeah," he said, "it's good, Elf."
>
> She stood where she was, smiling now, but with her mouth conspicuously closed. "You know what, Joe Lon, honey?"
>
> "No, Elf."
>
> "I made me a phone call this morning first thing."
>
> "Okay, Elf." . . .
>
> "You know who it was to?" said Elfie.
>
> "No," he said, "I don't know who it was to."
>
> "To the dentist in Tifton." Her voice was rising and lilting, full of surprised triumph. "I called the dentist, and I'm gone git these old sorry teeth of mine fixed."
>
> He turned his eyes from the window to look at her where she had retreated to the sink. He could see now what she was doing.

She was washing out baby diapers. Although he had not before, he now smelled the ammonia from his son's piss and he wished he didn't. He forced himself to smile at her as she still watched him over her shoulder.

"That's real good, Elf," he said. "You done real good to do that for youself." His throat felt very tight. "It'll make you feel better."

She left the sink and came to stand behind him. "I done it for you, Joe Lon, honey. I coulda done without it for myself." She moved closer to the back of his chair. Her thin soft hands touched him, one on each shoulder. "Me'n the babies love you, Joe Lon, honey."

He could only nod. He turned loose his coffee and took hold again of the table. He desperately wanted to howl.

Alice Walker grew up in Eatonton, Georgia. Her father was a sharecropper and the family was poor, but she received a scholarship to Spelman College and later continued her studies at Sarah Lawrence College. During the 1960s, she was involved in the civil rights movement in Mississippi, and she journeyed to Africa, she says, "in search of her roots." These experiences provide the subject matter for much of her fiction and poetry.

In 1973, Ms. Walker published "Everyday Use" (*Harper's* 246, April 1973), a short story told in the first person by a black woman whose ambitious daughter has come back to visit. The mother lives in a country shack with Maggie, her younger daughter. Maggie is slow and timid—disfigured by burn scars and destined to marry the "mossy-toothed" John Thomas. The mother considers the older girl, Dee, somewhat of a phenomenon. Dee now calls herself Wangero in honor of her African roots, and she professes great pride in her black heritage. Particularly, she wants her mother to give her some handmade quilts which have already been promised to Maggie.

"Mama," Wangero said sweet as a bird. "Can I have these old quilts?". . .

"The truth is," I said, "I promised to give them quilts to Maggie, for when she marries John Thomas."

She gasped like a bee had stung her.

"Maggie can't appreciate these quilts!" she said. "She'd probably be backward enough to put them to everyday use."

"I reckon she would," I said. "God knows I been saving 'em for long enough with nobody using 'em. I hope she will!" I didn't want to bring up how I had offered Dee (Wangero) a quilt when she went away to college. Then she had told me they were old-fashioned, out of style.

"But they're *priceless!*" she was saying now, furiously; for she has a temper. "Maggie would put them on the bed and in five years they'd be in rags. Less than that!"

"She can always make some more," I said. "Maggie knows how to quilt."

Dee (Wangero) looked at me with hatred. "You just will not understand. The point is these quilts, *these* quilts!"

"Well," I said, stumped. "What would *you* do with them?"

"Hang them," she said. As if that was the only thing you *could* do with quilts.

Maggie by now was standing in the door. I could almost hear the sound her feet made as they scraped over each other.

Walker has published a number of short fiction and poetry collections, including *You Can't Keep a Good Woman Down* (1981) and *In Search of Our Mothers' Gardens* (1983). Her best known work is *The Color Purple* (1982). This epistolary novel not only records the correspondence of Celie from adolescence to mid-life but also her growth from childish dependence to mature independence. She writes to God and to her sister, whose letters are also included in the novel. Celie has not finished high school, but she writes eloquently in nonstandard English. The style is natural and reflects Celie's dialect without employing distracting devices such as unusual punctuation or spelling. For this novel Walker received a Pulitzer Prize.

Visual Arts

The considerable achievement reached by literary expression in Georgia in the first half of the twentieth century was never complemented by similar achievement or vitality in the visual arts. This fact is perhaps most apparent when one becomes aware of the region's dearth of written criticism on the visual arts from this period, as compared with the existence of literary criticism. The lack of any truly reputable and cosmopolitan art schools before the 1940s meant that almost all talented artists sought an education in the Northeast or in Europe. Only a few returned. Of the artists working in the South, few were native to the region; rather, they were drawn to the area because of a perceived southern sensibility (again the myth) or by the beauty of the terrain.

One native Georgia artist, however, gained wide recognition working in the South. William P. Silva, a native of Savannah, (1859-1948), had studied for two years under the Impressionists in Paris before painting *Georgia Pines at Sunlight*. Silva's hazy treatment of a scene reminiscent of the low country of Chatham County depends on the French Impressionist techniques and seems imitative of Whistler. Silva, who in

1913 moved to California, attempted to articulate a southern sensibility to the environment and won many prizes and awards as a landscapist.

Sentimentalizing the southern environment was the canon of most southern artists of this early period. Their nostalgia was a retreat to the postbellum protective attitude that had expected the sacredness of the land to be maintained and that was, as we have seen, fostered by the Vanderbilt Agrarians. The protective attitude included rejection of any artistic style tainted by what were considered the revolutionary changes and liberal ideas of the Northeast.

Perhaps the myth was punctured most meaningfully by a Missouri native, Thomas Hart Benton. In 1928 and 1929, he travelled through much of rural Georgia and produced works such as the *Cotton Pickers, Georgia* and *Arts of the South*. Most apparent in these works is a lack of sentimentality in depicting the landscape. In *Cotton Pickers* (1928-29), the black sharecroppers may be placed in idyllic fields of white fluff, but the work they are doing is backbreaking and dehumanizing; it is paralleled by the delapidated condition of a wagon full of cotton and the home that sits behind it. Benton's *Arts of the South* (1932), shows little sympathy with a "mythical" locale; here it is strewn with refuse, as Benton foreshadows O'Connor in his depiction of evangelical fundamentalist religion.

Yet Benton was an outsider, and no matter how accepted his paintings would be in the North (the Metropolitan Museum of Art and the Whitney Museum of American Art), he was always portrayed as a northern liberal by the tradition-bound society of the South. Thus painting in the South continued to express the sentimental nature of the agrarian experience—"the conditions of life that have given art a meaning," according to *I'll Take My Stand*. Through the 1930s, painters harkened back to the theme of a legendary South that never existed: Albrizio's murals for the Louisiana State Capitol and MacKenzie's four historical panels in the dome of the Alabama Statehouse are examples. Much art work, especially for public buildings, was funded by the New Deal's federal art programs. While these programs poured money into the South, they tended to sectionalize even further the southern arts and artists. While Erskine Caldwell was enjoying the success of his social realism in New York City, southern painting was enjoying its neoromantic era.

In 1934, Georgia painter Lamar Dodd returned to the South. He had spent a few years in New York training with the Art Students League and at age twenty-five had already had several successful exhibitions. In 1936, Dodd received the prestigious Norman Waitt Harris Award at the Art Institute of Chicago's 47th annual exhibition of American painting and sculpture for his work, *The Railroad Cut*. Following this success were numerous purchase awards and recognitions: in 1937, he had a 10-year retrospective exhibition in Birmingham; in 1939, he was selected as one of 13 outstanding American artists; in 1940, the Metropolitan Museum of Art purchased one of his paintings; and in 1941, he had two one-man exhibitions—at Ferargil Galleries in New York and at the Corcoran Gallery in Washington, D.C.

In 1937, Dodd was appointed to the faculty of the University of Georgia and soon after was named head of the art department. Dodd's painting career developed even more within this academic environment. A native son whose broad vision carried him far beyond the sentimental agrarian representationalism of earlier southern painters, Dodd created a body of work that is eclectic both in style and subject matter. At times his subject is the southern locale in its most idyllic aspects—*Dew-Ag Hill* (1941) and *Skyward* (1944); at times social protest is the theme, as in *Copperhill* (1938) and *Cotton Pickers* (1945) shown below. During the late fifties and early sixties he expressed himself in the style of abstraction and representational expressionism. In 1963, he was one of seven artists invited by NASA to record the manned orbital flight of astronaut Gordon Cooper, and then in 1969 he was invited to record

Cotton Pickers (1945) by Lamar Dodd. This lyric painting reflects the artist's feeling for the Southeastern environment—the land and the people.

the Apollo 11 moon mission. Currently, Dodd's paintings have become metaphysical in orientation.

The South at the end of World War II was changing significantly, although paradoxically so. "The region was more an integral part of the Union and the world than ever before," wrote historian George Brown Tindall. "But its political leaders, (were) internationalist and parochial at the same time" (*The Emergence of the New South 1913-1945,* A History of the South, vol. 10 [Baton Rouge: Louisiana State University Press, 1967]). Progressive yet reactionary were the paradoxical characteristics of the region's painters. Although the myth of locale was subsiding, it still had a strong influence. Throughout the South, until the 1960s, one can find sentimental expression of the southern myth (e.g., Hobson Pittman's work), as well as some social protest work predominantly depicting the culture and condition of the southern black (e.g., the work of Romare Bearden). Yet, the expression of locale was gradually transmuted into a new form dominated by the combined techniques of expressive brush stroke, color, and shaped canvas—international influences that had become an integral part of the cosmopolitan New York scene. The Black Mountain School in North Carolina, boasting a prestigious visiting modernist faculty, is often credited with bringing change to the South.

What was really to bring an end to this gradualism, however, was the growth both of urban centers, particularly Atlanta, and of schools of art on the campuses of southern colleges and universities. On the campuses, change in the idiom of expression was being taught and produced. In the cities, networks were established by which artists could communicate and experiment, exhibit and sell. By the mid-1960s, the southern artist had been influenced by New York and European techniques and tendencies to the extent that regionalism and the concept of an art that is southern were transformed and subsumed. At the same time, the boundary line of what made up the South was in doubt both geographically and experientially: what had at one time stood out as the essential work of the South—the landscape rather than the cityscape—was now becoming merely emblematic.

In sum, the search for professionalism in technique and a rebellion against southern regionalism seem to have become the predominant motivating forces for visual artists working in the South. In the visual arts, perhaps more than in any other artistic endeavor, are reflected directly the economic, educational, and life-style changes taking place in the South. Two painters of Georgia whose works embody the new spirit of modernism as well as insight into the southern experience are Howard Thomas and Benny Andrews.

Thomas, a professor of art at the University of Georgia from 1945

A Soul *(1974) with Benny Andrews, the artist. Another of Andrews's works,* Flight, *can be viewed at Atlanta's Hartsfield Airport, in the north terminal.*

to 1966, has perhaps been considered a southern painter more for his use of the native soil for his pigments than for the subject and style of his paintings. He had a deep involvement with color—exemplified in his *Earth Red* (1964)—but he also had a love of Cezanne and cubism, and Chinese ceramic glazes. And he imposed such styles with his unique coloring upon what he termed his "interior landscapes" of the South, such as *Festival Mountain* (1970). However, even much of his earlier work deals with southern themes that had little to do with the fanciful myth—*Street Hound* (1941), *Hound Dog's House* (1941), and *Willie's Alley* (1941). His *Show Boat* (1946) with its sharp angular structures softened by thick creamy clouds circling around the edges of the composition is an example of his ability to express his southern vision with chromatic harmony and professional technique. Thomas died in 1971. In 1984, the Heath Gallery in Atlanta presented a retrospective exhibition of his work.

Benny Andrews, painter, book illustrator, and writer, was born in 1930 in Madison, Georgia, to a black sharecropper family, and grew up in a two-room shack with nine brothers and sisters. He attended Fort Valley State College and, in 1958, received a BFA degree from the Art Institute of Chicago. Andrews has had solo exhibitions in Atlanta, Boston, Hartford, Los Angeles, and New York, and his work is in numerous major collections throughout the country.

Andrews' best known works are those he gathered for the 1976 U.S. Bicentennial exhibition at the High Museum: *Symbols* (1971), *Trash* (1972), *Circle* (1973), and *Sexism* (1974). All these works are done in a series of panels, reaching heights of 10 and lengths of 36 feet. *Symbols* is made up of 11 sections folded inward at the ends to create an effect of beginning and end within the allegorical story that unfolds from left to right. Showing some relationship to the social narrative work of Benton, Andrews projects, on a huge scale, grotesque images (not unlike those described by O'Connor) that are both harsh satires and sympathetic portrayals of the black and white societies in rural Georgia. The other paintings in this series are similar in content. The artist is shown in the photo on page 267 with *A Soul* (1974).

Andrews' more recent work, a series of 21 collages exhibited in 1982, embodies little of the social protest or grotesque imagery of his earlier works. Dealing mostly with portraits of women and landscapes, the collages are airy mixtures of spray paint, torn or cut pieces of paper overlaid on each other, and magazine photographs. The collages command attention because of their starkness and simplicity.

Along with Andrews, contemporary Georgia artists Jim Herbert and Mike Nicholson were chosen by the critic/teacher Donald Kupsit for inclusion in the 1983 Virginia Museum of American Art exhibition, "Painting in the South: 1564-1980." Both artists are faculty members at the University of Georgia. Other popular painters—Herb Creecy, Katherine Mitchell, Tommy Mew, Wadsworth Jarrell, Art Rosenbaum, and others—are also associated with educational institutions. Of these, only Jarrell, a native Georgian, whose work is an attempt to synthesize his African heritage with his experience as an American and Georgian, and Rosenbaum who has focused on the folk heritage of the rural South, might be typified as Georgian and southern. Among the many painters who live in Georgia today, the presence of a style that might be typified as "southern" is exceptional.

Despite a wealth of excellent marble and rich clay deposits in Georgia, until recently sculptors were few in number. Marshall Daugherty, a Mercer University faculty member whose work has been predominantly portraiture, has had numerous small busts commissioned by organizations and individuals. Curtis Patterson, who teaches at the Atlanta College of Art, has received a commission from MARTA for his work *Mild Steel*; his media are metal and clay and he works in

—humanity, suffering, and death—William Thompson's Prisoners of War *memorial (1976) at Andersonville National Historic Site.*

the abstract mode. The work of University of Georgia professor William J. Thompson has been featured in several exhibitions. His most well-known works are his monumental sculptures of historic figures, especially *Senator Richard B. Russell* (1976) at the state capitol and the *Prisoners of War* (1976) of Andersonville, shown above. Also notable is his work with angels, crucifixes, and other Christian emblems, in which he achieves a mix of representationalism and abstraction.

Traditional Arts and Crafts

Twenty years ago a potter in Georgia was considered "odd." Today it is almost embarrassingly fashionable. (Charles Counts, potter, Rising Fawn, Georgia, 1983.)

The growing interest in Georgia not only in pottery but also in traditional arts and crafts in general is phenomenal. Individual craftmakers in Georgia identified positively when Andy Nasisse—a craftsman in clay from Athens and faculty member at the University of Georgia—received a large commission in the competition for works for the new Hartsfield Atlanta airport and when the interior walls of John Portman's buildings were graced with huge textiles by native craftsmen forced to compete with big name, out-of-state professionals. The work of several have withstood the competition: Edward Moulthrop in wood, Ken Weaver in textiles, Paul Bendzunas in glass, and Don Penny in clay.

Outside the intense activity of Atlanta, the individual craftmaker has a difficult time. A few that have kept their distance and stayed in touch with the clay are the indomitable Charles Counts, Rising Fawn; the late Virginia Dudley, Rome; teacher Bob Owens, Dahlonega; and blacksmith Ivan Bailey, Savannah.

Also present in Georgia are artists whom the Japanese would call "living treasures" and who are popularly called "folk artists" in the United States. Their work is characterized by an unaffected and almost instinctive simplicity that masks the discipline, courage, search for perfection, and loss of self that is involved in it. Two of the best known are the late Nellie Mae Rowe and Howard Finster.

Nellie Mae Rowe, a native of Fayette County, lived in Vinings for more than 50 years, worked as a maid, and died in 1982 at age 82. Her work, which includes drawings and small figurative sculpture, has been shown in major folk arts exhibitions, including "Black Folk Art in America 1930-1980" (1982) at the Corcoran Gallery of Art in Washington, and can be found in collections at the High Museum, the Library of Congress, and the Chase Manhattan Bank. In 1979, she had a one-person show in New York. Rowe, like Finster, has been acclaimed among the South's "visionary artists" who, according to critic Virginia Warren Smith, "have never been concerned with making mugs or baskets like their grandmothers did." Rather, says Smith, "their vision is of a New Heaven and a New Earth, not the propagation of the old order" (*Art Papers,* September-October 1984).

A self-proclaimed "man of visions" is folk artist Howard Finster of Summerville, Georgia. A preacher for 45 years, he tells of a 1976 religious experience in which God told him to "paint sacred art." For the Reverend Finster, art is a ministry that allows him to reach a greater audience. In 10 years, he has created more than 4,000 paintings, sculptures, and assemblages; nurtured a two-acre sculpture garden; and built with his own hands (but no plans) a multistoried chapel of art.

Finster works out of his grassroots experience and uses materials at hand. Most of his paintings are done with tractor enamel (for durability) and many are on wood, cut into symbolic shapes such as angels, cheetahs, and vises intended to be freestanding, mounted on a back-

Rev. Howard Finster and Chapel of Art at Summerville, Georgia (1985). Finster approaches art as a personal ministry, but has enjoyed remarkable national exposure as well as commercial success.

ground, or framed. Always his paintings include prose: bible verses, admonitions, prophesies, or credits to those who help spread the Word. Finster's art is life-affirming, and his subjects are often people who have worked in life-affirming ways—including inventors, authors, and politicians. In the variety and combinations of materials and techniques he uses in creating his assemblages, excitement and humor are evident. In describing his own work, the artist is direct: "this is dried paint art" and "this is a $500 piece."

Although he lives and works in a small northwest Georgia town far from the art scene, Howard Finster has reached a large buying public through shows across the country; workshops on college campuses ("workouts" he calls them); galleries in Atlanta, Los Angeles, New Orleans, and New York; and commissions for record jackets. So many people have made the pilgrimage to the sculpture garden-chapel-studio complex and purchased Finster's work directly off the easel that he finds it difficult to meet the demand. Says Finster, "I just can't keep enough of 'em."

Other folk artists are Bill Gordy of Cartersville, D.X. Gordy of Greenville, and the Meaders family near Gainesville.

Art Networks—Museums and Galleries

The art network in Georgia cities is a physical and often political system of places and spaces where artists and craftsmen can display their work.

The centerpiece of Atlanta's network is the High Museum of Art. In the fall of 1983, the High moved with considerable fanfare and excitement into a new building, the cost of which ran more than $20 million. The slogan for its fund-raising campaign was "Help Build a Museum Big Enough for Atlanta," and it is big—135,000 square feet of space on six levels. It contains ample exhibition space for the museum's permanent collections, of which the old building could display only 10 to 20 percent at one time. The building's sixth level is designed so that galleries can be combined into 15,000 square feet of space for special exhibitions on one level. The museum also has a 250-seat auditorium, classrooms, workshops, a junior gallery, a cafe, a skylight atrium, and a ramp system for visual connection between levels.

The new building places the High in a class with leading museums in the country and surely makes it the outstanding one in the Southeast. Designed by architect Richard Meier, the building is constructed of white enameled steel and glass on a concrete frame. In bright sunlight, according to *Newsweek's* critic Douglas Davis, it is transformed "into the purest and whitest of abstract visions or—depending upon one's taste—the world's sleekest deep freeze." The new High's early and wide acclaim, not as an art space, but for its architecture and its positive impact on property values in midtown Atlanta, led the same critic to observe:

> The meteoric success of this willful but brilliant architectural fantasy speaks worlds about how some cultural leaders now perceive the role of the art museum. In this sense, the most effective artist on exhibit in Atlanta at this moment is the tall, urbane Richard Meier himself. Whether his building's appeal will endure as the High tries to mount major exhibitions, display its growing collection and handle large crowds pressing in to see art, rather than architecture, is another question (*Newsweek,* Jan. 30, 1984).

In short order, the new museum had ample opportunity to display its capacity to handle major exhibitions and large crowds pressing in to see art. Museum-goers thronged to "China: 7,000 Years of Discovery" for three months in 1984-85 and "Masterpieces of the Dutch Golden Age" for two and a half months in 1985. In the latter year, membership in the High reached 22,000, among the largest in American art museums, and annual attendance was more than 532,000. However, with its successes the new High may be showing a tendency already strong among large museums to become involved with the "blockbuster" exhibit that will attract visitors and dollars. (Such a predilection could be to the detriment of the museum's obligations to share its rich collections with and to educate the public of the greater Atlanta area.)

The High's director, Gidmund Vigtel, is a strong supporter of regional and state art competitions and exhibitions. The junior gallery has often been used as space for exhibits of the works of Atlanta artists. For many years the High acted as home and host for the Artists of Georgia annual exhibit, and in 1985 it began a "Southern Expressions" series with shows of four Georgia artists.

Other museum-type spaces in Atlanta are provided by several Atlanta area colleges and universities. The Emory University Museum of Art and Archaeology opened in 1985, like the High in 1983, to considerable fanfare for its architecture. In sharp contrast to the modernist High, however, the Emory is a Beaux-Arts masterpiece of 1916, a thoroughly renewed space formerly occupied by the university's law school. Important in providing contemporary artists the opportunity to show their work are the galleries of the Atlanta College of Art, Georgia State University, Oglethorpe University, and Agnes Scott College.

Contemporary arts are also supported by commercial and community galleries. The Heath Gallery is an enterprise dedicated to modern art and to giving exposure to southern artists. Its owner, David Heath, in 1977 founded *Contemporary Arts/Southeast,* Atlanta's first major arts publication, which was subsequently absorbed by the influential *Art Papers.* Other Atlanta spaces which offer splendid exhibit opportunities for artists include the Fay Gold Gallery, a marketing gallery; and the Nexus Gallery, one of the city's alternative or community galleries. Increasingly, exhibit spaces are found in office buildings, shopping malls, and other unconventional sites.

Throughout the state a number of communities have attempted to establish exhibit space. In Dalton, the Creative Arts Guild moved into a new $750,000 facility in 1982. More than 10,000 square feet in size and housing a main and auxiliary gallery, two dance studios, an arts and crafts studio, and a music room, the new building in its first year of operation attracted more than 200 exhibitors to its annual arts and crafts festival and close to $13,000 in purchases by areawide businesses.

In the southwest section of the state, Columbus, Albany, and LaGrange have structures for the visual arts. The Columbus Museum of Arts and Sciences, after many years of searching for an identity and adding to its permanent collection, has a long-range plan of improvements and has been well supported in this endeavor by the National Endowment for the Arts and the Georgia Council for the Arts and Humanities. The Albany Museum of Art, a 17,056-square-foot structure, was completed in 1983 at a cost of almost $1.5 million. It has featured exhibitions from major national collections in its large central gallery; an adjacent small gallery houses shows of younger artists. LaGrange has the most active small-city art association in the Southeast, the Chattahoochee Valley Art Association (CVAA). It has two exhibits per month or shows part of its permanent collection at its own headquarters in LaGrange, the rehabilitated city jail. CVAA hosts three annual shows: the Harvest Heyday, the Affair on the Square, and the LaGrange National Competition and Exhibition in March. CVAA receives funds from the city of LaGrange, Troup County, the Georgia Council for the Arts and Humanities, and the Callaway Foundation, one of the richest foundations in the state. Such funds enable the group to make purchases from its shows for its own permanent collection. The CVAA has a strong relationship with LaGrange College. It was influential in developing the Lamar Dodd Art Center at the college, a handsome and large structure, where the work of many state craftspersons and artists has been exhibited.

Savannah's Telfair Academy, the oldest museum in the Southeast, is housed in Telfair Mansion (1819), a Regency-style building. The museum boasts in its permanent collection works by Jeremiah Theus, Charles W. Peale, John Wollaston, and Henry Benbridge, as well as a large collection of French and American Impressionist and Ash Can School realist paintings. In addition, Telfair owns one of the most important collections of the drawings and pastels of Kahlil Gibran. The museum has a comprehensive exhibition schedule throughout the year and provides a wide range of educational activities for schools and for the public. Telfair has received grant support from several local, state, and federal sources. In 1977, the first NEH challenge grant ($300,000) awarded in Georgia went to Telfair.

In addition to the Telfair, Savannah has several art galleries, studios, and schools, some of which are housed in old brick warehouses along the river front. Upriver from Savannah, Augusta has the Augusta-Richmond County Museum and the Gertrude Herbert Art Institute.

Athens, where cultural development is dominated by the University, is a center for arts and crafts activity because of its productive art faculty. There are several exhibition spaces on and off campus.

The major exhibition space in Athens, located on the university campus, is the Georgia Museum of Art. Established in 1945 with a gift of 100 paintings from Alfred H. Holbrook, in 1982 it was designated Georgia's official state museum of art by the General Assembly. Although the Georgia Museum has severe limitations in physical size and budget, it has presented several outstanding travelling exhibitions including the JMW Turner Watercolors from The British Museum and the Hemphill Collection of American Folk Art. The permanent collection, now numbering more than 5,000 works, has a dollar value of some $12 million. The present museum building is inadequate to store and display the holdings; less than 5 percent of the collection can be exhibited. Plans have been completed for a new 70,000-square-foot building designed by architect Edward Larrabee Barnes, who designed the Walker Art Center in Minneapolis and the Dallas Museum of Art.

Architecture

> I've been asked if glass boxes are finished. I'm not one who says glass boxes are either good or bad, that buildings must have arches, or buildings must be this or that. Form *per se* is not really what we should focus on. We should focus on the human being's involvement with environmental circumstances and let that tell us what the form should be.
>
> —John Portman, architect, 1985

The Europeans who settled Georgia in the 1730s were most certainly involved with environmental circumstances. Hot summers, damp winters, and the availability of wood, sand, clay, and oyster shells influenced the location, shape, and materials of their buildings. In general, the earliest houses were adaptations of English yeoman cottages and Indian huts of wattle and daub, woven branches covered with clay to close spaces between timbers. For more durable construction, especially fortifications, colonists along the coast used tabby—a mixture of lime, sand, and shells—which while moist was squeezed into wooden forms.

The trustees of the Georgia colony were especially concerned with the human environment, and Oglethorpe's plan for Savannah provided for building a sense of community among the settlers. Uniform 60' by 90' lots arranged around open squares provided the nucleus for neighborhoods of simple 16' by 24' clapboard houses.

Later, along with economic growth, more elegant structures appeared in colonial Georgia. The most prevalent style was the "Georgian," derived from English designs, which rose a story and a half on a high basement. A formal facade with a small porch marked the exterior, a central hall and staircase the interior. Both the porch and hall would highlight succeeding styles in the state.

In Georgia, the years between the Revolution and the Civil War witnessed the emergence of a distinctiveness in architectural style not matched since then. During the first half of the nineteenth century, Eli Whitney's cotton gin transformed the economic life of Georgia, bringing a prosperity that was reflected in a variety of residential architectural styles. Two especially noteworthy *high* styles—based on architects' plans—were the federal and the Greek revival. But, the vernacular—or tradition-based—architecture of the people, especially the dog-trot cabin and plantation plain-style house, deserves special mention.

After the revolutionary war, Savannah became a focal point for the federal style—a mixture of Georgian colonial, New England two-story designs, and English decorative ideas that was generally limited to coastal areas. Usually fronted by only a small porch or stoop, the federal house was often raised on basements to avoid the damp night air creeping in. Semicircular fanlights appeared above the door and windows, and neoclassical designs were imposed upon the exterior—foreshadowing the classical revival to come. Exteriors were commonly of brick, while inside walls were plaster with decorations. Curved and free-standing staircases trimmed with delicate designs beautified the central halls. A late example of the federal style in Savannah is the Davenport House, 1820, shown on the opposite page. In the 1820s, Savannah's vigor was sapped by a devastating fire which destroyed many eighteenth century buildings, an outbreak of yellow fever, and a national depression. By then, however, the great architectural achievements in Georgia were becoming centered in the upcountry.

In Georgia's early years as a state, settlers from Virginia and the Carolinas pushed into the heavily forested upcountry and developed several styles of log dwellings. Newcomers built single-room log cabins with a chimney at one end and, often, a sleeping loft reached by a ladder. Later, their cabins were expanded to two rooms. One design simply added a room using the chimney as a central heating source and room separation: this type is generally called a saddlebag cabin. A second design separated the two rooms with an open breezeway, commonly called a dog-trot, and had two chimneys.

In the early 1800s, the dog-trot cabin became vastly popular in the Coastal Plain, less so in the Piedmont. It had many practical values: cooking in the summer could be relegated to one side of the house or to the dog-trot, while eating, socializing, and sleeping could go on in a cooler environment. As families outgrew a two-room cabin, they might add two rooms above with access from the dog-trot. However, some dog-trot cabins were originally built with a story and a half, perhaps

Davenport House (1820), Savannah. The federal style is generally limited to coastal areas.

with a room over the dog-trot. An example of the latter is the Henry Lane Cabin, built around 1815 in Morgan County, pictured on the next page. In time, as porches and rooms and weatherboarding were added to the cabin, the dog-trot was often enclosed front and back with doors and windows to become a great central hall.

As plantation agriculture spread across Georgia in the early nine-teenth century, so did the plantation plain style of house. The plain style was a simple two-story, gable-roofed, frame house with exterior end chimneys. Its basic plan featured two rooms on each floor, the central hall, and a shed-roofed, full-width front porch. Often, shed rooms were added on the rear and the whole house sat on rock or brick piers. Oriented toward the southwest, the plain-style porch and central hall provided shade and cooling breezes and the setting for domestic and social activities in the hot Georgia climate. As the planter accumulated wealth, the plain-style house was often adorned with Greek revival embellishments.

In the three decades immediately preceding the Civil War, the emergence of Georgia as the "Empire State of the South" was accom-panied by the blossoming of the Greek revival style of architecture. The

Henry Lane Cabin (c. 1815), Morgan County (removed from site). Logs 43' 5" long were used for the sills and above the open dog-trot. Metal roofing (over shingles) is of recent vintage.

architectural movement known broadly as the classical revival dates from the late 1700s, drew on Roman as well as Greek styles, and was employed in all parts of the United States. Just as Greece and Rome were models for the American republic, architecture embodying the classical ideals of beauty, symmetry, reason, and truth seemed a proper model for the American people. Thomas Jefferson's home, Monticello, and the United States Capitol are early examples of neoclassical architecture.

The neoclassical movement reached its peak in the Greek revival style of the antebellum South. Georgians not only adopted architectural designs comparable to those of classic Greece, but they also gave Greek names to a few of their towns, e.g., Athens and Sparta. The Greek revival movement, which reached Georgia in the 1830s, was probably propelled by the Greeks' seven-year war for independence from Turkey (1821-28).

As the Greek revival was high style architecture, Georgia builders benefited from architectural plans, builders guides, and special millwork in their designs. The primary emphasis was the imitation of the colossal temple, especially the Parthenon. A construction of fluted columns supporting a pediment whose roof covered either a portico or the whole building was popular for commercial and public buildings as well as houses. The conventional house plan was four rooms over four rooms with a central hall. Such structures were well adapted to the Georgia environment: colonnaded porches, sometimes extending around the house, shielded interiors from the summer sun; and the central hall, high ceilings, and tall windows allowed good ventilation. Greek revival mansions were raised on basements or brick piers to obtain coolness without dampness.

Some Greek revival plantation houses evolved from indigenous architecture. Back and front rooms would be added, a porch with columns grafted on, the roof raised—the whole being adapted to the temple arrangement. Finally, the great mansion was painted a pure white in mistaken imitation of the ancient Greeks, who had actually painted their own architecture with bright reds and blues, colors that had been bleached out to white over the centuries. To complement the architecture, there were symmetrical boxwood gardens in front with flowers and evergreens at the sides.

Those Greek revival plantation houses, surrounded by fields of cotton, were the homes of a tiny minority of Georgians, but for many people even today they symbolize the myth of the southern experience. In truth, during the antebellum period most Greek revival mansions were built not in the countryside but in the towns and cities of the Piedmont where the wealthy cotton planters and merchants preferred to live. A representative example of one of these Greek revival town houses is the Taylor-Grady House, built around 1840 in Athens, pictured on the next page. Architectural historian Frederick Doveton Nichols summed up their meaning thusly:

> The solid, symmetrical Greek temples of Georgia, which stylistically emphasized rigid form over flexible convenience, were a visual representation of the region's belief in a stable, disciplined, hierarchical society (*The Architecture of Georgia* [Savannah: The Beehive Press, 1976]).

In the 1850s, the Gothic revival movement reached Georgia. Stone, wrought iron, parapets, castle-like doors and windows, and paint colored with earth pigments were used to imitate European villas for the wealthy. Perhaps the finest example of the style in the United States is the Charles Green House, built in Savannah in 1853, pictured on page 281. The short-lived Gothic revival marked the end of Georgia's great age of architectural distinctiveness.

Into the Mainstream

The long depression Georgia suffered from the end of the Civil War to World War II and great changes in the economic and social structure of the state influenced its buildings. The breakup of plantation agriculture, the beginnings of industrialization, and the extension of railroads,

Taylor-Grady House (c. 1840), Athens. An example of the Greek Revival style, this was once the residence of Henry W. Grady.

coupled with population increase, led to the growth of towns. New houses tended to be modest and to lack the regional quality of prewar houses, as builders chose designs from popular magazines and plan books over tradition-based architecture. The height of monotony and drabness was reached in the millworker houses of company towns erected around the new cotton mills. Scarcely more inspired were the Spartan tenant houses strung along country roads for the sharecropper families who worked former plantation lands. Georgians of means took to the Victorian style of asymmetrical plans; rambling porches; decorative brackets, lattices, scrolls, and railings; and stained glass. Others opted for Gothic, French, Tudor, and eclectic designs. In the 1890s, there was a Greek re-revival. Into the twentieth century, new one- and one-and-a-half-story bungalow style houses continued to feature the porch, but the center hall was often missing. The growth of towns, notably seats of government to serve the counties that proliferated in the half century following the Civil War, brought new public and commercial buildings of various styles, as well as houses.

Regional distinctiveness in architecture had faded by the time Georgia's economy began to prosper. The residences of Georgia's suburbs, where the bulk of post-World War II construction had occurred,

Charles Green House (1853), Savannah. This Gothic Revival mansion served as Gen. William Sherman's headquarters in the Civil War.

were of the same designs as suburban homes in other regions of the country. Automobiles, air conditioning, smaller families, the demise of cheap domestic labor, Sunbelt migration, an economic structure similar to that of the rest of the nation, the policies of federal lending agencies, and the mass marketing of simple anonymous styles of housing resulted in post-World War II housing in Georgia that is substantially the same as housing elsewhere in the United States. The mobile home, a type of housing especially popular in rural Georgia, represents standardization at its utmost.

Perhaps motivated by a mixture of impulses—the historical, the aesthetic, and the elitist—a movement to preserve the state's architectural heritage has developed in Georgia. Across the state, old houses are being resurrected as private homes, or adapted to new uses along with cotton warehouses, hotels, banks, and other relics of bygone commerce. The preservation that has taken place in Savannah is Georgia's stellar achievement in this movement and has received international acclaim. Other cities, such as Athens, Columbus, and Macon, after losing much of their heritage to modernization in the 1950s and 1960s, belatedly began preservation efforts. Ripe for restoration are the late nineteenth and early twentieth century commercial rows of many county seats that escaped being modernized after World War II because of lack of money to do so. A prime example of the latter is Sparta, whose Drummers hotel and Hancock County Courthouse are pictured below.

While Savannah embraces the past, Atlanta reaches for the future with concentrations of monumental modern architecture downtown, midtown, uptown, and on the I-285 perimeter. Hometown architect and entrepreneur John Portman has moved Atlanta to the forefront in architectural progress. Portman's Hyatt Regency Hotel, 1967, catapulted him to international fame and has served as a model for hotel design. It is highlighted by the outside world turned in: its 21-story atrium lobby, with exposed capsule-like elevators scaling its inner walls and foliage and sculpture rising in formal disarray, has been widely imitated. Since this triumph, Portman's dominant influence on Atlanta's architecture has been confirmed by the construction of the Peachtree Center complex; the 73-story Peachtree Plaza Hotel, a graceful cylinder with a 3-story revolving restaurant for its crown; and the Marriot Marquis Hotel with its 46-story atrium.

So rapidly is greater Atlanta abuilding that any listing of its major buildings is subject to continual revision. In the mid-1980s, downtown

Hotel (1840/1897), known as "The Drummers Home," and Hancock County Courthouse (1881), Sparta.

Atlanta was anchored by the Omni International Center, a massive futuristic construction with clashing lines of monumental walls and translucent roofs, and the 52-story Georgia-Pacific Building, a post-modernist form in red granite. Midtown was dominated by Colony Square—a complex of interrelated apartment residences, offices, shops, restaurants, and hotel rooms—and the Woodruff Arts Center and the High Museum of Art. Uptown, at Buckhead and Lenox Square, construction of office towers, hotels, condominiums, and retail businesses was so frenzied it raised fears that downtown was moving uptown. However, it is not here but at Atlanta's periphery that the greatest future construction activity is projected. This activity could exacerbate problems associated with unplanned growth, traffic congestion, and the abandonment of the inner city as a place to live and work.

Recently, John Portman directed his attention towards Atlanta's suburbs, where, he believes, people live isolated lives controlled by needs that only the automobile can answer. In his projected "pedestrian-only, European-style village" on Atlanta's northern perimeter, Portman has been influenced by the sense of community that he finds still present in large European cities like Paris and Venice.

Perhaps there is a double irony in Portman's plan. It, too, may exacerbate the problems of a downtown abandoned by people for suburban malls and subdivisions. Yet, in its focus on community, it reveals a kinship with Oglethorpe's plan for Savannah in 1733.

The Performing Arts

> I believe in the essentialness of the arts. I believe every word of it. I think other things try to bring sanity and wholeness to society, too. But it takes a giver and a taker, and it takes someone to listen, too. So I don't think society is going to be saved until the arts have as many listeners as singers. The arts may indeed not be the luxury of the few but the best hope of human beings to inhabit this planet with joy.
>
> —Robert Shaw, music director,
> Atlanta Symphony Orchestra, 1984

Music

Of all the forms of art, music displays best the dichotomy between popular and high culture. And the South is the ancestral home of contemporary popular music. From the religious and secular music of its black people came the South's native musical idiom—jazz. First known as the *blues,* because it often had a melancholy tone, early jazz was characterized by an untutored improvisational method and vigorous syncopated rhythms. An improvisational method also marked the traditional string music of the Scotch-Irish people of the Appalachian South. But the balladic subject matter of their vocal music, accompanied by banjo or fiddle, was unique to the mountain areas. Singing games, square dancing, and clogging developed from the mountain music. So too did "hillbilly" music, which became very popular during the 1930s.

During the years between World Wars I and II, popular music in Georgia was beginning to develop slowly and sporadically. Although New Orleans and Memphis were the acknowledged music centers of the South, Atlanta had its place. In 1923, the first country record ever, "The Old Hen Cackled and the Rooster's Gonna Crow" by Fiddlin' John Carson, was cut in Atlanta. In the next year, the first "race music," for black audiences, was recorded in Atlanta. In time, the long societal relationship between white and black cultures in Georgia would result in a musical heritage that included a host of popular musicians, from Blind Willie McTell in the 1930s to the B-52s in the 1980s.

Popular music may represent Georgia's most vital, creative output. No other state in the nation has produced such an abundance of artists in popular music. A highly selective listing would have to include Blind Willie McTell, one of the greatest 12-string guitarists of the pre-World War II period; Bill Anderson, Razzy Bailey and Norman Blake, top-ranked country music performers; Johnny Mercer, big band vocalist, leading Hollywood songwriter, and record industry executive; James Brown, perhaps the most influential black artist in the area of soul; Ray Charles, a legend in his own time who made popular the state song, "Georgia"; Gertrude "Ma" Rainey for the blues; Marion Brown for jazz; Piano Red and Little Richard for rock and roll; and Otis Redding for soul. In the 1970s, the musical prestige of Macon soared, mostly because of Capricorn Records' success with the Allman Brothers. Atlanta in 1983 had 26 recording studios and such a host of management, booking, and publishing firms that it was the fourth-ranked pop-music center in the United States. By the mid-1980s, Athens had gained national recognition with the appearance of the B-52s and R.E.M., the talk of an "Athens sound" (new wave), and the existence of a cult/underground music scene made up chiefly of Athens and Atlanta musicians.

Classical music has faced an uphill struggle in the state. Georgia's first professional orchestra, the Atlanta Symphony, had its genesis as recently as 1944. In that year, Henry Sopkin came from Chicago to develop a youth orchestra for Atlanta, made up of students from the city's high schools. Later, professionals were added as section leaders, and in 1947 the orchestra became the official Atlanta Symphony Orchestra (ASO). Three years later the American Symphony Orchestra League classified it as one of 25 major symphony orchestras in the United

States and Canada. Thirty years later, the ASO would be one of America's youngest orchestras to achieve national prominence.

The orchestra's prominence is due primarily to the appointment of Robert Shaw as music director and conductor in 1967. At the time, Shaw, an assistant to George Szell at the Cleveland Orchestra, was the country's leading choral conductor. National recognition came with the ASO's January 1977 concert at President Carter's inauguration. Its new status was reinforced over the next several years by performances in major U.S. cities, beginning with a 1978 tour of western states and a Beethoven series at New York's Carnegie Hall. In April 1980, Shaw took the Atlanta Symphony Orchestra and Chorus to New York to perform the requiems of Verdi, Berlioz, and Brahms on successive nights at Carnegie Hall. To attempt such a feat was unheard of. Said *New York Times* critic, Donal Henahan, following the Verdi performance:

> When it was first announced that Mr. Shaw was planning to offer this triptych of requiems, one wondered if he really had a chorus in Atlanta equal to the job. One should have known.

In 1980-81, the ASO had a four-day residency in Mexico City and made its Chicago debut, where its performance of the Beethoven *Symphony No. 7* received high praise from local critics. In 1983, upon the ASO's return to Carnegie Hall, *New York Times* critic Bernard Holland opined:

> The Atlanta has become an orchestra of solid quality under its music director, Robert Shaw. The strings have richness, the winds are well-tuned and the brass playing is equally accurate though not always very subtle.

Further enhancing the orchestra's reputation has been a series of well-received recordings beginning with the 1979 release by Telarc Records of the ASO's performances of Stravinsky's *Firebird Suite* and excerpts from Borodin's *Prince Igor,* a recording which received a Grammy nomination, and including major symphonic-choral works such as the *Messiah* of Handel and the requiems of Berlioz and Brahms. The orchestra's 1985 recordings received a total of 12 Grammy nominations.

While the ASO, more than any other local musical organization, deserves credit for erasing Georgia's image as a cultural desert (Mencken's usage), other musical groups have also contributed to Atlanta's becoming a performing arts center. The Atlanta Ballet Orchestra, formerly the Atlanta Chamber Orchestra, directed by John Naskiewicz, has for several years filled an important place in the classical music scene of the city. Although the orchestra had taken a quantum leap in quality in its 1982-83 season, performing a repertoire written for chamber groups and not suited for the symphony, its financial problems became so perilous that it almost disbanded. In 1985, four other professional groups of note were performing chamber music in Atlanta: the Atlanta Chamber Players, Atlanta Virtuosi, Georgian Chamber Players (composed of ASO principals), and Musica da Camera. Choral music is performed by the Atlanta Choral Guild conducted by William Noll, onetime assistant to Robert Shaw. Like the ASO Chorus, a volunteer group, it sings for free or receives performance fees only to help defray expenses. In March 1982, the Choral Guild appeared at Carnegie Hall and drew a rave review from the *New York Times*.

Savannah is the only city in Georgia outside of Atlanta to have a professional symphony orchestra. Founded in 1953 as a community orchestra of amateur players with a small core of professionals, today the symphony has a professional staff and is governed by a board of 27 leading citizens. The Savannah Symphony season includes a nine-concert Masterwork Series, a chamber series, four afternoon pop concerts, city and county sponsored concerts, and a youth orchestra series.

Among the state's community orchestras, which are made up of amateur musicians with a sprinkling of professionals, the Columbus Symphony Orchestra is one of the best. In addition to its regular season, the orchestra tours the surrounding area and performs at the annual Chrysanthemum Festival in Callaway Gardens at Pine Mountain.

Augusta is home of the Augusta Opera Association, a professional company. In addition to touring annually throughout the state and the Southeast, the company in 1983 mounted a production of Puccini's *Madame Butterfly* that was broadcast on a 28-state public television network.

Atlanta is well known for its love affair with the Metropolitan Opera of New York. Since 1910, the Met's spring visit to Atlanta has been a revered part of the city's cultural and social calendar, with almost every performance in the annual seven-opera series sold out months in advance. Homegrown opera, however, has never prospered in Atlanta. In 1968, Atlanta opera was shattered as a result of a $250,000 production of John Dryden's masque *King Arthur* that was a disastrous artistic and financial failure. There have been several attempts at revival: the Civic Opera, the Lyric Opera, the Phoenix Opera, and the Shoestring Opera. None has been artistically and financially successful. In 1985 and 1986, ASO Assistant Conductor William Fred Scott led a new Atlanta Opera company in successful summer seasons. That success plus the Met's decision no longer to go on tour presaged a new life for operatic performance in Atlanta.

Whatever the future brings for musical performance of the high-culture genre in Georgia will depend to a great extent on education. Music education in the state has not been strong. Until the 1940s, music education in primary and secondary schools was limited to weekly singing lessons. Musical performance attained legitimacy in the schools, however, through the back door of athletics. High school football had become a growing and exciting leisure-time activity for both rural and urban Georgians, and marching bands to increase the excitement were a natural development. In some school systems, the support for bands was extended to orchestras, then to school choruses, and finally to training in instrumental music.

Georgia does not have a nationally recognized professional school of music: the loss is not only in native talent to other parts of the country but also in performers, composers, and scholars who might otherwise be drawn to such an institution. Most professional music performances in Georgia depend on imported musicians. Regarding Atlanta's becoming a major musical center, Robert Shaw has repeatedly warned: "It *has* to have a school, an educational program for the development of young orchestral musicians and solo performers and young vocal performers. There's just no way *not* to accept responsibility for the regeneration of musical resources."

Dance

Dance in Georgia is centered in Atlanta. More than a dozen professional dance companies, dance education programs at the area colleges, an Atlanta School of Ballet and countless other private dance schools, and a host of visiting ballet and modern dance groups give Atlanta a lively dance scene.

The Atlanta Ballet is the city's oldest, largest, and most notable dance company. It was founded in 1929 by the late Dorothy Alexander, who received the prestigious Capezio Award in 1981 for her work in dance. The company has a national reputation. Its season generally includes a mix of the classics—such as *Sleeping Beauty, Giselle,* and the ever-popular *Nutcracker,* which drew about 50,000 persons to 15 performances at Christmas 1985—and some nonstandard fare such as recent highlights *Pas Trop Vite* and *Raja Manjkamaj* by Thor Sutkowski and the 1985 world premiere of John Fall's *The Watchers.* The Atlanta Ballet worked for more than a decade to return itself to financial solvency after suffering in 1968 from its participation in *King Arthur.* In 1983, its longstanding debt of $350,000 was wiped out by Atlanta's well-known "anonymous" donor, Robert Woodruff.

Of Atlanta's modern or contemporary dance companies, the Carl Ratcliff Dance Theatre and the Ruth Mitchell Dance Company are two of the oldest, continually presenting innovative and challenging performances. Dancer's Collective, a sponsoring organization and dance facility, plays an important role in Atlanta's dance scene by giving exposure to local and visiting modern dance groups.

Beyond Atlanta, dance activities are found in Savannah and Augusta. Until recently there were three dance companies in Savannah. Now there are two: The Ballet Guild and Ballet South. The Guild, founded in 1964 is classified as professional under standards of the state funding agency, the Georgia Council for the Arts and Humanities. It produces six sub- scription concerts per year, four performances for schools in Chatham County, and a regional touring program. Ballet South gives two public performances a year, and a number of community-wide service pro- grams. North of Savannah is the Augusta Ballet, which has been consistently judged among the best in the Southeast in regional competitions.

Professional dance companies radiate from the Atlanta area to per- form in many of the smaller communities of the state. Much of this activity is paid for jointly by the community and by the Georgia Coun- cil for the Arts and Humanities. In some cases, these companies have had extended engagements in communities, performed in the secondary schools, and involved the students.

Theatre

> Remember the actor's calling
> Is the finest in the world.
> Is it sometimes a little galling
> When, with lip politely curled
> And a supercilious smirk,
> You are told to your face
> That the theatre has no place
> Among important things?
> I tell you, it's an art
> That has its springs
> In the heart
> Of all mankind.
>
> —Sacha Guitry, *Deburau,* in an English version
> by Harley Granville Barker
> (New York: G.P. Putnam's Sons, 1921)

Atlanta's main cultural attraction, along with and alongside the High Museum, is the Robert W. Woodruff Arts Center, formerly known as the Memorial Arts Center. The center was built in memory of 122 Atlan- ta art patrons who on a High Museum trip to Europe died in a plane crash near Paris in June 1962. Completed in 1968, the $13 million center, financed almost solely by private donations, was designed to house the institutions that make up the Atlanta Arts Alliance: the Alliance Theatre, the Atlanta College of Art, the Atlanta Symphony, and the High Museum.

When the center opened in 1968, the Arts Alliance did not include a resident theatre. The theatre space was leased to an independent pro- ducer who, under the name Atlanta Municipal Theatre, inaugurated theatre at the Arts Center with the aforementioned *King Arthur* that devastated ballet and opera, as well as theatre, in Atlanta. It was seven years before any semblance of stability would return to theatre at the Arts Center.

The Alliance Theatre has become the centerpiece of Atlanta theatre over the past 10 years. By 1977 it had a subscription season, a partial resident company, and newly hired artistic and managing directors. The Junior League's Children's Theatre was merged with the Alliance and quickly became a highly respected training and production organization. However, the Alliance Theatre had a subscription audience of only 3,400 and was carrying a $26,000 deficit. The Alliance Board of Trustees discussed closing the theatre in 1978. Instead, an urgent and committed drive by the management put the theatre back on firm financial ground. The newest marketing techniques were used, and by 1983 the Alliance Theatre's season subscriptions numbered more than 21,000, making the Alliance the second largest nonprofit regional theatre in the country, runner up to the Mark Taper Forum in Los Angeles. For its 1984-85 season, the Alliance had a budget that approached $3.5 million and played to 144,330 patrons in its 784-seat mainstage theatre and 13,951 patrons in its 200-seat studio theatre. The Alliance has by far the largest theatre audience in Atlanta.

The Alliance's box office success has not been matched by artistic success. Alliance seasons for the mainstage have been mostly audience-safe: popular Broadway successes, musicals, and Shakespeare. Experimental or provocative plays were usually relegated to the studio theatre in the basement. Through 1984-85, the majority of Alliance mainstage productions had a community-theatre sense of the stage. At the end of the 1984-85 season, the Alliance had a change in artistic directorship and for 1985-86 a change was in evidence: the season opened with the first Alliance mainstage production of a locally written play, Sandra Deer's *So Long on Lonely Street*, and included a second work by a Georgia playwright, Jim Peck's *Flint and Roses*.

The studio theatre, a three-quarter round, thrust-stage space was designed for experimental works. Although some of its productions have had an "anything goes" attitude about them, one of the finest presentations at the Alliance in years was its 1984 studio production of Athol Fugard's *Master Harold . . . and the Boys*, performed by a visiting director and a mostly imported cast.

The Alliance's other activities include the Atlanta Children's Theatre, whose Umbrella Players take theatre into the schools, playing to more than 150,000 youngsters in 1984-85. And about 1,000 students take classes at the Alliance Theatre School.

The Academy Theatre, founded in 1956, is Atlanta's oldest resident company. After many years in makeshift playhouses, the Academy now has a splendid permanent home two blocks south of the Arts Center. The Academy's seasons regularly veer from the mainstream to include new and provocative works and to educate the theatre audience.

The Academy Theatre's space houses a second resident company, Jomandi Productions, a black theatre company. In 1985, Jomandi toured Germany, Denmark, and Sweden with its production, *Voices in the Rain.*

The Alliance Theatre, the Academy Theatre, Peachtree Playhouse (home of Just Us Theatre, the largest black theatre company in the Southeast), and Center Stage form the northern boundary of what has become an identifiable theatre district. Moving south on Peachtree Street, there are Theatrical Outfit, the Fox Theatre (for touring shows), and Onstage Atlanta. Nearby, the Civic Center presents mostly large touring Broadway musicals. On the fringe of Atlanta's downtown are Seven Stages, Southern Theatre Conspiracy, and Acme Theatre. Almost all the once popular dinner theatres have closed. In total, in the Atlanta area there are some 25 professional theatres.

At the northern end of the theatre district is the Center for Puppetry Arts, a splendid performing space, museum, and conservatory. The center, considered home for the puppetry arts in North America, has a mix of productions of storybook classics for children and evening performances for adult audiences. The museum program has continual exhibits of puppetry art. The puppetry library is in constant use, and the workshop and master classes of the conservatory in the art of puppetry are available from October through April of each year.

What then is the state of theatre in Atlanta? In terms of numbers—performances, companies, audiences, and budgets—it is thriving. The city has the largest theatre company in the Southeast, a lively theatre district, and the Atlanta New Play Project which with the cooperation of several resident companies stimulates the writing and production of new works. Yet, there are too often shortcomings of artistic discipline. These shortcomings can be attributed to a lack of experience and of directing ability; more seriously, they sometimes reflect a lack of respect for and responsibility to Atlanta's large audience.

Responsibility for the problems in theatre is also due in some measure to the lack of perceptive and thorough criticism from the city's newspapers. Some of the best theatre criticism has appeared, though infrequently, in *Art Papers* and the *Atlanta* magazine.

Professional theatre does not exist outside of greater Atlanta. The numerous community theatres are predominantly recreational or amateur groups. Two of note are in Columbus and Savannah.

The Springer Opera House, a magnificently restored theatre in Columbus is home to the leading performing arts group in Columbus who often produce plays on a par with professional productions in Atlanta. In addition to a wide variety of performances for adults and children, the Springer conducts its own school of theatre arts.

The Savannah Little Theatre, founded in 1950, is the city's oldest performing arts organization. Despite financial and management problems over the years, the theatre does good work. Its five-performance season is marked by more than the usual community theatre fare, its city-sponsored performances are very popular, it runs a theatre school, and it tours programs throughout Chatham County.

Film, Video, and Broadcasting

Most film and video production in the state takes place in the Atlanta area. Beyond screening notices, little news about what is happening reaches the public through the popular media. *Art Papers* and *Image* both review independent film and video screen activity. *Image* is the newsletter for the nonprofit media arts center, Image, on Peachtree Street. Founded in 1977, its film and video center promotes an annual film and video festival and assists local artists in production.

Noncommercial television production is handled by the Georgia Public Telecommunications Commission, whose aim is to serve the broad educational, cultural, and informational needs of the citizens of the state. Although limited funding prevents it from carrying many programs seen on other state public broadcasting systems, the commission has grown professionally with its own productions. It presented, in 1983, the Savannah Symphony's "Messiah" and the Augusta Opera Company's "Madame Butterfly." Its production of "Symphony: a Creative Conspiracy" won an Atlanta Emmy for outstanding achievement in cultural programming.

Public television in Georgia has the capacity to reach 96 percent of the citizenry. Public radio on the other hand, was limited to Atlanta and Savannah until 1985 when the four-station Peach State Public Radio network was established under the telecommunications commission. In 1987, it was slated to expand to six stations.

Cultural Funding and Cultural Change

Urbanization, rural population decline, Sunbelt migration, economic prosperity, civil rights, Atlanta's ascendancy to international status, improved public education—all contributed to the social and economic upheaval that characterized Georgia in the 30 years following World War II. With this upheaval, the culture of Georgia changed. In order, agriculture, the agrarian lifestyle, and the values that were inherent in working the land counted for less and less. The Georgia that had at once given challenge to the artistic talents of great writers but generally ignored the visual and performing arts was fading rapidly. A new outlook for all the arts—popular, folk, classic and contemporary—emanated from the changing culture within the state.

High culture has always been dependent upon a mixture of education, financial benefactions, and politics. Today, funding for such culture has become big business. Government and the private sector spend billions on cultivating the arts, on building cultural complexes, and on supporting arts-producing organizations and individual artists. While it is questionable whether or not they have had any effect on the *development* of culture in Georgia, there is no question that many Georgians have been exposed to the arts as the result of such funding.

In 1965, Congress created the National Endowment for the Arts (NEA) and the National Endowment for the Humanities (NEH). With that action, the national government made for the first time a financial commitment to the cultural growth of the United States similar to what had long ago been undertaken in European countries. Subsequently, state-level counterparts—in this state, the Georgia Council for the Arts and Humanities and the Georgia Endowment for the Humanities— were set up to channel a portion of federal funds and state matching funds to certain activities. While the endowments proved to be a bounteous blessing to some cultural institutions, artists, and scholars, they also proved to be a frustration and even a threat to others. The native cultural traditions that to a large extent direct the funding policies of European nations are decidedly less pluralistic than that of the United States. American culture (in the narrow sense) is a mixture of high culture (predominantly Western European), popular culture, and a variety of ethnic or folk cultures.

Since their inception, the endowments have been criticized for being elitist in their funding policies. In response, they have attempted at times to become more pluralistic. Most notable are NEA's programs in Expansion Arts, which encourage artistic expression of the nation's diverse cultural groups, and in Folk Arts, which encourage the preservation of traditional arts. Yet, the large well-established and well-to-do cultural institutions which disseminate a cultural product that is mostly traditional European or avant-garde in substance have received the lion's share of funding. This situation has serious implications when one considers that in a democratic society, taxpayers' money is being distributed with some inequity for the enjoyment of a well-to-do and select few.

In addition to funding artists and institutions directly and through their state agencies, the national endowments also spawned local arts agencies. In Georgia, communities from Dalton to Brunswick, and including places such as Moultrie and Madison, LaGrange and Pelham, Fitzgerald and Milledgeville, have arts agencies. Many of them bring visiting artists to town, launch community theatres and choruses, and sponsor arts festivals and construction and restoration projects. In general, most local arts agencies are in the business of arts exposure and not arts education. It is a common fallacy by arts boosters throughout the nation to believe that exposure to the arts is equivalent to education and appreciation of the arts. Yet public funding is predominantly for programs of exposure; what little formal education is attempted is almost entirely for children, not for adults. And many Georgia high schools, although much improved in this matter, still treat the arts as frill and fluff, one or two levels below athletics.

Conclusion

The flowering of artistic expression in the state began when Georgians rejected the myths of the past and sought the reality of southern life. This flowering, which reached its peak in literature, did not depend on cultural imports but was homegrown, born of the native experience with the ills, contradictions, values, and virtues of the region. Today, Georgia's richest area of arts production is likewise home grown.

Atlanta has become the arts center of the South. In theatres and music halls, galleries and museums, there is almost feverish activity in buying and selling art, both classic and contemporary. The large cultural institutions enjoy public and private subsidies. But the fine arts are trumpeted as being good for business: Mencken's diatribe still seems to haunt the urban landscape.

Elsewhere in Georgia, the works of some popular musicians and folk artists manifest what the literary works of Caldwell, McCullers, and O'Connor manifest, and what the paintings of Benny Andrews, Lamar Dodd, and Howard Thomas manifest: a high plateau in artistic expression reached through honest efforts to experience and render the reality of the life and values of the people of this state.

Regionalism—provincialism—may well be dead. Yet the South, particularly Georgia, still has a recognizable identity. To communicate that identity to contemporary audiences requires artists of talent, training, and honesty. To encourage artistic development, Georgia will have to provide an environment that nurtures artists and educates the public about the arts. Otherwise, there may be a great deal of thunder and lightning manufactured by the marketing specialists for the arts, but there will be little rain.

CHAPTER NINE

Five Communities

By Lawrence R. Hepburn and Allen B. Moore

What do Georgians think about the place in which they live? Certainly the census figures showing more in-migration than out-migration indicate that Georgia as a whole is seen by both natives and non-natives as a better place to live now than a few decades ago. But, other data in Chapter 4 indicate that some parts of Georgia are far more popular than others. Likewise, economic data from Chapter 3 showed that material wealth among Georgians differs greatly from one county to another. In sum, the numbers suggest a great diversity in the society and culture of Georgia.

How do these data translate into real life? Is life significantly different from one place to another? Is life in this or that place "great"? Of course, only the millions of people included in the statistics discussed in Chapter 4 can answer these questions. So we (the authors) asked Georgians themselves what they think about their communities.

Obviously, we couldn't ask some five million people for their opinions on life in Georgia. So, we decided to ask 1,000 of them, a number large enough to get a fair representation of the population. In a 1983 telephone survey, we asked them about six subjects related to community life: whether or not they were concerned about crime, jobs, housing, and health care; and whether or not they were satisfied with public education and their community in general.

Those who answered the phone were asked whether they agreed or disagreed with statements such as the following:

If I had to move away, I would look for a community just like this. (community satisfaction)

We have some of the best public school teachers in the country. (satisfaction with public education)

There are not enough good places for people to live around here. (concern for housing)

Health facilities in this area are not very good. (concern for health care)

Job opportunities in my area are becoming scarcer all the time. (concern for jobs)

It seems a lot of homes around here have been broken into lately. (concern for crime)

What we found was a rather remarkable degree of satisfaction among Georgians across the state. Overall, the people we talked to were satisfied with their communities (73%) and public education (61%). They were generally not concerned about health care (54%). They tended not to be concerned or expressed no strong opinion about crime (72%) and the availability of housing (80%). They were slightly concerned about jobs (58%).

However, a closer look at the data showed clearly that who you were, in what place in the community you fit, and where your community was located made a difference in how questions were answered.[1]

For example, blacks were more concerned than whites were about crime (40% compared to 26%), about jobs (75% to 59%), access to health care (31% to 18%), and the availability of housing (33% to 21%). Blacks were more satisfied than whites were with public education (74% to 61%), but blacks were generally less satisfied than whites were with their communities (60% to 75%).

Income also made a difference. People making less than $15,000 tended to be more concerned than were people making over $15,000 about the availability of housing (33% to 16%), about access to health care (26% to 13%) and about crime (35% to 20%). Likewise, Georgians with less than 12 years of education were more concerned than were persons with higher educational levels about such things as jobs (53% to 28%) and access to health care (25% to 12%).

Whether one's community was in north or south Georgia, and in an MSA or not in an MSA, also seemed to make a difference. South Georgians were more concerned than were north Georgians about jobs (72% compared to 58%) and the availability of housing (32% to 20%). Georgians living outside MSAs were more concerned than those living inside metro areas about jobs (74% to 55%) and access to health care (31% to 13%).

---

1. Of the people we phoned, 8 of 10 were white, 7 of 10 were homeowners, 6 of 10 were female, 5 of 10 were over 40 years old, and 4 of 10 had yearly incomes of $15,000 or more. Two of three lived in north Georgia and two of three had completed high school or advanced education.

All these numbers told us that just how great it is to live in Georgia depends on just where you live in Georgia. Also, whether a person is concerned or unconcerned, satisfied or unsatisfied with things in his or her community clearly depended on more than mere location. But, what the numbers didn't express were the real ideas of real people.

We decided to talk face-to-face with a few Georgians in a few communities. We limited ourselves to five places, places that we suspected were different enough from each other so that the expressions of the people who lived in them would reflect some of the diversity of life in Georgia.

Which five of the hundreds of communities in Georgia should we pick? We adopted and discarded several schemes for choosing our places and finally asked ourselves, "Why not just follow the route of the new faculty tour?" (See Foreword to this book.) We'd start at the Tennessee line with a mountain community, move into metro Atlanta for inner city and suburban communities, go to rural south Georgia for a farming community, and finally end up where it all started—on the coast at Savannah.

These five communities, although they cannot be said to represent the population of Georgia, do illustrate much of the diversity in Georgia.

We asked people face-to-face some of the same questions that were on the 1,000-person survey. People being interviewed like to talk about other things though, and their comments sometimes offer insight to what they think is important. In general, they told us what was so good about living in their Georgia communities, what the big problems were (and sometimes who they thought was causing them, but we won't print that), and why anyone would want to move there.

Like our telephone respondents, our 43 interviewees were generally positive. We heard over and over, "This is a good place to raise kids" and "I don't want to live anywhere else." Some, who knew we were interviewing residents of certain other communities volunteered some criticism of those other places. "I couldn't survive stuck out there in Snellville," said one person in West End. "Downtown Atlanta?" a Snellville resident recoiled: "we moved out here to get away from big city problems." Obviously, Georgians are not of one mind regarding the kind of community they want.

Just as we didn't pick the five communities scientifically, neither did we pick the persons to interview according to any rigid scheme. We learned the names of a few influential persons in each community, persons likely to know many other residents—such as bankers, lawyers, merchants, doctors, ministers, and government and civic organization leaders. We then asked these people to give us several more names. We asked for young and old, black and white, male and female interview prospects. We sought people who weren't necessarily influential in the community—ordinary as well as extraordinary people.

You will meet these people in the following pages. Their names are real and so are their comments.

Chatsworth

The Mountains and the Mills

In 1980, 2,493 people resided in Chatsworth, Georgia. Not surprisingly in the most homogeneously Anglo-Saxon region of the state, 98.6 percent of the people were white, and 82.6 percent were Georgia-born. The town sits astride U.S. 411, at the foot of the Blue Ridge Mountains, about 15 miles south of the Tennessee line and 90 miles north of Atlanta. The mountains, to the east, dominate the scenery around Chatsworth, but the mills dominate everything else.

Fort Mountain, the tallest of the forested heights, rises some 2,000 feet on Chatsworth's eastern edge. Near its crest, an 850-foot serpentine wall of stone, which gives the mountain its name, attests that people were drawn to settle here in prehistoric times. When Oglethorpe was planting his colony on the Savannah River, this was the heart of the thriving Cherokee Nation.

The first major encroachment of white Americans came with the 1805 Treaty of Tellico whereby the Cherokees permitted the United States to cut a "federal road" through their country to link Georgia and Tennessee. By 1832, the state of Georgia won a long fight to open the land to white settlement. Six years later, the last Cherokee holdouts were rounded up and sent west on the "Trail of Tears."

Later came the timber men who went into the mountains with teams of oxen or mules and portable sawmills to cut up the great stands of hardwoods. On the flat valley floor, farmers eked out a living from cotton, corn, hogs, and cattle. In the 1870s, commercial talc mining began in the nearby hills and the arrival of the L & N Railroad put Chatsworth on the map. The town was incorporated in 1906, and seven years later became the county seat.

Today, about 75 percent of Murray County is once again forest land, most of it in the Chattahoochee National Forest, Cohutta Wilderness area, and Fort Mountain State Park. The same natural features which drew earlier settlers still attract the hikers, campers, and vacationers to Fort Mountain State Park and federal recreation areas.

On the steps of the Murray County Courthouse, Attorney Dean Donahoo, born and raised in Atlanta, points at the mountains and states why he settled in Chatsworth: "I wouldn't live anywhere where I couldn't see a mountain. When I graduated from law school, I didn't put in an application in any area where you couldn't see a mountain. I came here because of the environment."

A few other newcomers have come, like Donahoo, for the mountains. But more of the non-natives have come because of the mills.

In front of the courthouse, through traffic on the old federal road (now U.S. 411 and 76) isn't very heavy today. Some vacationers, headed south from Knoxville, still take the scenic route, and some stop long enough to snap pictures of the courthouse. A few interstate haulers use it as an alternate to I-75. Mostly, though, the truck traffic originates here; for there is a bigger game in town than tourism—it is called tufting carpets. Along 411, "semis" stream in and out of town, their flanks emblazoned with brand-names that quickly establish that mill traffic dominates the road. At Kin's Restaurant, hard by 411 on the south side of Chatsworth, the mill talk dominates the conversations of the coffee-drinkers, clad in blue jeans, boots, and baseball caps: "How many shifts they running now? What mill's working seven days a week? Are they hiring? What about their working conditions? What kinds of benefits do they have? Who's going to give a big bonus this year?"

"The mills are the biggest topic?" I ask the waitress.

"Yes," she replies. "Mills and mill business, it's about all we have here."

It hasn't been this way for long. Agriculture used to dominate the local economy. In the 1950s, the public schools still took a break in the fall to allow pupils to pick cotton. "At two cents a pound, you could make three dollars a day if you picked 150 pounds," one man recalls. Today, no one grows cotton in Murray County. About 300 mostly small farms produce soybeans, corn, poultry, and cattle, but county agent Louis Canova will tell you he gets as many calls about backyard azaleas and rosebushes as he does about crops and livestock.

The big change began some 20 miles to the west around Dalton where, with the development of tufting machines, small "spread houses"—chenille bedspread plants—grew into carpet mills. Soon, Murray County farmers became commuters, working the mill shifts and keeping a chicken house on the side or a few row crops at home.

In the early 1970s, the carpet industry came to Chatsworth. "When the boom came," Dean Donahoo tells it, "they just turned chicken houses into carpet mills. Moved out the chickens one day and moved in the machines the next."

Chatsworth's own carpet industry is a source of community pride, and stories abound of how the local boys brought the industry home. Banker-legislator Tom Ramsey explains, "Some of those who gained the expertise over in Dalton said, 'If we can make this fellow a living, why don't we just come back to Murray and set up our own mill? We know what to do, we'll do it ourselves.'"

Bob McEntire was one of those who came back to do it himself. In a few years, he headed a carpet mill that was the third largest employer in Murray County. "We were founded on December 15, 1972. We were incorporated, we got a backer, an attorney, the name verbally approved by the Secretary of State, opened a bank account. . .all in one day. And, it's grown from that point. We're a little over 600,000 square feet, over 500 employees, and over $50 million in sales annually. . .from zero in 11 years."

By 1983, Murray County's 47 manufacturing plants, most of them part of the carpet industry, employed more than 4,200 people. Most remain small operations housed in one-story metal or brickfaced buildings along U.S. 4ll or the new four-lane to Dalton. Here are the jobbers; retail and wholesale outlets; vendors of carpet backings, yarns, and dyes, tufting machinery services; and tiny plants which cut remnants into doormats, sample swatches, drink coasters, and novelty items. Several of the big manufacturers with a hundred or more employees are clustered, in low brick buildings with green lawns, in the industrial park on the north side of Chatsworth.

The carpet industry has been good for the economy of Chatsworth and Murray County. In the 1970s, Murray County was one of the few non-MSA counties to register a more than 50 percent increase in new housing units. Some of those new housing units were occupied by newcomers to the county who came in response to the labor needs of the growing industry, but many were occupied by Murray County natives enjoying a new prosperity.

As in most of nonmetro Georgia, housing throughout Murray County is predominantly owner-occupied (73 percent) and single-family. About 22 percent of the housing is of the mobile home type, typically located on small acreage in the countryside, not in mobile home parks. The rise in new housing and the popularity of mobile homes reflect both the new prosperity and the influx of people mainly taking hourly jobs in the mills. Between 1970 and 1980, after decades of no growth, Murray County's population jumped from 12,987 to 19,685, a 52 percent increase. In 1979, a good year for the carpet industry, the median family income in Murray County was $16,652, about 95 percent of the state average and 36th among the 159 counties.

Most of the newcomers settled in rural areas, not in Chatsworth proper. In fact, the 1980 census showed the town's population had decreased by 213 during the 1970s and that its median family income was $15,382, or 88 percent of the state average. Chatsworth is mainly a low- to middle-income community. Of 945 households in 1979, 115 households, or 12 percent, had incomes of $25,000 or more while 417 households, or 44 percent, had incomes of less than $10,000. Compared to the countywide population, Chatsworth's population has a smaller percentage of children five years and under (6 to 10 percent), and a greater percentage of people 65 years and over (11 to 8 percent).

Around town, signs of the new prosperity are apparent. Fast-food places have appeared along the new four-lane to Dalton, some expensive homes are under construction on large wooded lots, and a modest renovation of Chatsworth's downtown has begun. But, some buildings stand vacant, some sorely needed fixing up, and a few—especially the old talc mill—are plain unsightly.

A Loose-knit Community

"The majority of the society here is rather loose-knit," says lawyer Donahoo, suggesting that a busybody would be out of place here. "It has to do with a lot of folks being from the mountain area. Privacy is important. Being able to live your own life in your own way is important. There's not much emphasis on conformity."

Such a characterization is consistent with the reputation of the people who settled the Appalachians. They were "the most individual of the individualistic Americans," said a British geographer describing the nineteenth century Anglo-Saxons of the upcountry South. The mountain farmers quickly established that they would not readily follow the lead of Georgia's dominant economic and political interests—whether antebellum planters or postreconstruction industrialists. Many opposed secession and the Confederate war effort, and their descendants have maintained pockets of Republicanism to the present. Before the turn of the century, leaders in reform politics, prohibition, and women's suffrage came out of this region. On the other hand, mountain Georgians were known to be hostile to outsiders, especially blacks. Louis Canova, himself a relative newcomer, notes, "Being county agent, I was accepted right away, but it seems like people come in and they may be kind of looked at for a spell before they are actually accepted...."

Physically, economically, and socially the region remained out of the mainstream of state affairs. From 1913 to 1983, no governor hailed from this region. Locally, the small farmer's penchant for separateness and their overriding concern for family and private enterprise, not public affairs, were reflected in their community institutions. Their stores, churches, and schools were scattered in the open country, as were their homes. Until the arrival of the mills, they counted among the poorest whites of the state.

Traditional rural values manifest themselves in many ways. The mills' workforce is nonunion. Not that labor organizers haven't tried. Mountain independence and unionism just haven't meshed easily. Add the rural tradition of hard work: local men and women may put in 60 to 70 hours a week in the mill. So, even though carpet manufacturing may be a relatively low-wage industry, one can have a good income. Few mill workers still farm on the side.

The traditional North Georgia outlook is evident in people's attitudes toward government. "They want services, but not extravagance or fancy things," observes Tom Ramsey, who has lived here all his life and represents Murray County in the Georgia legislature. "What country folks look for most from their tax dollars," he adds, "is good roads. An elected official can point to that bridge or that four-lane between Chatsworth and Dalton. Those are the things that rural people see for their tax dollars. . . . They don't really make that many demands because country folk know that the more you demand of government, the more it's going to cost you."

Public education is another issue. Because of the success in keeping property taxes as low as possible, Murray County schools are not as good as they could be, some community leaders acknowledge. "The parents are interested in sports, but not education itself," said one. Despite a big increase over the past 10 years in taxable commercial property, improvements in facilities have been modest, and salary supplements to attract teachers are low. While the majority of the community may be satisfied with the local system, some of the newcomers in middle-level management positions pay tuition to send their children to the better-financed schools in Dalton.

Of course, local people don't always have a free choice in determining how taxes will be spent. Recently, Chatsworth faced the problem of building a new jail. "There's no way around it; we're going to have to build it," admits Tom Ramsey. "The people in the community have heard about surrounding counties under court orders to build new jails. They tell me, 'Let's build one before the courts get a hold of us. . . . If we're going to have to spend our money, let's spend it like we want to, not like some federal judge tells us.'"

"We try to handle our own problems," adds Bob McEntire, "without calling up any government agencies to take care of our problems. I think other companies do the same thing. Families, too, take care of their own problems."

While the time-honored views of independence and family still hold sway, local people acknowledge some change in recent years. Dixie Jones was a newcomer some 20 years ago. She runs the Fort View Cleaners, two blocks north of the courthouse. "When we came over here from Dalton, our competitor told us we better not fix up too much because people wouldn't do business with us. That was the attitude: if people think you're doing too well, they won't do business with you. I grew up in the country and I'd heard people say, 'they're just getting too big for their britches,' but anyway we went ahead and we kept most of our customers. And we added to them as the town has grown. The customers today have more money and are more conscious of the quality of clothes. People have moved in from other parts of the country, and I think it's all been for the better. Chatsworth is more broad-minded than a lot of other towns this small because change has taken place faster here than elsewhere. But people don't have the time to stand and talk to you like they did 20 years ago. . . ."

Not only is the industry credited with breaking down old barriers to change within the community, but also with promoting acceptance of progress in the rest of Georgia. State Representative Tom Ramsey explains it this way: "At one time, if anything suited the metro areas, we didn't like it. If it was good for them, it certainly couldn't be good for us. But now we look at Atlanta as a major marketplace for our products. And as for Savannah . . . so much of our exports go through the port, and jute comes into the industry."

This border area's blooming identification with the rest of Georgia results from more than the coming of carpets. Because of the close proximity to Chattanooga, the area has a decidedly Tennessee flavor. Before cable TV came to the area, residents watched Chattanooga TV because of the poor reception from Atlanta, and those without cable still do. On Saturday nights, local people are more likely to drive to Chattanooga than Atlanta for entertainment.

What of the future? Even carpet mill owners agree that if the local economy is to be less susceptible to nationwide business cycles, it has to have more than carpets to stand on. The carpet industry itself is especially sensitive to fluctuations in the national economy, as it is so closely tied to housing construction and auto sales. From 1975 to 1979 to 1982, Murray County's unemployment rate ranged from among the highest in the state (11.8 percent), to one of the lowest (4.9 percent), to one of the highest (11.9 percent). For upwardly mobile educated young people, the carpet industry offers few opportunities: it requires far more hourly workers than salaried managers. In 1980, 33 percent of Murray County's work force were employed as machine operatives or in similar jobs. For the state as a whole, the comparable figure was 12 percent.

The effort to diversify, to bring in new industry, has a special imperative: keep the young people from leaving. The Chamber of Commerce and planning commission have had some success in attracting noncarpet industry. But according to Louis Canova, who was also president of the

Dixie Jones (left, with Annie Ree McConneaughey and Dean Donahoo):
"Chatsworth is more broad-minded than a lot of other towns this
small. . . ."

Chatsworth Kiwanis Club, "We have trouble getting enough people involved in a project to make it effective."

One organization that is successful in getting a large group involved in a project is the Murray County Saddle Club. Its project is Chatsworth's biggest annual event: The Appalachian Wagon Train. Each July, several hundred horse and mule enthusiasts from around the Southeast move in with their animals for 10 days of exhibitions, contests, trail rides, parades, and square dances. Some locals grumble about the visitors "who come in and rip around," but the huge event does suggest the potential for tourism.

Dixie Jones is pushing for that: "We have Fort Mountain State Park and the Grassy Mountain Wilderness Area up there and just a lot of beautiful scenery. But it's not been promoted like northeast Georgia. Some local people are not as enthusiastic as I am about the potential of the area. They've lived here and are happy with things the way they are...and they're not out trying to change it."

Snellville

For most Georgians who know where Snellville is, it's a place to go through, not a place to go to. That is especially true for countless University of Georgia Bulldog fans stuck in its traffic bottleneck on their way to Athens on football Saturdays. It's also true for commuters and others who travel through Gwinnett County on U.S. 78.

Although the highway was widened from two to three to five lanes, the ever-growing local traffic assured a continued bottleneck. To the long-suffering football fan, Snellville was a wonderment. It seemed to grow from one Saturday to the next. A few rural stores clustered at the crossing of U.S. 78 and Ga. 124 became a shopping center, then a commercial strip several miles long. Growth came so fast that as late as 1980, a pasture full of horses remained less than 1,000 feet from the highway intersection.

The visitor to Snellville, who discerns neither physical boundaries to distinguish the city from its surroundings nor any concentration of buildings to mark its center, may ask, "Where's the town?"

But many people have seen Snellville as a good place to live. Snellville is a bedroom community for people who work in other parts of metro Atlanta. Its residents are dependent on the automobile, which shapes the community's lifestyle. Spread along the highway are fast-food restaurants, gas stations, convenience and discount stores, supermarkets, home improvement and nursery suppliers, banks, schools, churches, offices for doctors, dentists, and realtors, dance and karate studios, and hairstyling and dog-grooming salons. All the services for comfortable living are here. Getting from one shopping section to another requires a car, and there's plenty of parking. Housing, too, is spread out, mainly in subdivisions. Sidewalks are rare. Rarer still are places to work, such as office buildings, plants, and warehouses. Those are heavily concentrated in the northern part of Gwinnett County, near I-85, and that's the way Snellville residents seem to like it: they get the benefits—jobs and tax payments for schools and local government—but not the headaches of industrial development.

A Homogeneous Community

Like so many developing suburbs across the nation, Snellville has a homogeneous population. Over 99 percent of the residents are white. Snellville's households seem to fit the American ideal of "mom, dad, and the two kids." In fact, of 2,481 households in 1980, 88 percent were married-couple families, about two-thirds of them with children under 18. Another way of looking at family structure: 89 percent of persons under 18 in Snellville lived in married-couple families. (The comparable figure for Chatsworth was 67 percent and for the city of Atlanta 43 percent.) Of persons age 25 and over, about 79 percent were graduated from high school and 44 percent went on to some years of college. Practically every employed person 16 and over (95.6 percent) drove alone or carpooled to work and 59 percent commuted to a job outside Gwinnett County. In 1979, 70 percent of the households had incomes between $20,000 and $50,000. Per capita income for Snellville that year was 133 percent of the state average. Only 2 percent of Snellville families had incomes below the poverty level. (For the state as a whole, 13 percent of families had incomes below the poverty level.)

With little social disparity among the residents, Snellville lacks the traditional political elite, or power structure, of similar-sized places in the South. Mayor Emmett Clower says emphatically, "We have no real poor and no socialites or blue bloods. Family doesn't count. There's no classifications. We don't have that. People have mixed real well. I guess we have Southern hospitality. We've had a lot of Northerners move in here and some foreigners, and everybody gets along just fine."

The influx of residents has made Snellville one of the fastest growing communities in the nation, but it had a slow start. Incorporated as a city in 1923, it had only 204 residents by 1940. T. W. Briscoe was mayor in 1965 when the city had a budget of $3,700, and he and the police chief, who doubled as water commissioner, had to track down leaks whenever the water pressure dropped. That was the year things began to change: "What happened when the boom started, there were two young boys, the Mason brothers, they bought 200 and something acres of land right here in the city limits which belonged to one family's farm. They started tearing down all these little tenant houses...and put in subdivisions."

Today, the subdivisions spread out from Snellville in all directions and 30,000 people live within a four-mile radius of its center. The city's population increase is part of the spectacular growth of Gwinnett County.

Year	Snellville Population	Percentage Increase	Gwinnett County Pop.	Percentage Increase
1960	468		43,541	
1970	1,990	325.2	72,349	66.2
1980	8,514	327.8	166,903	130.7

Note: Gwinnett County is growing so fast that the State Office of Planning and Budget estimates that its population will increase by 65 percent to 296,155 in 1990 and by another 49 percent to 441,680 by the year 2000.

Snellville's growth has been spurred by two familiar demographic phenomena: white flight and Sunbelt migration. In the mid-1960s, the prospect of integrated schools and integrated neighborhoods convinced thousands of white families in east Atlanta, southeast DeKalb County, and other close-in sections of metropolitan Atlanta to head for Gwinnett County. Historically a county with a relatively small black population, Gwinnett in 1980 still counted fewer than 5,000 blacks, and Snellville had only 13 black residents.

After the initial wave of newcomers in the 1960s, migration to the Sunbelt, not flight to the suburbs, accounted for Gwinnett's being one of the fastest growing counties in the nation. In 1980, about 41 percent of Gwinnett's population and 43 percent of Snellville's had been born outside Georgia.

The Napiers live in Summit Chase, a subdivision hidden in the hills away from the highway and the commercial strip. "We moved here because of our jobs," explains Pam Napier. She and her husband, John, are from Virginia. She works for Southern Bell in Atlanta and he teaches at the University of Georgia in Athens. "For me, it takes about an hour in the traffic; it's 30 miles each way. And, it takes John about an hour to go 42 miles the other way. . . ." "People feel safe with their families out here," John Napier points out. "We haven't had much trouble. We have good police protection—they circle us all the time."

Most of the residents of this subdivision are not natives. "On this block we have a North Carolina, a New York, Kansas, Wisconsin, two Nebraskas, and a Virginia." Pam Napier explains that the subdivision builder catered to people from out of state: "The builders would have contacts with the big companies and would meet their people at the airport, show them a film, and bring them out here. And when one family from a big company buys in here, several do. Six Rockwell families bought here and six Georgia-Pacific, too—in from Oregon—and several Southern Bell besides us. And the men John plays golf with. . .one is Safeco, one is Travelers Insurance, and one is Frigidaire. We have a Greyhound man, a couple of GM people, and the meat man from Food Giant."

Because Snellville has drawn its population from outside the area, Mayor Emmett Clower is a rarity in Snellville: he is a native. His father and grandfather, also named Emmett Clower, were natives, too. Mayor since 1972, Clower can remember when everyone knew everyone else in Snellville, but his interest lies with the new, not the old Snellville "We're not being revitalized; we're all new. Almost all our homes are less than 20 years old. A brand new city is just about what we are."

The homogeneity of Snellville's residents is matched by the homogeneity of its residences. According to the mayor, "We have a minimum of 1,350 square feet in the whole city. We have nothing smaller than that. By doing that, we've kept out a lot of things. We don't have a great number of apartments, and we don't have the trailer parks, the slums, the urban renewal that you find in a lot of other places. . .which does prohibit us from a lot of federal grants, but sometimes that's good, too. We don't have those problems."

Pam Napier: "Briscoe Park, practically everybody in Snellville goes there. The ducks are the best-fed anywhere."

Life in Snellville

Like Emmett Clower who followed him in the mayor's office, T. W. Briscoe is quick to point out Snellville's advantages. While squabbles over land development and local services abound in other parts of Gwinnett, he notes that Snellville's people have a countywide reputation for cooperating. "The new people and the old people worked together and made a town. I've been real pleased with the way things have gone—except for the traffic."

Briscoe is proud of the city park—T. W. Briscoe Park—which could serve a city much larger than Snellville. The 76-acre complex has softball and soccer fields, tennis and basketball courts, golf course, swimming pool, fishing lake, picnic grounds, and pavilion. On weekends, hundreds of children and their parents participate in the city recreation department's organized activities.

Elise Cotter has lived in Snellville 12 years, raised a family, and regards herself as a native. Besides working in real estate, she's involved in several community groups, organizes fund-raising for school and civic projects, and serves on the city council. "We have neighborhood clubs, community clubs, women's clubs—you have no trouble getting people involved. It's not like other suburbs where the only times people go outside is to cut the grass."

Of course, not everyone in Snellville is keen to be involved in community affairs. Many of the subdivisions have their own "residents only" pools and clubhouses that keep people at home. Summit Chase, Snellville's "PUD" (planned unit development), is a country-club-type subdivision complete with 18-hole golf course, tennis courts, swimming pool, and club. According to Pam Napier, many newcomers take little if any interest in civic affairs. "They travel in their jobs and don't have time for that. They come back here to escape, to play golf at the club and get away from it all. And then, start again on Monday morning. We're really part of the club environment because of the golf and tennis and swimming and all that. But, most everybody in the neighborhood is a member of a church: either the Catholic or Presbyterian or Methodist or Baptist."

Snellville counts over a dozen churches, some of them with growth problems of their own. The First Baptist is Snellville's largest church; a few years ago, its members were adding a three-story education wing and contemplated ways to accommodate 3,000 worshippers on Sunday morning. (Next door, the Methodists erected a new sanctuary to handle their growth.) The pastor, Rev. Ronnie Spillars, acknowledges, however, that the church has to make some adjustments in this kind of community. "We really have to set our priorities as a church, . . . to find out what is the most effective ministry that we can carry on in the least amount of time—so that we can allow families to be families. Churches have to make that adjustment . . . because you have school activities, recitals, sports—all the other activities that a community offers that people are going to become involved in . . . . We have to be respecting of that. And they of us. They basically respect Sunday, and most of the sports activities in the city respect Wednesday evening, but sometimes they schedule things on Wednesday, which puts families in a tension."

The influx of people from outside the Bible Belt has introduced living patterns that dismay older residents. Directly across the highway from First Baptist and Snellville Methodist, the "Super-Kroger," advertised as the largest supermarket in metropolitan Atlanta when it opened, operates 24 hours a day, seven days a week. Not too long ago, all Snellville business closed by sundown (noon on Wednesdays) and never opened on Sundays. Families came to town on Saturday to do their shopping. Of more concern however, was liquor-by-the-drink. The enforcement of Snellville's ban on drink sales was an irritant to some newcomers who felt that the only way they would get a "decent" restaurant in town would be to drop the prohibition.

Yet, newcomers join with older residents in voicing desire to keep things as they are. Developer proposals to build apartments, smaller one-family houses, or light industry are all rejected by a majority of the people. Even growth itself is less favored than a few years ago. "It would be nice to have the same population as 10 years ago," sighs a harried city official.

Particularly galling to some residents is the suggestion—earnestly made upon occasion to the city council—that the town's name be changed. The name, long the source of jokes in Atlanta, derives from the founding Snell family, many of whom still live here. "It's crazy, but they don't want to use Snellville as a mailing address or tell people they're from Snellville," says Elise Cotter, who recalls potential residents who would not move to Snellville because of the name. "A lot of people [living in Snellville] will say, 'I'm from Atlanta.'"

Government is rather personal here, and the mayor and council must be ready to answer complaints about overflowing sewage, teens hanging out at the video arcade, and of course traffic. Issues tend to be minor.

Public offenses also tend to be minor and smack more of small town mischief than big city crime. "This morning I was egged," Mayor Clower recounts more in resignation than anger. "Some kids threw eggs at the door. I'm sure they got a speeding ticket or something and they took out their frustrations on my door and the window, too. I've got to clean it up now. I've only had a couple other instances like that, but it bothers you sometimes."

U.S. 78 in Snellville. Traffic, here passing First Baptist Church, remains the most talked-about local problem.

What of the future? Many people worry about the problems that plague any rapid growth area. The fear of losing the small town character is real. Children are a main concern: many are left alone while father and mother are away at work, and many affluent teenagers drive around looking for something to do. "They can't all be in sports; we need more youth programs," several parents suggest. A civic center is proposed for Briscoe Park. Others see alienation creeping in. "We have to promote more of a neighborly type of attitude where people really care," warns Reverend Spillars.

And then, there's the traffic. A Snellville community survey showed that more than any other problem the people wanted the traffic flow improved. When asked about it, Reverend Spillars responds with a smile. "The traffic? When Georgia plays football, I can't get out of the church parking lot. You can burn a tank of gas waiting."

West End—Atlanta

Since 1946, Peggy Brady has stayed in her "poor man's Victorian" as she calls it, raising two sons amidst calamitous change in West End. "I preached, 'You don't let people run you away from your home. You do something about it.'"

A little brochure published by WEND, the West End Neighborhood Development association says, "West End is a community of poor, middle class, professional, black, white, old and young people...." Beyond that, it's rather difficult to pin down the makeup of West End. Even the boundaries of West End are open to dispute, for it's not an incorporated municipality like Chatsworth or Snellville; it's a neighborhood community in the west-central section of the city of Atlanta. It's about 15 blocks east-west and seven or eight north-south. Most residents agree that it is bounded on the north by I-20, an expressway, and on the east by the railroad tracks, but the south and west boundaries are open to discussion. Because no one knows exactly where West End begins and ends, all data about West End residents should be viewed as approximations.

In 1980, West End was home to approximately 3,652 people, about 80 percent black and 74 percent Georgia-born. Of Atlanta's five communities, West End has the most mobile population: 61 percent of the persons over five years of age lived in a different house in 1975. (The comparable figure was 55 percent for Snellville and 47 percent for the whole city of Atlanta.) West End differed from all of Atlanta in another way in 1980: while Atlanta's per capita income was 102 percent of the state average that year, West End's per capita income was only 65 percent of the state average. Yet, the percentage of West End families with incomes below the poverty level was only slightly higher than for the city as a whole: 26 percent compared to 24 percent. Clearly, West End had few wealthy people to boost the average per capita income; its residents were low to middle-income people.

Years of Change

West End is a neighborhood undergoing change, and Peggy Brady has witnessed those changes. "I've seen it go from being a very nice beautiful neighborhood—dogwood trees, the old homes were all kept up—it was just a nice place to live. Then it became crime-ridden, we had all kinds of problems. . . . I've seen it go downhill and I'm seeing it go back up. It's a delightful place to live, kind of like a small town community. Well, it is!"

West End was once a small city. Incorporated as a municipality in 1868, it was annexed into Atlanta in 1893. By that time, it had become a fashionable suburb and many prominent Atlantans were among the merchants, bankers, manufacturers, managers, and politicians who lived there. Only a mile and a half from Five Points—Atlanta's center of commerce—West End was a short ride to work, or home for lunch, on the new streetcars. On weekends, golfers rode the streetcar out to the West End Golf Course. The most prominent West Ender was Joel Chandler Harris, author of the "Uncle Remus" stories and editor for the *Atlanta Constitution.* Among the houses of the affluent were a few clusters of smaller houses of the black people who cooked and cleaned and washed and tended the gardens, horses, and children of the white residents.

By World War I, West End had ceased to be in fashion and Atlanta's affluent moved to the north side around Buckhead. West End settled into a comfortable middle-class stability.

World War II brought a hint of changes to come. Housing was scarce and Ft. McPherson was only a dozen blocks to the south. Some one-family houses were divided into apartments to accommodate the demand for housing.

West End began a slow slide into depression for 20 years after the war. Rural white and black migration to the city, urban renewal of low-income neighborhoods in other sections of the city, the building of suburbs and expressways, school integration—all contributed to the destabilization of West End.

Peggy Brady's neighbors moved out and turned their houses into rental property. "They didn't care who they rented to. We had some pretty rough customers, and they came in all colors. We had to call the police about shooting or drinking, disorderly conduct, cussing, just fighting. . . . Rental property doesn't have to be that way, but it can be...that's what created the problem here. Transient people don't usually care about a neighborhood; they know they'll be gone in a few weeks."

For over two decades, West End has received the attention of outside agencies. In 1963, as Atlanta's poor continued to converge on the neighborhood, the Community Council of Metropolitan Atlanta, with a grant from private sources, started the West End Project. The project, whose aim was to break the poverty cycle by helping the poor become employable, was by early 1965 engulfed by the federal War on Poverty. In the process, West End, which had been pinpointed by the Community Council, was given a massive dose of federal money.

In 1966, Atlanta's media featured the $14 million worth of projects that would allow West End to rise phoenix-like by its 100th birthday. Day care, family counseling, mental and physical health, and rent subsidies were included. The biggest project involved bulldozing West End's old commercial center—a block along Gordon Street between Lee and Ashby—for an in-town shopping mall anchored by a new Sears, Roebuck store.

The mall opened in 1970, but West End's slide continued. Mall tenants came and went, and Sears was ready to pull out. Citywide, West End's reputation was that of slums, crime, and dying businesses.

What West End needed was stable residents, not money and new buildings. In the early 1970s, only 10 percent of its houses remained owner-occupied. The others sheltered the short-term renters or stood vacant and vandalized. Property values had sunk so low that the one real estate agent who handled houses in West End was nicknamed "the junk man."

The beginning of West End's turnaround came in 1974 when architect Wade Burns purchased and started renovating a block of houses on Peeples Street. Burns' project, completed in 1978, did more than reclaim old houses; it attracted into West End the middle-income homeowners who could give the area the stability it had lacked for so many years. His success encouraged other urban "pioneers" to take a chance.

Many were young professionals: doctors, lawyers, college professors, artists, media people, and public administrators, including Atlanta's police commissioner. The census for 1980 showed that of the West End residents over 25 years old, 15 percent were college graduates. (Of our five communities, only Snellville had a higher percentage of college graduates, 21 percent.) Moreover, about 39 percent of the housing units in West End were owner-occupied.

Cleta Winslow, an administrative assistant to the county commission, was one pioneer: "I remember the first time coming into this house, I came in through the window. It was broken out; the stained glass had been taken. At that time, houses were going for between $3,000 and $10,000. The people who moved in, I guess, had a vision of something better later on down the line, in building something, not just in terms of a structure, but really in building a neighborhood. . . .They knew how rundown it was but were willing to take a risk."

James Dupuy, who oversees Georgia Federal's West End Branch, is credited for much of the creative financing that enabled many people to buy and fix up their own houses. With support from HUD and other institutions, a reconstruction mortgage was devised: the bank lent money based not on the current market value of an unrestored house, but on its potential value after restoration. Dupuy is emphatic about the benefits to the whole area: "It's an interesting cycle. . . .You had many old homes broken up, four units renting for $20 a week. You can imagine the income level in the community. What kind of merchandise do you think Sears went down to? Turn this around—an old home that wouldn't even meet the city code, buy it and put 30 to 35 thousand dollars into it. You have a totally different [situation]. Here you had four families living on welfare, now you have one family—maybe a professor at Emory and the husband a superintendent for a commercial contractor, with a combined income of 65 to 70 thousand dollars, and it's not just one family, it's 50, it's 100." Not only did Sears' merchandise mix change, but new businesses began popping up along Gordon Street as news of the residential renovation spread.

Community Action

Though West End is an old neighborhood, it is a young community. In 1980, of the 816 families in the neighborhood, 53 percent included children under 18 years of age. Only 15 percent of them were headed by a person 65 years or older. Again, of our five communities, only Snellville had a higher percentage of families with children under 18, 67 percent, and a lower percentage of familes with householders over 65, 5.5 percent. However, while 89 percent of Snellville's under-18 population lived in married couple families, only 40 percent of West End's young people did so. Of the five communities, West End had the highest percentage of families with children under 18 headed by a female householder with no husband present, 23 percent. At the other extreme were Chatsworth and Snellville, with 7.5 percent and 4.9 percent respectively. Cleta Winslow, who heads WEND, feels this kind of community looks out for children needing help. "Usually if they've got only one parent, then they'll find a substitute here [her own house] or someplace else."

Winslow also is quick to point out the difference between West End and other in-town neighborhoods. "The whites that have moved in know the make-up of the neighborhood. They could have moved someplace else, but chose to come here. . . . Normally in a predominantly black neighborhood you would not have whites coming in. . . . And all religious groups, they feel comfortable, not harassed. We may not understand or appreciate someone else's viewpoint or practices, but we tolerate, we respect."

Another resident, Janice Sykes, also notes West End's diversity. "I have neighbors who are architects, with CNN, retired. You have all kinds of couples, you know, racially-mixed as well as homosexual couples and heterosexual couples. It's a very diverse neighborhood." Janice Sykes is emphatic about the benefits of living in a thoroughly mixed community. A librarian at the Atlanta Public Library, she and her husband, Dann, a television producer, believe it's especially good for their children. "They can be introduced to all kinds of people who make up the world," she observed. "We want our children to have people skills, to be people who are leaders, who can deal with different kinds of individuals and personalities. And this is a church community, whether people go or not. You have Ralph Abernathy's church, St. Anthony's, which is one of the oldest Catholic churches in the city; the Muslim community— Islam; Reverend Jackson around the corner; the Church of God in Christ. Every couple of blocks there is a church, but there's a strong feeling that whatever you do in your house is fine."

Balancing West Enders' tolerance of individual differences is an overriding concern for community cohesiveness. According to Cleta Winslow, the young professionals who move here are into "neighborhoodness." "By that I mean they want to build a sort of unity, a community type family: watching out for each other, making sure vacant lots are cut, helping people out if something happens in their family. . . and there's a kind of forced closeness, forced by issues, by problems. That's usually when people come together, to fight for something."

West Enders have found that gaining the attention of city politicians is especially difficult in a neighborhood that those politicians were used to neglecting. Police protection, schools, street cleaning, and garbage pickup slipped as the neighborhood lost political clout. Regaining that clout was a slow process.

"I needed a new councilman for my community," explains Dann Sykes. "The old one was never here and didn't respond to the concerns of the community. He spent most of the time in midtown." So Sykes went to work for the candidate who eventually unseated the incumbent. "We had a coffee for him here in our house for the people in West End and we put his yard signs—dayglo—all up and down Gordon Street, so many it freaked him out." Cleta Winslow thinks the process has worked. "The relationship to City Hall is very good, the city has put money into West End. . .the response is very good. It took a while to get that, a lot of persistence: they finally realized we were serious."

West Enders meet. Left *to* right: *Wade Burns, Peggy Brady, Anne Baird-Bridges, Mr. and Mrs. Ed Winslow, and WEND President Cleta Winslow.*

Janice Sykes agrees. "The police know we demand a certain level from them as we demand from the school board. In fact, we have a pretty solid reputation of being harassing: when we descend on City Hall, *we descend!* When we descend on the school board, we descend!"

The redevelopment of West End has brought new problems, according to Winslow. "We want to make sure businesses don't encroach too much on the residential part. . .wanting to come in and change residential lots into commercial lots. . . .We hammered out a compromise with a developer who wanted to put two fast foods on one lot. We said, We've got enough fast foods!. . .Unless you demand things, people will not respect you."

James Dupuy is also concerned about problems of development and developer perceptions, but from a different perspective. As the banker who put together the loan packages for individuals who wanted to reconstruct their own West End houses, he sees West End development as part of the larger southside development of Atlanta. "Development in Atlanta has all moved north. If we continue, in another 10 or 15 years, our central business district will be up around Lenox [Square]. We can't afford that. We have got to start moving development south. Where do you start? There's only one place: West End. There's no damn reason why if you live on the south side you have to go to the north side for a job. Job-intensive development can take place in connection with residential development. We're on the number one leg of MARTA to the airport. If you were building a southeastern headquarters for a major insurance company, what place would be better than here? There's Hartsfield—phweet!—right here to West End, an office tower. You're still only three minutes to downtown, and we're right here at the interchange of 85, 75, and 20. You've got everything here."

But, as Dupuy readily admits, West End suffers from a problem in perception. "Prejudice. . .we've been fighting this for years. Not one day goes by that we don't have one shopping center in this city that has more crime than all the West End commercial area. No one thinks anything about going into Lenox Square, but if you say 'go to West End' they say 'Oh, Lord, I'm not going there.'. . . According to police records, West End is a low crime area, but, according to the perception. . . here again, prejudice. If an area is an old area, if it's a close-in area, if it's integrated, and if there are blacks, you know."

As the political and economic influentials discuss the wisdom of a "southside strategy," West End, whose future would be determined in part by that strategy, continues its comeback. Janice Sykes has a more intimate view of its continuing need: To make West End better, "we need to raise the consciousness level of some of the people who are very poor and really do not see themselves as part of the community. We have some houses that really need to be either torn down or fixed up, and the people in them need to be moved out. If they want to come back in and function as responsible tenants, then they should be offered that property first, but there are people who need to have their consciousness raised. I feel strongly about that. . . I'm not as liberal as some of my neighbors."

Peggy Brady, who has lived almost 40 years in West End, and is the neighborhood's oldest activist, is emphatic about her neighbors. What does West End need? "More of the same: people who are interested in improving the community. I've got some of the best neighbors I've had in my life, I love 'em to death. We work together, young, old, black, white. My neighbor, I wouldn't take a million dollars for her."

Ocilla

Mr. and Mrs. Oscar Powell have lived here for 20 years, raised a family, and are now retired—he from the bank, she from teaching. They are two of this small town's biggest boosters.

Mary Ann Powell remembers when a couple from up North happened upon Ocilla: "They were just riding down I-75 and heard on the radio of a lot for sale here. They are originally from, oh, 'Yankeetown'—I don't know exactly where, but they moved down here lock, stock, and barrel. And they do not want to go back North."

Oscar Powell corroborates his wife's story. "Yes, they just heard it on the radio and came off the highway."

A Stable Community

Ocilla hasn't had many newcomers in recent years, however. In 1980, the town's population stood at 3,436, an increase of 251 persons over 1970. Not only were 93 percent of Ocilla's residents Georgia-born, but 80 percent were living in the same house in 1980 as in 1975. Moreover, of the two in ten residents who did move during the five years, 82 percent had moved only from another house in Irwin County. In terms of residence, Ocilla is certainly the most stable of our five communities.

A major difference between a Snellville, to which migrants are flocking, and an Ocilla, where they are not, is reflected in the 1980 census figures. Whereas persons 18 to 44 years old—that is, younger adults starting families, building homes, and embarking on careers—composed 44 percent of Snellville's population, only 30 percent of Ocilla's population was in that age group. Conversely, 17 percent of Ocilla's population was 65 years or older; in Snellville, only 6 percent was.

In treating any population data for Ocilla, one must consider that the population is 51 percent black and 49 percent white, and that sharp distinctions exist between the two groups. For example, in 1980, 12 percent of the blacks were under five years old and 11 percent 65 years and over: that same year only 6 percent of the whites were under five, but 24 percent were 65 and over. In 1979, while 54 percent of the black persons had incomes below the poverty level, only 18 percent of the white persons had incomes below the poverty level.

Of course, economic opportunity is the primary motivation for migration. Thus, Snellville—located in the midst of the booming metro Atlanta region—boomed in the 1970s; Ocilla—in rural south Georgia—did not. Ironically, the nonmaterial aspects of a community—the caring attitude and neighborliness that Reverend Spillars said was needed in Snellville—are touted as advantages of living in Ocilla.

Mary Ann Powell talks about those advantages. "People say, 'come and pick peanuts out of my field, I'm fixing to plow it under, come and pick peanuts and boil them.' Or they'll say, 'You have a standing invitation to fish from my pond. I'll tell you where the best fishing places are.' We have people like that, you just love them to death. You go to your front door and there's some vegetables somebody just brought in. Sometimes they don't even let you know they were here."

"We probably know too much about individuals and their families, but that's the way of life here," observes Charles Harris, merchant and life-long resident. "I think really the thing about a community such as this one is that folks sincerely care about what happens to their neighbors or their friends—and they even care about what happens to folks they don't consider their friends."

Strong family and social ties extend out into the county, so when people talk about the community, they mean Irwin County as well as Ocilla. Yet, Ocilla the town is special.

Syd Blackmarr explains it this way: "People say about Ocilla that it seems to be a little bit, I don't like to say 'elitist,' but people here seem to be aware of the finer things of life—whatever that means." Blackmarr, who runs a state program to bring the arts to rural south central Georgia, surely knowns what that means. She knows most of the communities in the region. "Interest in the arts and in education is a little higher in Ocilla than in other communities of similar size and makeup."

Travelers coming in on U.S. 319 from Tifton find themselves in a residential section almost stereotypically smalltown America. The setting could as easily be the Midwest as the South. Bungalows and other modest, mostly pre-World War II houses predominate. They stand under big shade trees close by streets laid out in the grid style made popular in nineteenth century America. Streets are number-named east and west, tree-named north and south: Apricot, Elm, Maple, Pine. The school and schoolyard and two big brick churches, Ocilla Baptist and First Methodist, hold prominent spots. It is a pretty neighborhood.

Coming into Ocilla from the south on U.S. 129, one first encounters some of the town's newest residences, a neat public housing project, and then the older, often cramped houses of the black community. Ocilla's housing projects are visible signs that things have improved for black residents. "We're getting rid of the last unpaved streets in the black community," says Alfonso Owens, a retired school principal. "We've been without for years. I've lived on this street all of my life, 60-some odd years, and this street was just paved in June, but every street in the white community was paved. Now, with the federal money, they have torn down houses and built new houses—that money made the difference." Owens gives Ocilla's mayor much of the credit for the federal involvement in the black community. "He tries to get everything he can for the city."

Social life in rural communities has traditionally been centered in homes and churches and oriented toward families, and it remains so in Ocilla. As Charles Harris points out, "We still take time to visit each other here. In the cities they sometimes forget that families ought to visit." Other than the regular activities at church, or the athletic events of the high school, Ocilla's social life is carried on at home.

Although private homes are still the focus of social life in the white community, the last 20 years have brought change. "The ladies were very into big social gatherings. . . the silver teas and things of that kind when we came here," Mary Ann Powell recalls. "They used to say," recalls Oscar Powell, "that if you stopped at the red light long enough, they'd invite you to a silver tea."

Today, the young people are not buying silver punch bowls, and the white gloves are gone. Syd Blackmarr, who grew up in Ocilla, remembers when "there were women who didn't work, who had the time and resources, when things were simpler. Domestic help was easy and inexpensive to come by." She has seen all of that change.

But the old-fashioned virtues are given regular expression. "Folks here are sound, they're stable, they're conservative, they're not big spenders, not big party-ers," Charles Harris observes.

Concern for others is mentioned often as a community characteristic. Sometimes it means being sensitive to feelings, not making people uncomfortable, making life more pleasant. Sometimes it means active caring. People can readily call up incidents where a group of young farmers took over a hospitalized man's farming until he got back on his feet. In one case, the group-help went on for over a year. "There's an esprit de corps. Like the old-fashioned corn-shuckings or barn-raisings," Richard Williamson, assistant superintendent of schools, observes.

Farm talk permeates practically all conversation in Ocilla. Prices, insects, equipment, yields, and above all the weather are the topics of the day. People say Irwin County has some of the best soil and best farmers anywhere, and they can quote production figures to prove it. "All we need is the right sunshine and rain," according to Charles Harris.

Ocilla is what social scientists would call an agricultural service center. Although sawmills and turpentine stills were important in its earliest days, once the pine forests were cleared, the town was developed by and for agriculture. Here the farmer found the suppliers, buyers, processors, lenders and—because it was also the county seat—officials with whom he had to deal. With the prosperity that came from growing cotton and corn, and later peanuts and tobacco, there came the preachers and teachers, doctors and lawyers, and even more merchants, to meet the farm family's needs. Business, churches, schools, and residences of nonfarmers were all raised on agriculture.

Meeting the Future

Agriculture remains the backbone of the economy here, but changes in farming techniques, mainly mechanization, have proven a mixed blessing to the town itself. In the 1980s, a parcel of land that took the labor of five or six families to farm productively in the 1940s could be worked more efficiently by one family. From 1950 to 1970, Irwin County's population dropped from 11,973 to 8,036 as more and more farmers found their labor unneeded and headed for manufacturing jobs in the city. Fewer people meant less business activity in town. The population stabilized in the 1970s, but the development of new shopping centers in Tifton, Albany, and other larger places drew business away from Ocilla. Then I-75 carried off most of the Florida-bound tourists who used to roll through Ocilla on U.S. 129. Three especially dry summers, beginning in 1980, only made things worse for the local farm economy.

In the blinding summer sun, Ocilla's downtown, largely devoid of shade, has a bleached-out quality. Auto and pedestrian traffic is light. There's activity in the Osceola Cafe, Turk's Pharmacy, Harris's Department Store, and the two banks, but almost anyone can tell you Ocilla's downtown, with its vacant stores and listless air, needs new life. "What are we going to do about it?" is a regular expression of despair, not a question one is expected to answer. Some see that fixing up the downtown is not the real problem. For them, the sad condition is merely a concrete reminder that the community faces a big challenge: finding ways to meet the need for new sources of income, jobs. For some, it's a dilemma: how to meet that need for change and still preserve the good things threatened by change. Whatever is done, or not done, it will touch those things so important in the traditional South: family and place.

The need to do something, to ensure the future, is especially voiced by those who work with Ocilla's young people. Richard Williamson sees the problem as an educator.

"I can't blame young people; there's not that much here to attract a young person to come back. The majority of our high school graduates who have done some postsecondary schoolwork haven't come back here. It's a drain on the community. We're losing our best minds, people who probably in the future would have made something happen." (In 1980, of our five communities, Ocilla had the lowest percentages of persons over 25 with a high school diploma, 31 percent, and four or more years of college, 7 percent.)

Williamson has taken up the effort to attract industry to Ocilla. In the 1960s, before he moved here, a development corporation was formed and land obtained for an industrial park. A few firms, notably a mobile home builder (the community's major industrial employer in 1986) and a maker of children's clothes, did move in, but as the pace of development picked up in surrounding counties, it lagged in Irwin.

"We'll always have to be selective," Williamson admits. "Because of the conservativeness of the community, I think we couldn't have a Miller Beer company," he explains, alluding to that firm's brewery in another south Georgia county. What would fit the community? "Something related to agriculture," Williamson sighs. "They want to believe their

Ocilla is but one of many south Georgia towns once developed on agriculture and now competing for business and industry.

survival is based on agriculture, but most community members who are involved in agriculture today can tell you that we'll not survive on agriculture."

Gary Tankersley has been Irwin County's agriculture extension agent for two decades. He works closely with the county's farmers and runs the 4-H activities for their sons and daughters. For Tankersley, the problems of farming and young people come together. "We don't have the number of young people going into farming that we should, simply because it costs too much to get started. Farm income is too low at the present time. We just don't have those who are financially able to go into the business of farming."

The changes in agriculture have especially hit the black community. Mechanization meant wholesale displacement for blacks, most of whom were sharecroppers or farm hands, not landowners. For many blacks remaining here in town, Ocilla is practically a bedroom community; they drive to jobs in industry in Tifton, Fitzgerald, and Douglas. They also do most of their shopping in those out-of-county towns.

There are few black-owned businesses in Ocilla, and, by a curious twist of population change, no black churches pastored by preachers who live in Ocilla. On Sundays, visiting preachers serve the black congregations. As a result there is little monied or educated leadership in the black community.

Alfonso Owens retired after a long career in public education, including heading the county's black schools during segregation. Now, appointed to the county school board, Owens is still caught up in the problems facing black youngsters in Ocilla. Like their white classmates, many black students leave town as soon as they finish high school. But, Owens sees a difference.

"We don't have blacks in any positions other than menial positions like at the grocery store where blacks carry out. They don't even have a black cashier in there. Now you go to Fitzgerald, you can see black cashiers in all the big chain stores. They're in the banks in Tifton and all around. You see, that would be something that kids could look forward to. 'Well,' they could say, 'we got somebody down at the First State Bank or Bank of Ocilla, maybe one day I could work there.'"

Those who work in the public schools recognize that most of the young people will leave the community. The counseling programs, course offerings, and new computer equipment are there to help the youngsters make their way in the world. Generally, the schools get good marks, and good support, in the community. Of course, the school remains an important locus of social life in the rural community. And Irwin County High School football and basketball bring the whole community together as few other activities do. Indeed, high school athletics is often credited with smoothing the integration process in the early 1970s. "Black kids and white kids were thrown together. We were Ocilla Indians and everybody shared the success. We were state baseball champions in '73 and '75 and state football champions in '75 . . . right on the heels of integration," Williamson recalls.

Integration has unfortunately meant the loss of another group important to the community's future. "We don't have that many blacks with whom black children can identify in the school system now," Alfonso Owens points out. "The majority of the kids last year in the high school were black, but we had only one black high school teacher. It's difficult to get an educated black to come here to teach."

Getting people to come to Ocilla is an ongoing effort. Not only for Alfonso Owens trying to recruit black teachers, but also for Gary Tankersley trying to entice a young doctor to open a family practice here and for Richard Williamson trying to persuade an entrepreneur to come in. In all their efforts, they're competing with other communities offering higher teacher salaries, better medical facilities, and more developed industrial parks.

Enticing people who work elsewhere to come live in Ocilla is also bandied about. "Just put up some attractive middle-income housing."

"We need to do something to ensure Ocilla's future." Left to right:
Alfonso Owens, Stanley Hall, Mandy Roberts, and Richard Williamson.

But, others don't want Ocilla to be another "bedroom community," an adjunct to Tifton or Douglas.

Syd Blackmarr, in her office at Abraham Baldwin Agricultural College 20 miles away, views Ocilla's dilemma: "There is an element that wants to see Ocilla grow. But at the same time those of us who have lived there all our lives are reluctant to see it grow because we don't want to lose the sort of special qualities that seem to be dying out in the South—qualities of concern for others, graciousness, manners. . . .You can see two aspects: downtown, many businesses are closed up; in the residential area, beautifully well-kept homes are maintained."

One of the surviving businesses on Ocilla's main street is the A.S. Harris Department Store. "Irwin County's Trading Center," the sign out front proclaims. Inside is a sedate dry goods store. On one side, a few racks of dresses; men's suits along the opposite wall. Most of the merchandise is neatly folded and piled on counters. From the shoe section at the back, Charles Harris can survey his whole operation, and the traffic outside. Except for his years in college and Marine Corps service in World War II, he's lived all his life in Ocilla. He's been through the good years and the bad.

"My father was an immigrant from Russia who came to America when he was 13 years old. He went to Ellis Island. . .from New York to Savannah. At 16 he was peddling from a wagon, came to Ocilla and started this business in 1906. Opportunity is still present in rural Georgia towns for young men and women to make a living and be happy at what they're doing. Maybe you have to work at it a bit harder. You have to be better, price more competitively, maybe have a wider assortment. You have to work at being good. That's what you ought to do anyway. Everything changes, men and women who don't want to change with the times are going to fall by the wayside."

Savannah

> I sat in the sun in one of the city's squares, amid live oaks and Spanish moss and great explosions of azaleas. How beautiful this city is, I thought. It was as if parts of Dublin or London had been picked up and set down on some subtropical island. The houses were part of it, handsome but not too grand, built in the 1800s on profits from shipping cotton to England. But it was also the plan of the city. Seldom has one man marked a city's face so strongly as James Oglethorpe when he laid out Savannah on Renaissance ideals of balance and proportion. (John J. Putnam, "A Good Life in the Low Country," *National Geographic,* December 1983.)

Unlike Chatsworth, West End, Snellville, and Ocilla, Savannah is well known to millions of non-Georgians. Over the past quarter century, the city has been featured time and again, almost always with enthusiasm, in such magazines as *Architectural Forum, House Beautiful, National Geographic,* and *Newsweek.* Most of the copy has focused on the city's buildings and on its liveability:

> Savannah is more than a delight to the eye; it is a welcome measure of assurance that modernization need not be an esthetic disaster. ("A Hosanna to Savannah," *Newsweek,* Feb. 7, 1972)
>
> . . .Savannah is still a charming place to visit, as well as to live and work in. Anachronisms can be made to pay off in urban civilization. (Walter McQuade, "Two Cities, New and Old Show the Way to Urban Amenity," *Fortune,* July 1975)
>
> . . .Savannah has steadfastly restored hundreds of old houses and public buildings and, in the process, has become one of America's outstanding examples of convenient and comfortable city living at an affordable price. (Roger M. Williams, "Savannah: Historic Roots at an Affordable Price," *Saturday Review,* August 21, 1976.)

So easy on the eye is Savannah that even locals admit to focusing perhaps too exclusively on buildings. Native Savannahian John Alexander, himself an interior designer, recounts sending a book about his city to some friends in New York. "One wrote back and said, 'The book is beautiful, Savannah is a beautiful city, but I don't see any people in the book.' The book had been photographed without any people on the streets. So, the person was wondering, 'Where are all the people?'"

When it began, Savannah was all about people. In his city plan, Oglethorpe followed the ideals of balance and proportion not for beauty's sake alone but for very human reasons. He and the other trustees who established the colony thought the "worthy poor" of London who would settle Georgia were made poor by environmental conditions, not by any lack of human qualities. Plan the environment and those qualities would come to the fore. The social features of Oglethorpe's plan—no liquor, no slavery, limits on landholding, and regulated agriculture—proved unworkable. Only his physical scheme remained to shape Savannah's growth for 200 years.

On the 200th anniversary of the city's founding, however, Savannah's prospects looked dim. The prosperity of a hundred years (albeit with down periods—especially 1861-1865) as the East Coast's major shipping port for cotton and naval stores collapsed just as the nation sank into the Great Depression. In desperation, Savannahians welcomed the construction of what would become the world's largest paper mill. The mill brought sorely needed jobs, but it fouled the water and air.

With World War II came renewed activity on the docks, military training facilities, and prosperity. Building of suburbs (begun in the 1920s) resumed, and the white middle class abandoned the historic downtown shaped by Oglethorpe's plan. The mid-1950s found the central city a wasteland of neglected tenements and vandalized shells of early nineteenth century townhouses. Along the riverfront, decaying docks and the stench of industrial pollution completed the dismal scene.

Restoration of the City Core

The story of Savannah's renaissance has been retold many times in the popular magazines: how several socially prominent white women, agitated at the impending demolition of a historic house, bought it themselves and touched off the preservation movement; how two and a half square miles of the downtown were placed on the National Register as the nation's largest historical landmark, how the restoration of the historic district and development of the riverfront created a booming tourist industry for Savannah. Magazine writers and tourists, fascinated by this Cinderella story of historic Savannah, may not be aware that Savannah is a living community with all the complexities of a city of 141,390 people, and an MSA of 220,553. Savannah's people share the problems of other urban dwellers—crime, pollution, schools—and have some rather peculiar ones of their own.

"Everybody in Georgia wasn't born in a mansion," W. W. Law tells his audience of mostly black citizens, prominent in Savannah business and public life. "There are other kinds of properties that ought to be placed on the register. The simple houses are important, too, because these people did as much to make America great and Georgia great as the folks who lived in the big house. We all know that there was no wealth in Georgia until slavery was introduced in 1749. Everybody in Georgia—other than General Oglethorpe—was poor. . . ." The audience listens intently despite the stifling heat in the crowded classroom. They have come to this meeting at the Massie School, built in 1853 and 130 years later the school system's Heritage Interpretation Center, at Mr. Law's behest on a matter of urgency to the black community: the preservation of *their* heritage.

For many Savannahians, black and white, W. W. Law is a legend in his own time. In 1963, the local newspaper commented how unlikely was the meeting of a black letter carrier and the city's white leadership to negotiate a settlement to Savannah's civil rights turmoil. No ordinary postman, Law headed both the city and state NAACP organizations, led an 18-month boycott of white businesses to end discrimination in public accommodations, and guided the desegregation of the public schools. Twenty years later, he turned his attention to the preservation and study of the black heritage. For Law, the mentor of black youngsters selected to desegregate the schools, knowledge of that heritage is particularly crucial to the young. "I contend that if a people know their heritage, it's impossible for them not to achieve and to succeed. . . .The regrettable thing is that we allow people to grow into adults oftentimes without really exposing them to the things that really make them human, that make them great."

Already some historic black properties have been saved, Law recounts to his listeners, but what he proposes is far bigger: a survey of every black property with the potential for historic preservation. Other organizations (white) had done such surveys as the first step in their preservation of the "big houses."

The first survey of historic houses was made by the Historic Savannah Foundation, established in 1955, as part of its public awareness campaign. The purpose of the campaign was to save as many houses as possible and to encourage affluent whites to move back into the downtown. The foundation bought the shells of mainly brick houses built by nineteenth century merchants and resold them to persons who promised to restore them and live in them. By the early 1970s, the foundation had overseen the restoration of more than 1,000 buildings

W.W. Law: ". . . if a people know their heritage, it's impossible for them not to achieve and to succeed . . . ."

and the transformation of the historic district from a slum to a first-class neighborhood of upper-middle-class homeowners.

The restoration effort of 20 years has amounted to a $400 million investment in downtown Savannah that not only enhanced the beauty and liveability of the city but also provided hundreds of jobs. Moreover, the restoration stimulated a tourist industry income that grew from less than $200,000 per year in the late 1950s to more than $130 million per year in the early 1980s.

But the tourist who wanders just a block or two out of this restored area is apt to be shocked by another Savannah, one that is poor and mainly black. Some of these poor people were moved out to the periphery of the historic district in the course of its restoration. But, this juxtaposition of wealth and poverty, white and black, also has historical antecedents.

Explains John Alexander, "That's always been Savannah. Price Street separated white from black, Gwinnett Street separated white from black. This goes back to when blacks were freed in Savannah. We have always lived so close to each other. One street can separate a million dollars from a thousand dollars just like one historic community can be right next to an area that's run down."

Alexander lives in the Victorian District, younger by a half century than the restored historic district. Begun in the 1890s to accommodate Savannah's population growth, it features wood and porches and ginger-bread in contrast to the brick rowhouses of the early nineteenth century. Like the older district, the Victorian had also become a derelict by the 1950s. Twenty years later, it too was undergoing restoration, but with an important difference—the planned avoidance of displacement or "gentrification."

Gentrification or displacement are terms used to describe one consequence of the restoration of urban neighborhoods. From Hoboken and Washington to Atlanta and San Antonio, the young and affluent have rediscovered the charm—and real estate developers the market-ability—of inner-city properties previously abandoned to low-income groups. When developers buy low-income rental properties for renovation and resale, in the process tenants are displaced by "gentry."

Displacement is precisely what Leopold Adler wants to avoid in Savannah. For seven years in the 1960s, he was president of the Historic Savannah Foundation and points out that during his tenure he "never bought a building that was occupied at the time." In 1974, with the historic district effort winding down and local attention turning to restoration of the nearby Victorian District, the spectre of "gentrification" rose up—for most of the Victorian houses were renter-occupied, not abandoned. Unlike the renaissance of the historic district, the Victorian rebirth would not mean the wholesale immigration of affluent whites. Instead it would mean some homeowners, some tenants, some middle-income, some low-income, some black, some white.

To ensure this mix, Adler launched Savannah Landmarks, a non-profit corporation that acts like a landlord. In addition to preservation, its goal is to provide low-income Savannahians with a "decent, safe, sanitary place to live."

There were tremendous obstacles to what Landmarks proposed in 1974. Critics said the poor people would tear up their new apartments. At first, Adler admits the poor people too were skeptical "because they had been promised so much." But, with help from the local minority-owned Carver State Bank, the city of Savannah, and federal programs ranging from the National Endowment for the Arts to CETA and sub-sidized housing of Department of Housing and Urban Development (HUD), Landmarks began buying, renovating, and renting historic prop-erties. Its procedure is to buy a building outright, move tenants tempo-rarily out of it, renovate it, and move tenants back in. Low-income tenants

Leopold Adler (right) *and Joe Bell, Carver State Bank vice-president, stand in front of renovated Victorian houses.*

pay 25 percent of their income for rent; the difference between that and what HUD calls "fair market value" is provided in a supplement from the federal government for 20 years. The renter's share plus the federal supplement is enough not only to pay back the cost of rehabilitating the property but also provides for taxes and upkeep of the property. Unlike public housing, Landmark's properties remain on the tax rolls.

In 10 years of existence, Savannah Landmarks had redone some 400 houses. "We're providing," adds Adler in words reminiscent of those of Georgia's founders, "for the responsible poor people." Of course, not all who would like to can live in rehabilitated historic housing: some 1,000 people were on Landmark's waiting list. They represented but a small part of a big problem: for a city of Savannah's size, there are just too many poor people.

A Mixed Economy

"Half the black community lives below the poverty line," says Henry Moore, who can watch from his city hall office the ship traffic that brings Savannah much of its wealth. "In Savannah, when you isolate the wealth of the black community, it is really very poor. There are 194 households in the black community that earn more than $50,000, but in the white community, it's 1,275 households. Yet we're half the population." As Savannah's assistant city manager for development, Moore oversees municipal capital projects: streets, sewerage, water, housing, recreation, downtown revitalization. He carries the statistics in his head: "Sixty-seven percent of the black households earn less than $14,000, 50 percent less than $10,000, and 35 percent of households are headed by women."

The problem of female unemployment in Savannah has long been recognized. Manufacturing—wood and paper products, chemicals, transportation equipment—is overloaded toward traditionally male jobs. Moreover, child care is a sore need: in 1983 only 466 slots were available in public child care facilities for the children of low-income women.

Male unemployment gains more attention, though, because of another factor—crime. Between 1960 and 1980, Savannah's crime rate increased almost 400 percent. Media attention and official reaction were often greatest in the wake of crime perpetrated against residents and tourists in the historic district, but most Savannah crime was black-on-black in low-income neighborhoods.

John Finney, director of Economic Opportunity Authority-Savannah, assesses the situation: "In part it is economic frustration . . . part is people have just lost hope. We need jobs so people don't have to resort to crime." Finney estimates Savannah needs an industry to employ about 2,500 people. He recounts how the city lost out to Jacksonville, Macon, and other places in bidding for desirable industries. With a tone of urgency he concludes, "Now we need *whatever* we can get; if it's non-polluting, OK, if it's not. . . ."

Pollution! If there is a frequent qualifier placed on the consensus that Savannah needs new industry, it is that it be clean industry, "industry we can live with."

A half century's experience with heavily polluting industries and the need to protect the new tourist industry have made many Savannahians wary of industrial development. In 1970, the condition of the Savannah River was so bad that the Ralph Nader organization chose Savannah for its case study on environmental pollution. Since the mid-1930s, locals' overriding concern for industrialization had led them to give manufacturers license to dump whatever waste they had into the river. Because Union Camp Corporation built the world's largest kraft paper mill just a mile upstream; because Continental Can Company, American Cyanamid, and other industries had located on the river, and because the city—100,000 strong—dumped its own untreated sewage into it, the Savannah River had become an open sewer. For some Savannahians, especially those living on the west side of town, air pollution emanating from the paper mill was an even worse problem. The Nader report raised the anxiety of some officials who felt it stigmatized the city, but in general the response was favorable. What had to be said had finally been said, and it helped to catalyze public action. Industry was forced to adopt technologies to treat its effluents, and the city had to build sewage treatment facilities.

Savannahians have learned the personal benefits of a cleaner environment and its contribution to the tourist industry. Yet, when the wind blows westerly, they are cautioned anew about industrial development. In 1983, the *Savannah News Press,* warned that "Savannah ranks among the top metropolitan areas in the Southeast in the amount of air pollution generated by its industries." Said the paper, "Tourists frequently mention air pollution as the worst aspect of their visit."

The concern for environment has driven Savannah to seek clean high-tech industries. Through 1986, it had little success in this effort.

Dr. John Northrup, a physician, heads up Savannah's Clean Air Council. "The politicians in Atlanta and other places have not done their part to try to convert Georgia into a high-tech industry state. One of the reasons for this is very obvious. This is a great state for absentee landlords. It's a great state for someone in New York or New Jersey or Ohio to start a mill or something like that. . . ship down the interest and ship home the profits. They really don't care if they foul up the air or goof up the water. It doesn't make any difference to them as long as they fulfill the bottom line on the balance sheet. People are beginning to realize that the future is probably in tourists, military, and the port. Perhaps more so than low-tech polluting industries. That's where the battle lines are being drawn."

In recent years, as tourism blossomed and environmental concerns hardened, the search for industry focused on service industries that don't pollute. But, Savannah's location, so important to waterborne commerce, is not a positive factor in attracting service industries. Financial, information, and health service industries don't need a deepwater port. The coastal location places Savannah outside the main region of Sunbelt growth. Moreover, 50 to 100 miles of hinterland isolate Savannah from other population concentrations. A business seeking to service the Southeast is not likely to find Savannah the best place to locate its headquarters. Savannah's inability to attract service companies has brought attention back to industry likely to be attracted by its number one selling point: the port.

"I think you can have good industrial growth with the technology advances we've had, if the industry can afford the costs," says Tom Coleman, a businessman and banker who serves Chatham County in the state senate.

Local Issues

The growth issue has many facets: not only what kind of growth is most desirable, but also the location of growth must be considered. East side, west side, or downtown?—each has its advocates. Also there is strong "no growth" sentiment. All but surrounding the city are pristine marsh-lands, some of nature's most productive habitats, nurseries for marine life. Many Savannahians are adamant that the marshes must remain pro-tected from filling-in for development. If they are, Savannah can't grow.

Rabbi Saul Rubin perhaps best expresses the sentiment to keep Savannah small. "The city is unique. There is no skyline as you enter, the buildings are proper proportions, there are no towers to cast you into shadows. It helps the humaneness of people who are living here. If you go racing into town, you always have to stop at one of those squares, it slows you down to a different pace. It's a walking city. That has great appeal. . . slow pace."

If there is any consensus regarding the economy, it is that the port is Savannah's ultimate advantage. And, if Savannah is not to lose ship-ping business to other ports, it must have larger facilities to handle larger ships.

Being a port has also given Savannah a human advantage. In 1980, 38 percent of the residents were born out-of-state or abroad. "Like most port cities it's got a mix of ethnic groups which make it unique in Georgia," Irish Catholic Tom Coleman claims. "We've got some of everything: a large Irish Catholic contingent, a lot of Greeks, Jews, and plain old Georgia crackers. It's good for the city and has helped our race relations."

On race relations, W. W. Law attests that Savannah was rather peculiar compared to other places in Georgia. "In the old days we used to call folks who came here 'refugees' —who weren't old families— because Savannah was considered to be a pretty free town; Negroes got along, had the kind of freedom here that they didn't have elsewhere. Of course, that goes all the way back to colonial days when Savannah was a haven for runaway slaves. . . . Overall, we probably have had for a longer period of time better race relations in this city than almost any Georgia town. . . . From my earliest childhood, the blacks of our com-munity always felt as though the blue-bloods, or the native people, were pretty decent to deal with. And that the outsiders, or the rednecks, who came in, . . . well, it was that kind of situation."

Savannah's people were a diverse group from the outset. On July 11, 1733, just five months after Oglethorpe's first group of 114 settlers came ashore, 42 Jewish colonists from Spain—the largest single group of Jews to land in colonial America—arrived. By the next spring, enough German colonists, the "Salzburgers," landed to make the English-speaking colonists almost a minority!

Today, Savannahians readily publicize their ethnicity. There are the organized clubs such as the Hibernian Society and the St. Andrew's Society, the "Second Largest St. Patrick's Day Celebration in the U.S.," and a regular schedule of festivals such as "Greek Week."

In recent years, the most prominent ethnic has been the mayor, John Roussakis. "He's Greek," almost any Savannahian will announce before mentioning another of the mayor's qualities—longevity in office.

"Roussakis is the great compromiser, he gets all the groups to work together, that's why he's been reelected so many times," says Larry Thompson, a high school teacher and student of Savannah's history. The consensus opinion is that the man who has been mayor longer than previous Savannah chief executives has a talent especially needed in Savannah politics. The contentiousness of Savannah and Chatham County politics is almost legendary. "We take our politics very seriously," admits Tom Coleman, a city and county official prior to going to the legislature. "We like a good debate, a good fight; we like to disagree."

Nowhere is the penchant for argument more evident than in school politics. Though private education has a long and honorable history here, the more recent upsurge in private school enrollment has alarmed many. Some 25 percent of the children in Chatham County attend private schools, compared to the statewide average of 7 percent.

Many feel the local press hasn't helped the situation by stressing public schools problems and failing to note its qualities. Programs for the gifted, exceptional children, and community ties to business and the professions are notable. The heritage program, developed by Emma Adler (wife of Landmarks' founder) and based at the Massie School, is a model for any American city.

But infighting among school board members, threats and lawsuits, and continual hiring and firing of administrators have contributed to the public schools' negative image and boosted the private school alternative.

"Savannah has had a tradition of having mediocre to average public education," asserts Tom Tippett, administrator of Calvary Baptist School, one of the largest private school establishments in Savannah. "I don't know if this has anything to do with the number of nonpublic elementary and secondary schools. . . . This community is multi-ethnic; a lot of people tend to do what they want to do relative to their own ethnic community. . . . If someone has a controversy with a certain theory of education. . . they just go out and start their own school."

Not only alleged mediocrity but also busing to achieve racial balance is blamed for the public schools' loss of support. But, as Bob Porter, development director for the Memorial Medical Center, points out, "all private schools bus; the choice is private or public school busing. I don't think the private schools, except for one or two, are any better than the public schools."

In recent years, support for the public schools began to grow with the business sector's realization that success in economic development depended on success in public education.

Coming Back to Savannah

In spite of the community's fragmentation, of contentiousness, of inaction, of the tendency to muddle through, people are attracted to it. Perhaps it is because of these things. "Savannah takes to strangers," says Bob Porter. "New people fit right in—newcomers had a lot to do with historic restoration downtown. But, the peculiar thing about Savannah is that people (who go away) always come back; even the soldiers stationed at Hunter."

John Alexander is one of those who came back. After high school he went to New York, in 1965, to further his education because there was no theater program at Savannah State College. "New York opened the doors. . . letting me see what I wanted to pursue as a profession. It was probably always in me growing up in Savannah, but by not having the exposure, of being able to appreciate the beauty of Savannah, I needed to go outside of the city in order to come back and be able to appreciate what it had to offer. There's something here that you don't find in New York. There is an openness here. . . a handshake can mean as much as a contract here in Savannah. People respect you for your word. . . . Essentially we mind our own business. There's a tendency to protect that. We are our own institution. We keep to ourselves, stay within our own circle."

And there are others who eventually come back. "There's a great hunger to stay in Savannah," says Rabbi Rubin, "but the economic opportunity prevents that. I have served as rabbi many places, but this is the only town where I have the sense of people making the last pilgrimmage home. The kids have to leave, but at the end of life. . . this is home."

Index